I0090813

# INDONESIA'S
# ECONOMY
# SINCE
# INDEPENDENCE

The **Institute of Southeast Asian Studies (ISEAS)** was established as an autonomous organization in 1968. It is a regional centre dedicated to the study of socio-political, security and economic trends and developments in Southeast Asia and its wider geostrategic and economic environment. The Institute's research programmes are the Regional Economic Studies (RES, including ASEAN and APEC), Regional Strategic and Political Studies (RSPS), and Regional Social and Cultural Studies (RSCS).

**ISEAS Publishing**, an established academic press, has issued more than 2,000 books and journals. It is the largest scholarly publisher of research about Southeast Asia from within the region. ISEAS Publishing works with many other academic and trade publishers and distributors to disseminate important research and analyses from and about Southeast Asia to the rest of the world.

# INDONESIA'S ECONOMY SINCE INDEPENDENCE

THEE KIAN WIE

**LSEAS**

**INSTITUTE OF SOUTHEAST ASIAN STUDIES**

*Singapore*

First published in Singapore in 2012 by
ISEAS Publishing
Institute of Southeast Asian Studies
30 Heng Mui Keng Terrace
Pasir Panjang
Singapore 119614

*E-mail*: publish@iseas.edu.sg
*Website*: <http://bookshop.iseas.edu.sg>

All rights reserved. No part of this publication may be reproduced, stored in a retrieval system, or transmitted in any form or by any means, electronic, mechanical, photocopying, recording or otherwise, without the prior permission of the Institute of Southeast Asian Studies.

© 2012 Institute of Southeast Asian Studies, Singapore

*The responsibility for facts and opinions in this publication rests exclusively with the author and his interpretations do not necessarily reflect the views or the policy of the publisher or its supporters.*

### ISEAS Library Cataloguing-in-Publication Data

Thee, Kian Wie.
  Indonesia's economy since independence.
  (ISEAS current economic affairs series)
  1.  Indonesia—Economic conditions—1945–
  2.  Indonesia—Economic policy—20th century.
  I.  Title
HC447 T374                2012

ISBN 978-981-4379-63-2 (soft cover)
ISBN 978-981-4379-54-0 (e-book, PDF)

Cover photo: Aerial view of Tarumanegara University in Jakarta, March 2011. Courtesy of ANTARAFOTO.

Typeset by Superskill Graphics Pte Ltd
Printed in Singapore by Chung Printing Pte Ltd

*In memory of my parents*

# CONTENTS

# PREFACE

In the course of my academic career, I have incurred many debts to my colleagues and friends in Indonesia and overseas for their encouragement and help in my academic endeavours, and for their books and papers and particularly for their helpful comments and suggestions on my papers which have greatly contributed to the improvement of my work.

In Australia I would like to record my great appreciation to my colleagues and friends at The Australian National University, Canberra, particularly Hal Hill and Chris Manning, and Ross McLeod, Peter McCawley, Budy Resosudarmo, Terence Hull, Colin Barlow and Pierre van der Eng; Howard Dick, formerly at the University of Melbourne; Robert Elson, formerly at The University of Queensland; John Butcher, formerly at Griffith University; and Cassey Lee at the University of Wollongong.

In the U.S., I would like to express my great appreciation to Jeffrey Williamson at the University of Wisconsin; Madison, Wisconsin; Thomas Grennes at North Carolina State University, Raleigh, North Carolina, and William Liddle at Ohio State University, Columbus, Ohio.

In the UK I would like to express my great appreciation to Anne Booth, School of Oriental and African Studies (SOAS), University of London; and in The Netherlands to J. Thomas Lindblad, University of Leiden; to Cees Fasseur, formerly at the University of Leiden; Ewout Frankema, University of Utrecht; and Leonard Blusse, formerly at the University of Leiden, and Eddy (Adam) Szirmai at UNU MERIT, Maastricht. In Sweden I would like to express my appreciation to Fredrik Sjoholm, Research Institute of Industrial Economics, and Obrero University, Stockholm.

In Japan I would like to express my great appreciation to Eric Ramstetter, International Centre for the Study of East Asian Development (ICSEAD), Kitakyushu, and to Ichimura Shinichi and Takii Sadayuki, both formerly at ICSEAD.

In Korea I would like to express my great appreciation to Lee Jisoon, Seoul National University, and Baek Ehung-Gi of Sanmyung University, Seoul.

In Singapore I would like to express my great appreciation to Professor J. Soedradjad Djiwandono of the Rajaratnam School of International Studies, Nanyang Technological University, Singapore.

In Indonesia I would like to express my great appreciation to my younger colleagues M. Chatib Basri and Arianto Patunru, Institute of Economic and Social Research, Faculty of Economics, University of Indonesia (LPEM-FEUI); Sudarno Sumarto and Asep Suryahadi at the SMERU Research Institute; Dionisius Narjoko at the Economic Research Institute for ASEAN and East Asia (ERIA); to Haryo Aswicahyono, Raymond Atje, Pande Radja Silalahi, and Maria Monica Wihardja of the Centre for Strategic and International Studies (CSIS); and to Taufik Abdullah at the Indonesian Institute of Sciences; M.P.S. Tjondronegoro at the Bogor Agricultural University; and Bambang Purwanto at Gadjah Mada University.

I would also like to express my great appreciation to Darwin, Head of the Economic Research Centre, Indonesian Institute of Sciences (P2E-LIPI), Jakarta; for his inspiring leadership of the Centre, and to my younger colleagues, particularly Siwage Dharma Negara, at the Centre for their friendship and for sharing with me their newly-acquired knowledge upon their return from their postgraduate study overseas.

I also would like to record my great appreciation to Mr K. Kesavapany, Director of the Institute of Southeast Asian Studies (ISEAS), Singapore, for his support of my book project.

Last but certainly not least, I would like to express my heartfelt thanks and great appreciation to Mrs Triena Ong, Managing Editor and Head of the Publications Unit of the Institute of Southeast Asian Studies (ISEAS), Singapore for her positive response to the planned book and for her most valuable and constructive suggestions for the book, and to Mark Iñigo M. Tallara, also of the Publications Unit of ISEAS, for his very important role in getting this book to publication.

*Thee Kian Wie*
*1 August 2011*
*Jakarta*

# ACKNOWLEDGEMENTS

The chapters in this volume are taken from the sources listed below, for which the author and publishers wish to thank their editors, original publishers or other copyright holders for the permission to use their materials as follows:

1. KITLV Press for republishing my article 'Indonesianization: Economic aspects of decolonization in the 1950s', originally published in Thomas Lindblad and Peter Post (editors): *Economic Decolonization in Indonesia in Regional and International Perspective* (KITLV Press, Leiden, 2009, pp. 15–39).

2. Professor Bambang Purwanto, Professor of History, Gadjah Mada University, for republishing my article 'Indonesia's First Affirmative Programme: The *Benteng* Programme in the 1950s', in *Lembaran Sejarah* (History Papers), Vol. 8, no. 3, 2005, pp. 33–36.

3. Cambridge University Press for republishing my article 'The debate on economic policy in newly-independent Indonesia between Sjafruddin Prawiranegara and Sumitro Djojohadikusumo', which appeared in *Itinerario*, Vol. XXXIV, issue 1, pp. 1–22.

4. Taylor and Francis. Co. UK, for republishing my articles:

i. 'The Major Channels of International Technology Transfer to Indonesia: An Assessment', in *Journal of the Asia-Pacific Economy*, vol. 10, no. 2, May 2005, pp. 214–36.

ii. 'Indonesia's Two Deep Economic Crises: The mid-1960s and late 1990s', in *Journal of the Asia-Pacific Economy*, vol. 14, no. 2, February 2009, pp. 49–60.

iii. 'The Indonesian Wood Products Industry', in *Journal of the Asia-Pacific Economy*, vol. 14, no. 2, May 2009, pp. 138–49.

iv. 'The Development of Labour-intensive Garment Manufacturing in Indonesia', in *Journal of Contemporary Asia*, vol. 39, no. 4, November 2009, pp. 562–78.

5. Institute of Southeast Asian Studies (ISEAS), Singapore, for republishing my article 'Policies Affecting Indonesia's Industrial Technology Development', in *ASEAN Economic Bulletin*, Vol. 23, no. 3, December 2006, pp. 341–59.

6. Bureau of East Asian Economic Research, ANU College for Asia and the Pacific, School of Economics and Government, Australian National University, for republishing my article on 'Indonesia and the BRICs', available at the East Asia Forum website: <http://www.eastasiaforum.org/>.

**Note**: The following two papers:

1. 'Indonesia's Economic Development During and After the Soeharto Era: Achievements and Failings', appeared in the JICA/JBIC International Workshop Report *Asian Experiences of Economic Development and Their Policy Implications for Africa*, published by the Institute of International Cooperation, Japan International Cooperation Agency, Tokyo, May 2008, pp. 19–24.

2. 'The Impact of the Two Oil Booms of the 1970s and the Post-Oil Boom Shock of the Early 1980s on the Indonesian Economy', appeared in the *Proceedings of the Third AFC International Symposium 'Resources under Stress — Sustainability of the Local Community in Asia and Africa'*, published by the Afrasian Centre for Peace and Development Studies, Ryukoku University, Kyoto, 23–24 February 2008, pp. 239–51.

While the following two papers were unpublished papers:

1. 'Indonesia's Industrial Policies and Development Since Independence', which was originally presented at a Conference on Labour-intensive Industrialization in Southeast Asia, Kyoto, February 2008.

2. 'Indonesia's Auto Parts Industry', is an abbreviated and updated version of part 3 of the Final Report on *Indonesia's Industrial Competitiveness – A Study on the Garments, Auto Parts and Electronic Components Industries*, written by Haryo Aswicahyono, Raymond Atje and Thee Kian Wie for the Development Economics Research Group, The World Bank, March 2005.

**Note:** Some of these papers were published at different times in different books and journals, and for this reason may be repetitive. They were also written a few years ago, so some of the data may not be up-to-date.

# INTRODUCTION

## A short historical overview of Indonesia's economy since independence — Essays

This book contains a collection of papers on various aspects of Indonesia's economy and its industrial development since the early 1950s. This date is chosen because Indonesia only achieved effective sovereignty over the whole territory of the former Netherlands Indies, with the exception of Papua, after the official recognition of Indonesia's independence by the Netherlands government on 27 December 1949, even though on 17 August 1945 Sukarno and Hatta had officially proclaimed Indonesia's independence.

The Netherlands recognition of Indonesia's independence was only achieved after a bloody armed struggle by Indonesian freedom fighters against the returning Dutch army in late 1945. This armed struggle lasted until the delegations of the two contending parties (the Indonesian revolutionary government and the Netherlands government) under the auspices of the United Nations Commission on Indonesia (UNCI) at the Round Table Conference in The Hague in the autumn of 1949 agreed on the transfer of sovereignty from the Netherlands government to the government of the United States of Indonesia (*Republik Indonesia Serikat, RIS*) on 27 December 1949.

The Netherlands transfer of sovereignty to the federal Republic of the United States of Indonesia (RIS) was particularly galling to the revolutionary Republic of Indonesia based in Yogyakarta which had waged the armed struggle against the Dutch army. The reason was that it was forced to share power with 15 puppet states set up by the Dutch as a counterweight to the Republic. However, this federal structure proved to be fragile, as in the following months the puppet states one by one disbanded themselves to join the Republic.

At the celebration of independence day on 17 August 1950, President Sukarno was able to proclaim the restoration of the unitary state of the Republic of Indonesia (*Negara Kesatuan Republik Indonesia, NKRI*).

## Outline of the book

This book does not provide a thematic account of Indonesia's modern economic history, as contained in Anne Booth's pioneering book *The Indonesian Economy in the Nineteenth and Twentieth Centuries: A History of Missed Opportunities* (1998) or the chronological account provided in the book *The Emergence of a National Economy: An Economic History of Indonesia, 1800–2000*, written by Howard Dick, Vincent Houben, J. Thomas Lindblad and Thee Kian Wie (2002).

Instead, this book discusses various aspects of Indonesia's post-independence history which have not yet been discussed in the above two books or are discussed in greater detail than has been the case with the above two books.

This book is divided into two main parts, namely Overall Developments and Industrial Development.

The part on **overall developments** is divided into three periods, namely the early independence period in the 1950s; the Soeharto era (often referred to as the New Order era, 1966–98); and the ensuing two economic crises, namely the impact of the Asian Financial Crisis of 1997/98 and the Global Financial Crisis of 2008.

In the section on the early independence period in the 1950s three papers are presented, including:

– Economic aspects of decolonization in the early 1950s, which discusses Indonesia's efforts at economic decolonization after political independence was achieved;
– The *Benteng* programme in the 1950s which was aimed at countering Dutch and Chinese economic dominance over the Indonesian economy;
– the debate on economic policy in newly-independent Indonesia between Sjafruddin Prawiranegara and Sumitro Djojohadikusumo, who were two of Indonesia's most prominent economic policymakers in the early 1950s.

The section on the Soeharto Era contains two papers, namely 'The Indonesian economy during the Soeharto Era — Achievements and Failings' which argues that during the first two decades the New Order state was a 'developmental state', which during the third and last decade deteriorated into a 'predatory state' when economic policies were often designed to benefit President Soeharto's children and their cronies; and 'The Impact of the Two Oil Booms of the 1970s and the Post-Oil Boom Shock of the Early 1980s on the Indonesian Economy', which discusses the beneficial aspects of the two oil booms of 1973/74 and 1978/79 on the Indonesian economy, and the adjustment and deregulation (liberalization) measures which the Indonesian government had to take in early 1983 to restore macroeconomic stability and raise non-oil exports in response to the end of the oil boom era in 1982, when the price of crude oil in the international market steeply declined as a consequence of the economic recession in the major industrial countries.

The section on the Asian Financial Crisis of 1997/98, the Global Financial Crisis of 2008, and the prospects for rapid growth contains three papers, namely Indonesia's two deep economic crises, the mid-1960s and late 1990s' which compares the adverse impact of Asian Financial Crisis and the economic crisis of the mid-1960s on the Indonesian economy; the relatively mild impact of the Global Financial Crisis on the Indonesian economy; and a short discussion on the feasibility of Indonesia joining the BRIC (Brazil, Russia, India and China) group of rapidly-growing economies.

The second part on **Industrial Development** contains six papers, namely an overall discussion of Indonesia's industrial policies and industrial development since independence, a discussion on the Indonesian government's policies affecting Indonesia's industrial technology development; a discussion of the four major 'Channels of International Technology Transfer to Indonesia', specifically to its manufacturing sector; and three final papers on three of Indonesia's most important manufacturing industries, namely the labour-intensive garment industry'; 'the resource-intensive wood products industry'; and 'the medium-technology auto parts industry'.

# PART I

## THE EARLY INDEPENDENCE
## PERIOD IN THE 1950s

# 1

# INDONESIANIZATION: ECONOMIC ASPECTS OF DECOLONIZATION IN THE 1950s[1]

The late Professor Harry Johnson at the University of Chicago defined economic nationalism as 'the national aspiration to having property owned by nationals and economic functions performed by nationals' (Johnson 1972:26). Following this definition, the force of economic nationalism in Indonesia, especially during the early independence period, can be easily understood. Economic nationalism was, and still is, reflected in the Indonesian government's economic policies. To a higher degree than in other Southeast Asian countries, economic nationalism in post-colonial Indonesia has been, and continues to be, an important factor affecting government policy. Whereas economic nationalism during the 1950s was primarily targeted at continuing economic dominance of the Dutch and ethnic Chinese business interests, in the years following the Asian economic crisis in the late 1990s economic nationalism came to be directed primarily at perceived interference by international organizations, in particular the International Monetary Fund (IMF), in the formulation of Indonesia's economic policies in order to handle the crisis.

Despite strong economic nationalism, pragmatic considerations have more often than not overruled popular pressures of economic nationalism, particularly after the advent of the New Order government in 1966. As a result, pragmatic economic policies have often been able to offset adverse economic and political effects of virulent nationalism, except during the final years of President Sukarno's rule.[2]

In the following pages the so-called 'Indonesianization' policies pursued during the 1950s, when economic nationalism was very strong, will be discussed. Using Johnson's definition, 'Indonesianization' (*indonesianisasi*) is understood here as efforts by the Indonesian government to transfer property, or more correctly, productive assets owned by foreigners or foreign business, especially Dutch business, or residents viewed as foreigners, in particular Indonesians of Chinese descent, to indigenous Indonesians and to transfer economic functions performed by foreigners or residents viewed as foreigners to indigenous Indonesians. The drive towards 'Indonesianization' involved various measures taken by the Indonesian government in the 1950s aiming at an 'economic decolonization' considered all the more urgent since the Indonesian government already in early 1950 realized that political independence had not been accompanied by economic independence. 'Indonesianization' also formed an official response to the strong appeal by several nationalist leaders, such as Sujono Hadinoto of the Indonesian Nationalist Party (Partai Nasional Indonesia, PNI), who wished 'to convert the colonial economy into a national economy' (*merombak ekonomi kolonial menjadi ekonomi nasional*) (Hadinoto 1949:1).

## THE POLITICAL AND ECONOMIC CONSEQUENCES OF THE ROUND TABLE CONFERENCE

With the transfer of sovereignty to Indonesia on 27 December 1949, a new phase began in the often tortuous relations between Indonesia and the Netherlands. Sovereign Indonesia could now deal with the Netherlands on an equal basis. However, during the 1950s, Indonesian-Dutch relations were marred by the lingering aftermath of the colonial relationship. While President Sukarno's efforts from the early 1950s onwards were aimed at 'completing the national revolution', specifically the 'liberation of West Irian' (West New Guinea), still under Dutch control, the Netherlands attempted strenuously to hold on to what little was still left of its formerly vast colonial possessions (Houben 1996:160).

The uncomfortable legacy of the colonial past was a direct consequence of agreements reached at the Round Table Conference (RTC) held in The Hague from late August until early November 1949 where the terms of Dutch acknowledgement of Indonesia's independence were formulated. The Indonesian delegation at the RTC agreed to a number of controversial conditions under pressure of wanting a quick agreement with the Dutch. The expectation of substantial financial assistance from the United States also induced Indonesian leaders to make economic concessions to the Netherlands. However, concessions greatly outweighed the relatively paltry economic assistance in the form of a loan of $100 million from the United States Exim-Bank that was at long last extended. Moreover, this loan, that had to be repaid with interest, corresponded to only one–third of post-war credits by the same bank to the Netherlands. This was all Indonesia received after yielding to the insistence by Merle Cochran, the American observer at the RTC, that the United States government would shoulder the overseas debt bequeathed by the Netherlands Indies government to Indonesia (Kahin 1997:26).

Four provisions of the RTC agreement, two political and two economic, were particularly resented by the Indonesians (Dick et al. 2002:170). The first one was that the Netherlands would transfer sovereignty to the Republic of the United States of Indonesia (Republik Indonesia Serikat, RIS), a federation in which the Indonesian Republic (Republik Indonesia, RI), that had waged war with the Dutch, constituted only one state next to fifteen puppet states in various regions created by the Dutch in order to counterbalance the Republic. In addition, the Dutch insisted on the creation of a Netherlands-Indonesian Union along the lines of the British Commonwealth. However, within a few months after the transfer of sovereignty the fragile puppet states one by one dissolved themselves and joined the Republic. By 17 August 1950, five years after the proclamation of Indonesia's independence, RIS was dissolved and replaced by the present unitary Republic of Indonesia.

The second, far more contentious issue concerned the status of West New Guinea (named West Irian by the Indonesian nationalists, today's Papua). The Indonesian nationalists considered themselves the rightful inheritors of the Netherlands Indies. At the RTC the Dutch had refused to hand over West Irian to Indonesia, arguing that its Papuan population was racially, culturally and linguistically no part of the Indonesian nation. Since the Dutch adamantly refused to transfer sovereignty over West Irian, Dutch-Indonesia relations were doomed from the start and deteriorated until broken off altogether on 17 August 1960 (Houben 1996:173).

One economic matter that rankled Indonesian nationalists was the Dutch insistence that Indonesia would take over the foreign debt incurred by the Netherlands Indies government to the Netherlands to an amount of $1,130 million running with an interest rate of 3 per cent and due to be repaid in full no later than June 1964 (Kahin 1997:26; Sumitro Djojohadikusumo 2000:95). In addition, Indonesia was obliged to take over the rights and liabilities of the colonial government's external floating debt amounting to another $70 million (Kahin 1997:314). The total inherited debt obligation would have been even higher had Sumitro not at the RTC insisted that a large part of it consisted of military expenses by the Netherlands in its military campaigns to subdue the Republic (Kahin 1997:26; Sumitro 2000:95).

Despite resentment at the huge inherited debt, the Indonesian government faithfully fulfilled its international financial obligations. When the Burhanuddin

Harahap cabinet on 21 February 1955 abrogated the economic and financial agreement of the RTC as a result of the protracted West Irian dispute, only $171 million of the original $1,130 million remained to be repaid. No other former colony was obliged to take over such a large debt from its former colonial ruler as Indonesia (Kahin 1997:27).

The second, equally contentious economic issue was the guarantee that Dutch economic and business interests would be allowed to continue to operate in Indonesia without any hindrance, just like during colonial times. During the four-year armed struggle against the Dutch (1945–49), leading Dutch business firms had come to realize that trying to reoccupy Indonesia by military force was futile. Their top priority, therefore, was to rehabilitate and reconstruct their business establishments, estates, mines, and factories, which had been severely damaged during the Japanese occupation and the armed struggle against the Dutch (Lindblad 2002:141). Private Dutch business exerted heavy pressure on the Netherlands government to ensure that the RTC would yield an agreement safeguarding their extensive economic interests in independent Indonesia.

With these guidelines, the Dutch delegation at the RTC refused to make any concessions and insisted on obtaining necessary guarantees for unrestricted operations by Dutch business enterprises in independent Indonesia. Interestingly, on this issue the Indonesian and Dutch delegations quickly reached agreement formalized in the so-called Finec (Financieel-Economische Overeenkomst). This agreement secured the maximum possible economic and financial benefits for the Netherlands, in particular private Dutch business in Indonesia. Finec also included a clause to the effect that nationalization would only be permitted if it was in Indonesia's national interest and if both parties agreed. A judge would then decide on the amount of compensation to the owners on the basis of the real value of the nationalized enterprise (Meijer 1994:46-7).

Finec also contained provisions favouring Dutch economic interests, including a commitment by Indonesia that it would consult with the Netherlands whenever its fiscal and monetary policies would affect Dutch economic interests in Indonesia (Meijer 1994:46-7). No wonder that the late Professor Henri Baudet, a conservative Dutch economic historian, stated that the Finec contained the maximum attainable guarantees for the unhindered continuation of Dutch business (Baudet & Fennema 1983:213).

The achievement of political independence, yet without economic independence, posed a serious problem for the Indonesian government. Not being able to exert any control over important segments of the Indonesian economy clearly restricted the scope of action of Indonesia's economic policymakers. For instance, pursuing an independent monetary policy would be difficult if the Java Bank, the bank of circulation which acted as the country's central bank, was still in the hands of the Dutch. It also gave rise to the widely held notion that the economic phase of decolonization had not even started. The late Sutan Sjahrir, Indonesian prime minister during the early years of the revolution and chairman of Indonesia's Socialist Party (Partai Sosialis Indonesia, PSI), expressed the widely felt dissatisfaction in 1951 stating that 'continuing Dutch economic domination in Indonesia, and not West Irian, was the real fundamental problem adversely affecting Netherlands-Indonesia relations' (Meijer 1994:349).

Dutch economic domination over the Indonesian economy is, amongst others, reflected by the fact that only 19 per cent of the capital not invested in agriculture was owned by indigenous Indonesians. Economic gains for the Netherlands from continued operations of Dutch business in Indonesia were substantial: out of total profits pocketed by foreign private business in Indonesia in 1953, no less than 70 per cent (Rp449 million) were transferred to the Netherlands. In addition, Rp464 million or 83 per cent of total overseas transfers for social purposes (pensions, personal savings and the like) also went to the Netherlands in that year (Meijer 1994:349).

Indonesia's economic dependence on the Netherlands was in particular visible in inter-island shipping, which was largely controlled, or virtually monopolized by the Dutch shipping concern KPM (Koninklijke Paketvaart Maatschappij, Royal Packet Company). Realizing that inter-island shipping constituted the vital artery of trade in the Indonesian archipelago, the Indonesian government understandably wished to terminate the domination by the KPM. However, these early plans could not be realized, because the Indonesian government lacked the financial means to take over KPM (Meijer 1994:350) at a price acceptable to KPM.

Continuing Dutch economic dominance in the Indonesian economy is evident from an estimate by the late Professor Benjamin Higgins, a United Nations consultant to the Indonesian government in the early 1950s. Higgins calculated that the Dutch-owned segment of the modern sectors in the Indonesian economy accounted for about 25 per cent of the nation's GDP and about 10 per cent of total employment (Higgins 1990:40). Many senior positions in the fledgling Indonesian public service were occupied by Dutch officials, whose loyalty to newly-independent Indonesia could not readily be taken for granted. According to one estimate, after the transfer of sovereignty about 17,000 Dutch public servants entered Indonesia's public service, although many of them were soon relegated to unimportant positions. Their incomes were eroded because of the monetary measures of the Indonesian government to curb inflationary pressures (Houben 1996:171). Eurasians, that is persons of mixed Dutch and Indonesian descent, were also removed from the bureaucracy. They were distrusted by the Indonesians because they had sided with the Dutch during the revolution (Houben 1996:171).

The president and most directors of the Java Bank (which had functioned as the bank of circulation during the colonial period) were still Dutch (Higgins 1990:40). The head of the Foreign Exchange Control Board was also a Dutchman. The Board was an independent government body that in the colonial period had reported directly to the Governor-General. Sumitro observed that, when he became minister of finance in 1952, he entered a department full of Dutch officials who, as he caustically noted, had no clue about economics, but were very good at administrative procedures (Sumitro Djojohadikusumo 2003:59).

## INDONESIANIZATION AND MEASURES TO REDUCE DUTCH ECONOMIC PREDOMINANCE

Despite unhappiness with the continuing Dutch predominance in the economy, the leading economic policymakers in the early 1950s, including vice president Mohammad Hatta, Sumitro Djojohadikusumo, Sjafruddin Prawiranegara and Djuanda, were pragmatic men who, while attracted to socialist ideals, did not adhere to any rigid ideological doctrine (Booth 1986:13). They did not constitute a cohesive group and adhered to views about several economic issues such as the role of foreign direct investment or the feasibility of crash industrialization. However, as pragmatic politicians they realized that top priority had to be given to economic stabilization and rehabilitation. Since a large part of the modern export sector, including large estates and several mines, were still owned and operated by Dutch private firms, these policymakers realized that they had to protect the legal rights of the Dutch enterprises, unpalatable though this was. The Dutch enterprises could therefore operate without any official restrictions, although this policy was often criticized by more radical nationalists. Yet, the pragmatic policymakers also realized that the Dutch export-oriented large estates and mines generated much-needed foreign exchange revenues to import food, raw materials and capital goods.

Despite constraints imposed by Finec, the pragmatic economic policymakers were determined to match Indonesia's hard-won political independence with meaningful economic sovereignty, even though they appreciated that it would take a long time and great effort. Since Finec provided the legal basis for nationalization under specified conditions, the Indonesian government soon took steps to nationalize key economic institutions and enterprises of singular economic or strategic importance.

The first important economic institution to be nationalized was the Java Bank, the bank of circulation during the colonial period that had been chosen as the nation's central bank also after 1949. On 30 April 1951, Yusuf Wibisono, minister of finance, announced that the Indonesian government intended to nationalize the Java Bank as soon as possible. He explained to the press that the Masyumi party, of which he was a member, at its national conference in Yogyakarta in December 1949 had already urged for nationalization, and that he was proud to be able to implement that decision (Saubari 2003:71-2).

But Yusuf Wibisono had made his announcement in the press without consulting the Dutch (Sjafruddin 2003:81). Not surprisingly, the Dutch initially attempted to retain control over the Java Bank, but in the event the nationalization of the Java Bank proceeded relatively smoothly as the Dutch accepted that control of money and credit was an essential ingredient of sovereignty (Anspach 1969:137).

On 3 July 1951, the Sukiman cabinet, dominated by Masyumi, installed a committee on the nationalization of the Java Bank authorized to take all necessary preparatory steps towards nationalization, including drafting the required legislation. Members of the committee were Sumitro, Moh. Sediono, Soetikno Slamet, T.R.B. Sabaruddin, A. Oudt and Khouw Bian Tie (Saubari 2003:72).

Upon advice of the committee, the government decided that nationalization would be implemented through the purchase of shares from both domestic and overseas shareholders. To speed up the purchase of shares, the government sent two officials to the Netherlands, Moh. Saubari, secretary-general at the department of finance, and Khouw Bian Tie, advisor of the Java Bank. Their talks with Piet Lieftinck, the Dutch minister of finance, and the Dutch association for trade in securities in Amsterdam went smoothly, resulting in a decision to suspend trading of Java Bank shares on the Amsterdam Stock Exchange. The announcement was signed by Moh. Saubari and published in Het Financieel Dagblad (Financial Daily) on 3 August 1951 (Saubari 2003:72).

In Indonesia, Wibisono issued a statement on the same day about the government's offer to purchase privately held shares at 120 per cent of the nominal value when expressed in Dutch guilders or 360 per cent when expressed in Indonesian rupiah. The purchase of the shares proceeded well and within a couple of months 97 per cent of all shares had already been acquired by the government. On 6 December 1951 the law on the nationalization of the Java Bank was enacted (Saubari 2003:72-3).

A. Houwink, the last Dutch president of the Java Bank, had resigned and been succeeded by Sjafruddin Prawiranegara already before the nationalization took place. Sjafruddin, former minister of finance in the cabinets headed by Moh. Hatta and Moh. Natsir, was at first reluctant to take up the position at the Java Bank as he wanted to retire from public life. Sjafruddin wanted to earn enough money for the education of his children but was only in a position to do so in a private capacity as he, possibly as a result of his Dutch-styled education, did not want to abuse his power as a public servant to make money (Sjafruddin 2003:80). Sjafruddin therefore put forward as a condition that his salary, and that of all Indonesian staff, should not be changed to an Indonesian level and that privileges which the Dutch staff enjoyed should also be made available to the Indonesian staff. The government agreed and Sjafruddin became the first Indonesian president of the Java Bank. His candidacy was also supported by the staff at the Java Bank, including his predecessor Houwink (Sjafruddin 2003:80). In 1953, the Java Bank was transformed into Bank Indonesia with Sjafruddin Prawiranegara as its first governor.

Nationalization also affected other Dutch-owned enterprises occupying a key position in the Indonesian economy, for instance the railways in Java and public utilities such as electricity and gas companies (Burger 1975:170). Domestic air transport was transferred from the Koninklijke Nederlandsch-Indische Luchtvaart-Maatschappij (KNILM, Royal Netherlands Indies Airlines) to Garuda Indonesian Airways, Indonesia's national carrier. This airline was initially established as a joint venture between the Royal Dutch Airlines KLM and the Indonesian government. However, in 1954 Garuda was transformed into a fully state-owned airline with the role of KLM limited to providing technical assistance and advice (Burger 1975:170).

However, efforts to nationalize the Dutch-controlled KPM, which in 1956 still dominated inter-island shipping, did not succeed. However, the newly established Indonesian shipping company PELNI (Pelayaran Nasional Indonesia), the state-owned, inter-island shipping company which received financial assistance from the Indonesian government was able to make steady inroads into the market dominated by KPM. For instance, while in 1956 PELNI carried 25 per cent of the cargo, in 1957 it was able to increase its share to 29 per cent. Although in the passenger trade, the KPM was better able to keep its dominance with 94 per cent of the traffic, the introduction in 1956 of six new passenger ships enabled PELNI in 1957 to double the number of passengers carried (Dick, 1987: 18).

The nationalization of the Java Bank and other enterprises deemed to be of crucial importance to the Indonesian economy proceeded relatively smoothly. Both the Dutch government and the owners of the enterprises in question realized that no sovereign government could leave its central bank, public utilities and vital modes of transport in the hands of foreigners.

Other efforts to counter Dutch economic control included vice president Hatta's instruction to the executive board of Central Trading Company (CTC), Indonesia's first government-owned, trading company established in Bukittinggi in 1947, to challenge the monopoly of the 'Big Five', the five leading Dutch trading companies (Daud 2003:256). The establishment of the CTC had been urged by Hatta who did not approve of the involvement by Indonesian revolutionary army units in smuggling agricultural commodities to Singapore and British Malaya in order to acquire military equipment and arms for the struggle against the Dutch. Therefore, Hatta wished to legalize these trading by separating smuggling from military operations through the establishment of a formal trading house, CTC (Daud 2003:255).

Heeding Hatta's instruction to challenge Dutch control over Indonesia's export and import trade, yet lacking any business experience themselves, the two directors of the CTC, Teuku Moh. Daud and Teuku Abdul Hamid Azwar, realized they had to look for people possessing the required experience and skills, especially with regard to international business. At the time, the only people who had such business experience and skills were Indonesians of Chinese descent. They therefore approached some Sino-Indonesian managers employed in the few large companies owned by Sino-Indonesians such as the Liem Goan Seng and Kian Gwan firms (Daud 2003:257).

At first, Daud and Azwar experienced some difficulty persuading CTC's board of trustees to recruit mainly Sino-Indonesian managers. They eventually succeeded because it was obvious that Daud and Azwar were not playing politics, and were only concerned with making CTC an efficient and viable corporation. This would be imperative to achieve the first task of CTC of reducing the domination of the Dutch companies over the Indonesian economy (Daud 2003:257).

Daud and Azwar were successful in recruiting a senior manager from the Liem Goan Seng company, Koo Liong Bing, who was willing to join CTC. Through Koo, CTC was able to recruit several other Sino-Indonesian managers, mainly from the Kian Gwan company. Later Koo himself became one of the directors of CTC (Daud 2003:257).

Another measure to try to counter the 'Big Five' was the so-called *Benteng* (fortress) programme launched in 1950 (Sumitro 2003:59). This programme was also the first major official strategy to further the development of a strong indigenous Indonesian business class. The *Benteng* programme focused on securing national control over the import trade by reserving import licenses in certain restricted categories of easy-to-sell goods exclusively for indigenous Indonesian importers. The provisions of the programme, however, did not specifically exclude ethnic Chinese businessmen who possessed Indonesian citizenship (Mackie 1971:47-8). In fact, however, the *Benteng* programme was primarily aimed at countering both Dutch and Chinese economic domination.

To promote the development of an indigenous Indonesian business class, the government established new financial institutions providing credit to eligible businessmen. Such institutions included the Bank Industri Negara (State Industrial Bank, BIN), extending credits to large-scale agricultural enterprises and manufacturing and mining enterprises, the Bank Negara Indonesia (Indonesian State Bank, BNI), that gave loans to exporters and importers, and also the Yayasan Kredit (Credit Foundation) which provided guarantees for loans for which the customary business collateral was not available (Burger 1975:171).

Another important measure to 'indonesianize' the Dutch companies was a 'gentlemen's agreement' between the Indonesian government and the Dutch firms that 70 per cent of the companies' personnel had to be (indigenous) Indonesians. However, this 'indonesianization' (*indonesianisasi*) programme turned out to be limited to the lower functions in the companies. In fact, the Dutch companies in general were little motivated to train their Indonesian personnel in order to enable them to occupy higher functions and include the most competent among them in the companies' board of directors, as stipulated in provision 12 of Finec. At the estates the top function occupied by Indonesian personnel was usually that of *mandor* (supervisor) (Meijer 1994:352).

Very much aware of the fact that the Dutch companies were reluctant to promote their Indonesian staff to higher and managerial positions, the Wilopo cabinet (April 1952 – June 1953) resorted to reducing drastically the work permits for Dutch citizens in Indonesia. While in 1950 Dutch citizens could still freely enter Indonesia, after 1951 strict entry quotas were introduced, which gradually reduced the number of Dutch citizens given work permits and in 1953 only 1000 work permits were issued (Meijer 1994:353).

The Dutch companies soon experienced great difficulties because of the tiny visa quotas. Despite offering higher salaries and other favourable incentives, the firms were unable to slow down, let alone stop the steady outflow of Dutch employees. While remaining Dutch staff was initially able to take over the tasks of those who had repatriated, over time this was no longer possible as more and more Dutch employees were leaving (Meijer 1994:352-3).

The outflow of Dutch employees seriously threatened continuity in the operations of Dutch business in Indonesia. The companies therefore reluctantly started to train Indonesian staff in greater numbers to occupy the higher functions left vacant by departing Dutch employees. To this end, Dutch import and export companies established a trade school for their Indonesian staff. In general, however, numbers of participants in the training programmes remained limited as the directors of most Dutch companies were concerned that to elevate their Indonesian staff to senior managerial positions or to allow participation of Indonesian capital would pave the way to nationalization of their enterprises (Meijer 1994:353).

## THE CURTAIN FALLS:
## NATIONALIZATION OF ALL DUTCH ENTERPRISES

Relations between Indonesia and the Netherlands deteriorated rapidly from the mid-1950s because of the Dutch government's adamant refusal to discuss the status of West Irian (Papua). When the Indonesian government in November 1957 failed to persuade the United Nations General Assembly to adopt a resolution calling on the Netherlands to negotiate a settlement with Indonesia on the West Irian issue, anti-Dutch demonstrations broke out in Jakarta. On 3 December 1957 workers of militant labour unions affiliated with the Indonesian Nationalist Party (PNI) started taking over Dutch enterprises and business offices (Meier, 1994: 584).

The head office of the Dutch interisland shipping company KPM in Jakarta, a prime symbol of Dutch economic dominance, was the first to be taken over by the workers. Another symbol of Anglo-Dutch economic power, Royal Dutch Shell, was not taken over as it was partly British-owned.

On 5 December 1957 the Department of Foreign Affairs called the Dutch *charge d'affaires* and presented him with a note that all Dutch citizens had to leave the country within the shortest possible time. The subsequent Dutch exodus proceeded relatively smoothly, and by March 1959 30,000 of the last remaining Dutch had repatriated, leaving only about 6,000 Dutch citizens behind. These people had stayed on because they were either working under contract with non-Dutch foreign enterprises (about 3,500), or were serving as missionaries (about 1,600) (Meier, 1994: 585, 592).

During the following two weeks this action was followed by similar takeovers of other Dutch enterprises all over the country. Although the Indonesian government had not initiated the takeovers, it did not attempt to resist the actions (Glassburner 1971:92). Some senior government officials, notably Sjafruddin Prawiranegara, governor of Bank Indonesia, openly spoke out against the takeovers (Sjafruddin 2003:81). Sjafruddin felt that Indonesians through education and training first had to acquire the required skills to manage and run the modern Dutch enterprises.

Concerned about the economic and political chaos caused by unauthorized takeovers, General Nasution, the army chief of staff, took control of events on 13 December 1957 by issuing an instruction to the army to manage the seized enterprises. The PKI and SOBSI, anxious to avoid an open confrontation with the army, promised to support the military forces by keeping the seized enterprises operating (Ricklefs 1994:261).

In December 1958 the legal foundation was laid down for the nationalization of seized Dutch enterprises and this was effectuated for various categories of enterprises during the first half of 1959. All nationalized companies became state property (Dick et al. 2002:184). With one drastic action, the powerful Dutch business firms that had operated in Indonesia since the second half of the nineteenth century, were eliminated. Unlike the nationalization of the Java Bank and the public utilities at an earlier stage in the 1950s, which had been achieved by mutual consent, the nationalization of Dutch enterprises in 1959 was a unilateral measure taken by the Indonesian authorities in response to the collapse of Dutch-Indonesian relations because of the acrimonious dispute about West Irian.

## DEALING WITH THE 'CHINESE PROBLEM'

The nationalization of Dutch enterprises went a long way towards satisfying the national aspiration 'to convert the colonial economy into a national economy' in Hadinoto's formulation. The nation's important productive assets, formerly owned by the Dutch, were now Indonesian-owned and important economic functions, formerly performed by the Dutch, were now filled by Indonesian nationals. But this conversion was still not felt to be complete as the large indigenous Indonesian population was still facing the economic dominance of ethnic Chinese businessmen, including both Indonesian as well Chinese nationals, who since colonial times had played a major role in the economy, particularly intermediate trade, rice milling, and money lending. Their economic dominance, and the perceived usurious activities of Chinese moneylenders (*Cina mindering*) caused much resentment, if not outright hatred, among indigenous Indonesians. For this reason the late Professor Everett Hawkins, an American economist who had worked in Indonesia in the 1950s and early 1960s, once referred to the 'double colonialism' that had prevailed in Indonesia.[3]

Next to efforts to limit Dutch economic dominance, the Indonesian government therefore in the early 1950s also took steps to reduce the economic role of ethnic Chinese. However, taking measures to limit Chinese economic activities proved to be more difficult than eliminating Dutch economic interests. For one thing, the number of ethnic Chinese was much larger than the Dutch. Through intermediate trade and money lending, their economic activities in the rural areas were also far more intertwined with the economic activities of the indigenous population than the Dutch activities had ever been.

Moreover, the large ethnic Chinese group included Indonesian citizens as well as citizens of the People's Republic of China and a small group of pro-Taiwan 'stateless' citizens. It was therefore difficult for the Indonesian government to take measures directed at all ethnic Chinese, as this category included a relatively large group of Indonesian citizens. Having fought against Dutch colonialism and its implied racism, many Indonesian leaders found that overly discriminatory policies against its citizens of Chinese descent did not accord well with the ideals of the Indonesian revolution. Nevertheless, given strong political pressure, the Indonesian government did initiate measures in the early 1950s to reduce the economic role of the ethnic Chinese and promote the development of indigenous Indonesian (*Indonesia asli*) entrepreneurs. Such measures are discussed in detail in the following.

## THE *BENTENG* (FORTRESS) PROGRAMME

Pressure to promote the development of indigenous Indonesian business grew stronger but, by and large, economic activities of indigenous Indonesians were confined to small-scale agriculture, small retail stores, and small-scale industries, such as batik, handicrafts, and clove cigarettes. To promote the development of indigenous entrepreneurs, Djuanda, minister of welfare, in April 1950 issued a regulation which gave priority to indigenous businessmen to import goods from abroad. To facilitate their import trade, indigenous businessmen were given priority access to cheap credit (Siahaan 1996:168). As noted above, the *Benteng* programme was primarily aimed at countering the dominance of the 'Big Five' Dutch trading companies in import and export trade.

Protection to the indigenous importers was provided by reserving the imports of specified categories of goods, referred to as *Benteng* goods, solely for indigenous importers, and by channeling credits to these importers through the state-owned BNI Bank Negara Indonesia (BNI) (Sutter 1959:1017-8). The required qualifications for receiving preferential treatment through the *Benteng* programme were, at least on paper, quite stringent.

Choosing import trading as the first major economic activity to promote indigenous entrepreneurship was understandable, as at the time almost all export and import trade was handled by Dutch and ethnic Chinese firms (Suhadi 1967:218). Focusing on the import trade to secure indigenous Indonesian dominance appeared to be the most feasible option since this line of business was considered the most responsive to state direction through controls over the allocation of import licenses (Robison 1986:44). The import trade was also the most accessible to indigenous businessmen. They could easily set up business with a minimum of overhead investment and concentrate on products sufficiently standardized to require a minimum of business experience, and also specialize in goods that were protected by import restrictions (Anspach 1969:168).

The *Benteng* programme attracted a great deal of interest. While in 1951 some 250 businessmen had registered with this programme, in 1952 the numbers had increased to 741, and to 1,500 in 1953 and to 2,211 in 1954 (Siahaan 1996:68). As a result, the percentage of total government foreign exchange credit allocated to the *Benteng* importers increased from 37 per cent in 1952/3 to 76 per cent in late 1954 (Robison 1986:45). By the early 1950s around 70 per cent of the import trade was reportedly done by indigenous Indonesian businessmen (Burger 1975:171).

Many of the new indigenous Indonesian importers receiving preferential treatment under the *Benteng* programme, lacking capital and/or business experience, engaged in business practices which, although not in violation of the letter of the law, did offend ethical standards. There were of course several other new, capable indigenous importers whose companies grew into viable companies. However, there were many more cases which could hardly be named 'bonafide' enterprises, but rather 'Ali-Baba' enterprises involving indigenous importers and ethnic Chinese businessmen (whether Indonesian citizen or foreign national). Such enterprises in fact proliferated under various forms, such as fronts and strawmen and the selling of import licenses to genuine, mostly ethnic Chinese, importers (Sutter 1959:1027).

The *Benteng* programme failed to foster a strong, self-reliant indigenous merchant class, but rather furthered a group of licensed brokers and political fixers, in short what we now call unproductive 'rent-seekers' or 'rent-harvesters'. These importers were often referred to as 'brief case importers' (*importir aktentas*), whose sole qualification as an importer was that they carried a briefcase (Siahaan 1998:168).

As the *Benteng* programme progressed, it became increasingly apparent that this programme was not effective in nurturing a viable group of indigenous entrepreneurs. To eliminate abuses, Roosseno, the minister of economic affairs from November 1954, introduced a foreign exchange auction system in the textile sector. He also banned discrimination on ethnic grounds, and thus allowed Sino-Indonesian businessmen to openly participate in the import trade. The auction system, however, turned out to be unsuccessful, as it did not give indigenous importers with inadequate financial resources access to the auctioned foreign exchange quota. Hence, such indigenous importers continued to serve as agents for ethnic Chinese businessmen (Anspach 1969:174-5). Indonesia's experience with its first affirmative programme to promote a strong and self-reliant indigenous business class proved a failure and in the second half of the 1950s came to an inglorious end when the Indonesian government realized that its aim of fostering a strong indigenous Indonesian class of entrepreneurs had not been achieved. However, the *Benteng* programme was never officially abolished.

## LIMITATIONS ON ETHNIC CHINESE ACTIVITIES IN THE WEAVING INDUSTRY

In 1954 the Indonesian government issued a regulation that foreign entrepreneurs (*pengusaha golongan asing*) were not allowed to expand the capacity of their weaving mills beyond prewar capacity. To circumvent the restriction, Chinese mill owners turned to subcontracting and recruited indigenous (*asli*) weavers but this practice enhanced the bargaining position of indigenous weavers vis-à-vis their contractors, namely the Chinese weavers (Keppy 2001:156).

Subcontracting in the weaving industry was in a sense illegal as it involved unlicensed weaving capacity and production based on weaving yarn that had been purchased in the black market. Because of its nature as a 'hidden business', subcontracting was vulnerable to punitive action by the government. Moreover, several of the ethnic Chinese weavers were small businessmen lacking the political protection and patronage which the big Chinese businessmen, notably the textile king Thee Tjie Tjhoen, were able to enjoy (Keppy 2001:156-7).

## BAN ON OWNERSHIP OF RICE MILLS, STEVEDORING, HARBOUR TRANSPORT AND WAREHOUSES BY ALIENS

Since the Dutch colonial period, Chinese businessmen had owned and operated most of the rice mills in Indonesia. In 1952 no less than 138 out of 154 rice mills in East Java were owned by ethnic Chinese (Anspach 1969:182). In view of the great economic importance of these rice mills, the Indonesian government in 1954 issued a regulation that Chinese-owned rice mills had to be transferred to indigenous Indonesians by March 1955. The regulation decreed that no new licenses for operating rice mills would be issued to foreign nationals, while existing mills had to be transferred to indigenous Indonesians, specifically persons having only Indonesian citizenship. Since the Indonesian citizens of Chinese descent still had, at the time of the regulation, dual citizenship, the 1954 regulation also affected them (Suryadinata 1992:132). However, because of the difficulties in implementing this regulation, the government still granted licenses to Chinese citizens on an annual basis (Suryadinata 1992:32).

Although until late 1957 most enterprises handling stevedoring, harbour transport and warehouses were owned and operated by the Dutch, some enterprises were owned and operated by Chinese. For this reason the government issued a decree in 1954 that these Chinese-owned enterprises had to be transferred to indigenous Indonesians by 1956. However, because of the difficulties in implementing the decree, this date had to be continuously extended, with the last extension running to June 1959 (Anspach 1969:184).

## MEASURES AGAINST PRO-TAIWAN LOCAL CHINESE

Angered by the support of the Taiwan government and the 'stateless' Taiwan-oriented local Chinese to the PRRI and Permesta rebellions in respectively West Sumatra and Sulawesi, the Indonesian government in 1958 closed down all Chinese organizations, schools, newspapers and enterprises officially and unofficially associated with Taiwan. Taiwan-oriented community leaders who were pro-Kuomintang were also arrested (Suryadinata 1992:175). Yet this measure did not seriously affect economic activities of the ethnic Chinese in Indonesia because of the relatively small number of pro-Taiwan Chinese. The government of the People's Republic of China predictably applauded these measures but its satisfaction did not last long as in the following year, 1959, the Indonesian government took a far more drastic measure to curtail economic activities by 'foreign' Chinese, specifically the citizens of the People's Republic.

## BAN ON RETAIL TRADE BY ALIENS IN RURAL AREAS

With the nationalization of all Dutch enterprises in 1959, the Chinese community emerged as the strongest element in the economy, aside from the government itself. In rural areas the Chinese had since the Dutch colonial period built a position of dominance in retail trade, rice milling and rural finance (Mackie 1971:9). Given Chinese economic dominance, deteriorating economic conditions and general distrust of the political loyalty of the ethnic

Chinese, it was only a matter of time before the Chinese, particularly those who were nationals of the People's Republic, would be the next target of government action.

A major step was an attempt in 1959 to break the Chinese hold on intermediate trade throughout the country by eliminating all 'foreign' Chinese from retail trade in rural areas (Somers Heidhues 2003:238). In May 1959, Rachmat Muljomiseno, then minister of trade and a strong supporter of the strongly anti-Chinese Assaat Movement[4] announced a regulation banning foreign nationals from rural trade requiring them to transfer their businesses to Indonesian citizens by 30 September 1959 (Suryadinata 1992:135). Rachmat's regulation adversely affected the traditional Chinese economic role as middlemen in collecting agricultural produce for the towns or for export and in the distribution of city-produced or imported goods in rural areas (Somers Heidhues 1964:24). Before the minister could implement this regulation, a new cabinet headed by President Sukarno himself was installed on 5 July 1959 introducing Sukarno's 'Guided Democracy and Guided Economy' (*Demokrasi Terpimpin dan Ekonomi Terpimpin*).

The new cabinet was equally committed to Rachmat's plan and on 16 November 1959 Government Regulation no. 10 of 1959 (*Peraturan Pemerintah, PP 10/1959*) was issued. It decreed that as from 1 January 1960 foreign nationals would be banned from rural trade and would have to transfer their business to Indonesian nationals (Suryadinata 1992:135). Although Indonesian nationals benefiting from this decree could in principle also include Indonesian citizens of Chinese descent, the government hoped that much of the rural trade run by the 'foreign' Chinese would be taken over by co-operatives and businesses owned and run by indigenous Indonesians.

Although *PP 10/1959* applied to all foreign nationals, it was mainly an army-instigated move to hurt the foreign Chinese who, the strongly anti-communist army suspected, could be a fifth column for China, and also to weaken Jakarta's (i.e. Sukarno's) growing friendship with China, and, finally, to embarrass the PKI. Although the Chinese government put heavy pressure on the Indonesian government not to carry out, if not rescind, this decree, the army in late 1959 began forcibly moving the 'foreign' Chinese from rural areas, specifically rural areas below the district (*kabupaten*) levels, to the towns and cities of Java. As a result of this expulsion, in the course of 1960-1961 about 119,000 Chinese nationals repatriated to China (Ricklefs 1993:267). The ban also caused a serious rupture in the political relations between Indonesia and China.

Since most co-operatives and/or indigenous businessmen were not able to replace the Chinese traders, or to engage in rural trade with equal efficiency, the ban caused considerable economic disruption. At least in the short run, the ban caused above all hardship to the villagers it was supposed to help (Somers Heidhues 1964:28). In order not to weaken the position of Sukarno, who was viewed as a strong ally of China, and since it had difficulty accommodating the large number of repatriated Chinese, China soon tuned down its anti-Indonesia rhetoric. Sukarno himself, realizing the danger to both the country's economy and his own position if the anti-Chinese campaign were be continued, eventually succeeded in curbing the anti-Chinese actions. Although *PP 10/1959* was never officially repealed, its further implementation was temporarily suspended. (Suryadinata 1992:137).

As economic conditions continued to deteriorate in the early 1960s and Sukarno's and the army's attention increasingly focused on reclaiming West Irian from the Dutch, a resumption of the implementation of *PP 10/1959* did not take place. Moreover, with the emphasis on 'Indonesian-style socialism', pursuing new affirmative programmes to promote indigenous private businessmen was no longer a priority.

## CONCLUSION

While the nationalization of the Dutch enterprises in 1959 was considered a crucial step in satisfying aspirations of economic nationalism, in the short run this measure caused serious economic disruption. The nationalized Dutch enterprises were turned into state enterprises, mostly managed and run by military officers not familiar with running commercial enterprises efficiently. Not surprisingly, the performance of these nationalized enterprises declined rapidly.

Since the ethnic Chinese minority had owned and run important economic activities since colonial times, measures against the Dutch were followed by measures to curtail the economic activities of the ethnic Chinese. Although many ethnic Chinese businessmen experienced great difficulties during the 1950s, the anti-Chinese measures during the period 1950–1965 did not appreciably reduce their economic importance. In fact, in view of the shortage of experienced indigenous businessmen, the niches created through the nationalization of Dutch enterprises paved the way for the entry of ethnic Chinese businessmen into wholesale trade and other activities formerly dominated by Dutch enterprises.

## Notes

1.   "Indonesianization: Economic Aspects of Decolonization in the 1950s", by Thee Kian Wie, first published in *Indonesian Economic Decolonization in Indonesia*

*in Regional and International Perspective,* edited by Thomas Lindblad and Peter Post, Leiden: KITLV Press, 2009.

2.  I acknowledge the helpful comments and suggestions of Professor Anne Booth and Dr Peter Keppy on an earlier draft of this contribution. However, I alone remain responsible for remaining errors and shortcomings.

3.  Personal communication from Professor Everett Hawkins.

4.  In 1956 Assaat, former president of the short-lived Republik Indonesia when it was a constituent part of the United States of Indonesia (Republik Indonesia Serikat), January–August 1950, launched the Assaat Movement (Gerakan Assaat) aimed at ending Chinese domination over the Indonesian economy. The Assaat movement was subsequently discredited when Assaat joined the anti-Sukarno PRRI rebellion in West Sumatra in 1958.

## References

Anspach, Ralph. "Indonesia". In *Underdevelopment and Economic Nationalism in Southeast Asia*, edited by Frank H. Golay et al., 111-202. New York: Cornell University Press, 1969.

Baudet, Henri and M. Fennema. *Het Nederlands belang bij Indië*. Utrecht: Spectrum, 1983.

Booth, Anne. "The colonial legacy and its impact on post-independence planning in India and Indonesia". *Itinerario* (1986): 10-1:1-30.

Burger, D.H. *Sociologisch-economische geschiedenis van Indonesië; II. Indonesia in de 20e eeuw*. Amsterdam: Royal Tropical Institute, 1975.

Daud, Teuku Moh. "Recollections of My Career". In *Recollections: The Indonesian economy, 1950s–1990s*, edited by Thee Kian Wie, 253-63. Singapore: Institute of Southeast Asian Studies. Originally published in 1999 in: *Bulletin of Indonesian Economic Studies* (2003): 35-3:41-50.

Dick, H.W. *The Indonesian Inter-Island Shipping Industry — An Analysis of Competition and Regulation*. Singapore: Institute of Southeast Asian Studies, 1987.

Dick, Howard, Vincent Houben, Thomas Lindblad and Thee Kian Wie. *The Emergence of a National Economy: An Economic History of Indonesia, 1800–2000*. Crows Nest, NSW: Allen & Unwin, 2002.

Glassburner, Bruce. "Economic policymaking in Indonesia, 1950–57". In *The economy of Indonesia; Selected readings,* edited by Bruce Glassburner, 70-98. Ithaca, NY: Cornell University Press, 1971.

Hadinoto, Sujono. *Ekonomi Indonesia: dari ekonomi kolonial ke ekonomi nasional*. Jakarta: Yayasan Pembangunan, 1949.

Higgins, Benjamin. "Thought and action; Indonesian economic studies and policies in the 1950s". *Bulletin of Indonesian Economic Studies* (1990): 26-1:37-47.

Houben, Vincent. *Van kolonie tot eenheidstaat; Indonesië in de negentiende en twinstigste eeuw*. Leiden: Vakgroep Talen en Culturen van Zuidoost-Azië en Oceanië, Rijksuniversiteit te Leiden [Semaian 16], 1996.

Johnson, Harry. "The Ideology of Economic Policy in New States". In *Chicago Essays in Economic Development*, edited by David Wall, 23-40. Chicago: University of Chicago Press, 1972.

Kahin, George McT. "Some recollections from and reflections on the Indonesian Revolution". In *The Heartbeat of the Indonesian Revolution*, edited by Taufik Abdullah, 10-27. Jakarta: Gramedia, 1997.

Keppy, Peter. *Hidden Business: Indigenous and Ethnic Chinese Entrepreneurs in the Majalaya Textile Industry, West Java, 1928–1974*. Ph.D. thesis, Free University of Amsterdam, 2001.

Lindblad, Thomas. "Politieke economie en de dekolonisatie in Indonesië". In *Macht en majesteit; Opstellen voor Cees Fasseur* edited by Thomas Lindblad and Willem van der Molen, 132-46. Leiden: Opleiding Talen en Culturen van Zuidoost-Azië en Oceanië, Universiteit Leiden [Semaian 22], 2002.

Mackie, J.A.C. "The Indonesian Economy, 1950–63". In *The Economy of Indonesia; Selected Readings,* edited by Bruce Glassburner, 16-69. Ithaca, New York: Cornell University Press, 1971.

Meijer, Hans. *Den Haag–Djakarta; De Nederlands-Indonesische betrekkingen. 1950– 1962.* Utrecht: Spectrum, 1994.

Ricklefs, M.C. *A History of Modern Indonesia Since c. 1300* [Second edition]. London: Macmillan, 1993.

Robison, Richard. *Indonesia: The Rise of Capital*. Sydney: Allen & Unwin, 1986.

Saubari, Moh. "Reflections on Economic Policymaking, 1945–51". In *Recollections: The Indonesian Economy, 1950s–1990s*, edited by Thee Kian Wie, 69-73. Singapore: Institute of Southeast Asian Studies. Originally published in 1987 in: *Bulletin of Indonesian Economic Studies* (2003): 23-2:118-21.

Siahaan, Bisuk. *Industrialisasi di Indonesia; Sejak hutang kehormatan sampai banting stir.* Jakarta: Pustaka Data, 1996.

Sjafruddin Prawiranegara. "Reflections on Economic Policymaking, 1945–51". In *Recollections: The Indonesian Economy, 1950s–1990s*, edited by Thee Kian Wie, 69-73. Singapore: Institute of Southeast Asian Studies. Originally published in 1987 in: *Bulletin of Indonesian Economic Studies* (2003): 23-3:100-8.

Somers Heidhues, Mary. "Peranakan Chinese politics in Indonesia". Interim report Modern Indonesia Project, Ithaca, NY: Cornell University, 1964.

Suhadi Mangkusuwondo. *Industrialization Efforts in Indonesia: The Role of Agriculture and Foreign Trade in the Development of the Industrial Sector*. Ph.D. thesis, University of California, Berkeley, 1967.

Sumitro Djojohadikusumo. *Jejak perlawanan begawan pejuang*. Jakarta: Sinar Harapan, 2000.

Suryadinata, Leo. *Pribumi Indonesians, The Chinese Minority and China* [Third edition]. Singapore: Heinemann Asia, 1992.

Sutter, John. "Indonesianisasi: A historical survey of the role of politics in the institutions of a changing economy, from the Second World War to the end of the general elections, 1940–55". Ph.D. thesis, Cornell University, Ithaca, New York, 1959.

Thee Kian Wie. "Recollections of My Career". In *Recollections: The Indonesian Economy, 1950s–1990s*, edited by Thee Kian Wie, 253-63. Singapore: Institute of Southeast Asian Studies. Originally published in 1986 in: *Bulletin of Indonesian Economic Studies* (2003): 22-3:27-39.

# 2

# INDONESIA'S FIRST AFFIRMATIVE POLICY: THE *BENTENG* PROGRAMME IN THE 1950s[1]

To a much greater degree than has been the case in the other newly-independent countries in Southeast Asia, economic nationalism in Indonesia has remained a potent force until the present. Although its contemporary manifestations has in general become less aggressive and less strident than they were in the 1950s, economic nationalism remains a driving force that to a large extent still influences economic policies today. Whereas economic nationalism during the early years of independence in the 1950s was mainly directed at the continuing economic dominance of the Dutch and ethnic Chinese business interests, in the years following the Asian economic crisis in the late 1990s economic nationalism was mainly aimed at the perceived interference of international organizations, particularly the IMF, in the formulation of Indonesia's economic policies.

Despite the strong economic nationalism, pragmatic considerations have more often than not over-ruled ill-considered economic nationalism. In this way, pragmatic policies have often been able to mitigate the adverse economic and political effects of emotional economic nationalism. This was, as will be argued in this paper, evident when the Indonesian government in the second half of the 1950s, terminated the unsuccessful *Benteng* programme, its first affirmative programme to promote indigenous Indonesian entrepreneurs.

## ECONOMIC NATIONALISM DURING THE EARLY YEARS OF INDEPENDENCE

During the early years of independence in the 1950s a basic aspiration of Indonesia's economic nationalism was the need 'to convert the colonial economy into a national economy'. This popular demand appealed to many Indonesians, as during the Dutch colonial period Indonesia had become an outstanding example of a *colonial primary export economy*. The growth dynamics of such an economy was primarily determined by the rapid expansion and diversification of primary exports at the expense of traditional economic activities (Pauuw, 1983: 9). While primary export expansion had brought some welfare to the Indonesian population, it had not laid the basis for sustained economic growth and successful transformation into a more diversified economy. Moreover, during the colonial period the production of primary commodities for export had been initiated and managed by Dutch and other Western enterprises, while the Indonesian population only played a subordinate and passive role as lessors of land and/or as unskilled, lowly-paid workers. Not surprisingly, rapid primary export expansion did not lead to a substantial increase in the skills, productivity and incomes of the Indonesian population (Paauw, 1983: 9–10).

However, if economic nationalism in newly-independent countries is defined as the national aspiration to have nationals own and control the productive assets owned by foreigners or residents considered as aliens and perform the important economic functions hitherto performed by foreigners or resident aliens (Johnson, 1972: 26), the major target of Indonesia's economic nationalism during the early 1950s was the elimination of Dutch economic dominance, particularly over the modern sectors of the economy. Under the terms of the Financial-Economic Agreement (Finec), reached at the Round Table Conference (RTC) in The Hague (23 August – 2 November 1949), the Indonesian government guaranteed that Dutch business could continue to operate in Indonesia without any hindrance. Nationalization of Dutch enterprises would only be permitted if it was considered to be in Indonesia's national interest and only when it was mutually agreed by both parties. The amount of compensation for the nationalization of the enterprise would be decided by a judge on the basis of the real value of the nationalized enterprise (Meier, 1994: 46–7).

The success of the Dutch delegation at the RTC in persuading the Indonesian delegation to agree with most of the items contained in Finec, including the guarantees, concessions, and rights accorded to Dutch business in independent Indonesia, and the financial and trade relations between the two countries, could be attributed to the determination of the Dutch government to secure the maximum possible economic benefits from Finec (Meier, 1994: 46). In return, the Dutch were prepared to make political concessions to the Indonesians.

On its part, the Indonesian delegation, led by Vice-President Hatta, was prepared, though reluctantly, to yield to the Dutch demands because it realized that for the foreseeable future Indonesia would, whether it liked it or not, still need Dutch capital and enterprise for the reconstruction of its war-ravaged economy and generate the export revenues needed to import foodstuffs and raw materials and capital equipment for its manufacturing industries. As a pragmatic nationalist, Vice-President Hatta realized that no matter how unpalatable the continuing Dutch economic dominance would be to the Indonesian people, there was in the short run no viable alternative.

Having achieved political independence without meaningful economic independence, the Indonesian government took several steps to counter Dutch economic dominance insofar as this was possible within the constraints of Finec. One of the most important early measures was the nationalization of the Java Bank, the former bank of circulation in the Netherlands Indies, through the purchase of shares of from both domestic and overseas shareholders. The purchase of shares proceeded smoothly, and on 6 December 1951 law no. 24 of 1951 on the nationalization of the Java Bank was officially enacted (Saubari, 2003:72), and under its new name Bank Indonesia became the central bank of Indonesia. Sjafruddin Prawiranegara, former Minister of Finance in the Hatta and Natsir cabinets, was appointed as the first Governor of Bank Indonesia.

Other measures to reduce Dutch economic dominance included the replacement of the Netherland Indies Airline Company (*Koninklijk Nederlands-Indische Luchtvaart Maatschappij, KNILM*) by Indonesia's new national airline Garuda Indonesian Airways. The Indonesian government also took over several Dutch enterprises deemed of strategic economic interest, including the railways on Java and several public utility companies, such as electricity and gas companies (Burger, 1975: 170). Since initial plans to nationalize KPM (*Koninklijke Paketvaart Maatschappij, Royal Packet Company*), the inter-island shipping company, were not successful, the Indonesian government in 1952 founded the limited liability company *Pelayaran Nasional Indonesia* or *PELNI* (Indonesian National Shipping with a nominal capital of Rp200 million (Dick, 1987: 16–7). In addition, Indonesia first general trading company, the Central Trading Corporation (CTC) which had been established in

Bukittinggi in 1947 during Indonesia's war of independence, was given the task of challenging the monopoly of the 'Big Five' Dutch general trading companies (Daud, 2003: 256).

Throughout the first half of the 1950s heated political debates raged about the pace at which the vestiges of Western (i.e. Dutch) capitalism should be eliminated in order to build up a national economy which, most nationalist leaders agreed, would not be built along capitalist lines. A vocal group of radical nationalists advocated the establishment of state-owned enterprises (SOEs) occupying the 'commanding heights of the economy' and cooperatives for the 'economically weak groups in society' to replace the foreign-owned capitalist enterprises. Arrayed against them was a smaller, less cohesive group of pragmatic nationalists, who argued that the pace of eliminating capitalist enterprises, particularly the foreign-owned ones, would have to be gradual to prevent serious economic disruption (Paauw, 1983: 207).

While these political debates proceeded, political relations with the Netherlands deteriorated rapidly after the mid-1950s as a result of the unresolved political conflict over the status of West Irian (West New Guinea, now called Papua province). When in the autumn of 1957 the Indonesian government failed to persuade the United Nations General Assembly to force the Netherlands to negotiate with Indonesia about the status of West Irian, militant trade unions took over the headquarters of KPM, the prime symbol of Dutch economic control. In the following unruly days more and more Dutch enterprises were taken over by trade inions. To re-establish order and wrest control from the communist-oriented trade unions, General Nasution, the army chief of staff, ordered the seized enterprises to be placed under the supervision of local army commanders (Dick, 2002: 164). In February 1959 all the seized Dutch enterprises were formally nationalized. With this one sweeping measure, the powerful Dutch business presence in Indonesia, which had operated in Indonesia since the early 1870s, was eliminated.

## PROMOTING INDIGENOUS INDONESIAN ENTREPRENEURS: THE *BENTENG* PROGRAMME

The nationalization of Dutch enterprises went a long way towards satisfying the national aspiration 'to convert the colonial economy into a national economy'. However, this conversion was not felt as complete, as the large indigenous population was still facing the economic dominance of ethnic Chinese businessmen, including Indonesian citizens as well as resident aliens, which continued to dominate important sectors of the economy, particularly the intermediate trade. Ethnic Chinese economic dominance of the important intermediate trade alongside Dutch economic dominance of the modern sectors of the economy (plantations, mining, large-scale manufacturing, banking system and public utilities) led an American Indonesianist, the late Professor Everett Hawkins, to refer to a case of 'double colonialism' in Indonesia.[2]

Building a 'national economy' (*ekonomi nasional*) gave expression to the national aspiration for an economy which would be controlled by indigenous Indonesians (*Indonesia asli*)[3] rather by 'foreign' groups, like the ethnic Chinese, regardless of whether they were citizens or not (Coppel, 1983: 3).

In view of the historically weak position of Indonesian businessmen since the Dutch colonial period, Indonesian policymakers since the early 1950s put a high priority on promoting the development of indigenous Indonesian entrepreneurs. Aside from the above-mentioned measures to counter Dutch economic dominance, the Indonesian government also took steps to reduce the economic role of the ethnic Chinese.

However, in view of the above factors, taking measures to curtail Chinese economic activities proved to be more difficult than eliminating Dutch economic interests. For one thing, the number of ethnic Chinese was much greater than the Dutch, and their economic activities in the rural areas were much more intertwined with the economic activities of the indigenous population than the Dutch activities had ever been. Moreover, the large ethnic Chinese group included Indonesian citizens as well as citizens of the People's Republic of China and a small group of pro-Taiwan 'stateless' citizens.[4] It was therefore quite difficult for the Indonesian government to take measures directed at all ethnic Chinese, as this group also contained the relatively large group of Indonesian citizens. Having fought against Dutch colonialism and its implied racism, many Indonesian leaders found that overly discriminatory policies against its citizens of Chinese descent did not accord with the ideals of the Indonesian revolution.

In transforming the 'colonial economy into a national economy', many Indonesian nationalists aspired to build a national economy along socialist lines. In actual practice, however, successive Indonesian governments, at least until Guided Democracy and Guided Economy were introduced by President Sukarno in 1959, for pragmatic reasons were not prepared to dismantle the 'capitalist' economic structure inherited from the Dutch colonial government (Mackie, 1971: 44).

Trying to analyse what Indonesian leaders in the early 1950s actually meant by 'socialism', two different views stand out. For many nationalists, 'socialism' was mainly interpreted as 'Indonesianization'. This implied that foreign economic dominance by Dutch capitalists in the plantation, mining, large-scale manufacturing, and wholesale trade, and by ethnic Chinese in the intermediate trade had to eliminated. However, whether this was to be achieved by nationalization of these foreign enterprises or by the promotion of private indigenous businessmen was for a long time an unresolved argument (Mackie, 1971: 44). The other view about socialism in Indonesia emphasized that a national economy should take the form of a 'collectivist' organization of the economy and be based on the 'family principle' (*azas kekeluargaan*), as enshrined in the Constitution of 1945 or on '*gotong royong*' (mutual help) tradition of performing certain agricultural tasks as practiced in the villages (Mackie, 1971: 44).

Since the early 1950s pressures for preferential treatment of indigenous Indonesian businessmen grew stronger. In general the only fields in which indigenous Indonesians operated was in small-scale agriculture, a few medium-sized modern retail stores, and small-scale industries, such as batik and clove cigarettes. To promote the faster development of indigenous entrepreneurs, Djuanda, the Minister of Welfare, in April 1950 issued a regulation which gave priority to indigenous businessmen to import goods from abroad. To facilitate this import trade, indigenous businessmen were given easy access to cheap credit. This programme was called the *Benteng* (Fortress) programme (Siahaan, 1996: 168).

Besides building up a class of indigenous businessmen, the *Benteng* programme was also aimed as yet another measure to counter Dutch economic dominance (Sumitro, 2000: 144), particularly the power of the Dutch trading houses. Although Sumitro himself was responsible for the implementation of the *Benteng* programme when he was Minister of Trade and Industry in the Natsir cabinet (1950–51), as an academically trained economist he basically considered market forces as the best way to ending the import monopolies of the Dutch general trading companies. By liberalizing the import trade, the market power of the Dutch companies could be eroded by import competition. However, most other economic nationalists viewed the Western-trained Sumitro with great suspicion, and wanted to continue the prewar system of import controls which had been introduced during the early years of the Great Depression in the early 1930s. This time the import controls, however, had to benefit indigenous rather than the Dutch import companies (Booth, 1998: 222).

Protection to the indigenous importers was to be provided by reserving the import of certain categories of goods (which were referred to as *benteng* goods) solely for indigenous importers and by channeling credits to these importers to the state-owned bank BNI (*Bank Negara Indonesia*) (Sutter, 1959: 1017–8). The required qualifications for receiving preferential treatment through the *Benteng* programme were, at least on paper, quite stringent. For instance, to qualify for such protection, an indigenous businessman had to be 'a new Indonesian importer' and a legal entity, such as a corporation, silent partnership or partnership, and possess a minimum amount of working capital of Rp100,000, an office large enough for 'several full-time employees', and officers with previous business experience. Another qualification was that at least 70 per cent of the capital had to be provided by indigenous Indonesians (*bangsa Indonesia asli*), while foreigners could at most provide 30 per cent of the capital. However, among these provisions there was no reference to non-indigenous Indonesians (Sutter, 1959: 1018).

The reference to 'indigenous Indonesians' led Siauw Giok Tjhan, member of parliament and a representative of the ethnic Chinese, to question the government what it meant by 'indigenous Indonesians' and to suggest that racial discrimination was contrary to the national ideal of every citizen of foreign descent of becoming a genuine Indonesian patriot and democrat, as stipulated in the government manifesto of 1 November 1945. According to Siauw, such a discriminatory measure would hamper healthy cooperation between fellow citizens and lead to a system of fronts at a time when all the capital and energies of Indonesian citizens were needed for national economic reconstruction (Sutter, 1959: 1018).

Responding to Siauw's remarks, Djuanda observed that the requirement that the required 70 per cent of the capital to be provided by indigenous Indonesians was based on the government's view that although it did not practice racial discrimination, it was the government's full right to make regulations to protect the economically weak groups. Djuanda went on to state that indigenous Indonesians as a group were included in the economically weak groups, while the non-indigenous Indonesians, with some exceptions, form the economically strong group. With this statement, Indonesian citizens of foreign descent (read: citizens of Chinese descent) were given notice that they could not expect a more favourable treatment than that given foreigners (Sutter, 1959: 1019).

Choosing the import trade as the first major economic activity, on which policies to promote indigenous entrepreneurship would be focused, was understandable, as at the time almost all the export and import trade were in the hands of the Dutch and the Chinese (Suhadi, 1967: 218). Focusing on the import trade to secure indigenous Indonesian dominance appeared to be the most feasible, as this trade seemed to be most responsive to state direction through controls over the allocation of import licenses (Robison, 1986: 44). The import trade also appeared the most accessible to indigenous businessmen, as they could easily set up their business with a minimum of overhead investment, could concentrate on products sufficiently standardized which only required a minimum of business experience, and could deal in goods that enjoyed a seller's market because of import restrictions (Anspach, 1969: 168).

Moreover, prospective indigenous importers could learn from the example of the 'Big Five' Dutch general trading companies (Borsumij, Jacobsen van den Berg, Geo Wehry, Internatio and Lindeteves), which had used their activities in the import trade as a springboard to diversify into plantation agriculture, internal distribution, insurance and the manufacture of various import-competing goods (Anspach, 1969: 168). Learning from the experience of these Dutch general trading companies, several indigenous importers, such as Dasaad Musin, had diversified into tea cultivation and the weaving industry, while Djohan Djohar had moved into rubber cultivation and brick manufacture, and Rahman Tamin had diversified into textile manufacturing (Anspach, 1969: 168). The government hoped that like these indigenous business pioneers, the *Benteng* importers could use their activities in the import trade as a base for capital accumulation which would sustain the expansion of indigenous capital into other sectors (Robison, 1986: 44).

To assist the indigenous importers, the government selected certain kinds of goods which could only be imported by the *Benteng* importers. Most of these goods were simple consumer goods which could be easily sold, such as yarn, textiles, paper, stationery, matches and sundries. To enable the *Benteng* importers to import the selected goods, the government allocated Rp65 million for this purpose, of which Rp40 million was allocated for the import of textiles, Rp12 million for weaving yarns, and Rp7 million for sundry goods (Suhadi, 1967: 218).

## IMPLEMENTING THE *BENTENG* PROGRAMME

The *Benteng* programme attracted a lot of interest. While in 1951 some 250 businessmen had registered with this programme, in 1952 this number had increased to 741, and to 1,500 in 1953 and to 2,211 in 1954 (Siahaan, 1996: 168). As a result, the percentage of total government foreign exchange credit allocated to the *Benteng* importers increased from 37 per cent in 1952–53 to 76.2 per cent in late 1954 (Robison, 1986: 45).

This great interest was not surprising, since the government, making ample use of the existing system of import control, allocated scarce foreign exchange to the favoured indigenous importers who, as a result, could earn windfall profits from importing various goods. Lobbying to obtain an adequate share of the foreign exchange, the indigenous importers formed a group which, after the *Benteng* programme, was called the *Benteng* group (Suhadi,

1967: 218). As a result of this programme, by the early 1950s around 70 per cent of the import trade was conducted by indigenous businessmen (Burger, 1975: 171).

Another group which attempted to obtain a share in the rents created by the foreign exchange control system of the *Benteng* programme was the relatively small group of indigenous industrialists who realized that their prospects for making good profits depended very much on the opportunity of purchasing imported raw materials and capital goods at official prices. As the Indonesian government since the early years of independence had been anxious to promote industrialization, it had put important industrial raw materials in the category of essential goods in its approved list of imports. Imported raw materials were therefore charged with low tariffs or sometimes could be imported duty free. However, as it were the indigenous importers who were free to sell their imported goods, it was they who benefited most from the rents created by the foreign exchange control system and not the industrialists (Suhadi, 1967: 219–20).

From the time that the new indigenous importers had started receiving preferential treatment under the *Benteng* programme, with several of them lacking capital or business experience or both, engaged in certain business practices which, although not in violation of the letter of the law, did offend ethical standards. There were of course several other new indigenous importers which had established a bonafide cooperation between their indigenous companies and non-indigenous or foreign companies. However, there were many more cases which could hardly be named 'bonafide' enterprises, in which indigenous importers and ethnic Chinese businessmen (whether Indonesian citizen or foreign national) had set up so-called 'Ali-Baba' concerns. In fact, 'shotgun weddings' between new indigenous importing companies and the older importing companies owned by ethnic Chinese businessmen proliferated under various forms, such as fronts and strawmen and the selling of import licenses to genuine, mostly ethnic Chinese, importers (Sutter, 1959: 1027).

Several of the new indigenous importers also turned out to be individuals associated with powerful officials in the government bureaucracy or in the political parties, who controlled the allocation of import licenses and credit.

These bogus importers also often failed to repay the credits they had received from the state-owned BNI bank (Robison, 1986: 45). Hence, the *Benteng* programme had not fostered strong, self-reliant indigenous merchant class, but a group of licensed brokers and political fixers, in short what are now called unproductive 'rent-seekers' or 'rent-harvesters'.

Reflecting on the record of the *Benteng* programmes, Sudarpo Sastrosatomo, a highly successful indigenous businessman whose business managed to survive throughout three turbulent periods in Indonesia's history (the Sukarno era, the Suharto era and the 'Reformasi' era) caustically observed that under the *Benteng* programme import licenses were given to people who were not even remotely businessmen, but who believed that they were entitled to enjoy the facilities granted by the government as the fruits of the Indonesian revolution. The result was a disaster, as these new class of importers did not even understand the first steps of the importing business, not even how to document imports, or how to finance them. As a result, they had to turn mainly to Chinese traders who knew the business, but they carried this feudal idea that these traders were an inferior class. The result was the creation of a trading community that was doomed from the beginning (Soedarpo, 2003: 154).

No wonder that Professor Sumitro Djojohadikusumo, Minister of Trade and Industry at the time the *Benteng* programme was introduced and a strong proponent of the industrialization programme as contained in the Indonesian government's Economic Urgency Programme, of which the *Benteng* programme was an important part, later observed that he 'had no illusions about what might happen, but that if you gave assistance to ten people, seven might turn out to be parasites, but you might still get three entrepreneurs' (Sumitro, 2003: 59).

In contrast, Sjafruddin Prawiranegara, former Minister of Finance and the first Indonesian Governor of Bank Indonesia, stated that from the outset he had been opposed to the *Benteng* programme. Sjafruddin held that '*people would have to be educated in management and technology first before rushing into forced industrialization. If we did not educate first, we would just create Ali Babas!*' (Sjafruddin, 2003: 82).

Most of the registered indigenous importing companies were indeed companies on paper only. Many of these importers did not even have an office, while their "capital" often consisted only of a stamp, paper, and a brief case. Not surprisingly, these importers were often referred to as 'brief case importers' (*importir aktentas*), whose only qualification as an importer was that they carried a briefcase (Siahaan, 1968: 168).

Although the government was obviously aware of these malpractices, in practice it was often difficult to draw a line between bonafide cooperation and malpractices, which had existed from the beginning of the *Benteng* programme. However, these malpractices only began to proliferate when Iskaq became Minister of Economic Affairs (Sutter, 1959: 1027), and Ong Eng Die became Minister of Finance in the first Ali Sastroamidjojo cabinet

(1953–55). Both of them were members of the Indonesian Nationalist Parties (*Partai Nasional Indonesia, PNI*) and, according to Professor Sumitro, did not care much about finance. With the first general elections coming up in 1955, Iskaq and Ong, according to Sumitro, 'began blatantly using the import licensing system to buy political supporters'. Then I saw how much harm was done, and what chaos the uncertainty caused in the business world' (Sumitro, 2003: 61).

As the *Benteng* programme progressed, it became increasingly apparent to the government that the programme was not successful in achieving its stated aims. In 1953 the government started screening the officially registered indigenous importers, and as a result was able to reduce the number of registered importers by more than half from about 4,300 to about 2,000 (Burger, 1975: 171).

This measure, however, turned out to be ineffective, as in August 1954 the Central Office of Imports estimated that about 90 per cent of the registered national importers were not bonafide. This estimate was confirmed by another screening in 1955 ordered by Roosseno, the new Minister of Economic Affairs, who had replaced Iskaq. Even Iskaq, former Minister of Economic Affairs who had been a strong supporter of the *Benteng* programme acknowledged that import licenses were being sold at 200 to 250 per cent of their nominal value (Anspach, 1969: 174).

To eliminate the abuses of the *Benteng* programme, Roosseno introduced a foreign exchange auction system in the textile sector. He also banned discrimination on ethnic grounds, and thus allowed Sino-Indonesian businessmen to openly participate in the import trade. The auction system, however, turned out to be unsuccessful, as it did not allow indigenous importers with inadequate financial resources with access to the auctioned foreign exchange quota. Hence, indigenous importers with inadequate financial resources continued to serve as agents for ethnic Chinese businessmen (Anspach, 1969: 174–5).

Thus Indonesia's experience with its first affirmative programme to promote a strong and self-reliant indigenous business class proved to be a failure and in the second half of the 1950s came to an inglorious end, even though this programme was never officially abolished. By then, however, economic conditions started deteriorating rapidly, partly as a result of the nationalization of all Dutch enterprises in 1959 and the actions against the foreign Chinese community, such as the expulsion of foreign Chinese traders from the rural areas, and partly because of the regional rebellions in West Sumatra and North Sulawesi. With the introduction of Guided Democracy and Guided Economy by President Sukarno in 1959 and his call for an Indonesian-style socialism (*sosialisme a la Indonesia*), the promotion of indigenous private entrepreneurs took a backseat, as the new state enterprises, which had been established from the expropriated Dutch enterprises, were now given a leading and controlling role over various aspects of the economy.

## CONCLUSION

The nationalization of the Dutch enterprises did not facilitate a more rapid development of indigenous businessmen, as the vacuum left by the departure of Dutch business was filled by ethnic Chinese businessmen. The emphasis on 'Indonesian-style socialism' also prevented the introduction of new affirmative programmes to promote indigenous private businessmen.

Under the 'New Order', with its emphasis on accelerating economic growth, ethnic Chinese businessmen, with their greater business acumen and experience and better access to financial resources, were in general able to prosper. This did not only apply to the regime's Chinese business cronies, who in cahoots with the political power holders established large conglomerates, but also to the medium-sized and smaller businesses the majority of which, however, unlike the Chinese conglomerates, had to survive by their own wits.

Nevertheless, the rise of powerful Chinese conglomerates under the patronage of President Soeharto and other senior military officers and government officials created social tensions and gave rise to the strong public perception in the late Soeharto era about the widening gap between rich and poor and between the *non-pribumi* (non-indigenous) and *pribumi* (indigenous) citizens. In the end these social tensions erupted in various racial riots, particularly in Solo and Jakarta, on the eve of Soeharto's fall in May 1998.

At present these racial tensions have abated, as other social conflicts, sometimes religious and sometimes ethnic in nature, have arisen following the collapse of the strong authoritarian state under Soeharto. The attention of the successor governments under Presidents Habibie, Abdurrachman Wahid and Megawati Soekarnoputri have also been absorbed by the strong need to re-establish political stability and achieve economic recovery. With the urgent need to achieve strong economic recovery and restore economic growth, and with the emergence of new indigenous successful and confident entrepreneurs and a skilled and experienced indigenous managerial class, opportunities for a more fruitful and mutually profitable business cooperation between *pribumi* and *non-pribumi* businessmen appear to be better than they seemed only a few years ago.

## Notes

1. "Indonesia's First Affirmative Policy: The *Benteng* Programme in the 1950s", by Thee Kian Wie, first published in *Lembaran Sejarah* (History Papers), Vol. 8, No. 3 (2005): 33–46.
2. Personal communication to the author.
3. Since the 'New Order' era the term used for indigenous Indonesia was '*Indonesia pribumi*'.
4. As Indonesia only recognized the People's Republic of China as the only legitimate government of China, pro-Taiwan Chinese were treated as stateless citizens.

## References

Anspach, Ralph. "Indonesia". In *Underdevelopment and Economic Nationalism in Southeast Asia*, edited by Frank Golay, et al. Ithaca and London: Cornell University Press, 1969. pp. 111–201.

Booth, Anne. *The Indonesian Economy in the Nineteenth and Twentieth Centuries: A History of Missed Opportunities*. London: Macmillan Press, 1998.

Burger, D.H. Sociologisch-Economische Geschiedenis van Indonesie, Deel 1. Indonesia voor de 20e eeuw (Sociological-Economic History of Indonesia, Vol. 1. Indonesia before the 20th century. Amsterdam: Koninklijk Instituut voor de Tropen, 1975.

Coppel, Charles. *Indonesian Chinese in Crisis*. Singapore: Oxford University Press, 1983.

Daud, Teuku Mohamad. "Recollections". In *Recollections: The Indonesian Economy, 1950s–1990s*, edited by Thee Kian Wie, 251–63. Singapore: Institute of Southeast Asian Studies, 2003.

Dick, H.W. *The Indonesian Interisland Shipping Industry: An Analysis of Competition and Regulation*. Singapore: Institute of Southeast Asian Studies, 1987.

Dick, H.W., et al. "Formation of the Nation State, 1930s–1966". In *The Emergence of a National Economy: An economic history of Indonesia, 1800–2000*, 153–93. Crows Nest, NSW: Allen and Unwin, 2002.

Dick, H.W. et al. *The Emergence of a National Economy: An Economic History of Indonesia, 1800–2000*. Crow Nest, NSW: Allen & Unwin, 2002.

Golay, Frank, Ralph Anspach, M. Ruth Pfanner and Eliezer B. Ayal. *Underdevelopment and Economic Nationalism in Southeast Asia*. Ithaca and London: Cornell University Press, 1969.

Johnson, Harry. "The Ideology of Economic Policy in New States". In *Chicago Essays in Economic Development*, edited by David Wall. Chicago: University of Chicago Press, 1972.

Meier, Hans. *Den Haag–Djakarta: De Nederlands-Indonesischebetrekkingen, 1950–1962* (The Hague — Djakarta - Dutch — Indonesian Relations, 1950–1962). Utrecht: Uitgeverij Het Spectrum, B.V., 1994.

Paauw, Douglas S. *The Economic Legacy of Dutch Colonialism to Independent Indonesia.* Paper presented at the Conference on Indonesian Economic History During the Dutch Colonial Period, Research School of Pacific Studies, The Australian National University, Canberra, 12–13 December 1983.

Robison, Richard. *Indonesia: The Rise of Capital.* Sydney: Allen & Unwin, 1986.

Saubari, Mohammad. "Recollections". In *Recollections: The Indonesian Economy, 1950s–1990s,* edited by Thee Kian Wie, 69–73. Singapore: Institute of Southeast Asian Studies, 2003.

Siahaan, Bisuk, 1996. *Industrialisasi di Indonesia: Sejak HutangKehormatan sampai Bintang Stir* (Industrialisation in Indonesia — Since the Debt of Honour until the Turn-Around), Pustaka Data, Jakarta.

Sjafruddin Prawiranegara. "Recollections". In *Recollections: The Indonesian Economy, 1950s–1990s,* edited by Thee Kian Wie. Singapore: Institute of Southeast Asian Studies, 2003. pp. 75–86.

Soedarpo Sastrosatomo. "Recollections". In *Recollections: The Indonesian Economy, 1950s–1990s,* edited by Thee Kian Wie. Singapore: Institute of Southeast Asian Studies, 2003. pp. 141–63.

Suhadi Mangkusuwondo. *Industrialisation Efforts in Indonesia: The Role of Agriculture and Foreign Trade in the Development of the Industrial Sector,* Ph.D. thesis, University of California, Berkeley, 1967.

Sumitro Djojohadikusumo. *Jejak Perlawanan Begawan Pejuang* (The Resistance Footsteps of an Honourable Fighter), Jakarta: Pustaka Sinar Harapan, 2000.

——— "Recollections". In *Recollections: The Indonesian Economy, 1950s–1990s,* edited by Thee Kian Wie, 49–65. Singapore: Institute of Southeast Asian Studies, 2003.

Sutter, John O. "Indonesianisasi: A Historical Survey of the Role of Politics in the Institutions of a Changing Economy, from the Second World War to the End of the General; Elections (1940–1955)". Ph.D. thesis, Cornell University, June 1959.

Thee, Kian Wie. *Recollections: The Indonesian Economy, 1950s–1990s.* Singapore: Institute of Southeast Asian Studies, 2003.

Wall, David. *Chicago Essays in Economic Development.* Chicago: University of Chicago Press, 1972.

# 3

# THE DEBATE ON ECONOMIC POLICY IN NEWLY-INDEPENDENT INDONESIA BETWEEN SJAFRUDDIN PRAWIRANEGARA AND SUMITRO DJOJOHADIKUSUMO[1]

## THE INDONESIAN ECONOMY AFTER THE TRANSFER OF SOVEREIGNTY

In 1949, after a four-year long armed struggle, Indonesia finally achieved effective control over its entire territory, with the exception of West Irian (now Papua). Nevertheless, the young nation faced serious political and economic problems. The Japanese occupation and the long fight against the Dutch had seriously impoverished the Indonesian people. The new government also faced armed insurrections and secessionist movements in various regions such as Aceh, West Java, South Sulawesi, and the Moluccas, which threatened the country's territorial integrity. In late January 1950, scarcely one month after the transfer of sovereignty, Raymond Westerling (a rogue member of the Dutch army) along with a few hundred troops under his command, carried out an audacious but quixotic plan to occupy Bandung and Jakarta.[2] Although this plan immediately failed, it increased the sense of vulnerability of the Indonesian government.

The economic problems facing Indonesia in the early 1950s were no less urgent. The Indonesian people had suffered greatly during the Japanese occupation and the armed revolution against the returning Dutch. Basic goods and services — food, clothing, dwellings, health and education services — were all in short supply. Therefore, the Natsir cabinet, which replaced the Hatta cabinet in late August 1950, focused its efforts on raising the welfare of the people.[3] This focus was crucial since standards of living, as expressed by real per capita GDP, had declined by roughly one-third from what was already a low level before the Pacific War, from $1,252 (at 1990 prices) in 1941 to $840 in 1950.[4]

The profitable agricultural estates, industrial plants, and much of the physical infrastructure (including irrigation networks and power stations), had been badly damaged during the Japanese occupation and subsequent Indonesian Revolution. Food crop production was estimated at merely 70–75 per cent of pre-war output, whereas smallholder tree crop production was down to 30–35 per cent and estate production even lower at 20–25 per cent of pre-war levels.[5] The output of the sugar factories had declined from more than 1.5 million tons in 1939 to 261,000 tons in 1950, which was barely enough to meet domestic demand.[6] Sugar exports had fallen from 1.2 million tons in 1939 to only 1,000 tons in 1950. Exports rose to 7,000 tons in 1951 but dropped again to 1,000 tons in 1952. During subsequent years, sugar exports gradually increased, reaching 217,000 tons in 1955, which, however, corresponded to only one-sixth of the level of exports in 1939.[7] The output of coconut oil had similarly declined by almost one-half from around 200 million kilograms per year before the Japanese occupation to 112 kilograms in 1950.[8]

Next to problems in production, the Indonesian government was saddled with the heavy burden of a large foreign debt not of its own making. At the Round Table Conference in The Hague during the autumn of 1949 the Indonesian delegation had agreed to take over the staggering foreign debt of the Netherlands Indies' government, which amounted to $1.13 billion. This debt had to re-paid fully by June 1964. Although the Dutch delegation had argued that much of the post-war foreign debt of the Netherlands Indies Civil Administration (NICA) had been incurred to raise the economic welfare of the Indonesian population, in practice much of this debt had been used to benefit the Dutch.[9] Sumitro Djojohadikusomo, a member of the Indonesian delegation, disputed the total amount of debt to be borne by Indonesia. According to him, a large portion of the debt consisted of an internal component of approximately $800 million (the equivalent of 3 billion guilders) which had been incurred as military expenses by the Netherlands Indies government in its four-year long effort to subdue the Indonesian Republic.[10]

The Indonesian delegation grudgingly accepted to take over the debt incurred by the Netherlands Indies government in expectation of substantial economic assistance from the United States, which had been fostered by Merle Cochran, the American observer at the Round Table Conference. Sumitro had vigorously protested against Indonesia accepting this huge foreign debt, especially the part of it that was connected to Dutch military operations against the Indonesian Republic.[11]

However, after hard bargaining by the Indonesian delegation, the Dutch did agree to leave out that part of the post-war debt which had been used to finance Dutch military operations to fight Indonesian independence. Vice President Moh. Hatta, head of the Indonesian delegation, overruled further objections by Sumitro in accepting the remaining debt.[12]

Ironically, the large foreign assistance which Cochran had dangled before the eyes of the Indonesian delegation came down to a loan by the US Export-Import Bank of $100 million that had to be repaid with interest. This loan corresponded to only one-third of the amount which this bank lent to the Netherlands after the Second World War.[13]

Another matter also grated on Indonesia's sensitivities — under pressure from the Dutch delegation, the Indonesian delegation at the Round Table Conference agreed that the extensive Dutch business interests in newly-independent Indonesia would be allowed to continue operating without any hindrance. Under this agreement, laid down in the Financial and Economic Agreement, Finec (*Financieele en economische overeenkomst*), nationalization of the Dutch enterprises was only allowed if deemed to be in Indonesia's national interest, with affected parties agreeing and compensation paid. The amount of compensation would be determined by a judge on the basis of the real value of the nationalized assets.[14] The Finec agreement contained a number of provisions regarding the Dutch-Indonesian relations in finance, foreign trade and economic cooperation. It offered guarantees of rights, concessions, licenses and operations of Dutch businesses. With respect to trade with European nations, the Netherlands and Indonesia agreed to enter only into joint commercial treaties. Trade policies of the two countries with respect to trading partners outside Europe were to be harmonized as much as possible, although no joint treaties were required. The Finec agreement also included an obligation of the Indonesian government to consult with the Netherlands government whenever financial and monetary policies would affect Dutch interests, as long as the debt had not been fully repaid.[15]

It need not surprise us that the conservative Dutch economic historian Henri Baudet concluded that the Finec agreement contained the maximum in attainable guarantees for continued operations by Dutch enterprises in

Indonesia.[16] On the other hand, many Indonesian nationalist leaders strongly criticized the provisions of Finec that infringed on Indonesia's sovereignty. For instance, Ruslan Abdulgani, a prominent member of the PNI (*Partai Nasional Indonesia*, Indonesian National Party) and later Minister of Foreign Affairs, stated that "his party found it unacceptable that the Netherlands still was in control of its [the nation's] economic interests".[17] No wonder that Indonesia's nationalist leaders were determined to terminate Dutch economic power in Indonesia sooner rather than later.

For the Indonesian government, the first priorities were to raise the standards of living, lay the foundations for a sound national economy, increase production and stimulate commerce and industry.[18] The pressing short-run economic problem facing the Natsir government in 1950 was how to finance the rehabilitation of the severely damaged physical infrastructure and the production apparatus (estates, mines, industrial plants) from the government's limited budget, which in 1950 showed a deficit of Rp1.7 billion. In 1951, however, a sudden increase in export revenues generated a budget surplus as well as a balance of payments surplus of Rp1 billion.[19]

Rising export revenues during the Korean War boom emanated from the rapid increase in demand by the American government for strategic raw materials such as oil, rubber, bauxite, sisal and vegetable oils. Yet the boom proved to be short-lived.[20] During the second quarter of 1952, prices of Indonesia's major commodity exports dropped dramatically, bringing a sharp decline in export earnings. Imports, however, continued to increase as they were related to income some months ago rather than to current cash flows. As a result, a deficit was recorded in the balance of payments. Since government finance was highly dependent on trade taxes, the decline in export earnings caused a deficit in the government budget as well.[21]

By the middle of 1952 it became apparent to the Indonesian government that the country was facing a serious financial crisis. During the following year the government was especially devoted to implementing stop-gap measures to check the drain on the foreign exchange reserves and to offset inflationary pressures arising from the budget deficit.[22]

This brief survey underscores the enormous challenges the Indonesian government faced in the early 1950s in both maintaining macroeconomic stability (by restraining inflationary pressures and reducing balance of payments deficits) and rehabilitating the badly damaged physical infrastructure and production apparatus whilst attempting to raise standards of living and repaying a large foreign debt. The Indonesian government was confronted with having achieved political independence without obtaining economic independence. The scope of economic policy was severely restricted by the inability to exert full control over key segments of the economy where extensive Dutch business interests were still firmly entrenched.[23]

The continued economic predominance by foreign and non-indigenous Indonesian (primarily ethnic Chinese) economic interests is well illustrated by an estimate that of all consumer imports in 1950, 60 per cent were handled by eight Dutch firms with the largest four accounting for no less than 50 per cent of the total. The central bank (Java Bank — *Javasche Bank*) was largely a Dutch-owned private corporation, controlled by Dutch managers. Private commercial banking was largely owned and controlled by seven foreign banks, three of which were Dutch.[24]

Few, if any, of the newly-independent nations were left with a more crushing external financial burden and such severe limitations in economic policy-making than Indonesia. The consequences were political instability due to sharp conflicts between moderate and radical leaders and a steadily deteriorating relationship with the Netherlands, which culminated in the takeover and subsequent nationalization of most remaining Dutch enterprises in the late 1950s. As a consequence, Indonesia only embarked in earnest upon a path of independent economic development after 1966, seventeen years after the transfer of sovereignty.

## ECONOMIC POLICYMAKERS IN THE EARLY 1950s

The economic and political constraints facing Indonesia's economic policymakers in the early 1950s were of such a magnitude that conditions were bound to change sooner or later. This applied in particular to countering and eventually eliminating Dutch economic predominance over the modern sectors of the economy through promoting both state-owned enterprise and private companies owned by indigenous Indonesians. These companies were nurtured by state-owned banks such as the *Bank Negara Indonesia* (BNI) and the *Bank Industri Negara* (BIN), which provided credit, as well as the *Yayasan Kredit* (Credit Foundation), which offered guarantees for loans for which no collateral was offered.[25]

The main task of the Hatta and Natsir cabinets in the early period was to stabilize and expand an economy that was both foreign-dominated and privately owned.[26] Most Indonesian political leaders were not only dedicated nationalists but also socialist in their ideological orientation, so their aversion to this situation is understandable. However, to design sound economic policies which would also satisfy the ideological demands of the more radical leaders was difficult, if not impossible.

Thus it was fortunate that in the early 1950s economic expertise was virtually monopolized by sober, Dutch-trained, pragmatic social-democrats. In the early 1950s there were only two qualified economists, Moh. Hatta and Sumitro Djojohadikusumo, who had both studied at the *Nederlandse Economische Hogeschool* (Netherlands School of Economics) in Rotterdam. In addition, there were a few other economic policymakers whose experience and inclinations possibly qualified them as economic experts, notably Sjafruddin Prawiranegara, Djuanda Kartawidjaja, and Jusuf Wibisono.[27] Perhaps Ong Eng Die, Minister of Finance in the first Ali Sastroamidjojo cabinet (July 1953 – July 1955), could also be considered an economic expert, although he had not studied economics, but social geography at the University of Amsterdam. Unlike several other policymakers, Ong Eng Die cannot be considered a pragmatic policymaker but rather an overtly political minister, appointed by the PNI and bent on serving the political interests of the PNI — that is, winning the general elections in 1955 rather than serving the interests of the national economy.

The four most influential economic policymakers in the period of 1950–57 were undoubtedly Sumitro, Sjafruddin, Hatta, and Djuanda. Nonetheless, in spite of their considerable capabilities, personal integrity, and their pragmatic orientation, these four economic policymakers never worked together as a team, which distinguishes them from the tightly-knit "Berkeley Mafia" during the New Order.[28] This lack of cooperation and cohesiveness among the economic policymakers in the early 1950s is not surprising, as they were members of different political parties, except for Vice President Hatta and Djuanda, who was above all an apolitical technocrat. Sjafruddin and Wibisono were both members of the modernist Moslem party Masjumi, whereas Sumitro was a member of the PSI (*Partai Sosialis Indonesia*, Indonesian Socialist Party).

As pragmatic policymakers, they realized that top priority had to be given to economic stabilization and rehabilitation. Since most of the modern export industries (agricultural estates and mines) were still owned and operated by the Dutch, the policymakers realized that they had to, whether they liked it or not, protect the legal rights of the Dutch companies, as was indeed laid down in the Finec agreement. The Dutch enterprises were therefore allowed to operate without official hindrance, often in the face of strong opposition from radical nationalists such as Sujono Hadinoto of the PNI, who called for the "transformation of the colonial economy into a national economy".[29]

Benjamin Higgins, a Canadian economist who in the 1950s worked in Indonesia as a United Nations economic expert, referred to the relatively young, largely foreign-trained, economic policymakers (who gave high priority to Indonesia's economic and social development), as the "economics-minded" group. Many of these "economics-minded" leaders felt that Indonesia's economic development would in large measure have to follow Western lines, and they were therefore willing to cooperate with the Western countries with a view to receiving investment capital and technical assistance.[30]

Opposed to this group were, in Higgins's terminology, the "history-minded" leaders, the more radical leaders who were nationalist and often isolationist. They, including President Sukarno, attached the highest priority to "completing the national revolution", which implied the elimination of foreign control over Indonesian economic resources. The attitude of this group can best be attributed to the country's long history of resistance to foreign invaders, which culminated in the national revolution of 1945–49. That is why Higgins, not very accurately or clearly, labeled this group as the "history-minded" group.[31]

Higgins's classification of the two groups of nationalists competing for political influence in the 1950s is similar, although not identical, to the contrast that Herbert Feith, an Australian political scientist, had constructed between "administrators" and "solidarity makers". The "administrators" were the leaders with the administrative, technical, legal and foreign language skills required to run the apparatus of a modern state. The "solidarity makers" were political leaders skilled as mediators between groups at different levels of modernity, as mass organizers and manipulators of integrative symbols.[32]

The "administrators" competed for power on the basis of their technical skills and the status which they had enjoyed on account of their technical merits and accomplishments. They claimed leadership positions in the bureaucracy and political parties on the grounds that the educated elite had a right to govern. The "solidarity makers", by contrast, competed on the basis of their mass appeal and the status they had acquired as a result. They claimed leadership positions, both in the government and the government bureaucracy, on the grounds that they were close to the people and understood its wishes.[33]

The pragmatic "administrators" did their best to tackle the problems of economic stabilization, rehabilitation and economic development. Aiming at maximum production, they defended the continued presence of Dutch business as a necessity, even though, as nationalists, they too did not like Indonesia's continued dependence on Dutch business.[34] However, confronted by strong nationalist sentiments to independently own and control the country's productive assets, and inflamed by the continued refusal of the Netherlands to hand over its remaining colonial position in western New Guinea, the "administrators" or "economics-minded" policymakers steadily lost out in the 1950s to the "history-minded" leaders or "solidarity makers" who were more concerned with revolutionary nationalistic rhetoric than with economic development.[35] One contemporary foreign observer, Bruce Glassburner, who was teaching macroeconomics at the Faculty of Economics, University of Indonesia in the late 1950s, aptly made the following assessment: "From the point of view of economic policy, the years 1950 to 1957 in Indonesia are best understood as years of a hopeless losing battle on the part of a very small group of pragmatically conservative political leaders against an increasingly powerful political opposition of generally radical orientation."[36]

By late 1957 and early 1958, the pragmatic political leaders had not only lost the political battle, but had either withdrawn from political life (in December 1956 Hatta had resigned as Vice President) or had joined the PRRI rebellion in West Sumatra (Sjafruddin and Sumitro) and/or the Permesta rebellion in North Sulawesi (Sumitro).

## SUMITRO DJOJOHADIKUSUMO VERSUS SJAFRUDDIN PRAWIRANEGARA

The following account presents the gist of the debate between Sumitro Djojohadikusumo and Sjafruddin Prawiranegara and offers an insight into the views of leading economic policymakers in the early 1950s about how to solve the economic problems of the newly-independent nation and about which path of economic development path to choose.

Although there were other policymakers who also played an important role in the various cabinets during the first half of the 1950s, only Sumitro and Sjafruddin articulated their views in public. Hatta was also a prolific writer. As a student of economics in the Netherlands in the late 1920s, he wrote articles in Dutch and Indonesian about, amongst others, the economic ideas of the Western economic thinkers he was reading during his study in Rotterdam. After independence, Hatta also wrote several articles, mostly advocating cooperatives as the most appropriate expression of Indonesian social ideals.[37] As Indonesia's Vice President, however, Hatta refrained from writing policy-oriented articles, but rather focused on articles of a more normative nature.

Sjafruddin, who had graduated from the *Rechtshogeschool* (Law School) in Batavia in 1939, served as Minister of Finance in the third cabinet of Sjahrir during the Indonesian Revolution, and again held this post in the cabinets of Hatta (December 1949 – September 1950) and Natsir (September 1950 – March 1951). After the nationalization of the Java Bank in 1951,

Sjafruddin became the first Indonesian Governor of the Java Bank, which subsequently, in 1953, became Bank Indonesia, Indonesia's central bank.[38]

Sumitro served as Minister of Trade in the Natsir cabinet (September 1950 – March 1951), and as Minister of Finance in both the Wilopo cabinet (March 1952 – June 1953) and the Harahap cabinet (August 1955 – March 1956).

The debate between Sjafruddin and Sumitro was conducted in Dutch in March 1952 in the Dutch-language newspaper *Nieuwsgier*.[39] The views of Sjafruddin were first voiced in Indonesian in the Masjumi newspaper *Abadi* (entitled "Reorientation in the field of economics") and subsequently elaborated in a speech in Palembang, which was reported in the Dutch-language newspaper *Nieuwsgier*.[40] The accounts of Sumitro's views were all published in the *Nieuwsgier* in March 1952. It must be pointed out that when Sjafruddin's and Sumitro's views were published, neither of them was a cabinet minister. They were both criticising the then current Sukiman cabinet (April 1951 – February 1953).

## SJAFRUDDIN'S VIEWS

While reflecting on the preceding two years (1950 and 1951), Sjafruddin identified several unfavourable developments next to encouraging achievements that did not bode well for the future.[41] He surveyed five areas of economic policy: macroeconomic conditions, rice provision, conditions for industrialization, nationalization and foreign direct investment, which all warrant a brief introduction and a comment.

## MACROECONOMIC CONDITIONS

Sjafruddin noted that foreign exchange revenues had increased considerably due to the Korea War boom, resulting in foreign exchange reserves of Rp. 1,150 million. Part of the foreign exchange earnings, the equivalent of $100 million, had been used to purchase gold to enlarge reserves at the Java Bank. With respect to public finance, Sjafruddin noted the budget surplus in 1951 which amounted to Rp1.3 billion. This surplus allowed a reduction of the accumulated budget deficit from Rp1.8 billion to Rp500 million. In view of these developments, the inflationary pressures of 1950 were reduced, if not halted. But inflation would rear its head again if the government in 1952 and following years would not be able to keep the budget balanced. Sjafruddin ascribed the shortage of funds, felt by importers in particular, to dire poverty, which had been aggravated by the Japanese occupation and the Indonesian Revolution. This bottleneck could not be alleviated by the government just printing more money. Complaints of the importers demonstrated that they had been purchasing too many goods during the Korea War boom without keeping sufficiently in mind the limited purchasing-power of the Indonesian population. Sjafruddin argued that pumping money into the economy to speed up economic growth should not be done. All injections of money, including loans, into the economy should in principle be directed at productive purposes with payment of salaries of civil servants forming the sole exception to the rule. The extension of credit needed to be based on the assumption that production could be increased so that the loans could be repaid with interest. Without such guarantees, money injections in the form of credits would not improve economic conditions but rather cause deterioration.

The increase in foreign exchange earnings was not the result of Indonesia's own efforts, but the outcome of external factors, in particular the Korean War boom. Hence, Indonesia's economic position was unstable. Even with the monetary measures taken in 1950 when foreign exchange certificates were issued, Indonesia would have been in a precarious situation had not the Korean War bolstered demand for export products such as oil and rubber. In addition, much of the government budget in the preceding year had been spent on unproductive uses. If the government in 1951 had spent more on productive activities, both government and society would have prospered.

Given developments abroad, Sjafruddin thought it unlikely that the favourable conditions of 1950 would be repeated. Prices of Indonesian export commodities in overseas markets were already declining. Therefore, export production would have to be enlarged unless imports could be curbed. But various factors hampered efforts to increase production, including disturbances of law and order, theft or burnings of estate crops, strikes, unfavourable labour relations, increases in wages, land rents, rice prices, and so on. All these factors adversely affected the output of sugar, rubber, tobacco, coffee, other estate crops and cassava, which inflicted losses of millions of rupiah.

Sjafruddin's warning about the inflationary effect of loose fiscal and monetary policies pressures was correct. Borrowing by the Indonesian government from the central bank to finance the budget deficit did indeed cause prices to rise. Since government expenditures in 1952 rose by much more than government revenue, the budget deficit by the end of 1952 amounted to a massive Rp4.3 billion (five per cent of gross national income), against a budget surplus of Rp1.2 billion in 1951.[42] Sjafruddin was also correct in criticizing the spendthrift policy of the government frittering away windfall foreign exchange earnings on too many imported consumer goods, including durables such as cars, rather than spending the surplus on productive purposes.

## THE RICE PROVISION

Despite a rapidly increasing population, by 1940 Indonesia had been "self-supporting" in rice. However, since the transfer of sovereignty, several hundred thousand tons of rice had to be imported every year. In fact, rice imports were, as Sjafruddin pointed out, steadily increasing. Not much money would have to be spent in order to restore self-sufficiency in the nation's major food crop, at least not as much as would be required to build up a national industry. For instance, the government had allocated Rp120 million to construct a cement factory in Surabaya. With this amount, at least 60,000 hectares of *sawah* (irrigated rice fields) could have been opened up yielding 60,000 tons of rice. This harvest could then have been sold against a price of Rp2 per kg generating revenue of Rp120 million.

Sjafruddin calculated that an investment of Rp1.2 billion was needed to raise rice production by 600,000 tons, thus restoring self-sufficiency. In the current situation this amount had to be allocated to purchases of rice from abroad. By rehabilitating irrigation facilities, the time required for opening up new fields — for instance, in Kalimantan and Sulawesi, among others — could be significantly shortened. He argued that the rehabilitation of irrigation works should be delayed no longer.

Although Sjafruddin was right in emphasizing the need to increase rice production, he underestimated the considerable costs and time required to open up new *sawah* land and to construct irrigation works in Kalimantan and Sulawesi.

## CONDITIONS FOR INDUSTRIALIZATION

A large industrialization plan would cost billions of rupiah. This money could be obtained by foreign borrowing, but the key question, as Sjafruddin saw it, was who would provide such loans and under what conditions. Foreign loans were not being provided on the basis of economic and financial considerations, but exclusively on political grounds. He referred to the Mutual Security Agreement (MSA), concluded with the United States, that had created an uproar among Indonesia's political leaders. In addition, the government needed to choose between foreign borrowing or attracting foreign direct investment. Other Asian countries, notably India and Pakistan, were doing everything they could to attract foreign investors.

Foreign direct investment could be beneficial for Indonesia, particularly in terms of generating tax revenue and creating employment opportunities. To attract foreign capital, it was essential that foreign investors could transfer net profits to their home country and depreciate corporate assets in Indonesia. Sjafruddin underestimated or ignored these unfavourable conditions for foreign direct investment (FDI) in Indonesia during the 1950s. Considering the potency of economic nationalism in Indonesia at the time, it would have been unrealistic for Indonesia to rely on foreign investment to finance and implement its industrialization.

## NATIONALIZATION

Plans for the nationalization of foreign companies of vital importance, such as public utilities, railroads, oil companies and the like, did not meet with Sjafruddin's approval. The Indonesian government simply lacked the means to carry out such plans. Nationalization could only be justified for the most vital enterprises, such as the Java Bank. From an economic point of view, nationalization amounted to a transfer of ownership to the state; however, this certainly did not imply an increase in production for the benefit of society as a whole. Nationalization could therefore not result in an increase in national income and higher standards of living.

Sjafruddin's sober view on nationalization, particularly in regard to the Dutch companies, was unusual among Indonesian political leaders, most of whom were rankled by the continued operations of Dutch firms after the transfer of sovereignty. Apart from the nationalization of the Java Bank in 1951, the Indonesian government in the early 1950s nationalized several Dutch-owned enterprises that fulfilled key functions in the economy such as railroads and gas and electricity companies.[43]

## FOREIGN DIRECT INVESTMENT

Sjafruddin wrote:

> We may have 1,001 objections to attracting foreign investment in Indonesia, but we have to be conscious of the fact that closing the foreign enterprises in Indonesia without establishing new companies, for which we lack the capital and the skills, will not improve the people's welfare. We may have 1,001 objections to foreign companies because they produce mainly for the export market, but we should not forget that there is no country on earth, including the US and Russia, which can live from its own production only. We should be glad that we can export a lot of produce, because in this way

we can import products which we cannot yet produce ourselves, but which we badly need, such as capital goods for industrial development.[44]

These words reflect the pragmatic outlook of Sjafruddin, notwithstanding that in the early 1950s, attracting new foreign companies was politically inconceivable because of the bitter resentment of the presence of many foreign, particularly Dutch, companies.

## SUMITRO'S VIEWS

Sumitro's comments on Sjafruddin's views, as expressed in successive issues of the *Nieuwgier* in March 1952, are discussed in this section.[45] I distinguish between points of agreement and disagreement between Sumitro and Sjafruddin.

### Points of Agreement

Sumitro found himself in agreement with several points made by Sjafruddin, although he did not underwrite Sjafruddin's conclusions. The "therapy" which Sjafruddin offered to solve the economic problems of the time, differed significantly from the solutions advocated by Sumitro. However, Sumitro was keen to emphasize that his observations did not detract from his great appreciation for the quality and approach of Sjafruddin's analysis and his honesty in conveying the facts to public attention.

Sumitro wrote:

> I certainly agree with Sjafruddin that in 1951 the level of economic activities and of production is still very low. It is indeed true that the increased foreign exchange earnings from our commodity exports is not based on a higher level of production, but on external factors beyond our control, namely the Korean War. This constitutes an unstable basis for the position of our country. We also have to realise that no less than 60-70 per cent of our foreign exchange earnings are generated by only a very few commodities, namely rubber and tin. This fact has also been pointed out by Sjafruddin and also by me on several occasions.

Sumitro continued:

> I also completely agree with Sjafruddin's complaint about the wasteful government expenditures on consumption goods, including consumer durables. I also agree with Sjafruddin's criticism that the government has been negligent in not carrying out various projects in the sphere of production, which I consider as a neglect of the people's interests. Sjafruddin rightly

criticised the current rice situation, which is a clear example of the impotence of the current cabinet to solve the rice problem. Because of its negligence, this year 600,000 tons of rice have to be imported. It is clear that the policy pursued by the current government has put too much emphasis on trade, while lacking a clear and consistent policy on raising production.[46]

## Points of Disagreement

Sumitro stated that

> based on the developments Sjafruddin has observed, he has interpreted and drawn some conclusions which in his view would lead to improvements. But it is precisely these interpretations, conclusions and recommendations with which I in principle cannot agree. It is regrettable that Sjafruddin's formulation of the problems is unclear. He discussed several subjects in such a way that it seemed as if they were not inter-related. However, for the sake of clarity I would like to highlight certain aspects of our current economic conditions (Sumitro: Nieuwsgier, 17 Maart 1952).

He then focused on the structure of the Indonesia economy:

> Indonesia's current economic conditions can only be fully understood against the background of the history of our country. The factors, which affected economic conditions in the past, still to a high degree affect current economic conditions. When our country was a colony, its economic function was to supply the industrial countries with raw materials and serve as a market for the products of these industrial countries. History has shown that in the economic relations between the industrial countries and the primary-exporting countries, the social progress of the Southeast Asian countries was severely hampered. Through monopolistic systems and other measures the interests of the industrial countries were always given priority, so that the development of the raw material-producing countries was always hampered, particularly in the field of trade, shipping, and industrial development. This economic position has persisted until the present, and has led to a one-sided pattern of production and activities, namely the production of raw materials for overseas industries. This has meant that economic activity has been limited to agrarian activity, and that the greater part of production is destined for export.

> The people's welfare is therefore highly dependent on this one-sided pattern of production, a basis which is very narrow. Its consequence is a very weak economic position of the people, which is reflected by its low purchasing-power. The economic weakness is also reflected by the low level of development of the people in the economic field. For this reason the

productivity of the people has remained at a very low level which, in turn, is reflected by the low standard of living. Such a basis and characteristic of production aimed at limited interests therefore means a neglect of the interests of the people. As long as policies are not focused on eliminating or reducing these limitations, our society will not change (Sumitro: Nieuwsgier, 17 Maart 1952).

Sumitro took issues with Sjafruddin as follows:

The ways indicated by Sjafruddin will, I fear, not lead to a correct solution of the economic problems of Indonesia but, instead, will only be perpetuated, and even weaken the economic resilience of the Indonesian people. In short, Indonesia's economic structure and pattern of production up to World War II was aimed at producing agrarian products for the export market, and hardly enough for satisfying the primary needs of the people, including foodstuffs. When two years ago our independence was recognized, we immediately faced a worrying situation: a disorganized and chaotic government bureaucracy, a domestic market which was empty as regards the consumption goods for the people, and a totally neglected agrarian production apparatus of food crops as well as export crops. Compared to the needs of the people, the imports from 1940 to 1949 were minimal. Up to the present, the total import volume is far from adequate according to the normal pre-war volumes. Besides the increased need for essential consumption goods and the shortage of import goods, the people's purchasing-power has also declined among broad layers of the population.[47]

He continued:

The challenge is therefore how the purchasing-power of the people can be increased by broadening Indonesia's economic basis and stimulating the activities in the production sectors. This should be achieved by a clearly delineated financial and economic policy. During the past years financial policy was, according to my conviction, of little use for economic activity. It did not provide a stimulus for developing the possibilities for economic progress. Financial policy was pursued in such a way as if it was disconnected from economic activity and production. This was one of the causes of the present economic difficulties which led to the current deflation (Sumitro: Nieuwsgier, 18 Maart 1952).

Then Sumitro focused on the issue of inflation versus deflation:

Sjafruddin argues that at present we are experiencing inflation. However, his conclusion that there is inflation is unclear and unconvincing. Sjafruddin argues that inflation has appeared because of the creation of new money amounting to Rp1.8 billion, which was used to cover the budget deficit of 1950, and which could not be fully covered by the budget surplus of 1951. According to Sjafruddin, this budget surplus amounted to about Rp1.3 billion, so there was a remaining deficit of Rp500 million. If the total amount of money in circulation is used as a criterion to judge whether there is inflation or deflation, who will judge whether this amount is too large or too small? Or will this amount be compared with the total needs of society? In this case the total needs will always exceed by far the money in circulation (Sumitro, Nieuwsgier, 18 Maart 1952).

He continued:

We can also use a more "objective" criterion, namely the total reserves of the Java Bank, the bank of circulation. After the recent devaluation, the exchange rate of the US dollar to the rupiah was set at one US dollar = Rp3. Because of this our gold reserves are now worth Rp3.2 billion. Compared with the liabilities of the Java Bank of Rp4 billion, the Java Bank's gold reserves, considering that the reserve requirements of the Java Bank have to be 20 per cent, amount to no less than 77 per cent, thus almost four times as much as the required reserve requirements. In this case we can talk about a shortage of money in the sense of contraction of money. We can clarify this matter by also including the foreign exchange reserves in the reserves of the Java Bank together with the gold reserves, as is the case in several other countries [underlined by Sumitro]. Our foreign exchange reserves amount to Rp3,450 million which, in combination with the gold reserves of Rp3,180 million, amount to a total amount of reserves of Rp6,630 million or 165 per cent of the Java Bank's reserves (Sumitro: Nieuwsgier, 18 Maart 1952).

Sumitro proceeded to state:

How far will we go with "hoarding" such a large amount of reserves? Except for Switzerland, no other country pursues such a policy of "hoarding" foreign exchange reserves as we do. Is it the purpose that we accumulate reserves to an unlimited degree until all economic activities in this country grinds to a halt? Under present monetary conditions as well from an economic and formal legal point of view the value of our gold reserves need to be expressed in rupiah. If this procedure is followed, then the government budget deficit of Rp500 million, as mentioned by Sjafruddin, is incorrect. In fact, the reverse is the case. If we combine the budgets of both years [1950 and 1951] we don't have a budget deficit, but instead a surplus. Hence, the government does not have a debt with the Java Bank, but instead the Java bank has a debt with the government, since all profits arising from the devaluation accrue to the government. Because of this, the argument that the government budget deficit caused inflation is invalid, since one cannot say that a monetary expansion had taken place. Instead, a monetary contraction has taken place. I therefore do not agree with Sjafruddin's statement that the balance of payments and the government budget are the most important barometers of Indonesia's economic and financial conditions, since these conditions are closely related to the economic activities taking place in society.[48]

Sumitro's arguments on this issue seem rather contrived. There was no evidence of deflation. On the contrary, by mid-1952, the budget deficit had undeniably led to strong inflationary pressures.[49]

Sumitro also discussed the balance of payments and government budget at some length. He wrote:

We cannot just conclude that a budget surplus or a foreign exchange surplus in the balance of payments is a favourable phenomenon. We have to ask the important question what the function is of a budget deficit or surplus in connection with the level of production and economic activity, national income, employment etc. It is clear that the above budget surpluses during the past years were obtained by sacrificing the public interest, namely by neglecting the production and economic activities of our people. This has led to the worrisome condition in which we are now in. Sjafruddin himself stated that the large budget surplus was made possible because several productive projects were not implemented. On the other hand, government expenditures were often squandered. This can only yield one conclusion: exploitation of the people by the state (Sumitro: Nieuwsgier, 18 Maart 1952.

He continued:

My greatest criticism of the financial and monetary policies during the past years is that the government treasury is considered to be a sovereign or autonomous field, which has led to the total neglect of economic activity and the process of economic development. Financial policy should be focused on economic activity, so that government money will be an active tool for opening up possibilities for economic development.[50]

Sumitro's view on foreign exchange reserves differed quite markedly from that of Sjafruddin. Sumitro wrote:

Foreign exchange reserves themselves cannot be considered unconditionally as a good phenomenon, as Sjafruddin does. A foreign exchange surplus can occur if imports are low. More than a year ago I warned about the dangers which threatened the domestic economy because of the insufficient supply of goods for the domestic market. The important problem is not mainly having gold and foreign exchange reserves, but what is of crucial importance is how an adequate supply of goods, required to meet the minimum needs of the people, can be guaranteed. Although I agree with Sjafruddin's observation about the low level of production, the low level of economic activity, and the unstable economic conditions, I would like to add that the financial and monetary policies pursued during the past few years have not or only contributed very little to developing the possibilities of production and economic activity.[51]

A comment on Sumitro's criticism of the government's economic policies is warranted. In 1952 and 1953, the Indonesian government made serious efforts to raise production, especially of rice and other foodstuffs. To achieve this goal, an agricultural improvement programme was launched that included repair and improvement of existing irrigation systems, increased use of fertilizer (made possible by financial assistance from the United States), better seed selection and expansion of planted acreage.[52]

The issue of autarchy versus foreign trade also came up in the debate between Sumitro and Sjafruddin. On this topic, Sumitro wrote:

> Sjafruddin has actually weakened his own argument by touching on the subject of autarchy. Autarchy has never been an issue in Indonesia's economic development, and there has never been an issue of "autarchy or foreign trade". Although for Indonesia's economic development we have to search for new possibilities, this does not mean that we have to go back to a closed economy. The development of underdeveloped areas will be characterized by an expansion of trade and better exchange of goods and services with other countries. History has shown that trade between the industrial countries has increased rather than decreased. I would like to emphasize that the concept of autarchy and the aspiration for autarchy is not in order, since we don't intend to narrow the basis of our economic life, but intend to expand and broaden the basis of our economy and our future life.[53]

Sumitro was absolutely correct in pointing out that autarchy was not a viable economic alternative to Indonesia. Being a vast, archipelagic country with a very long coastline, autarchy would not be feasible.

Another topic of discussion concerned the balance between agriculture and industry in economic development. Sumitro stated:

> Industrialization does not mean that the agrarian foundation should be fully replaced by an industrial foundation. In fact, we have to strive for complementarity, that is, we have to view the industrial sector as an important complement to the still one-sided agrarian economic base of Indonesia. We

have to achieve a balance in the economic structure of Indonesia in view of the unstable and narrow basis of our economy. Since our production is primarily agrarian, labour productivity and the level of development in our country have remained low (Sumitro: Nieuwsgier, 19 Maart 1952).

He continued:

Sjafruddin himself pointed out the importance and possibilities of industrial development, although he pointed this out in another context, namely in regard to the role of foreign investment. However, Sjafruddin maintains that the state should focus its attention on agriculture. Perhaps his views have been influenced by his concern about the rice problem, a concern shared by everybody with a sense of responsibility. Sjafruddin's concern is understandable, and I completely agree with Sjafruddin that far too little attention has been paid to the production and distribution of foodstuffs. I would also like to note that I consider the problem of increasing rice production and improving the organization and purchase of rice of crucial importance. On the other hand, I am against any policy which focuses exclusively on agrarian production, while neglecting the promotion of industrial development. Such a policy would be irresponsible, since this would mean that the economic disparities would be maintained in the future. It would even cause a steady decline in the standard of living and the way of life of the Indonesian people (Sumitro: Nieuwsgier, 19 Maart 1952).

And further still:

Although Sjafruddin agrees that wages in the industrial sector are higher than wages in the agricultural sector, he thinks that this would only apply to a few thousand industrial workers. This argument, however, indicates a naive simplicity. Sjafruddin does not mention the "multiplier" effects of constructing, say, a cement plant. Establishing a plant of such importance will stimulate the establishment of and employment in other industries, secondary industries, which in turn will stimulate the establishment of tertiary industries. Aside from this, Sjafruddin does not consider the development of the rural, small and cottage industries. If one wants to raise the standard of living of the people, the development of small and cottage industries in the rural areas should not be overlooked. This is of even greater importance in densely-populated areas, such as in various regions in Java.[54]

Economic and social development can only take place if accompanied by industrial development, including the development of small and cottage industries in the rural areas. The history of other countries has also shown that an improvement in agrarian production can only be achieved in combination with the development of the industrial sector, since the spirit and attitude to life of the agrarian population can then become dynamic.

## Comment

Sumitro was quite correct in emphasizing that both agricultural and industrial development would be required to achieve a balanced structure of the Indonesian economy and sustained economic growth. No developing country would be able to achieve rapid and sustained economic growth if it were to focus only on agricultural development, while neglecting or deferring industrial development.

## SPECIALIZATION BETWEEN AGRARIAN AND INDUSTRIAL COUNTRIES

Referring to the economic motive or principle, Sjafruddin argues that we have to produce as many goods as possible, which we can produce as cheaply as possible. This economic principle is often advanced to justify specialization between the various regions in the world, namely the agrarian countries which have to keep supplying raw materials and the industrial countries which have to concentrate on industrial products. The needs of these various countries can then be met by mutual exchange of these products.

However, there is no reason at all for us to accept the present relations as being the best and allow it to perpetuate until the end of time. The present emphasis on our export products can only be justified if the present structural relations and the economic constellation is considered to be immutable and unchangeable.

The present condition in the world market for raw materials shows the great uncertainty in the relations between import products and export products. Our great dependence on foreign countries highlight this. The prices of our raw materials are declining, while the prices of the products we buy overseas remain high and are difficult to procure, even if we are willing to pay a good price for them. Moreover, the decline in the prices of our products can often not be offset by increasing the export volumes. Often an increase in the export volumes will lead to a further decline in the prices of our raw materials. These difficulties are aggravated by certain measures of the industrial countries which depress the prices of our raw materials — for instance, in the case of rubber and tin. On the other hand, we cannot do anything to counteract these measures by our own strength.

## Comment

The point raised here by Sumitro is related to the previous point, namely that it would not be sensible if Indonesia continued to specialize in agricultural production, and import manufactured products from the advanced industrial countries. The experience of the East Asian newly-industrializing economies (NIEs) has shown that rapid, labour-intensive, export-oriented industrialization led to rapid economic growth and a rapid decline in unemployment and absolute poverty.

## INDUSTRIALIZATION TO BE TOTALLY INITIATED BY FOREIGN, PRIVATE CAPITAL?

Sjafruddin underlines the weakness of our economic position as an agrarian country. He also does not reject the industrial development of our country. However, he feels that we have to concentrate mainly on agrarian development, while leaving industrial development to foreign capital.

Assuming that we follow the viewpoint of Sjafruddin, the question arises whether the industries we consider important will indeed be developed. It also remains to be seen whether such an industrial development will strengthen our economic basis.

In a country with an economic structure like Indonesia, industrial development will be quite different than in countries which already have an industrial foundation. In these latter countries — with well-developed societies and well-functioning transport apparatuses, high quality workers, well-organized stock exchanges, capital and labour markets — newly established industries can immediately profit from the external benefits of such a society. However, in less developed countries, such as Indonesia, conditions are quite different. A newly constructed plant will under present circumstances not directly experience the favourable impact of "external economies". Such plants will have to bear for a certain period the risks and costs which are very high compared to those in the industrial countries.

Under an open economic system new industries would only acquire a competitive strength in the market after a certain period of time. Support to new industries according to a clear and focused government policy are absolutely required. Without a determined economic protectionist policy (these words were underlined by Sumitro in his article in *Nieuwsgier* of 20 March 1952) in the so-called 'underdeveloped countries', leaving industrial development to the private sector will leave the new infant industries to compete against forces which already have a big head start.

In a country with a social structure like ours, government should go forward in making direct investments in various sectors to stimulate economic activity and private investment. If this does not happen, then there is little hope for industrial development, based on private initiative, of both domestic and foreign capital. Before the various industrial projects, the state should first invest in electrical energy, road construction, and transport infrastructure. There are sectors of vital and strategic importance, which cannot be left to private foreign capital. In these sectors, the state needs to take a leading role by direct investments. For this reason Sjafruddin's view that industrial development should all be left or largely left to private initiative and capital is not acceptable.

If our attention is only focused on agrarian production and industrial development is left to foreign private capital, than the distorted, power relations between the various groups in society will be maintained and the level of development of our people will remain low. Our people will then remain an object of various manipulations by foreign interests. In a country like Indonesia with an economic and social structure of a colonial or of a former colonial country, concepts such as "free enterprise" and "free competition" are empty phrases, because they do not conform to the reality of economic life.

There will be no freedom if everything is left to "free competition". One should not lose sight of the fact that in the social structure of our country certain groups completely dominate economic life because they <u>occupy monopolistic positions</u> (underlining by Sumitro) or possess <u>oligopolistic power</u> (underlining by Sumitro) in the economic field. These groups represent interests which are not organically rooted in society. Hence, leaving economic life in general, and industrial development in particular, to "free enterprise" would mean surrendering oneself to these monopolistic powers.

One should also not forget the development of small and cottage industries in the rural areas, which should be stimulated by the state. Industries which do not have a direct strategic interest, but because of their nature exert a direct impact on other industries should be reserved for participation by Indonesian interests, either with capital of the state, or with private capital. The remaining industries will provide enough opportunity for foreign private capital.

In other words, capital and workers from abroad are welcome on the condition that they are attracted in accordance with the needs of the people and are based on the interests of Indonesian society. By playing a constructive role in the development process of Indonesian society, domination of the interests of the people by foreign capital will be prevented.[55]

## Comment

Sumitro's argument with regard to the role of foreign capital in Indonesia's economic development, in particular industrialization, is convincing and certainly in line with the economic aspirations of many Indonesians. In fact, it was inconceivable that any developing country, except for a small city-state such as Singapore, would be prepared to entrust industrial development to foreign direct investment. Moreover, foreign investors might not be interested in committing funds to industries considered to be of strategic importance by the governments of developing countries. That would include basic heavy industry requiring large amounts of investment capital and long gestation periods.

Just like Sjafruddin, Sumitro entered into the public discourse at the time concerning nationalization. He wrote:

> Since the interests of the people are the sole criterion I consider "nationalization" not as a dogmatic or doctrinaire concept that, without taking into consideration special conditions, should be implemented. The core of the problem lies in the question where and under which circumstances nationalization has to be carried out in order to be of benefit for the people. This needs to be decided on the basis of cool calculation and business considerations and not on the basis of sentiment. What is equally important, besides the problem of ownership, is that the management of a nationalized enterprise should be focused on meeting the interests of Indonesian society [underlined by Sumitro]. This applies to the bank of circulation (Java Bank), the electricity company and other nationalized companies. Even if a company is taken over by the state but without a change in the focus of the management of the nationalized company, this will mean that the interests of the people will continue to be neglected. The only difference is that this will now be done with the money of our people. It is therefore of utmost importance to determine how and for what purpose the nationalized company was taken over. In this respect there appears to be agreement between my and Sjafruddin's views.[56]

With respect to the issue of nationalization, Sumitro and Sjafruddin both held pragmatic, non-ideological views and agreed that merely nationalising foreign companies would not be in the national interest if not focused on meeting the needs of the people.

The policy of transmigration was discussed by Sumitro as follows:

> Transmigration should not be viewed as a mechanical transplant of a great number of people, as if they were lifeless objects. Transmigration should be conducted as part of the opening up and real development of new regions, hence as a direct and integral part of the possibilities of industrialization and other economic activities in these new regions. We have to prevent that the future will be a repetition of what is happening in Java today. When a great number of people are just being moved from Java to other regions

without creating new job opportunities, then it can be foreseen that the increase in population and the limited nature of their economic activities will result in overpopulation, as is the case in Java now. Making economic activity more dynamic as part of the opening-up of new regions…has to be combined with the design and development of industrial, forestry and other job opportunities, which should be an integral part of transmigration. Those people being resettled in new regions should not view themselves or be viewed as the 'economic garbage' of our society. On the contrary, if transmigration is implemented according to our conception about the opening up and development of new regions, these resettled people should be considered as pioneers, since they open up new job opportunities.[57]

Despite Sumitro's criticism of the views of the late J.H. Boeke about "static expansion", he did stress the need for transmigration to amount to more than the resettlement of people from densely-populated Java to the sparsely-populated Outer Islands which might only lead to overpopulation. Instead, Sumitro was one of the early proponents of transmigration as a means of creating dynamic economic activities in the Outer Islands by encouraging initiatives in industrial production, forestry and other branches of the local economy.

Sumitro's general conclusion runs as follows:

In these above series of articles I have offered my views on the views of Sjafruddin. I thought it important to indicate that the path indicated by Sjafruddin is not the right way to get out of the present impasse, and even less to achieve progress. My objections are not directed at the basis or the spirit of Sjafruddin's views, which create the impression as if the real problem is being avoided. His views create the impression that the most logical solution is found, but in fact his views mean that the solutions he offers are a resignation with the difficulties being faced at present and in the future. In this way our people will remain at the level of illiteracy and low development. Without detracting from my appreciation for the views of Sjafruddin, it needs to be emphasized that only by pursuing policies according to the guidelines I have indicated, there is reason for hope for an increased level of production, increase in income, strengthening of the level of development of our people in order to achieve real progress of Indonesian society.[58]

## CONCLUSION

This account of the debate between Sjafruddin and Sumitro in March 1952 is of interest since both of them were pragmatic policy-makers. They were aware that Indonesia had to tolerate the continued presence of Dutch enterprises, at least for the time being, because of the foreign exchange earnings and employment that these firms generated and the imports they required. While both Sjafruddin and Sumitro had Indonesia's national interest at heart, they differed not only in their interpretation of the economic problems the nation faced in the early post-independence period, but particularly with regard to the economic policies to be pursued in order to solve Indonesia's economic and social problems.

Comparing Sjafruddin's and Sumitro's views, one notices Sjafruddin's more moderate and gradualist policy suggestions, which were unlikely to be accepted by most nationalist leaders. While Sjafruddin acknowledged that Dutch companies continued to dominate the economy even after the transfer of sovereignty, he also argued that the Indonesian government had the political power to reduce the economic leverage of these firms, which could be achieved through reasonable means. Sjafruddin also saw education as a basic tool to solve social problems. To achieve that, however, Indonesia needed a genuinely democratic educational system with equal access for all. Sjafruddin therefore counselled patience, since economic conditions could not be solved in the short run. For this reason, Sjafruddin, at great political risk, spoke out against the takeover of Dutch enterprises in December 1957.[59]

Although he was also a pragmatic policymaker, Sumitro held views in 1952 that revealed a far more realistic grasp of Indonesia's short- and long-term economic problems. As a university-trained economist, Sumitro was also better able to articulate his views in a persuasive way. Sumitro's views are of special interest since several of his views and beliefs are still relevant today, as some of the problems he discussed almost sixty years ago have persisted until today. For instance, his view on the importance of industrial development; the important but supplementary role that foreign direct investment could play in Indonesia's development, although limited to non-strategic sectors; the crucial role which the state enterprises should play in strategic sectors, the need to promote small-scale and cottage industry in rural areas and the disproportionate economic power which certain groups in society enjoyed.

While Sumitro was certainly not a racist, he correctly identified, though cautiously, the great challenge the Indonesian government faced in reducing the wide economic gap between the more prosperous ethnic Chinese Indonesians and the *pribumi* (indigenous) Indonesian majority. The sad fact is that after more than sixty years of political independence, this economic gap has widened rather than narrowed. That issue, however, will be the topic of another paper.

## Notes

1. "The Debate on Economic Policy in Newly-independent Indonesia between Sjafruddin Prawiranegara and Sumitro Djojohadikusumo", by Thee Kian Wie, was first published in *The Indonesian Economy in the Early Independence Period*, edited by J. Thomas Lindblad. *ITINERARIO*, Cambridge University Press for the Centre of the History of European Expansion, Leiden University, March 2010. The author would like to acknowledge the valuable comments and suggestions given by Dr Jeroen Touwen at the University of Leiden on an earlier draft of this article. I alone remain responsible for errors and shortcomings.
2. Houben, *Van kolonie tot eenheidsstaat*, 163.
3. Sumitro, *Jejak perlawanan begawan pejuang*, 136.
4. Booth, "Government and Welfare", table 1.
5. Booth, "Growth and Stagnation", 402–3.
6. *Bank Industri Negara*, 9.
7. Ibid., 61.
8. Ibid., 9–10, 61.
9. Sumitro, *Jejak perlawanan Begawan pejuang*, 94–5.
10. Kahin, "Some Recollections", 26.
11. Meijer, *Den Haag-Djakarta*, 47.
12. Sumitro, *Jejak perlawanan begawan pejuang*, 96–7; Meijer, *Den Haag-Djakarta*, 47.
13. Kahin, "Some Recollections", 26.
14. Meijer, *Den Haag-Djakarta*, 45–7.
15. Ibid., 46–7.
16. Baudet and Fennema, *Het Nederlands belang bij Indie*, 213.
17. Meijer, *Den Haag-Djakarta*, 284.
18. Sumitro, *Facing the Situation*, 5.
19. Ibid., 8.
20. Dick, Houben, Lindblad, and Thee, *The Emergence*, 174.
21. Higgins, *Indonesia's Economic Stabilization*, 2.
22. Ibid., 2.
23. Thee, "Introduction", 8.
24. Glassburner, "Economic Policymaking", 79.
25. Burger, *Sociologisch-economische geschiedenis*,171.
26. Glassburner, "Economic Policymaking", 80.
27. Ibid., 81.
28. Booth, "The Colonial Legacy", 13.
29. Thee, "Introduction", 10.
30. Higgins, *Indonesia's Economic Stabilization*, 103.
31. Ibid., 103.
32. Feith, *The Decline*, 113.

33. Ibid., 114.
34. Ibid., 605.
35. Thee, "Introduction", 10, 20.
36. Glassburner, "Economic Policymaking", 71.
37. Mackie, "The Indonesian Economy", 44.
38. Sjafruddin, "Recollections", 100.
39. The three Dutch-language newspapers in circulation in Jakarta in the early and mid-1950s were the *Java Bode, Bataviaasch Nieuwsblad,* and *Nieuwsgier.*
40. Since the relevant issues of *Abadi* were not available in the National Library (*Perpustakaan Nasional*) in Jakarta, my account of Sjafruddin's views is based on the report in *Nieuwsgier* and, indirectly, on Sumitro's reactions.
41. Sjafruddin, "Naast verheugende resultaten", 1–2.
42. Higgins, *Indonesia's Economic Stabilization,* 6.
43. Burger, *Sociologisch-economische geschiedenis,* 170.
44. *Niewsgier* 13 March 1952.
45. Sumitro, "Indonesi"'s economische opbouw".
46. *Nieuwsgier* 17 March 1952.
47. Ibid.
48. *Nieuwsgier* 18 March 1952.
49. Higgins, *Indonesia's Economic Stabilization,* 2.
50. Sumitro, "Indonesi"'s economische opbouw".
51. Ibid.
52. Higgins, *Indonesia's Economic Stabilization,* 7.
53. Sumitro, "Indonesi"'s economische opbouw".
54. *Nieuwsgier* 19 March 1952.
55. *Nieuwsgier* 20 March 1952.
56. *Nieuwsgier* 22 March 1952.
57. Ibid.
58. Ibid.
59. Sjafruddin, "Recollections", 104.

# References

*Bank Industri Negara 1951–1956.* Jakarta: Bank Industri Negara, 1957.
Baudet, H. and M. Fennema. *Het Nederlands belang bij Indie.* Utrecht: Spectrum, 1983.
Booth, Anne. "The Colonial Legacy and its Impact on Post-Independence Planning in India and Indonesia". *Itinerario* 10:1 (1986): 1–30.
———. "Government and Welfare in the New Republic: Indonesia in the 1950s". *Itinerario* 34:1 (2010).
———. "Growth and Stagnation in an Era of Nation-Building: Indonesian Economic Performance from 1950 to 1965". In *Historical Foundations of a National Economy*

*in Indonesia: Indonesia, 1890s–1990s*, edited by J. Thomas Lindblad, 401–23. Amsterdam: North-Holland, 1996.

Burger, D.H. *Sociologisch-economische geschiedenis van Indonesie*. Amsterdam: Koninklijk Instituut voor de Tropen, 1975.

Dick, Howard, Vincent Houben, J. Thomas Lindblad, and Thee Kian Wie. *The Emergence of a National Economy: An Economic History of Indonesia, 1800–2000*. Sydney: Allen & Unwin, 2002.

Feith, Higgins. *The Decline of Constitutional Democracy in Indonesia*. Ithaca, NY: Cornell University Press, 1962.

Glassburner, Bruce. "Economic Policy-making in Indonesia, 1950–1957". In *The Economy of Indonesia*, edited by Bruce Glassburner, 70–98. Ithaca, NY: Cornell University Press, 1971.

Higgins, Benjamin. *Indonesia's Economic Stabilization and Development*. New York: Institute of Pacific Relations, 1957.

Houben, Vincent. *Van kolonie tot eenheidsstaat; Indonesie in de negentiende en twintigste eeuw* Leiden: Vakgroep Talen en en Culturen van Zuidoost-Azie en Oceanie, 1996.

Kahin, George McTurnan. "Some Recollections from and Reflections on the Indonesian Revolution". In *The Heartbeat of Indonesian Revolution*, edited by Taufik Abdullah, 10–27. Jakarta: Gramedia, 1997.

Mackie, J.A.C. "The Indonesian Economy, 1950–1963". In *The Economy of Indonesia*, edited by Bruce Glassburner, 16–69. Ithaca, NY: Cornell University Press, 1971.

Meijer, Hans. *Den Haag-Djakarta; De Nederlands-Indonesische betrekkingen, 1950–1962*. Utrecht: Spectrum, 1994.

Sjafruddin Prawiranegara. "Herorientatie di lapangan ekonomi". *Abadi* 6, 7 and 8 March 1952.

———. "Naast verheugende resultaten reden voor bezordheid voor de toekomst; Mr. Sjafruddin over de financieel-economische ontwikkeling; Dreigende inflatie in 1953 indien de begroting niet in evenwicht wordt gebracht". *Nieuwsgier* 13 March 1952.

———. "Recollections of My Career". *Bulletin of Indonesian Economic Studies* 23:2 (1987): 100–108.

Sumitro Djojohadikusumo. *Facing the Situation*. Jakarta: Ministry of Information, 1952.

———. "Indonesi"s Economische Opbouw; Aantekeningen op de beschouwing van mr. Sjafruddin Prawiranegara". *Nieuwsgier* 17, 18, 19, 20, 21 and 22 March 1952.

———. "Recollections of My Career". *Bulletin of Indonesian Economic Studies* 22:3 (December 1986): 27–39.

———.*Jejak perlawanan begawan pejuang*. Jakarta: Sinar Harapan, 2000.

Thee Kian Wie. "Introduction". In *Recollections: The Indonesian Economy, 1950s–1990s*, edited by Thee Kian Wie, 3–43. Singapore: Institute of Southeast Asian Studies, 2003.

# PART II

## THE SOEHARTO ERA: 1966–1998

# 4

---

# INDONESIA'S ECONOMIC DEVELOPMENT DURING AND AFTER THE SOEHARTO ERA: ACHIEVEMENTS AND FAILINGS[1]

## INTRODUCTION

After presenting a brief overview of Indonesia's rapid and sustained economic growth during Soeharto's New Order era and its performance after the Asian economic crisis, this paper discusses the country's economic and social achievements as well as its serious shortcomings during the New Order era. The paper then discusses the challenges which the post-Soeharto governments faced in solving the serious economic and social problems currently facing Indonesia.

## THE INDONESIAN ECONOMY DURING AND AFTER THE SOEHARTO ERA: AN OVERVIEW

### The achievements of Soeharto's New Order (1966–98)

During the late Sukarno years in the mid-1960s, Indonesia was experiencing stagnating output, widespread poverty and hunger, crumbling infrastructure and a hyperinflation of almost 600 per cent because of runaway deficit-financing. However, after a successful stabilization and rehabilitation programme designed by a new team of capable economic advisers (the so-called 'Berkeley Mafia'[2]), Indonesia since the late 1960s embarked on a period of rapid and sustained economic growth averaging 6.7 per cent annually which lasted for three decades until the Asian economic crisis struck Indonesia in 1997/98.

Meanwhile, a successful family planning programme reduced population growth from an average of 2.4 per cent in the period 1965 to 1.8 per cent in 1980–1996 (World Bank, 1992: 268; 1998: 43). The resultant average population growth of 2.0 per cent led to an average, annual GNP per capita growth of 4.7 per cent, one of the highest rates among the world's fast-growing, emerging economies (World Bank, 1998: 25). While per capita GNP was around $100 in the mid-1960s, it had reached $580 in 1982, and almost $1,000 in the early 1990s, enabling Indonesia to 'graduate' from the ranks of the 'low income' into the ranks of the 'lower middle income economies' (Thee, 2002: 198).

Indonesia's rapid economic growth was underpinned by a rapid and sustained growth in gross domestic investment, including investment in human capital, averaging 9.2 per cent on the average during the period 1965–1997, on a par like the two other, rapidly growing Southeast Asian economies, Malaysia and Thailand (World Bank, 1999: 16–9). Indonesia's rapid growth was also driven by high rates of total factor productivity (TFP) growth (World Bank, 1993: 28-29; 40–48).

Indonesia's rapid and sustained growth was also accompanied by a steady reduction in the incidence of absolute poverty. This decline took place in both the urban and rural areas (Table 1).

In a context of growing population during the above period, the corresponding number of poor people fell from around 54 million people in 1976 to 23 million people in 1996 (BPS). This steep reduction in poverty was quite remarkable, as reflected by a comparative World Bank study on

### TABLE 1
### The Decline in Absolute Poverty in Indonesia, 1976–1996
### (% of people under official poverty line)

| Year | Urban areas | Rural areas | Total |
|------|-------------|-------------|-------|
| 1976 | 38.8 | 40.4 | 40.1 |
| 1978 | 30.8 | 33.3 | 33.3 |
| 1980 | 29.0 | 28.4 | 28.6 |
| 1981 | 28.1 | 26.5 | 26.9 |
| 1984 | 23.1 | 21.2 | 21.6 |
| 1987 | 20.1 | 16.1 | 17.4 |
| 1990 | 16.8 | 14.3 | 15.1 |
| 1993 | 13.5 | 13.8 | 13.7 |
| 1996 | 9.7 | 12.3 | 11.3 |

*Source*: Central Agency of Statistics (BPS), Jakarta.

poverty alleviation in developing countries. This study found that over the period 1970–1987 the average annual reduction in absolute poverty in Indonesia was much higher than in the other developing countries (World Bank 1990: 45).

During the 1970s this remarkable achievement was caused by the successful stabilization of food prices which, particularly on Java, meant that the poor experienced a lower rate of inflation than the rich. The steady growth in agricultural production during the 1970s and early 1980s was made possible by the government's commitment to broad-based rural development, as reflected by the successful dissemination of new production technologies in the food crop (particularly rice) sector, which generated new employment opportunities in production, processing, and marketing. The two oil booms in the 1970s (1973/74 and 1978/79) also spurred rapid growth in the non-tradable sectors, including construction and trade, which created new employment opportunities for the large number of unskilled workers (Booth, 2000: 81).

Even after the end of the oil boom era in 1982 which forced the government to pursue tight fiscal and monetary policies to restore macroeconomic stability, absolute poverty kept falling. The reason was that the budget cuts after 1982 were made in the capital-intensive sectors, including energy, and in the transmigration (resettlement) programme and the subsidies to state-owned enterprises, which died not have a large effect on employment (Booth, 2000: 85).

After the resumption of rapid growth in the late 1980s poverty declined at a slower rate, particularly in the rural areas, as the agricultural sector was given a lower priority compared to large-scale, capital-intensive and technology-intensive (e.g. aircraft assembly) manufacturing, modern services and physical infrastructure. Hence, since the late 1980s economic policies became less pro-poor (Booth, 2000: 89–90).

Rapid economic growth was also accompanied by rapid social development, as reflected by a number of social indicators, including rising net primary enrollment ratios which for both boys and girls were close to 100, infant mortality rates which showed a sharp decline compared to 1970, and a rising percentage of the population having access to safe water (World Bank, 1999: 16–19). In fact, by 1980 Indonesia's net primary enrollment ratios of both male and female students were already quite high as a result of the government's large investments in the expansion of primary education, particularly in the rural areas. This expansion was made possible by the oil boom windfall gains in the 1970s (Jones, 1994: 164). By the late 1980s the goal of universal primary education had largely been achieved, assisted by slower growth of the primary school age education due to the successful family planning programme introduced in the 1970s.

Indonesia's three decade-long rapid economic growth was driven by rapid growth of all three main sectors, including agriculture, manufacturing, and services. During this period Indonesia's manufacturing sector grew at a faster rate than the two other main sectors (Table 2).

### TABLE 2
### Economic Growth in Indonesia, 1965–1996
### (average annual growth rates (%)

|               | 1965–1980 | 1980–1990 | 1990–1996 |
| ------------- | --------- | --------- | --------- |
| Agriculture   | 4.3       | 3.4       | 2.8       |
| Manufacturing | 12.0      | 12.6      | 11.1      |
| Services      | 7.3       | 7.0       | 7.4       |
| GDP           | 7.0       | 6.1       | 7.7       |

*Source*: World Bank: World Development Indicators, successive issues.

As a result of the much faster growth of the manufacturing sector than the other sectors, the Indonesian economy experienced a rapid structural transformation as the contribution of the manufacturing sector rose from 8 per cent of GDP in 1965 to 25 per cent in 1996, while the agricultural sector contracted from over 45 per cent to 16 per cent during the same period. During this same period, Indonesia's manufacturing sector on the average also grew faster than most of the other East Asian emerging economies, except for South Korea. Table 3 presents data on the rapid industrial transformation which Indonesia experienced during the New Order era in comparison with the three other large ASEAN countries.

The data in Table 3 show that although in 1965, the full last year that President Sukarno held power, Indonesia had a much smaller manufacturing sector than the Philippines (which had been the most industrialized country in Southeast Asia since the early 1950s) and Thailand. However, after a sustained double-digit industrial growth in the following three decades, by 1996 Indonesia had the largest manufacturing sector in Southeast Asia. Table 3 also shows that while manufactured exports (mostly processed commodities) only accounted for four per cent of Indonesia's total exports in 1965, they accounted for 51 per cent in 1996. This was the outcome of a series of deregulation measures, including a series of trade reforms to reduce the 'anti-

## TABLE 3
## Indonesia's Industrial Development in ASEAN Perspective, 1965–1996

|  | MVA (millions of US$) | | MVA as % of GDP | | ME as % of TE | |
|---|---|---|---|---|---|---|
|  | 1970 | 1996 | 1965 | 1996 | 1965 | 1996 |
| Indonesia | 994 | 58,244 | 8 | 25 | 4 | 51 |
| Malaysia | 500 | 34,030 | 9 | 34 | 6 | 76 |
| Philippines | 1,622 | 18,908 | 20 | 23 | 6 | 84 |
| Thailand | 1,130 | 51,525 | 14 | 29 | 3 | 73 |

Notes: 1. MVA = manufacturing value added
2. ME = manufactured exports
3. TE = total exports
Source: Thee Kian Wie, 2002, as quoted from World Bank: World Development Indicators, successive issues.

export bias' of the highly protectionist trade regime, which the government had introduced after the end of the oil boom in 1982.

These deregulation measures, including the trade reforms, to spur the development of a more efficient and competitive private sector and increase non-oil exports, particularly manufactured exports, to offset the decline in oil and gas exports, proved to be very successful. Since the late 1980s the manufacturing sector had replaced the oil sector, not only as the major source of export earnings, but also as the major engine of growth. In turn, the rapid growth of the manufacturing sector was mainly driven by the rapid growth of manufactured exports.

During the oil boom era of the 1970s, Indonesia had pursued an import-substitution pattern of industrialization which, after the end of the 'easy' phase of import-substitution in the mid-1970s, was followed by a second-stage import substitution in the late 1970s. Flush with the proceeds from the oil boom, the second stage of import substitution was initiated to establish a range of upstream, basic, resource-processing industries (steel, aluminum ingots), to be financed largely by the proceeds from the oil boom, and to be initiated and operated by state-owned enterprises (Thee, 2002: 222).

As a result of its considerable economic and social achievements, the World Bank in its famous but controversial report of 1993, 'The East Asian Economic Miracle — Economic Growth and Public Policy', classified Indonesia, along with Japan, South Korea, Taiwan, Hong Kong, Singapore, Malaysia and Thailand, as one of the eight 'High-Performing Asian Economies' (HPAEs) (World Bank, 1993: 1). While other developing countries had grown equally rapidly, none had achieved such high and sustained rates for such a long period. Because of its recent good performance in manufactured exports, Indonesia, together with Malaysia and Thailand, was also classified as one of the three *newly-industrializing economies* (NIEs) in the World Bank report (World Bank, 1993: 1).

## THE ASIAN FINANCIAL AND ECONOMIC CRISIS AND ITS AFTERMATH

However, only four years after the release of the East Asian Miracle report, and only two months after a fairly upbeat World Bank of May 1997 which projected that the Indonesian economy would continue to grow at an average annual rate of 7.8 per cent (World Bank, 1997: 29), market sentiments about the Southeast Asian economies, including Indonesia, suddenly turned worse. As a result, the currency markets in these countries, including Indonesia, came under increasing pressure, causing the currencies, including the Indonesian *rupiah*, to depreciate rapidly, as foreign investors and creditors scrambled to purchase US dollars to reduce their exposure to these countries, including Indonesia. This sudden reversal was ironic, since before the crisis the Indonesian authorities were concerned about the strength rather than the weakness of the *rupiah* (Hofman, et al. 2007: 70).

When several attempts by the Indonesian authorities, including a steep increase in interest rates, tight monetary and fiscal policies and the floating of the *rupiah* by Bank Indonesia, Indonesia's central bank, failed to stem its downward slide, the Indonesian government in late October 1997 turned to the IMF for financial assistance. In return for a large standby loan offered by the IMF, the Indonesian government in its Letter of Intent (LoI) to the IMF pledged to implement a comprehensive reform programme, including sound macroeconomic policies, restructuring the financial sector, and undertaking structural reforms. It was hoped that, with the availability of the IMF standby loan backed by a credible financial and economic reform programme, confidence in the *rupiah* could be restored (Sadli, 1999: 17).

The involvement of the IMF, however, failed to stem the downward slide of the *rupiah* and the ensuing economic crisis because, as some Indonesian critics argued, the IMF had prescribed 'one size fits all' reforms without taking account the peculiar economic conditions of Indonesia. For instance, in the first agreement with the IMF, it was stipulated that Indonesia had to tighten its fiscal policies, similar to the policies the IMF had prescribed to some Latin American countries which had run up large budget deficits because of loose fiscal policies. Before the onset of the crisis, however, the Indonesian government had run up a budget surplus. The decision to close 16 private insolvent banks, prescribed by the IMF, also proved fatal, since it led to a bank rush and the collapse of the entire banking system.

As a result the Indonesian government had to establish the Indonesian Banking Restructuring Agency (IBRA) to restructure the troubled banks through closures, mergers, recapitalization and to arrange the sale of its equity stake in these troubled banks. It was also to recover the transferred bad loans, and to monitor and sell the corporate assets transferred to IBRA from former bank owners as collateral for the liquidity credits provided by Bank Indonesia (Pangestu & Habir, 2002:21) The recapitalization of the troubled banks by issuing bonds to these banks proved to be an extremely costly effort for the Indonesian government which until the present still has to pay costly interest on these bonds, a heavy burden on the government budget.

On the other hand, many critics of President Soeharto argued that the IMF involvement failed to halt the steady depreciation of the *rupiah* because of his reluctance to implement the agreed reforms vigorously, particularly the structural reforms. These latter were seen as aimed at hurting his children's many business interests.

Although the Asian economic crisis hit Indonesia in mid-1997, GDP in 1997 was still able to grow at 4.6 per cent (compared to 7.8 per cent in 1996), since all the sectors still managed to grow at positive though lower rates of growth. The full adverse impact of the crisis was only felt in 1998 when GDP contracted by an unprecedented −13.1 per cent. In 1999, however, the economy recovered slightly with an anemic but positive growth of 0.8 per cent. As the economy slowly but steadily recovered in the subsequent years, GDP started growing at a more rapid rate, reaching 6.5 per cent in 2007 (Table 4).

In line with Indonesia's economic recovery, poverty rates also steadily declined after reaching a peak of 23.5 per cent in 1999 (Table 5).

In September 2006 the Central Agency of Statistics (BPS) announced that the poverty rate had increased from 16.0 per cent in February 2005 to 17.8 per cent in March 2006, corresponding to an increase in the number of poor people from 35 million to 39 million over this short period. It was the second time that the measured poverty rate had risen in recent years, the first and much more severe increase having occurred in 1998–1999 following the sharp contraction of the economy in 1998 (Lindblad & Thee, 2007: 30).

According to a recent World Bank study, three-quarters of the additional four million people falling below the poverty line did so as a result of the 33 per cent rise in rice prices between February 2005 and March 2006 rather than the fuel price increase, asserted by some critics of the government. The rice price increase was mainly caused by the ban on rice imports. According

## TABLE 4
## Indonesia's Economic Growth after the
## Asian Economic Crisis, 1998–2007
## (% annual growth)

| | |
|---|---|
| 1998 | −13.1 per cent |
| 1999 | 0.8 per cent |
| 2000 | 4.8 per cent |
| 2001 | 3.8 per cent |
| 2002 | 4.3 per cent |
| 2003 | 4.8 per cent |
| 2004 | 5.1 per cent |
| 2005 | 5.6 per cent |
| 2006 | 6.1 per cent |
| 2007 | 6.5 per cent |

*Source*: BPS (Central Agency of Statistics), Jakarta.

## TABLE 5
## The Incidence of Poverty after the Asian Economic Crisis, 1996–2007

| Year | Percentage of population under the poverty line | Number of poor people (millions) |
|---|---|---|
| 1996 | 17.6 * | 34.5 |
| 1999 | 23.5 | 48.4 |
| 2001 | 19,0 | 37.3 |
| 2002 | 18.4 | 38.4 |
| 2003 | 18.2 | 37.3 |
| 2004 | 17.4 | 36.1 |
| 2005 | 16.0 | 35.0 |
| 2006 | 17.8 | 39.3 |
| 2007 (preliminary estimate) | 16.6 | 37.2 |

*Note*: * After the Asian economic crisis, the Central Agency of Statistics revised its poverty estimates based on a better method to estimate the incidence of poverty.
*Source*: Central Agency of Statistics (BPS), Jakarta.

to the World Bank study, the Unconditional Cash Transfer Programme (UCT), which provided direct cash transfers to 19.2 million poor and near poor households, were able to offset the negative impact of the fuel price increase on these households (World Bank, 2006: x).

Although economic conditions continued to deteriorate and incidence of absolute poverty rose, the authoritarian Soeharto government proved unable to deal effectively with the serious financial and economic crisis, which eventually led to a serious political crisis, which forced President Soeharto to step down on 21 May 1998 after a reign of 32 years. Hence, within a time span of only one year, Indonesia had turned from a 'booming economy', extolled by the international aid community and many foreign observers as a development model worthy of emulation by other developing countries, into a 'melted-down economy' dependent for its survival on aid flows from the international aid community (Thee, 2003a: 184).

## WAS INDONESIA UNDER THE NEW ORDER A 'DEVELOPMENTAL STATE?'

In view of its high and sustained economic growth over three decades, and particularly in raising the standards of living of the Indonesian people, the question might be raised whether New Order Indonesia was a 'capitalist developmental state' as defined by Chalmers Johnson. Quoting Manuel Castells, Johnson described the capitalist developmental state as:

'A state is developmental when it establishes as its principle of legitimacy its ability to promote and sustain development, understanding by development the combination of steady high rates of economic growth and structural change in the productive system, both domestically and in relationship to the international economy' (Johnson, 1992: 25, quoting Castells, 1992).

Referring to Japan's case of a 'capitalist developmental state', Johnson further argued that 'the power of the Japanese state has not been delegated to it by the elected representatives of the people; instead the state has imposed its economic achievements on the people and won their allegiance in doing so' (Johnson, 1992: 26).

In view of Indonesia's remarkable growth performance under the New Order, one might refer to New Order Indonesia as a 'developmental state'. What accounted for the success of the New Order state, and what factors accounted for its collapse after the onset of the Asian economic crisis?. Were there factors at work which, behind the facade of economic success, were undermining the economic and political foundations of the authoritarian New Order state? More specifically, did New Order Indonesia pursue an industrial policy, like Japan and the East Asian newly-industrializing economies (NIEs), such as South Korea and Taiwan, which led to the development of an internationally competitive manufacturing sector?

After suppressing the alleged communist coup on 30 September 1965, General Soeharto, Commander of the Army Strategic Reserve Command (Kostrad) was able to consolidate his power, and subsequently emerged as

Indonesia's effective leader after President Sukarno had transferred executive power to him. In March 1968 the Provisional People's Consultative Assembly (MPRS) deposed President Sukarno, and appointed General Soeharto as Indonesia's second president.

Having witnessed the misery in which the large majority of Indonesians lived during the late Sukarno years, President Soeharto realized that the people of Indonesia had suffered unduly because of President Sukarno's predilections for playing politics (Elson, 2001: 150). Being preoccupied with 'completing the national revolution', including the liberation of Dutch-occupied West Irian (West New Guinea), and building an 'Indonesian-style socialism', and waging the 'Crush Malaysia' campaign in 1963, Sukarno had little interest in solving the country's serious economic problems.

Hence, on assuming power, Soeharto was convinced of the need for economic development and the crucial role that economic development might play in political pacification. Reflecting on this period, Soeharto in his memoirs stated that 'all the deterioration that we experienced before 1966 had their origins in the neglect of economic development' (Elson, 2001: 150). Hence, while Sukarno had obtained his political legitimacy as the primary leader in the revolutionary struggle against the Dutch, Soeharto had to obtain his legitimacy through economic development.

Facing the urgent need to solve the country's economic problems, notably hyperinflation, Soeharto turned to a group of five economists (Widjojo Nitisastro, Ali Wardhana, Mohamad Sadli, Emil Salim and Subroto) from the Faculty of Economics, University of Indonesia (FEUI), for economic advice. Soeharto had known these economists when he, as a participant at the Army Staff and Command School (*SESKOAD*) during the final years of the Sukarno government, had been taken courses in introductory economics given by these economists (Thee, 2003b: 21). According to Professor Sadli, one of the FEUI economists, Soeharto had obtained his basic knowledge about economics from these FEUI economists (Sadli, 1993).

Upon assuming power, Soeharto asked his team of economic advisers, ably led by Professor Widjojo, to draw up a Programme for Stabilization and Rehabilitation. The main objective of the programme was economic stabilization by stopping the hyperinflation by establishing the principle of a balanced budget, which prohibited the government from printing money to finance a budget deficit (Thee, 2003b: 23). The Rehabilitation Programme involved the rehabilitation of the rundown infrastructure and productive apparatus.

From the outset Soeharto realized that Sukarno's anti-Western attitudes had been part of the problems Indonesia faced (Hollinger, 1996: 25). He therefore decided to abandon the bankrupt 'inward-looking policies' of the Sukarno government, and henceforth pursue 'outward-looking policies' by pursuing more liberal trade and foreign investment regimes. To this end, the New Order government decided to re-establish good relations with the Western countries and Japan. These good relations were deemed crucial to rescheduling repayments of the large foreign debts inherited from the Sukarno government; to obtaining foreign aid to support the balance of payments and the budget; and to attracting new foreign direct investment (Posthumus, 1971: 12). Pleased with the turn away from anti-Western and anti-capitalist policies, the international aid community responded favourably to Indonesia's request for rescheduling debt repayments and obtaining new foreign aid. At the initiative of the Netherlands government, an international aid consortium for Indonesia, the Inter-Governmental Group on Indonesia (IGGI), chaired by the Netherlands, was established in 1967.(Posthumus, 1971: 12).

In contrast to the Sukarno government, the New Order government abandoned the 'statism' (the state as dominant player in the economy) of the Sukarno government. The stigma of private enterprise , characteristic of the Sukarno era, was removed (Sadli, 1988: 358). Henceforth, private enterprise, both domestic and foreign, was encouraged to invest in various economic activities to foster economic growth and employment. To this end, in 1967 a Foreign Investment Law was enacted in 1967 and a Domestic Investment Law in 1968. The 'open door' policy towards foreign investment attracted new foreign investment flows into the country, particularly in the oil sector, other mining projects and the mining sector (Hill, 1988: 81).

The Stabilization and Rehabilitation Programme carried out by the economic team and with the strong political support of Soeharto resulted in an impressive economic recovery. Hyperinflation was quickly brought under control by tight monetary and fiscal policies, which resulted in a rapid decline in the rate of inflation from 636 per cent in 1966 to only 9 per cent in 1970 (Grenville, 1981: 108). The restoration of and subsequent maintenance of macroeconomic stability enabled the New Order government to embark on a period of rapid economic growth which was generally sustained for the next three decades and which, as we have seen, led to a steep reduction in the incidence of absolute poverty, and a general increase in the welfare of the Indonesian people, as reflected by the improvement in several social indicators.

Despite these achievements, it is incorrect to characterize the authoritarian New Order state as a quintessential 'developmental state', similar to Japan, South Korea, Taiwan and Singapore. The reason for this are the failings and shortcomings of the New Order State, as described below.

## FAILINGS OF THE NEW ORDER STATE: THE DESCENT FROM A 'DEVELOPMENTAL STATE' INTO A 'PREDATORY STATE'

Despite the initial successes of the New Order government, shortcomings of the New Order 'developmental state' soon became apparent. In response to critical press reports and criticism by dissidents of increasing corruption, President Soeharto in 1970 appointed a four-man commission (Commission of Four), headed by Wilopo and assisted by Mohammad Hatta, the respected former prime minister respectively former vice-president under Sukarno, to investigate and report on corruption (Elson, 2001: 195).

After serious investigations and intensive interviews with officials suspected of corruption, the commission submitted several reports to President Soeharto, reporting on corruption committed by several generals close to Soeharto, and financial improprieties and irregular modes of operation by state enterprises, including Pertamina, the state-owned oil company, Perhutani, the state-owned forestry company, and agencies, such as Bulog, the Food Logistics Board, and questionable connections between state-owned enterprises and private individuals. However, concerned about antagonizing his political supporters, particularly the generals, Soeharto was unwilling to take strong steps against high-level corruption (Elson, 2001: 195, 197).

Over time corruption became increasingly blatant, until by the end of the increasingly oppressive and corrupt New Order regime in the mid-1990s the acronym KKN (corruption, collusion and nepotism) became synonymous with the New Order. This was reflected by the fact that by the late 1980s rising concern was voiced about the blatant corruption at all levels of government, collusive relationships between political power holders and their business cronies, and the proliferation of policy-generated barriers to domestic competition in the form of restrictive regulations and restraints on domestic competition and trade issued by the central and regional governments and sometimes by officially sanctioned trade and industry associations (World Bank, 1995: 45). These regulations and restrictions increased the costs of doing business in Indonesia, reduced efficiency and limited productive economic opportunities for bona fide entrepreneurs, including small and medium-scale enterprises (Thee, 2006: 141). These KKN practices also distorted market incentives by providing good opportunities for highly lucrative '*rent-seeking activities*' by well-connected businessmen and their political patrons in the government bureaucracy. These practices, as reflected by the blatant preferential treatment given to well-connected businessmen, several of them Sino-Indonesian tycoons, led to the explosive growth of large conglomerates which, unlike the highly competitive *chaebols* (Korean conglomerates), were not internationally competitive, since the bulk of their output was sold in the protected domestic market. With rapidly expanding interests in various sectors, including forestry, estate agriculture, manufacturing, banking and real estate, the stranglehold of these conglomerates in the economy was likened to that of an octopus (Thee, 2002: 213).

Not surprisingly, the rapid rise of big conglomerates reinforced the perception that there was a 'widening economic gap' between rich and poor, and between the Sino-Indonesian minority and the indigenous (*pribumi*) majority, which was undermining the social cohesion required for political stability and national development (Thee, 2002: 213–14). Some Indonesian critics also argued, with some justification that the rise of conglomerates has been at the expense of the development of a more broadly based entrepreneurial class, which in turn would be more representative of the country's diverse ethnic groups. In addition, most of the various government programmes to promote small-scale, indigenous (*pribumi*) Indonesian enterprises turned out to be inadequate (Booth, 1998: 322) in fostering economically viable enterprises.

To a large extent the rapid and sustained growth during the New Order era can be attributed to the ability of the economic technocrats to maintain macroeconomic stability. They were able to do this thanks to the strong support, particularly during times of economic distress, given by President Soeharto, who over the years was able to strengthen and consolidate his position as the undisputed leader of the country. However, in the early 1990s the strict financial discipline which had been maintained by the economic technocrats since the late 1960s started to erode, largely because of the waning influence of the economic technocrats, many of whom had by that time retired. While a younger group of capable economic technocrats had succeeded them, they did not enjoy the trust and rapport with President Soeharto which the older generation of economic technocrats, particularly Professor Widjojo, the leader of the economic team, had enjoyed (Thee, 2003: 35).

The waning influence of the economic technocrats was reflected by rising off-budget expenditures, that is government transactions not recorded in the official budget of the government, and thus not under the strict control of the Department of Finance, but under the direct control of President Soeharto. These off-budget expenditures were allocated to ailing state-owned enterprises, the companies of well-connected businessmen, and the 'strategic industries', including the aircraft industry, controlled by Dr B.J. Habibie, the powerful Minister of State for Research and Technology (Nasution, 1995: 19), and, last but not least, the companies owned and controlled by President Soeharto's children.

The erosion of financial discipline was a worrying development, as it clearly reflected the waning influence of the economic technocrats because during the last decade of the New Order. Some senior economic posts passed to non-economists, many of them engineers, the so-called 'technologists', who under the dynamic leadership of Dr B.J. Habibie favoured 'hi-tech projects', such as the aircraft assembling industry (Thee, 2002: 214). Their political ascendancy was primarily due to the strong support they received from President Soeharto.

Economists, however, worried that these expensive hi-tech projects were projects of questionable economic viability, since they had been established without regard to the economy-wide scarcity of resources or the impact on the size distribution of income. Without a prudent policy that took proper account of resource constraints, ambitious projects would, it was feared, become devouring 'tape worms', as one critical economist put it (Nasution, 1995: 3–4).

Is there a reason why the strong tendency to engage in rent-seeking activities was so large in Indonesia during the New Order and still continues until the present. Is it due to the 'natural resource curse' which allegedly afflicts many resource-rich countries, such as Indonesia, and which therefore deflected it from consistently focusing its efforts on developing a prosperous and equitable society underpinned by an efficient and an internationally competitive manufacturing sector?

The 'natural resource curse' is that slow economic growth in resource-rich countries is due to a failure to sustain efficient factor use, especially in industrial sectors where the potential for productivity gains is highest. Referring to Sachs and Warner, Coxhead argued that there is a negative relationship between GDP growth rates and natural resource wealth, as indicated by the experience of a large sample of countries (Coxhead, 2005: 71–72).

There are several explanations for this phenomenon. First, there are the adverse 'Dutch disease' effects of the boom in natural resource exports on the other, non-booming export industries because of the real appreciation of the exchange rate as a result of the large inflow of foreign exchange earnings. However, in the case of Indonesia the adverse 'Dutch Disease' effects were relatively mild, since the Indonesian government took several measures to protect those sectors and industries producing tradable goods. In the manufacturing sector a combination of high tariffs and quantitative restrictions on various consumer durables and cars and motor cycles effectively insulated domestic producers from foreign competition (Booth, 1992: 25). Unlike Nigeria where the oil boom led to a severe disruption of the agricultural economy, Indonesia managed to avoid serious economic disruption of its agricultural sector, because of the government's emphasis in the 1970s on agricultural development, particularly the rice crop sub-sector in order to achieve food self-sufficiency. Rice production grew by 4.2 per cent annually from 1968 to 1978 and by 6.7 per cent from 1978 to 1984, largely because of rapid increases in rice yields (Pinto, 1987: 432), made possible by the government's ability to benefit from the 'Green Revolution', involving the development of high-yielding, fertilizer-responsive seed varieties developed by the International Rice Research Institute (IRRI) in Los Banos, The Philippines, in the late 1960s and early 1970s (Thee, 2002: 217).

Second, it is also argued that exploitation of natural resource wealth reduces the return to human capital, and thus diminishes incentives for educational attainment. Resource-rich countries therefore encounter a form of low-level equilibrium trap in their attempts at industrial and technological upgrading because of their weakness in skilled manpower (Coxhead,. 2005: 72-73). Despite the rapid expansion of primary, and to lesser extent secondary, education in Indonesia during the New Order, secondary and particularly tertiary education has lagged far behind its East Asian neighbours, particularly South Korea, Taiwan, Hong Kong and Singapore (World Bank, 1999). No wonder this has hampered Indonesia's industrial and technological upgrading.

Third, it has also been argued by political economists that resource wealth promotes the ascendance of the *'predatory state'* over the *'developmental state'*, either by actively encouraging the former through corruption related to resource rents, or by undermining the latter when revenue flows associated with resource extraction reduce the efficiency of policy and administration (Coxhead, 2005: 73, quoting Auty, 2001). We have seen that in the late New Order era, with its extensive and blatant KKN practices as described above, the New Order state increasingly acquired the characteristics of a 'predatory state'.

As the power of the centralized New Order state accumulated over time at the expense of society and, if threatened, was sustained by violence, authoritarianism eventually led to self-serving policies, including the exploitation of natural resources of resource-rich regions for the benefit of the central government and the ruling elite. Eventually this led to discontent and separatist movements, notably in Aceh and Papua, which undermined the foundations of the unitary state and an integrated national economy (Thee, 2002: 240–41).

In her generally positive analysis of development under the New Order, Professor Booth, a keen observer of the Indonesian economy, implicitly recognized that the oppressive and corrupt New Order state (particularly in its latter years), had deteriorated into a 'predatory state'. This recognition was reflected by the final paragraph at the conclusion of her perceptive book where she stated that

> 'at the end of the 1990s, Indonesia is rapidly reaching the stage where apathy and acceptance of the state's rules, no matter how repressive, are giving way to challenges from new economic forces demanding the removal of the final vestiges of the predatory state'(Booth, 1998: 336).

In the end, it was not the new economic forces from within Indonesia which led to the downfall of the predatory New Order state, but the Asian economic crisis which revealed the brittle nature of the New Order state.

## POSTSCRIPT: DEVELOPMENTS AFTER THE ASIAN ECONOMIC CRISIS

After the fall of Soeharto, the oppressive, authoritarian and highly centralized New Order state was overnight transformed into a democratic and highly decentralized state. Wide-ranging reforms were carried out at both the national and local levels, with the new government designing new structures of state power and implementing a new electoral system. The reforms opened the way for new arenas of political participation, new actors and power constellations, and new forms of political interaction (Erawan, 2007: 58).

In 1999 the first free general elections since 1955 were held, and in 2004 for the first time direct presidential elections were held, which led to the election of Susilo Bambang Yuidhoyono (SBY) as the first directly elected president of Indonesia with about 60 per cent of the popular vote. Subsequently, direct local elections were held all over the country to elect local parliaments and local heads (*Pilkada*). Thus far, however, President Susilo, has not been able to utilize this broad popular mandate to push through needed economic and political reforms because he has been stymied by the lack of cooperation, even opposition from various political factions in the parliament. This relative weak position of the president is caused by the fact that the 1945 Constitution, which provided for a strong executive, was revised to provide for a much stronger legislature. In the present legislature elected in the general elections of 2004, president Susilo's party, the Democrat Party (*Partai Demokrat*) was unable to win a majority, obtaining only 10 per cent of the seats, and thus requiring it to forge a coalition with much bigger political parties, including the large Golkar party.

Based on the enactment in 1999 of two new decentralization laws, Law no. 22/1999 on Local Autonomy and Law no. 25/1999 on Financial Balance between the Central and Local Governments, a wide-ranging decentralization was introduced in early 2001 which marked a fundamental change in the landscape of the central-local political relationship (Erawan, 2007: 58). Under this decentralization programme, executive authority was devolved not to the provincial, but to the district (sub-provincial) governments.

The experience of regional autonomy thus far has indicated that the extent to which local (district) governments have been able to introduce policy reforms, building a societal support network and political coalition, and insulate their programmes from capture by vested interests, has been shaped by the ability of local actors (governments) to isolate their programmes from personalistic and partisan demands and, at the same time, create networks of supporters. These two factors have in turn been influenced by the existing shape of local political and economic circumstances (Erawan, 2007, 68–69).

Despite the political upheavals in post-Soeharto Indonesia, (having had four presidents during the decade since 1998), Indonesia's economy has steadily grown faster after it gradually recovered after its severe contraction in 1998 (–13.1 per cent), as the data in Table 4 show, This economic recovery and subsequent faster growth, particularly since 2005, has been underpinned by the adherence to sound macroeconomic policies, as reflected by a low, single digit inflation, a current account surplus, and a relatively stable exchange rate. Although investment has been growing at only single digit rates in the post-crisis years, it has grown at slightly higher rates over the past year, growing at 7–8 per cent annually since early 2006, with indications of faster growth in the near term. The value of exports of agricultural and mineral commodities (accounting for one third of total merchandise exports) have increased by 18 to 42 per cent since early 2007 as a result of the international commodity boom, while manufactured exports (accounting for around on half of total exports) also increased at a robust rate of 15 per cent, with forestry products up by 24 per cent (World Bank, 2007: 1).

Fiscal deficits too have narrowed significantly in recent years, from over 4 per cent of GDP in 1995 to 0.9 per cent in 2006 and 1.5 per cent in 2007. The larger budget deficit in 2007 was caused by temporary factors (e.g. large, once- for- all settlements of arrears in VAT payments arrears and spending for disaster relief) as well as more lasting factors (increased spending on priority areas (health, education and welfare) and higher fuel subsidies because of the rapid rise in oil prices. Over the past few years the ratio of government debt to GDP is estimated, despite larger budget deficits, to drop further from 39 per cent of GDP in late 2006 to less than 35 per cent in late 2007 because of continued strong growth (World Bank, 2007: 2).

Despite these improved macroeconomic indicators, criticism has been leveled at the SBY government for failing to reduce employment and absolute poverty significantly, despite its promises during the campaigns to increase employment and reduce poverty. Despite the fact that the incidence of absolute poverty in Indonesia had declined to 16.6 per cent in 2007, this still meant that 37.2 million Indonesians were still living in absolute poverty. Moreover, large income disparities remain between relatively more prosperous Western Indonesia and poorer Eastern Indonesia, with the poverty incidence in the provinces of Papua, Maluku (Moluccas) and the two Nusa Tenggara provinces being 41 per cent, 26 per cent, and 23 per cent respectively. There is also a persistent disparity in the incidence of absolute poverty between the rural areas (20 per cent in 2007) and the urban areas (13 per cent) (World Bank, 2007: 19), because of a persistent *urban bias* in Indonesia's development. Moreover, millions more people were living precariously just above the poverty line (the near poor), thus were vulnerable to fall below the poverty line again in the event of external shocks or natural disasters which struck Indonesia in several places since late 2004.

To reduce the high unemployment rate (slightly less than 10 per cent in 2007), but with around 40 per cent being disguised unemployed, a more rapid growth of the real sector (agriculture, mining and manufacturing) is required. This will require a rapid rise in investment, including foreign direct investment (FDI). However, this rise in investment in turn requires a substantial improvement in Indonesia's investment climate which, unfortunately, is still rated as one of the worst in the developing world. For instance, in the World Bank- International Finance Corporation report on Doing Business 2008 which compared business regulations in 2007, Indonesia ranked as number 123 out of a large sample of 178 countries surveyed in terms of the ease of doing business in Indonesia (World Bank-IFC, 2007: 126). In other words, doing business in Indonesia is still considered difficult by foreign and domestic investors alike, which accounts for the relatively low investment growth, though over the past year investment has grown at a slightly higher, though still single digit growth. Without higher investment growth required for higher employment growth, poverty rates are unlikely to decline more rapidly.

The above account of Indonesia's current economic conditions and short-term economic prospects shows that Indonesia's immediate development strategy and priority should be directed at increasing investment rates by improving its poor investment climate. Higher investment in the real sector will create more employment and reduce absolute poverty. Dreams of national grandeur by building up 'strategic, hi-tech industries promoted by a strong 'developmental state' should be abandoned in favour of the much more urgent task of raising the still low standards of living of the Indonesian population by increasing employment, and reducing poverty by improving the public goods of primary health care, extending and improving education at all levels and improving the dilapidated infrastructure.

## Notes

1. "Indonesia's Economic Development During and After the Soeharto Era: Achievements and Failings", by Thee Kian Wie, first appeared in the JICA/JBIC International Workshop Report on *Asian Experiences of Economic Development and Their Policy Implications for Africa*. Tokyo: Institute of International Cooperation, Japan International Cooperation Agency, Tokyo, May 2008.
2. The group of Soeharto's economic advisers were named the 'Berkeley Mafia' since many of them, though not all, had pursued their postgraduate study in economics at The University of California, Berkeley.
3. The first general and free elections in newly-independent independent Indonesia were held in 1955. During the New Order 1966–1998) six general elections were held which were rigged in favour of the ruling government party Golkar.

## References

Arndt, H.W. & Hal Hill. *Southeast Asia's Economic Crisis: Origins, Lessons and the Way Forward*. Institute of Southeast Asian Studies, Singapore, 1999.

Bebbington, Anthony & Will McCourt. *Development Success: Statecraft in the South*. Palgrave Macmillan, Houndmills, Basingstoke, Hampshire, 2007.

Booth, Anne & Peter McCawley. *The Indonesian Economy During the Soeharto Era*. Kuala Lumpur: Oxford University Press, 1981.

Booth, Anne. "Introduction". In *The Oil Boom and After: Indonesian Economic Policy and Performance in the Soeharto Era*, edited by Booth 1992a.

_____. *The Oil Boom and After: Indonesian Economic Policy and Performance in the Soeharto Era*. Singapore: Oxford University Press, 1992b.

_____. *The Indonesian Economy in the Nineteenth and Twentieth Centuries: A History of Missed Opportunities*. London: Macmillan Press, Ltd., 1998.

_____. "Poverty and Inequality in the Soeharto Era: An Assessment". In *Bulletin of Indonesian Economic Studies*, Vol. 36, no. 1, April (2000): 73–104.

Coxhead, Ian. "International Trade and the Natural Resource 'Curse' in Southeast Asia: Does China's Growth Threaten Regional Development?". In *The Politics and Economics of Indonesia's Natural Resources*, edited by Budy P. Resosudarmo, pp. 71–91, Singapore: Institute of Southeast Asian Studies, 2005.

Dick, Howard; Vincent Houben; J. Thomas Lindblad & Thee Kian Wie. *The

*Emergence of a National Economy: An Economic History of Indonesia, 1800–2000*, Crows Nest, NSW: Allen & Unwin, 2002.

Elson, Robert E. Suharto: *A Political Biography*. Cambridge: Cambridge University Press, 2001.

Erawan, I Ketut Putra. Tracing the Progress of Local Governments since Decentralisation, In *Indonesia: Democracy and the Promise of Good Governance*, edited by Ross H. McLeod, Andrew MacIntyre, pp. 55–69. Singapore: Institute of Southeast Asian Studies, 2007.

Grenville, Stephen. "Monetary Policy and the Formal Financial Sector". In *The Indonesian Economy During the Soeharto Era*, edited by Booth and McCawley, pp. 102–25. Kuala Lumpur: Oxford University Press 1981,

Hill, Hal. *Foreign Investment and Industrialisation in Indonesia*. Oxford University Press, Singapore, 1988.

————. *Indonesia's New Order: The Dynamics of Socio-Economic Transformation*. Crows Nest, NSW: Allen and Unwin, 1994.

Hofman, Bert; Ella R. Gudwin & Thee Kian Wie. "Managing the Indonesian Economy: Good Policies, Weak Institutions". In *Development Success — Statecraft in the South*, edited by Anthony Bebbington and Willy McCourt. Palgrave Macmillan, July 2007.

Hollinger, William C. *Economic Policy Under President Soeharto: Indonesia's Twenty-Five Year Record*. United States – Indonesia Society, Washington, D.C., 1996.

Ichimura, Shinichi. *Indonesian Economic Development: Problems and Analysis*. Japan International Cooperation Agency, Tokyo, 1988.

Johnson, Chalmers. *Capitalism: East Asian Style*, The 1992 Panglaykim Memorial Lecture, Jakarta, 15 December 1992.

Jones, Gavin W. "Labour Force and Education". In *Indonesia Assessment: Population and Human Resources*, edited by Terence Hull and Gavin W. Jones, Singapore: Institute of Southeast Asian Studies, 1994.

————. "Demographic Perspectives". In *Indonesia's New Order*, edited by Hal Hill, Honolulu: University of Hawaii Press, 1944, pp. 120–78. 1994.

Lee, Cassey and Cheong May Fong. *Competition Policy in Asia — Models and Issues*. Faculty of Economics and Administration and Faculty of Law, University of Malaya, Kuala Lumpur, 2006.

Lindblad, Thomas and Thee Kian Wie. "Survey of Recent Developments". *Bulletin of Indonesian Economic Studies*, Vol. 43, no. 1 (2007).

McLeod, Ross H. and Andrew MacIntyre. *Indonesia: Democracy and the Promise of Good Governance*. Singapore: Institute of Southeast Asian Studies, 2007.

Nasution, Anwar. "Survey of Recent Developments". *Bulletin of Indonesian Economic Studies*, Vol. 31, no. 2 (1995): 3–40.

Pangestu, Habir and Manggi Habir. *The boom, bust and restructuring of Indonesian banks*. IMF Working Paper no. 02/66, Washington D.C.:IMF, 2002.

Pinto, Brian. "Nigeria During and After the Oil Boom: A Policy Comparison with Indonesia". The World Bank Economic Review, Vol. 1, no. 3 (1987): 419–45.

Posthumus, G.A. *The Inter-Governmental Group on Indonesia*. Rotterdam University Press, Rotterdam, 1971.

Resosudarmo, Budy P. *The Politics and Economics of Indonesia's Natural Resources*. Singapore: Institute of Southeast Asian Studies, 2005.

Sadli, Mohamad. "The Private Sector", in Ichimura (editor), 1988.

———. "Recollections of My Career". *Bulletin of Indonesian Economic Studies*, Vol. 29, no. 1 (1993): 35–51.

———. "The Indonesian Crisis". In *Southeast Asia's economic crisis: origins, lessons, and the way forward*, edited by Heinz Wolfgang Arndt and Hal Hill. Singapore: Institute of Southeast Asia, 1999.

Thee, Kian Wie. "The Soeharto Era and After: Stability, Development and Crisis". In *The Emergence of a National Economy: An Economic History of Indonesia, 1800–2000*, edited Dick; Houben; Lindblad & Thee, pp. 194–243. Crows Nest, NSW: Allen & Unwin, 2002.

———. "The Indonesian Economic Crisis and the Long Road to Recovery". *Australian Economic History Review*, Vol. 43, no. 2, July (2003): 183–96.

———. "Introduction". *Recollections: The Indonesian Economy, 1950s–1990s*, edited by Thee Kian Wie. Singapore: Institute of Southeast Asian Studies, 2003.

———. *Recollections: The Indonesian Economy, 1950s–1990s*. Singapore: Institute of Southeast Asian Studies, 2003.

———. "Indonesia's First Competition Law: Issues and Experiences". In *Competition Policy in Asia: Models and Issues*, edited by Cassey Lee and Cheong May Fong. Faculty of Economics and Administration and Faculty of Law, University of Malaya, Kuala Lumpur, 2006.

World Bank. *World Development Report 1990: Poverty*. Oxford University Press, New York, 1990.

———. *World Development Report 1992*. Oxford University Press, New York, 1992.

———. *The East Asian Miracle: Economic Growth and Public Policy*. Oxford University Press, New York, 1993.

———. *Indonesia: Improving Efficiency and Equity Changes in the Public Sector's Role*. Washington, D.C., July 1995.

———. *Indonesia: Sustaining High Growth with Equity*. Washington, D.C., May, 1997.

———. *Indonesia in Crisis: A Macroeconomic Update*. Washington, D.C., 1998.

———. *World Development Indicators 1999*. Washington, D.C., 1999.

———. *Making the New Indonesia Work for the Poor: Overview*. Washington, D.C., November 2006.

———. *Indonesia: Economic and Social Update*. Washington, D.C., November 2007.

World Bank & International Finance Corporation. *Doing Business 2008: Comparing Regulations in 178 Economies*. Washington, D.C., 2007.

# 5

# THE IMPACT OF THE TWO OIL BOOMS OF THE 1970s AND THE POST-OIL BOOM SHOCK OF THE EARLY 1980s ON THE INDONESIAN ECONOMY[1]

## INTRODUCTION

Over the period 1974–1981 the Indonesian economy grew at a high and sustained average annual rate of 7.7 per cent. This rapid growth was to a large extent attributable to the considerable improvement in the country's international terms of trade caused by the two oil booms Indonesia experienced during the 1970s.

The first oil boom of 1973/1974 was caused by the decision of the Organization of Petroleum-Exporting Countries (OPEC), the international oil cartel of which Indonesia was a member, to quadruple the price of oil by reducing its combined oil exports. The second oil boom of 1979/1980 was caused by the temporary closure of Iran's oil industry as a result of the revolution against the Shah's regime. This closure had a great impact on world oil prices, since Iran was OPEC's second-largest oil producer and exporter after Saudi Arabia. The resulting imbalance between the world's oil supply and demand led to further doubling of the price of oil to about $30 per barrel by early 1980. In nominal terms the price of Indonesia's crude oil rose from $1.60 per barrel in 1970 to $35 in 1980 (Odell 1981: 255–56). However, in 1982 Indonesia experienced a third external shock, this time caused by a steep decline in the price of oil caused by a weakening of the world oil market which led to substantial deterioration in Indonesia's external terms of trade.

This paper describes the impact of these two oil booms on the Indonesian economy, and in particular the policies which the Indonesian pursued in response to these oil booms. This paper will also describe the policies of the Indonesian government in response to the end of the oil boom in 1982.

## 1. The First Oil Boom, 1973–74

Even before the Saudi Arabia, the largest oil exporter, and the other Arab countries had imposed an embargo on their oil exports as punishment for America's strong support to Israel during the fourth Arab-Israeli War in late 1973, the price of oil had been inching upward from $2.93 per barrel in April 1972 to $3.70 in April 1973 to $4.75 in October 1973, before it jumped to $11.70 a barrel in April 1974 as a result of the oil embargo (Grenville 1974: 2; Arndt, 1974: 1).

As a result of the steep rise in the price of oil, the value of oil exports rose steeply after 1973. The table below also shows that even before the oil boom of 1973/74 oil exports had started rising rapidly in view of rising world demand (Table 1).

The resulting surge in Indonesia's oil exports naturally widened the options for economic policymaking because it loosened up the financial and foreign exchange constraints faced by Indonesia during the 1950s and 1960s which had greatly hampered economic growth during these two past decades (Booth and McCawley 1981: 11–12). Because of this, the oil bonanza also transformed Indonesia's economic prospects in the short and even in the medium term. It added to the external resources available for development on a scale undreamed of even a year earlier. It was hoped that these resources could be used to achieve the social objectives of the Second Five-Year Plan

### TABLE 1
### Indonesia's Oil Exports, 1969/70–1975/76*
### (millions of US)

| | |
|---|---|
| 1969/70 | 384 |
| 1972/73 | 965 |
| 1973/74 | 1,729 |
| 1974/75 | 3,727 |
| 1975/76 | 4,204 |

*Note*: * Until 2000 Indonesia's fiscal year ran from 1 April to 31 March the following year.
*Source*: Grenville (1974: 2).

(Repelita II) for 1974/75–1978/79. On the other hand the oil bonanza also added fuel to an already rapidly accelerating inflation in 1974 which made the maintenance of fiscal/monetary and administrative discipline difficult. The oil boom therefore caused difficulties in economic management, namely in maintaining reasonable price stability which had been one of the main achievements of the young Soeharto regime (Arndt 1974: 1, 3–4).

In the months following the steep rise in the price of oil, the Indonesian government made three important decisions. First, in April 1974 the sales price of Indonesia's crude oil exports was further raised from $10.80 per barrel to $11.70 per barrel.

Secondly, the income-sharing arrangements with foreign oil companies were revised. Before this revision, the foreign oil companies operating under the older contracts of work (CoWs), including Caltex and Stanvac, were required to pay 60 per cent of their net earnings (that is, after deduction of costs) to the state-owned oil company Pertamina which, in turn, transferred the whole amount to the Indonesian government. Companies operating under the newer production sharing contracts were required to pay Pertamina 65 per cent of their net earnings (after deducting costs of up to 40 per cent of the gross value of production), and in some cases even 67.5 to 70 per cent of their net earnings, of which Pertamina passed on 60 per cent to the Government. Under the new arrangement, Indonesia's share was raised to 85 per cent of net earnings in excess of a price of $5 per barrel. Of this, Pertamina was entitled to retain the equivalent of 5 per cent of net earnings. For earnings up to the price of $5 per barrel the sharing arrangements remained unchanged.

Thirdly, in order to continue encouraging oil exploration by the foreign oil companies, the Indonesian government decided not to insist on a reduction in the 40 per cent limit to deductible costs under the production sharing contracts. This reduction had, amongst others, been advocated in the press (Arndt 1974: 3).

As a result of the oil boom, the government's budget also received a substantial boost by the large increase in oil revenues due to the large increase in tax revenues from the foreign oil companies following another rise in the export price of crude oil. This rise was due to the increase in the price of oil by 90 cents per barrel to $12.60, which raised the oil revenue in 1974/75 by almost Rp1.500 billion. This enabled the government to increase its expenditures for subsidies on sugar, fertilizer and imported rice (Rosendale 1974: 1, 9–10).

As a result of the vast increase in tax revenues from the oil companies (that is the share of oil company profits appropriated by government (Booth and McCawley 1981b: 127), the government budget of 1974/75 set a lower target rate of increase in tax revenue, indicating a slackening in tax efforts. The buoyant oil revenues were clearly responsible for the less effective enforcement of non-oil income and corporation taxes and the imposition of higher taxes on luxuries, including urban real estate (Rosendale 1974: 11).

Because of the oil bonanza, reinforced by capital inflow, primarily foreign aid, Indonesia's balance of payments position was comfortable. However, there was reason for concern because of Indonesia's growing dependence on a single export commodity, oil, and on large capital inflows. Concern also arose because non-oil exports were declining (Booth and Glassburner 1975: 3).

In early 1975, however, the government's development plans experienced a sudden setback because of the unexpected bankruptcy of Pertamina, the powerful state-owned oil company. The roots of this unexpected setback was that Pertamina, despite the establishment of a ministerial Board of Commissioners in early 1972, was accountable to no authority below the President. Unless and until President Soeharto exercised this authority, Pertamina was on major policy issues a law into itself (Arndt 1975: 3).

Pertamina was involved in a wide range of operations, including in the oil sector and activities directly servicing it, and in non-oil activities. The oil sector alone had become a large vertically integrated combine, covering all phases from exploration and development of oil and gas, to production, refining and marketing. The activities directly servicing the oil sector included Pertamina's tanker fleet, oil supply centres and office buildings for its own use, its telecommunications company, its own airline, and the provision of community services, such as roads, schools, hospitals, water supply and housing, in centres associated with the oil industry. Pertamina's non-oil activities included large fertilizer factories, an insurance company, a shipping line, real estate investments, the Krakatau steel project, an industrial estate and tourist project on Batam Island, a rice estate in South Sumatra province, and several other projects (Arndt 1975: 3).

Despite its size and importance, Pertamina had only the veneer of a sophisticated multinational corporation. Beneath the surface, however, Pertamina lacked systems, controls, management and experience (Prawiro 1998: 104).

Believing that Indonesia's finances had to be managed carefully and systematically to avoid inflation and to allocate funds for maximum economic growth, the economics ministers imposed restrictions on medium-term borrowing by Pertamina to fund its many projects. Pertamina circumvented this restriction by taking off-shore short-term or long-term loans that is loans repayable in less than one year or over fifteen years. However, in February 1975 the roof fell in on Pertamina when it missed a payment on a small loan from the Republic National Bank of Dallas, a small, unknown bank. Pertamina's default created considerable difficulties not only for Pertamina, but also for the Indonesian government, since it generated negative attention, and finally brought to light Pertamina's financial problems (Prawiro 1998: 107).

To contain the damage, the Indonesian government had to step in by announcing that it guaranteed repayments of all of Pertamina's short-term foreign loans. On 12 March 1975 Bank Indonesia, the central bank, paid off two loans. To prevent a recurrence of Pertamina's freewheeling ways, the government also announced that henceforth all foreign borrowing by Indonesia's state-owned enterprises would be through Bank Indonesia or the Department of Finance. The government moved promptly to deal with the crisis that threatened Indonesia's credit standing (Arndt 1975: 6–7). The government also moved to steadily divest the Pertamina conglomerate of most of its non-oil activities, to reschedule its debts wherever possible, and to reorganize the remainder of the company so that the lines of authority were made clearer and less centralized (McCawley 1976: 8). The costs of the Pertamina crisis were reflected in the balance of payments, which showed an estimated fall in reserves of $240 million for 1975 instead of the hoped for increase of $400 million. In mid-1975 the private capital account showed an outflow of over $600 million, which was balanced by a rise of over $1.4 billion in expected official capital inflow, that is foreign aid. The downward revision of the private capital inflows was primarily due to the debt repayments on Pertamina's behalf. It was estimated that over $1.5 billion of the capital outflow in fiscal 1975/76 was directly attributable to the bailout of Pertamina (McCawley 1976: 8–9).

A decline in oil revenues, combined with the financial obligations to repay Pertamina's debts as well as a reluctance to curb other expenditures led to a sizable increase in overseas borrowing. Consequently, the proportion of development expenditures covered by the 'rupiah financing' item (that is the excess of domestic revenue over routine expenditures) fell (McCawley 1976: 18). Hence, because of Pertamina's bankruptcy, a considerable part of the government's oil revenues were wasted bailing out Pertamina (Thee 2002: 210). Reflecting on the Pertamina crisis, Professor Sadli, the then Minister of Mining, observed that the losses of Pertamina were an 'enormous school fee, a bitter lesson', and said that it was no use blaming anyone party because 'we were all at fault'. Professor Sadli also observed that the oil boom of 1973/74 had led to wasteful practices and the disregard of the sound 'rules of the game' that should have governed official arrangements for borrowing and spending money (McCawley 1976: 5).

The principal means the government used to recoup the Pertamina losses was to extract more money from the foreign oil enterprises by taxing them more heavily, specifically by reducing the profits gained by oil companies on each barrel of crude oil they produced. This required a renegotiation of the contracts with all the foreign oil firms in which the government was able to impose a change in the basic split of 65 per cent to 35 per cent in the government's favour to 85 per cent to 15 per cent in the government's favour (Bresnan 1993: 186–87).

After the economic technocrats had solved the Pertamina crisis, Professor Widjojo, the leader of the economic technocrats, designed a new law for Pertamina which was aimed at putting Pertamina under strict government supervision. This Law provided for a Board of Supervisors, the members of which all had ministerial rank. Professor Sadli, the Minister of Mining, was made ex-officio chairman of the Board, with the other ex-officio members including the Chairman of the National Planning Board (BAPPENAS) and the State Secretary. In this way the power and autonomy of Pertamina were gradually trimmed, particularly by prohibiting Pertamina to keep revenues from the production-sharing agreements, and by requiring it to hand them over directly to the government (Sadli 1993).

The Pertamina crisis occurred just as the first oil boom was reaching a peak. If this crisis had not occurred, the economy might possibly have grown at 8 perhaps even 9 per cent because of the boost caused by the oil boom revenues. Instead, in 1975 the economy grew at only 5 per cent. While Indonesia's foreign exchange reserves grew from $576 million in 1972 to $1.5 billion in 1975, it had dropped to $594 million because of Pertamina's failure to contribute its share of revenues to the government. Worse, Indonesia's indebtedness rose since the government was forced to seek commercial loans to pay off Pertamina's debt and safeguard the country's liquidity (Prawiro 1998: 110).

## 2. The Second Oil Boom, 1979–80

Concerned that the oil boom was over and that the economy was facing serious structural problems caused by the 'Dutch disease' effects of the oil boom, particularly the modest growth or even decline of the non-oil tradable sectors (except timber), the government on 15 November 1978 devalued the *rupiah* by 50 per cent to offset the real appreciation of the *rupiah* over the 1972–1976 period because of the higher inflation in Indonesia vis-à-vis its major trading partners (Garnaut 1979: 21; Prawiro 1998: 117). The government took this step because it thought that devaluation was necessary to revive the non-oil tradable sectors by giving them a temporary price advantage while an undervalued *rupiah* would gradually rise to a new equilibrium against the US dollar and other currencies (Prawiro 1998: 117).

While the economy was still recovering from the adverse effects of devaluation and adjusting to large increases in the world market prices for its non-oil exports, in mid-1979 events suddenly took another turn when Indonesia experienced a second oil boom. Like in the first oil boom, the second oil boom led again to a huge increase in oil export earnings and fiscal revenues (Garnaut 1979: 1).

The second oil boom of 1979–1980 was caused by the temporary closure of Iran's oil industry when a revolution broke out against the repressive regime of the pro-American Shah of Iran. This closure greatly affected world oil prices, since Iran was OPEC's second-largest oil producer and exporter after Saudi Arabia. The resulting imbalance between the world's oil supply and demand led to further doubling of the price of oil to about $30 per barrel by early 1980 (Odell 1981: 255–56).

During the final months of 1979 a strongly rising trend in the real price of oil on world markets was detected and given further impetus by the continued strength of the spot market price of over $30 per barrel. Despite further switching of oil supplies by several OPEC members from long-term contracts to the spot market, demand for oil on the world market was buoyed by large-scale speculative stock-building. Several OPEC members, including Indonesia, increased their contract prices in late 1979. Although in the OPEC meeting in December 1979 no agreement was reached on the maximum level of combined output or the structure of prices, members were free to set their prices in accordance with their individual market situations. The weighted average price of Indonesia's crude oil exports rose from $21.76 per barrel during the period 15 July–16 November 1979 to $30.32 on 4 February 1980 (Rosendale 1980: 2, 4).

Once again Indonesia was faced with the benefits and problems of how to manage the sudden large increases in oil windfall earnings. In particular, Indonesia was once again faced with the problem of new inflows of oil money which could lead to renewed inflationary pressures and an economy out of balance again (Prawiro 1998: 118) because of the adverse effects of the 'Dutch Disease'.

In spite of the surge in oil prices in late 1979/early 1980, the outlook for world oil prices in 1980 was uncertain. The scope for further increases in posted or long-term contract prices was dependent on the trend in the spot price, which until then had been supported by speculative stock-building. In the meantime, oil production was running well ahead of demand, while stocks were at high levels. This factor and the expected impending recession in the industrial countries and the problems created by the high level of oil prices for the many non-oil producing developing countries led to concern that some softening of the level of real oil prices might occur later in the year (Rosendale 1980:6). However, in the short run this possibility was of little concern to Indonesia since the steep rise in the price of oil had led to a substantial change in the balance of payments constraint on medium term policy and planning (Rosendale 1980: 6).

The immediate response of the government to the second oil boom appeared rather slow compared to the quicker response to the first oil boom. Following the oil price rises of 1973/74, the government responded by importing large quantities of rice and fertilizer to spread the benefits of the oil boom to the needy groups in society. After the second oil boom, the government at first appeared not to recognize immediately that a big increase in *rupiah* spending, as urged upon by some circles, would increase inflation and thus dissipate the gains in the purchasing power of the public sector as well as the enhanced international price competitiveness of the non-oil traded goods caused by the devaluation of November 1978. Instead, the government raised the salaries of government employees by 50 per cent, even though they had already received a 'thirteenth' and 'fourteenth' month salary increase during the fiscal year of 1979/80. Paradoxically, while Indonesia's national income rose as a result of the considerable improvements in the country's terms of trade because of the oil boom, the devaluation-induced inflation actually decreased the real purchasing power of many groups in society (Rosendale 1980: 29).

However, despite these misgivings, the Indonesian economy performed quite well in 1980, growing at 7.1 per cent, compared to the much slower growth in 1979 when the economy grew only at 4.9 per cent due to the uncertainty caused by the expected *rupiah* devaluation in November 1979. The much better performance in 1980 could be attributed to the improved terms of trade caused by the second oil boom, increased domestic activity, and the stimulus of a surplus in both the overall balance of payments ($2.7 billion) and the current account ($0.9 billion) (Healey 1981: 1).

Table 2 presents the GDP growth rates of Indonesia during the two oil booms. The data in Table 2 show that most sectors grew at much higher rates in 1980 compared to 1979, including the manufacturing sector which grew much stronger in 1980 (11.6 per cent) following this sector's sluggish growth in 1979 as a result of the devaluation.

Indonesia's more rapid growth during the 1970s was not only stimulated by increased investment, as reflected in increased imports of capital goods, made possible by the oil boom revenues, but also by the more modern and

TABLE 2
**Growth Rates of Indonesia's Gross Domestic Product by
Sector of Origin in 1973 Constant Prices, 1975–1980**

(Unit: %)

| Year/Sector | 1975 | 1976 | 1977 | 1978 | 1979 | 1980 |
|---|---|---|---|---|---|---|
| Agriculture, forestry, fisheries | 3.7 | 4.7 | 1.3 | 5.2 | 2.5 | 5.0 |
| Mining & quarrying | −3.6 | 15.0 | 12.4 | −2.0 | −0.5 | −1.3 |
| Manufacturing | 12.3 | 9.7 | 13.8 | 11.3 | 8.8 | 11.6 |
| Construction | 14.1 | 5.5 | 20.5 | 14.0 | 6.4 | 7.8 |
| Commerce | 5.7 | 4.4 | 6.4 | 6.4 | 7.1 | 8.0 |
| Transport & Communication | 5.2 | 13.2 | 24.8 | 14.5 | 10.4 | 10.2 |
| Banking & Financial Services | 15.9 | 14.7 | 29.1 | 9.3 | 10.3 | 15.4 |
| Public administration & Defense | 27.3 | 5.5 | 16.0 | 11.3 | 4.8 | 13.2 |
| Services | 2.6 | 2.5 | 2.1 | 2.4 | 2.4 | 2.3 |
| Gross Domestic Product | 5.0 | 6.9 | 8.8 | 6.9 | 4.9 | 7.1 |

*Source*: Healy (1981: 34 [Appendix table 1, derived from BPS (Central Agency of Statistics), Jakarta.

sophisticated process and product technologies embodied in the imported capital goods (Sundrum 1986: 63–64).

## 3. The Outcomes Of The Oil Boom Era

Although the oil booms did relieve Indonesia from its long balance of payments and budget constraints, enabling the economy to grow faster, the oil windfall was in some respects worth less to Indonesia than most other oil-exporting country. Because of its large population, much larger than the other OPEC-member countries, Indonesia's oil windfall in dollars per capita was quite modest compared to the other OPEC countries. Even in total dollars, Indonesia's oil revenue was considerably smaller with better established oil industries, such as Nigeria and Venezuela. Because of its much wider resource base, Indonesia's oil windfall as a percentage of GDP was also smaller than in the other OPEC countries, such as Algeria (Bresnan 1993: 190).

As Indonesia's net energy exports rose from about $1 billion in 1973 to $13.3 billion in 1980, the share of energy exports (oil and gas) in total exports rose from 45 per cent to 70 per cent, while the government's reliance on oil taxes accounted for 70 per cent of the government's domestic revenues (that is revenues excluding foreign aid) in the budget of fiscal 1981–1982. As a result, the government did not feel the necessity to broaden the tax base (Bresnan 1993: 190).

Due to the higher oil revenues, the Indonesian government was able to launch several ambitious development programmes. These new programmes included promoting development in the outlying regions of the vast archipelago, social development, expanding physical infrastructure and establishing large-scale basic (heavy) industries. To promote regional development, the government recycled part of its oil revenues through the so-called 'Presidential Instruction', or *Inpres (Instruksi Presiden)* programmes to the various provinces (Thee 2002: 208). Most of these Inpres grants were allocated to the three tiers of local government — the province, district and sub district — to be spent on rural infrastructure development (Prawiro 1998: 175).

A subsidiary aim of these *Inpres* programmes was to improve the quality and effectiveness of local public administration. To qualify for the *Inpres* grants, the local governments had to prepare plans and budgets and, at the end of each fiscal year, submit reports on the activities financed by these grants. In view of the modest tax base of the local governments, the large central government grants, made possible by the oil revenues, greatly enhanced the power of the central government *vis-a-vis* the provincial and sub-provincial governments, both in control of financial resources and decision-masking authority (Mackie 1997: 29–30).

During the oil boom era an increasing part of the government's oil revenues was also recycled into social development, particularly education, health care and family planning. Government spending on these three sectors steadily increased from 11 per cent of the development budget during the First Five-Year Development Plan (1969/70–1973/74) to almost 15 per cent during the Second Plan period (1974/75–1978/79) and subsequently to 19 per cent during the Third Plan period. (1979/80–1983/84) (Thee 2002: 209). The strong commitment to social development persisted, even after the oil boom era had ended in the early 1980s (Prawiro 1998: 175).

Since the early 1970s first foreign aid and subsequently the increased oil revenues were also spent on rehabilitating and expanding the long-neglected physical infrastructure, particularly in the rural areas. Vast amounts were also spent on expanding and modernizing the transport infrastructure, including roads, railways, harbours, airports and communications, including the establishment of an International Direct Dialling (IDD) Facility in 1974 and the launching of the Palapa telecommunications satellite in 1976. Through this communications satellite, an integrated telephone system covering the whole of Indonesia, and linking this to the International Subscriber Dialling (ISD) system, was created (Dick and Forbes 1992: 265, 274, 280).

The first oil boom in the mid-1970s happened to coincide with the end of the first (easy) phase of import-substituting industrialization, that is the substitution of imported consumer goods by locally made ones behind protectionist barriers. Instead of moving into export-promoting industrialization as the East Asian newly-industrializing economies (South Korea and Taiwan) had done a decade earlier, the government embarked on an ambitious state-led programme of 'industrial deepening' or second phase of import-substitution. This second-phase involved the establishment of state-owned, upstream, basic, resource-processing industries. In addition, in 1978 a new Minister of State for Research and Technology, Dr B.J. Habibie, initiated the establishment of a range of 'strategic industries', including a hi-tech aircraft assembling industry (Thee 2002: 209–10).

The architect of the plan to develop a range of basic industries was A.R. Soehoed, the Minister of Industry during the period 1978–1983. During his term in office Soehoed proposed the establishment of 52 basic industries in which the government would have to take the initiative, because at the time private entrepreneurs were not yet ready. The problems with establishing basic industries were, in Soehoed's view, that a considerable amount of capital was needed, that the gestation period was quite long, the physical infrastructure had to be laid out, and the profit margins were generally low (Soehoed 1988).

In Soehoed's view, once a strong foundation of a range of basic industries, financed with the rapidly growing oil revenues, was established, industrial development would accelerate by itself. Although Soehoed's plan was not fully implemented because of the end of the oil boom in 1982, many industrial projects could be implemented during his term in office, including fertilizer and cement plants, the Asahan aluminium smelter in North Sumatra, paper and plywood mills and the nucleus of a steel and engineering industry (Soehoed 1988).

## 4. The Post-oil Boom Era

When in 1979 the Indonesian government was suddenly overtaken by the second oil boom which unexpectedly and vastly increased its revenues from oil taxes and its earnings revenues from oil exports, it could not have foreseen that in 1982, only three years after the second oil boom, it would again be overtaken by an unexpected event, namely the steep decline in the world price of oil. This steep decline was due to a sudden weakening of the world oil market, and heralded the end of the oil boom era for Indonesia.

The developments of 1979/80 and 1982 again underlined the vulnerability of the Indonesian economy to both international and domestic exogenous shocks. The domestic exogenous shock was the severe drought in 1982 which hit the agricultural sector hard and adversely affected most of the main rice-growing areas. The adverse effect of the long drought was particularly felt in the rice sector where rice output was estimated to fall by 5 to 10 per cent in 1983 (McCawley 1983: 1).

The Indonesian government's responses to the two oil booms of the 1970s, as described above, indicated that it had been both willing and able to implement the required macroeconomic stabilization policies (McCawley 1983: 3–4). This was confirmed again by the government's speedy response to the steep decline in oil earnings.

In response to the worsening external conditions, the Indonesian government in early 1983 initiated a broad-based adjustment program aimed at restoring macroeconomic stability. To deal with the rising current account deficit, the government devalued the *rupiah* in March 1983 (Thee 2002: 210). In response to the tightened fiscal position, the government pursued tight fiscal policies by, for instance, limiting the supply of government vehicles for senior officials, stopping the construction of new buildings for government departments, reducing the number of seminars and meetings, service visits abroad and ceremonial visits to the regions. On the revenue side, a departure tax was levied on Indonesian nationals leaving the country for overseas trips (McCawley 1983: 18–19). In addition, the implementation of several ambitious, large-scale, public sector projects, including the planned basic industries, were either deferred or cancelled altogether.

In response to the falling government revenues, a new tax law was introduced in December 1984 aimed at increasing non-oil taxes, particularly personal and corporate income taxes and a new value-added tax (VAT) to offset the decline in oil company taxes. To improve the efficiency of the banking system and the better mobilization of domestic funds, a banking deregulation measure was introduced in June 1983. To this end, the state-owned banks, which at the time still accounted for about 80 per cent of total bank assets, were now allowed freely to set their interest rates, while credit ceilings were lifted (Thee 2002: 210–11).

In addition to the stabilization measures to restore macroeconomic stability, the government also introduced several adjustment measures and structural policy reforms in 1983 aimed at weaning the economy away from its high dependence on oil (and gas) exports and at improving economic efficiency and private sector initiatives. To achieve this objective, the government introduced fairly comprehensive and far-reaching deregulation measures to improve the investment climate for both domestic and foreign investors by dismantling the complex regulatory framework (World Bank 1989: xiii) which had greatly hampered private sector activities.

The deregulation measures also included a series of trade reforms which were taken in 1985 and early 1986 aimed at reducing the 'anti-export bias' of its trade regime. These trade reforms included an:

a)   An across-the-board reduction in tariff rates in March 1985, and
b)   Measures to provide internationally-priced inputs to export-oriented companies (initially defined as companies exporting at least 85 per cent of their output, but later lowered to 65 per cent of their output), which was announced on 6 May 1986.

This scheme was designed to protect Indonesian exporters from the 'high cost' local economy by allowing producer-exporters to import their inputs free of import duty and VAT payments. The 6 May scheme extended beyond duty/tax exemptions, since it also allowed exporters to avoid the cumbersome import license restrictions. To implement the 6 May scheme, a duty drawback facility was established to enable indirect exporters to reclaim import duties (World Bank 1989: 59).

In addition to these trade reforms, the government pursued a supportive exchange rate policy to improve the international competitiveness of non-oil exports, including manufactured exports. In September 1986 the government devalued the *rupiah* following a second, even steeper decline in the price of oil in early 1986. Thereafter Bank Indonesia, the central bank, pursued a managed floating exchange rate by allowing the *rupiah* to depreciate by 4–5 per cent annually to offset the differential between Indonesia's higher inflation rate and those of its major trading partners. By keeping inflationary pressures under control and pursuing an active managed float, the government was able to keep the real effective exchange rate from appreciating, and to keep the local costs levels in line with those of its major international competitors (Pangestu 1996: 19).

The stabilization measures and structural reforms soon bore fruit, as domestic and foreign direct investment in export-oriented projects rose steadily after 1986. As a result, non-oil exports, particularly manufactured exports, rose rapidly. The surge of manufactured exports was so rapid that in 1996 manufactured exports accounted for more than 50 per cent of Indonesia's total exports, as compared to only 4 per cent in 1965 (Table 3). The rapid growth of manufactured exports fuelled the rapid growth of the manufacturing sector which, in turn, fuelled the growth of the whole economy. Hence, within a relatively short time, the manufacturing sector had replaced the oil sector as a major engine of growth and as a major source of export revenues.

## TABLE 3
### Indonesia's Industrial Growth in ASEAN Perspective, 1965–1996

| | Manufacturing value added (millions of US$) | | Manufacturing value added as % of GDP | | Manufactured exports as % of total exports | |
|---|---|---|---|---|---|---|
| | *1970* | *1996* | *1965* | *1996* | *1965* | *1996* |
| Indonesia | 994 | 58,244 | 8 | 25 | 4 | 51 |
| Malaysia | 500 | 34,030 | 9 | 34 | 6 | 76 |
| Philippines | 1,622 | 18,908 | 20 | 23 | 6 | 84 |
| Thailand | 1,130 | 51,525 | 14 | 29 | 3 | 73 |

*Source*: Thee (2002: 221) as quoted from World Bank: *World Development Indicators*.

The data in Table 3 also show that Indonesia's rapid industrial development enabled the country to develop Southeast Asia's largest manufacturing sector, despite the fact that in 1970 its manufacturing sector was much smaller than that of the Philippines and Thailand.

Despite the resumption of rapid economic growth in the late 1980s which was sustained until the onset of the Asian economic crisis in mid-1997, several disturbing developments indicated the emergence of various factors which undermined the resilience of the Indonesian economy, including corrosive corruption, collusion between influential power holders and their business cronies, and nepotism, as reflected by brazen preferential treatment given by President Soeharto to the many businesses of his six greedy children and their cronies (Thee 2002: 213–14).

Another worrisome development was the waning influence of the economic technocrats who had been responsible for designing the sound macroeconomic policies which had led to the rapid and sustained growth of the Indonesian economy, and who had largely retired. Their place was subsequently occupied by younger and competent economists who, however, did not enjoy the trust and confidence which President Soeharto had bestowed on the older technocrats. One manifestation of the diminished influence of the younger technocrats was the proliferation of off-budget expenditures to finance inefficient state-owned enterprises, the companies of the President's children and their cronies, and the 'strategic industries', which led to an erosion of financial discipline, which for a long time had been the hallmark of the economies policies of the Soeharto government. These conditions set the stage for the economic meltdown following the onset of the Asian economic crisis.

## CONCLUSION

The above account of the two oil booms in the 1970s and the post-oil boom shock of the early 1980s underlined the vulnerability of the Indonesian economy to external shocks which always threatened macroeconomic stability as well as the country's growth prospects. However, the above account also showed that the economic technocrats were able, though with considerable difficulty because of the opposition of vested interests, to push through the necessary policy measures required to overcome these shocks.

However, when in 1997/98 the Asian financial and economic crisis hit Indonesia, the Soeharto government proved for the first time to be unable to come to grips with the crisis. This was in part caused by the inappropriate policy measures which the IMF imposed on Indonesia after Indonesia had turned to the IMF for financial assistance. These included, amongst others, the requirement that the government had to pursue tight fiscal and monetary policies, even though the Indonesian government, unlike the Latin American countries which had also sought IMF assistance, had a fiscal surplus. Another shortcoming of the IMF 'recipe' was its demand to liquidate 16 insolvent banks, even though no credible deposit insurance was in place at the time. This understandably led to a bank run which eventually led to the breakdown of the whole banking system. Hence, in the case of Indonesia, the financial crisis was aggravated by a serious banking crisis.

However, Indonesia's steady economic deterioration was to a large extent also due to the reluctance of President Soeharto to faithfully implement the provisions of the agreement with the IMF, particularly the structural reforms which he saw as threatening the business interests of his children. As economic conditions continued to deteriorate, a serious political crisis arose which led to the inglorious fall of President Soeharto in May 1998 after a reign of 32 years.

## Note

1. "The Impact of the Two Oil Booms of the 1970s and the Post-Oil Boom Shock of the Early 1980s on the Indonesian Economy" by Thee Kian Wie, first appeared in the *Proceedings of the Third AFC International Symposium on Resources under Stress: Sustainability of the Local Community in Asia and Africa.* Kyoto: Afrasian Centre for Peace and Development Studies, Ryukoku University, 23–24 February 2008.

## References

Arndt, H.W. "Survey of Recent Developments". *Bulletin of Indonesian Economic Studies* 10 no. 2 (1974): 1–34.

———. "Survey of Recent Developments". *Bulletin of Indonesian Economic Studies* XI no. 2 (1975): 1–29.

Booth, Anne and Bruce Glassburner. "Survey of Recent Developments". *Bulletin of Indonesian Economic Studies* XI no. 1 (1975): 1–40.

Booth, Anne and Peter McCawley. "The Indonesian Economy Since the Mid-Sixties". In *The Indonesian Economy During the Soeharto Era*, edited by Anne Booth and Peter McCawley, 1–22. Kuala Lumpur: Oxford University Press, 1981a.

———. "Fiscal Policy". In *The Indonesian Economy During the Soeharto Era*, edited by Anne Booth and Peter McCawley, 126–61. Kuala Lumpur: Oxford University Press, 1981b.

———. *The Indonesian Economy During the Soeharto Era*. Kuala Lumpur: Oxford University Press, 1981.

———. *The Oil Boom and After: Indonesian Economic Policy and Performance in the Soeharto Era*. Kuala Lumpur: Oxford University Press, 1992.

Bresnan, John. *Managing Indonesia: The Modern Political Economy*. New York: Columbia University Press, 1993.

Dick, Howard, Vincent Houben, Thomas Lindblad and Thee Kian Wie. 2002. *The Emergence of a National Economy — An Economic History of Indonesia, 1800–2000*. Allen and Unwin, St. Leonards, NSW and KITLV Press, Leiden.

Dick, Howard, and Dean Forbes. "Transport and Communications: A Quiet Revolution". In *The Oil Boom and After: Indonesian Economic Policy and Performance in the Soeharto Era*, edited by Anne Booth, 258–79. Kuala Lumpur: Oxford University Press, 1992.

Garnaut, Ross. "Survey of Recent Developments". *Bulletin of Indonesian Economic Studies* 15 no. 3 (1979): 1–42.

Grenville, Stephen. "Survey of Recent Developments". *Bulletin of Indonesian Economic Studies* 10 no. 1 (1974): 1–38.

Healey, D.T. "Survey of Recent Developments". *Bulletin of Indonesian Economic Studies* 17 no. 1 (1981): 1–35.

Mackie, J.A.C. *Indonesia: Economic Growth and Depoliticisation*. Unpublished paper, Canberra, 1997.

McCawley, Peter. "Survey of Recent Developments". *Bulletin of Indonesian Economic Studies* XII no. 1 (1976): 1–43.

———. "Survey of Recent Developments". *Bulletin of Indonesian Economic Studies* 19 no.1 (1983): 1–31.

Odell, P.R. Oil and World Power. Harmondsworth: Penguin, 1981.

Pangestu, Mari. *Economic Reform, Deregulation and Privatization: The Indonesian Experience.* Jakarta: Centre for Strategic and International Studies, 1996.

Prawiro, Radius. *Indonesia's Struggle for Economic Development — Pragmatism in Action.* Kuala Lumpur: Oxford University Press, 1988.

Rosendale, Phyllis. "Survey of Recent Developments". *Bulletin of Indonesian Economic Studies* X no. 3 (1974): 1–25.

———. "Survey of Recent Developments". *Bulletin of Indonesian Economic Studies* 16 no. 1 (1980): 1–33.

Sadli, Mohammad. "Recollections of My Career". *Bulletin of Indonesian Economic Studies* 29 no. 1 (1993): 35–51.

Soehoed, A.R. "Reflections on Industrialization and Industrial Policy in Indonesia". *Bulletin of Indonesian Economic Studies* 24 no. 2 (1988): 43–57.

Sundrum, R.M. "Indonesia's rapid economic Growth, 1968–81". *Bulletin of Indonesian Economic Studies* 23 no. 3 (1986): 40–69.

Thee, Kian Wie. The Soeharto Era and After: Stability, Development and Crisis: 1966–2000. In *The Emergence of a National Economy: An Economic History of Indonesia, 1800–2000,* by Dick, Howard, Vincent Houben, Thomas Lindblad and Thee Kian Wie, 194–243. Allen and Unwin, St. Leonards, Leiden: NSW and KITLV Press, 2002.

World Bank. *Indonesia: Strategy for Growth and Structural Change.* Report no. 7758-IND. Washington, D.C. 3 May 1989.

# PART III

# THE ASIAN FINANCIAL CRISIS AND THE GLOBAL FINANCIAL CRISIS

# 6

# INDONESIA'S TWO DEEP ECONOMIC CRISES: THE MID-1960s AND LATE 1990s[1]

This chapter discusses the two deep economic crises experienced by Indonesia, namely the crisis of the mid-1960s and the crisis of the late 1990s. The two deep economic crises of the mid-1960s and late 1990s led to a serious economic contraction, –3.0 per cent in 1963 and an even more serious –13.1 per cent in 1998, and to a steep rise in poverty. The crisis of the mid-1960s was caused by internal factors, namely the utter neglect of sound economic policies. By contrast, the crisis of the late 1990s was triggered by external factors, namely a sudden shift in market sentiments among foreign creditors and investors which led to panic. Comparing these two deep economic crises is of interest since it indicates that an economy depending on only one but unsustainable institution, a strong president, is vulnerable to internal or external shocks. These crises in their different origins and manifestations show the importance of 'good governance' and strong, viable institutions.

## INTRODUCTION

This paper discusses the two most serious economic crises experienced by Indonesia since independence, namely the crisis of the mid-1960s and the crisis of the late 1990s. While Indonesia had experienced other economic crises, notably in the early 1980s following the end of the oil boom era, this crisis only led to a slower growth. The two deep economic crises of the mid-1960s and late 1990s, however, led to a serious economic contraction, –3.0 per cent in 1963 (World Bank 1998: 2.1) and an even more serious –13.1 per cent in 1998, and to a steep rise in the incidence of absolute poverty. The economic crisis of the mid-1960s was accompanied by a serious political crisis which led to the ignominious downfall of Indonesia's first President. The economic crisis of the late 1990s led to a serious political crisis which, like in the mid-1960s, also led to an equally ignominious downfall of Indonesia's second president.

The crisis of the mid-1960s was primarily caused by internal (domestic) factors, specifically the supremacy of political over economic considerations, which led to an utter neglect of sound economic policies. This led, not surprisingly, to an economic breakdown and an unprecedented hyperinflation which greatly impoverished the population. Production and investment in most key sectors had steadily declined since 1950, and real per capita income was probably below that of the prewar years of the late 1930s. In the early 1960s budget deficits had reached 50 per cent of total government expenditures, while exports had declined (Booth & McCawley, 1981a: 1).

The manufacturing sector accounted for less than 10 per cent of GDP, much lower than in most of the other Asian developing countries. The manufacturing sector was also characterized by very substantial excess capacity. It was estimated that in the mid-1960s the manufacturing sector was operating at less than 30 per cent of capacity because the shortage of foreign exchange led to a serious shortage of imported raw materials and spare parts (McCawley, 1981: 64).

In line with the policy of substantial direct government intervention in the market, various schemes were introduced to assist small-scale firms. These included attempts to provide traditional producers such as hand loom weavers with sufficient raw materials to continue operating by rationing yarn supplies through government-sponsored cooperatives. However, in practice the system turned out to be ineffective. Industrial policies during the early 1960s reflected the worst kinds of protectionist and *etatist* policies, and as a result industrial production stagnated (McCawley, 1981: 64).

In contrast, the crisis of the late 1990s was triggered by external factors, namely a sudden shift in market sentiments among foreign creditors and investors which subsequently led to panic. The panic, which first started in Thailand in mid-1997, through contagion soon spread to the other East Asian countries, including Malaysia, the Philippines and Indonesia. Gripped by panic, foreign investors and creditors hurriedly withdrew large amounts of capital, which led to a steep depreciation of the currencies of these countries, including the Indonesian rupiah. The Indonesian government's inability or reluctance to deal speedily and effectively with the currency crisis led to a serious financial and economic crisis, and subsequently to a serious political crisis, which ultimately led to the fall of President Soeharto in May 1998 after a reign of 32 years.

The Indonesian crisis of the late 1990s was also aggravated by internal factors. Although, unlike the early 1960s, the Indonesian government pursued sound economic policies, it apparently did not realise the adverse consequences of the rapid increase in private external debt, much of which was short-term and unhedged. In fact, monetary policy targets and a quasi-fixed exchange rate combined with an open capital account encouraged steadily rising capital inflows. A flawed banking system often violated central bank regulations, for instance exceeding the limits imposed on intra-group lending, without being penalized. Poor governance led to pervasive corruption. Political uncertainty also played a role because of the concern about the durability of President Suharto because of his advanced age and failing health (World Bank, 1998: 1.8–1.11; Hill, 1999: 54–70).

Owing to its weak financial and economic structures and institutions, Indonesia was unable to deal effectively with the severe shock of the steep depreciation of its currency. In the wake of the financial and economic crisis, a political crisis arose that rendered a speedy economic recovery more difficult than in the two other worst-affected countries, Thailand and Korea.

Both the crisis of the mid-1960s and late 1990s led to a steep fall in per capita GDP (van der Eng, 2001: 182). These steep declines severely affected the economic welfare of the Indonesian population, particularly the low income group of the population.

Comparing these two deep economic crises is of great interest since it clearly indicates that an economy depending on only one but unsustainable institution, a strong president ruling in an authoritarian way, is quite vulnerable to internal or external shocks. Hence, both these crises in their different origins and manifestations show the great need for 'good governance' and strong, viable institutions which can establish and enforce the basic rules, particularly on the government, but also on private companies and the public.

This paper will take a closer look at the economic conditions prevailing in the early 1960s and mid-1990s which preceded these crises and the economic policies which were pursued before and after these crises. The paper will conclude by comparing the factors which led to these two crises and the outcomes of the measures taken to deal with these crises.

## I. THE ECONOMIC CRISIS OF THE MID-1960s

### Economic conditions in the early 1960s

By the mid-1960s the Indonesian economy was experiencing an unprecedented economic breakdown. The chronic inflation which had plagued Indonesia since the early 1950s had, as a result of a rapid acceleration in monetary expansion since the early 1960s, turned into a crippling hyperinflation which reached 135 per cent in 1964 and almost 600 per cent in 1965 (Grenville, 1981: 102, 108).

As a result of this hyperinflation, financial institutions atrophied because they were unable to attract funds and therefore were unable to provide commercial loans. During this period the banking system, specifically Bank Indonesia, the central bank, served mainly to finance the growing government budget deficit (Grenville, 1981: 102–3). Since its establishment as Indonesia's central bank in 1953, Bank Indonesia had, like in most other market-oriented economies, enjoyed a level of independence from political decision-making. By law, money in circulation was not allowed to exceed five times Bank Indonesia's holdings of foreign exchange reserves and gold. However, following the decline of parliamentary democracy in 1957, Bank Indonesia's independence came to an end. Bank Indonesia subsequently became a *de facto* instrument of the central government when it started printing increasing amounts of money to finance the rapidly growing budget deficit, thus violating the existing restrictions on deficit spending. Henceforth, government spending increased rapidly without corresponding increases in government revenues (Prawiro, 1998: 3).

The growing government budget deficit was caused by the fact that tax collection had been steadily falling further behind uncontrolled government expenditures (Arndt, 1984: 3). During the greater part of the 1950s the bulk of government revenues was obtained from taxation on foreign trade. Since the late 1950s, however, these taxes on foreign trade began to decline as a percentage of total revenues. The reasons for this decline were the weakening of the world market for rubber and other export commodities and the rapid increase in smuggling to Singapore as a result of the overvalued exchange rate of the rupiah (Booth & McCawley, 1981b: 126) Since it was impossible to offset the decline in the taxes on foreign trade by raising other sources of domestic revenues, the government was forced to resort to deficit financing to finance the desired levels of expenditure (Booth & McCawley, 1981: 126).

Although the government was unable to raise revenues, it was unable or unwilling to reduce expenditures. Government expenditures had been rising rapidly for several reasons. Since 1961 a rising part of these expenditures were spent on military actions, including the military campaign to reclaim West Irian (currently Papua province) from the Dutch and the 'Crush Malaysia' campaign. The rising deficit spending was also caused by large expenditures on rice imports and subsidies on basic wage goods, especially rice and petroleum; spending on 'prestige projects', such as the large sports stadium at Senayan, Jakarta, the National Monument (*Monas*) on Merdeka Square, Jakarta (partly funded by the Japanese war reparations) and a large building to accommodate the Conference of the Newly Emerging Forces (*Conefo*); and the allocation of discretionary funds, including the so-called 'Revolution Fund' (*Dana Revolusi*) to finance various projects and to reward friends of the Sukarno government (Prawiro, 1998: 4–5).

The data in Table 1 show how the budget deficit as a percentage of government revenues rose rapidly in 1965 as compared to the already large budget deficit in 1964.

**TABLE 1**
**Government Revenues and Expenditures, 1964–65**
**(millions of rupiah)**

| Year | Revenues | | Expenditures | | Budget deficit | |
|------|----------|--------|--------------|--------|--------|-------------------------|
|      | Estimated | Actual | Estimated | Actual | Actual | As % of actual revenues |
| 1964 | 200 | 283 | 688 | 681 | 398 | 141 |
| 1965 | 671 | 923 | 965 | 2,526 | 1,603 | 174 |

*Source*: Radius Prawiro: Indonesia's Struggle for Economic Development — Pragmatism in Action, Kuala Lumpur: Oxford University Press, 1998, Table 1.1, p. 22, based on Bank Indonesia's Annual Reports.

Indonesia was also in default of a large foreign debt which by the end of 1965 amounted to almost US$2.4 billion (around 25 per cent of Indonesia's GDP). Of this amount US$ 1.4 billion (60 per cent) was owed to the Socialist countries, particularly the Soviet Union (US$990 million) and the other East European Socialist countries. The large loans from the Socialist countries, particularly from the Soviet Union, which had been largely obtained as Indonesia's relations with these countries had grown increasingly closer since the late 1950s, were largely used to purchase modern military equipment.

In view of Indonesia's strategic importance, the U.S. took a great interest in the country's political stability. Despite rising concern about Indonesia's tilt to the socialist countries, the U.S. continued to provide modest amounts of development aid to the government. However, after Indonesia launched its military confrontation against Malaysia after the establishment of the Malaysian federation on 16 September 1963 which it had strongly opposed from the outset, diplomatic relations with the U.S. deteriorated rapidly in view of America's strong support of Malaysia. American aid came to a halt when President Sukarno in March 1964 defiantly stated that the U.S. could 'go to hell with its aid'.

With total foreign exchange earnings (including oil revenues) for 1966 estimated at only US$450 million (around five per cent of Indonesia's GDP), Indonesia was unable to pay for the minimum import requirements estimated to be US$560 million, let alone service its foreign debt of US$530 million (Arndt, 1984: 5.14). By December 1965 foreign exchange commitments could no longer be met. Bank Indonesia, the central bank, was unable to honour cash letters of credit and had to suspend payments on some foreign trade credits (Palmer, 1978: 7).

During the early 1960s production of rice and most other cereals was not sufficient to replace banned rice imports. Production of rubber, one of Indonesia's major export crops, in 1964/65 slightly increased after the low point in 1963 when drought and the long-term problems adversely affected production. Fortunately, the takeovers of American and British estates in 1964 following the 'Crush Malaysia' campaign did not affect a sufficiently large acreage to have a significant affect on output. Rubber smallholders, who accounted for about two thirds of rubber output, were offered special bank facilities to encourage promotion but these facilities and the government-sponsored seed distribution and land clearing could not immediately affect output (S.A.; J.G. & L.C., 1965: 8).

The output of sugar, which during the early twentieth century had been Indonesia's major estate crop, experienced a steep decline so that during the post-war decade it generated only three per cent of the country's export revenues. In 1961 sugar even had to be imported (Mackie, 1971: 37). Without better seed cane, rehabilitation of irrigation works, further supplies of fertilizer and especially expansion of effective refining capacity, there was little prospect of a substantial increase in sugar output (S.A.; J.G. & L.C., 1965: 8)

In mining, only petroleum experienced a steady increase in output and substantial new investments (Mackie, 1971: 35). Despite the fact that oil exploration had ceased after Japan occupied Indonesia in 1942, oil output rose rapidly during the 1950s from 8 million to 18 million tons per annum (Hunter, 1965: 70). This increase was mainly due to the contribution of Caltex, one of the three major oil companies operating in Indonesia (the two other ones being Shell and Stanvac). Exports of crude oil also increased because the Caltex oil refineries were located outside Indonesia (Thomas & Panglaykim, 1973: 91).

Despite the increasing anti-Western stance of the Indonesian government since the late 1950s, rational considerations still exerted some influence as reflected by the fact that the Indonesian government signed exploration agreements with several small foreign oil companies. To encourage Indonesia to maintain an open-door stance in regard to oil exploration, the United

States used its aid, including educational and military aid, not only to stop the ascendant Indonesian Communist Party (PKI) from gaining more power, but also to keep Indonesian oil under Western control (Dick, 2002: 188).

However, when in the early 1960s the three major oil companies operating in Indonesia needed new concessions to search for oil, political instability in Indonesia and rising anti-Western attitudes caused by Western support of Malaysia in the face of Indonesia's 'Crush Malaysia' campaign, prevented the granting of new concessions. As a result, the future of the oil industry by the mid-1960s as a major source of export revenues was in serious doubt (Thomas & Panglaykim, 1973: 91).

Growth of the manufacturing sector, the output of which accounted for less than 10 per cent of Indonesia's net national product, was sluggish, since many industries dependent on imports were experiencing difficulties due to shortage of spare parts and raw materials. Due the above problem, the textile industry was only operating at an average of 5 to 10 per cent of capacity (S.A.; J.G. & L.C., 1965: 9).

Except for government services, the major sectors of the economy, grew at a sluggish rate during the first half of the 1960s. During this period the average annual growth of the Indonesian economy was lower than during most of the 1950s. According to the Central Bureau of Statistics, the average annual growth rate of net national product during the period 1958–65 was only 1.7 per cent, slightly lower than the population growth rate of 2.0–2.2 per cent (Mackie, 1971: 17; Booth, 1998: 65). In 1963 the economy even contracted by –3.0 per cent (World Bank, 1998: 2.1). Although economic growth in 1964 and 1965 was again positive, it was at an average annual rate of less than 2.0 per cent still very low, certainly lower than population growth. Hence, per capita GDP during this period experienced a gradual, but steady decline. In fact, per capita GDP in 1965 was lower than the pre-war level in 1940 (Booth, 1998: 65). Standards of living of the Indonesian population by the end of the Sukarno era were therefore lower than they were by the end of the Dutch colonial era in the early 1940s.

## Economic Policies Since the Late 1950s

The economic breakdown of the mid-1960s was the logical outcome of poor economic policies which had become a major feature of government policy since the late 1950s. To cope with the regional rebellions and the danger of national disintegration, General Nasution, the army chief of staff, persuaded President Sukarno to proclaim martial law in early March 1957 (Rickleffs, 1993: 255–56). With the proclamation of martial law, President

Sukarno and the army had established themselves as the major forces on Indonesia's political scene. President Sukarno subsequently consolidated his political power by creating an extra-parliamentary emergency business cabinet (*zakenkabinet*), named the 'Work Cabinet' (*Kabinet Karya*), headed by President Sukarno himself (Legge, 1972: 288). On 5 July 1959 President Sukarno further consolidated his political leadership by disbanding the legally elected Parliament and Constituent Assembly (*Konstituante*) and reinstated the Constitution of 1945. Under the 1945 Constitution the President was both head of state and head of government. Supported by both the army under Army Chief of Staff General A.H. Nasution and the ascendant Indonesian Communist Party (*Partai Komunis Indonesia, PKI*), President Sukarno ushered in the period of Guided Democracy and Guided Economy (1959–65).

Under Guided Democracy, Sukarno stated that Indonesia would have a political system which would reflect distinctively Indonesian values and which would enable a national consensus to emerge — under his guidance that is (Legge, 1972: 309–10). Under Guided Econom Indonesia would develop a 'Socialist Economy with Indonesian features' or '*Sosialisme a la Indonesia*', as Sukarno put it. How this goal of building a 'just and prosperous society' (*masyarakat adil dan makmur*) under Indonesian Socialism was to be achieved in practice, however, was not specified.

Since the advent of Guided Democracy, acceptance of the principles of 'Indonesian Socialism' and Guided Economy became a condition of participation in legal politics (Castles, 1965: 13). Under President Sukarno's leadership, economic policy was regarded as an integral part of general political strategy. It was obvious that in President Sukarno's view, politics came first. Political success, he believed, and nothing else, would ultimately solve the country's economic problems (S.A.; J.G. & L.C., 1965: 1).

Those officials trying to cope with practical problems, such as rising budget deficits and foreign exchange shortages, often had to resort to ad hoc policies which were not in line with achieving the goal of Indonesian socialism. To allay the doubts of the 'true' socialists, the thrust of these ad hoc policies was 'concealed' behind politically satisfying slogans (Castles, 1965: 18–19). Having neither the interest nor understanding of the country's economic problems, President Sukarno was not inclined to seek economic advice from the country's few qualified economists. Being preoccupied with what he saw as the country's major unfinished problem, namely 'completing the national revolution', President Sukarno did not take sufficient precautions to minimise the adverse effects of his policies (Legge, 1972: 328–29). Despite the official rhetoric of building a 'just and prosperous society', there was increasing evidence that declining per capita incomes was accompanied by widening income disparities between rich and poor, particularly in Jakarta and the other big cities.

Despite the severe economic difficulties, President Sukarno in his speech on 17 August 1965, commemorating the twentieth anniversary of Indonesia's independence, said little about the state of the economy despite the stirring title of the speech 'Reach to the Stars — A Year of Self-Reliance'. To achieve this goal, the President added, the acceptance of hardship was the price of revolutionary achievement and the forgoing of privileges for the welfare of the public (J.G., 1965: 1). Hence, on the eve of the so-called *Gestapu* coup on 30 September 1965, the Indonesian economy was in shambles as a result of the utter disregard of sound economic policies.

## II. THE ECONOMIC CRISIS OF THE LATE 1990s

### The course and causes of the crisis

Unlike Indonesia's economic crisis of the mid-1960s which many people had predicted because of the reckless disregard of sound economic policies, the economic crisis of the late 1990s was quite unexpected. Moreover, unlike the sluggish growth during the early 1960s, the Indonesian economy during the period 1989 through 1996 grew at an average annual real rate of 8 per cent, led by strong investment growth. Macroeconomic fundamentals also appeared to be strong, since inflation at 10 per cent a year, though a little higher than the other East Asian economies, was still low by developing country standards. The overall fiscal balance was in surplus after 1992, while public debt as a share of GDP had fallen as the government used privatization proceeds to repay a large amount of foreign debt (IMF, 2003: 11).

Although Indonesia's macroeconomic indicators on the eve of the crisis looked good, one could in hindsight identify some worrisome early warning indicators, particularly the rapid increase in foreign borrowing by the private sector since the early 1990s. Due to the large difference between the domestic and foreign interest rates and the semi-fixed exchange rate, many Indonesian firms were tempted to borrow large funds overseas without hedging (World Bank, 1998: 4). On their part, foreign investors from the advanced industrial countries scrambled to lend to borrowers in the emerging markets, including Indonesia, which looked attractive as their growth prospects looked good and higher yields could be obtained since interest rates in their own countries were low. As a result, by 1996 total foreign debt financing of Indonesian firms accounted for slightly more than 40 per cent of their total debt, out of which slightly more than one half (or 20 per cent of the total) was short-term debt (ADB, 1999: 27).

Although it was argued that Indonesia's foreign exchange reserves on the eve of the crisis were quite adequate to cover three months of imports, the country's vulnerability would be more evident if one looked at the short-term debt to foreign exchange reserves ratio (Hill, 2000: 124). Seen from this viewpoint, Indonesia during the second quarter of 1997 with a short-term debt to foreign reserves ratio of 1.70 was indeed more vulnerable to external shocks than the other crisis-affected Southeast Asian countries. Only South Korea had a higher short-term foreign debt to foreign exchange reserves ratio (Table 2).

### TABLE 2
### Short-Term Foreign Debt and Foreign Exchange Reserves of the Crisis-Affected East Asian Countries, Second Quarter of 1997*

| Country | Short-term debt (billions of US$) | Foreign exchange reserves (US$ billions) | Short-term debt to foreign reserves ratio |
|---------|-----------------------------------|------------------------------------------|-------------------------------------------|
| Indonesia | 34.7 | 20.3 | 1.7 |
| Malaysia | 16.3 | 26.6 | 0.6 |
| Philippines | 8.3 | 9.8 | 0.9 |
| Thailand | 45.8 | 31.4 | 1.5 |
| South Korea | 70.2 | 34.1 | 2.1 |

*Note*: * Rounded figures
*Source*: Asian Development Bank: Asian Development Outlook, 1999, Oxford University Press, table 1.3, p. 26.

The course and cause of Indonesia's financial and economic crisis of 1997/98 is by now well-known. The trigger was a crisis in Thailand where foreign investors' confidence was undermined by the sharp decline in export growth in 1996, particularly that of labour-intensive manufactured exports, and the widening current account deficit. This triggered a capital outflow and speculation against the Thai *baht* as a devaluation was expected to stem the fall in export growth. Once these expectations arose and portfolio capital fled the country, the process gained momentum (Warr, 1998: 55).

From mid-1996 through the first half of 1997 the Bank of Thailand tried to defend the *baht* (which had been pegged to the US dollar) against speculative attacks. To this end the Bank of Thailand intervened on the spot foreign exchange market by using more than US$23 billion out of its total reserves of nearly US$39 billion. These attempts failed. On 2 July 1997 the Bank of Thailand was obliged to float the *baht* which subsequently fell far more than its purchasing parity value (Nidhiprabha, 1999: 71). Through the contagion effect, the currency crisis spread from Thailand to the other Southeast Asian countries, including Malaysia, the Philippines and Indonesia. In these countries borrowers and offshore investors rushed to buy foreign currency in order to protect themselves against a possible currency devaluation, such as had occurred in Thailand. Their fears soon turned into a self-fulfilling prophesy (McLeod, 1998: 37).

Only three weeks after the *baht* was floated, the Indonesian rupiah came under strong pressure as foreign investors and creditors scrambled to reduce their exposure to Indonesia by moving their capital offshore. Indonesian companies followed suit. Bank Indonesia responded by widening the intervention margins of the crawling peg regime from 8 to 12 per cent. However, when speculation continued and pressure on the rupiah was unabated, Bank Indonesia floated the rupiah on 14 August 1997. Following the float, Bank Indonesia raised the interest rates of one-month central Bank certificates (SBI) and tightened liquidity by transferring a large amount of public sector deposits out of commercial banks (IMF, 2003: 12).

When these measures failed to stem the steady depreciation of the *rupiah*, the government turned to the International Monetary Fund (IMF) for financial assistance. In return for a large standby loan from the IMF, the government in its Letter of Intent (LoI) to the IMF pledged to implement a comprehensive reform program, involving sound macroeconomic policies; restructuring of the weak financial sector, including the closure of insolvent financial institutions; and structural reforms (Djiwandono, 2000: 54). It was hoped that the IMF good housekeeping seal would restore market confidence (Sadli, 1999: 17).

Market confidence, however, was not restored when the government, in accordance with the IMF programme, in November 1997 closed 16 insolvent banks to show its determination to deal decisively with financially troubled banks. This measure, however, led to a loss of confidence in the whole banking system. To prevent a panicky bank run by the public, Bank Indonesia issued a huge amount of emergency credits — referred to as Bank Indonesia's Liquidity Support (*Bantuan Likuiditas Bank Indonesia, BLBI*) to ensure that the other banks did not collapse (World Bank, 1998: 1.4–1.6). The currency crisis was now aggravated by a serious banking crisis. Not surprisingly, several critics faulted the IMF for what they considered the unnecessarily hasty closure of the 16 banks which destabilized the whole financial system and subsequently led to the insolvency of the entire banking system (Ramli, 2003: 11).

Meanwhile, the *rupiah* continued to depreciate further between December 1997 and January 1998. A second LoI to the IMF, signed by President Suharto in January 1998, failed to restore market confidence in the *rupiah*, which by mid-January 1998 dropped to Rp17,000 to the US dollar, that is one-seventh of its pre-crisis level (Hill, 1999: 19–20). It became increasingly evident that the President seemed reluctant to implement the IMF program fully and wholeheartedly, as several provisions, notably relating to the structural reforms, would hurt the business interests of his children.

While economic conditions in the other crisis-affected Southeast Asian countries, notably Malaysia and Thailand, slowly began to recover in March and April 1998, when exchange rates and stock markets began to recover slightly (Hill, 1999: 19–20), in Indonesia market confidence failed to recover. The inability of the government to deal effectively with what by then had become a full-blown economic crisis led to a prolonged political crisis which in May 1998 forced President Suharto to step down after a reign of 32 years. Suharto's clinging to power for months on end without being able to come to grips with the crisis cost the country dearly, not only in an economic sense but also in terms of political and social stability.

## The socio-economic effects of the crisis

Although the economy was hit by the crisis in mid-1997, rapid growth during the first half of 1997 still enabled the economy to grow at 4.6 per cent in 1997. The full impact of the crisis was only felt in 1998 when the economy contracted by an unprecedented –13.1 per cent, with almost all sectors, except agriculture, mining and public utilities, experiencing a sharp contraction. This economic contraction was much worse than the economic contraction of –3.0 per cent in 1963. During this period inflation rose to more than 80 per cent.

The sharp economic contraction in 1998 adversely affected the economic welfare of the Indonesian population, particularly in the urban areas, because many workers were laid off in the labour-intensive manufacturing, construction and service industries. However, many, though not all, of the displaced workers found lower income employment in agriculture and the urban informal sector, particularly in trade, the largest informal sector in urban areas (Manning, 2000: 127–28). As a result, real wages in both the tradeable and non-tradeable sectors declined sharply as adjustments in nominal wages failed to keep with the rise in inflation. Real wages paid to casual workers in the rice sector also fell in both Java and the Outer Islands, although the decline in the Outer Islands was less than in Java. Apparently, the social impact of the crisis was worse in Java than in the Outer Islands (Manning, 2000: 128–30).

As a result of increased private consumption, in 1999 the severe economic contraction was reversed when the economy recorded positive growth again, although at a miniscule 0.8 per cent. In 2000 the economy experienced a stronger recovery by growing at 4.8 per cent, fuelled largely by strong growth in private consumption and exports. However, in 2001 economic growth slowed down again to 3.3 per cent, but in 2002 growth rose slightly to 3.5 per cent, and then rose steadily to 4.8 per cent in 2003, to 5.1 per cent in 2004, 5.6 per cent in 2005, 6.1 per cent in 2006, and 6.3 per cent in 2007.

The loss of jobs in the formal sector, the subsequent shift to lower income activities in agriculture and the urban informal sector, and the hyperinflation and attendant drop in purchasing power during the sharp economic contraction in 1998 led to a significant increase in the incidence of absolute poverty, which before the crisis had steadily gone down. However, as the economy slowly began to recover in 1999, the incidence of absolute poverty began to decline until in 2002 it was almost down to the pre-crisis level of 1996. Although the poverty rate in 2006 rose again to nearly 18 per cent, largely because of the ban on rice imports (since rice is a major consumption item of the poor), it declined again to just over 16 per cent in 2007 as growth continued its steady growth.

### TABLE 3
### Percentage of Indonesia's Population
### Below the Poverty Line, 1996–2007

|         | (%)  |
|---------|------|
| 1996*   | 17.6 |
| 1999    | 23.4 |
| 2001    | 19.0 |
| 2002    | 18.4 |
| 2003    | 18.2 |
| 2004    | 17.4 |
| 2005    | 16.0 |
| 2006    | 17.8 |
| 2007**  | 16.6 |

*Notes*: * Revised estimates by the Central Agency of Statistics (BPS)
    ** Preliminary estimates
*Source*: World Bank, 2007, based on BPS's National Socio-Economic Survey (SUSENAS)

## Indonesia's economic crises of the mid-1960s and late 1990s: a comparison

A major difference between the crisis of the mid-1960s and the late 1990s is that the crisis of the mid-1960s was preceded by a steady economic decline during the previous five or six years caused by a total disregard of sound macro-economic policies. During this period sound economic policies were totally subordinated to the politics of President Sukarno 'to complete the national revolution' and mobilise the *'newly emerging forces'* (*Nefos*) in Asia and Africa against the *'old established forces'* (*Oldefos*), that is the Western capitalist countries. In his confrontational stance against the capitalist West and close alliance with the Socialist countries, President Sukarno was motivated primarily by his distrust of the Western countries, his preference to build an Indonesian-style socialist economy and his conviction that Indonesia's national interests would be better served by a closer alliance and cooperation with the Socialist countries. Since the early 1960s this approach had involved the forging of much closer relations with the People's Republic of China (PRC) at the expense of relations with the Soviet Union.

By contrast, the severe economic crisis of the late 1990s was triggered by external factors, namely the sudden shift in market sentiments among foreign investors and creditors about the economic prospects of the Southeast Asian countries, including doubts about whether the fixed or semi-fixed exchange rates in the region could be maintained. The negative shift in market sentiment started in Thailand, but through a process of contagion spread to other Southeast Asian countries, including Indonesia. This led to the panicky withdrawal of large private capital funds which had entered Indonesia during the boom years of the early 1990s, which in turn led to a steep depreciation of the rupiah. But the economic impact of the currency crisis was aggravated by domestic factors, namely Indonesia's basic economic and institutional weaknesses, particularly its weak financial and economic structures and institutions, which rendered the country more vulnerable to the currency crisis. The inability and unwillingness of President Soeharto to take the necessary decisive steps to deal speedily and effectively with the economic crisis ultimately led to a serious political crisis, which culminated in the fall of the President himself. The political weaknesses of the three successor governments of Presidents Habibie, Abdurrachman Wahid and Megawati Soekarnoputri rendered a speedy economic recovery much more difficult and intractable than in South Korea and Thailand, the other two East Asian countries worst affected by the Asian economic crisis.

Another major difference with the crisis of the mid-1960s was that the crisis of the late 1990s was preceded by three decades of rapid and sustained economic growth. Growth during this period led to an unprecedented rise in the standards of living in Indonesia, as reflected by a steady decline in the incidence of absolute poverty. This long period of rapid and sustained economic growth was the outcome of sound macroeconomic policies and the re-integration of the Indonesian economy with the world economy which from the outset was strongly supported by President Soeharto. It was Indonesia's tragedy that in the end Indonesia's national interests were increasingly subordinated to the business interests of Soeharto's children and his cronies.

## Note

1. "Indonesia's Two Deep Economic Crises: The mid-1960s and late 1990s", by Thee Kian Wie, first published in *Journal of the Asia-Pacific Economy*, vol. 14, no. 2, February (2009): 49–60. The author would like to acknowledge the valuable comments and suggestions of two anonymous referees on an earlier draft of the paper.

## References

Arndt, H.W. *The Indonesian Economy: Collected Papers*. Singapore: Chopmen Publishers, 1984.

Asian Development Bank. *Asian Development Outlook, 1999*. New York: Oxford University Press, 1999.

Booth, Anne and Peter McCawley. "The Indonesian Economy Since the Mid-1960s". In *The Indonesian Economy During the Soeharto Era*, edited by Anne Booth and Peter McCawley, pp. 1–22. Kuala Lumpur: Oxford University Press: 1981a.

———. "Fiscal Policy". In *The Indonesian Economy During the Soeharto Era*, edited by Anne Booth & Peter McCawley, pp. 121–61. Kuala Lumpur: Oxford University Press, 1981b.

Booth, Anne. *The Indonesian Economy in the Nineteenth and Twentieth Centuries — A History of Missed Opportunities*. London: Macmillan Press, 1998.

Castles, Lance. "Socialism and Private Business: The Latest Phase". *Bulletin of Indonesian Economic Studies* 1 (1965): 13–39.

Dick, Howard et al. *Formation of the nation-state, 1930s–1966*. Crows Nest: Allen & Unwin. 2002.

———. *The Emergence of a National Economy: An Economic History of Indonesia, 1800–2000*. Crows Nest: Allen & Unwin. 2002.

Djiwandono, J. Soedradjad. "Bank Indonesia and the Recent Crisis". *Bulletin of Indonesian Economic Studies* 36 no. 1 (2000): 47–72.

van der Eng, Pierre. "Indonesia's economy and standard of living in the 20th century". In *Indonesia Today — Challenges of History*, edited by Grayson Lloyd and Shannon Smith, pp. 181–99. Singapore: Institute of Southeast Asian Studies, 2001.

Garnaut, Ross. "The East Asian Crisis". In *East Asia in Crisis: From Being A Miracle to Needing One?*, edited by Ross McLeod and Ross Garnaut, pp. 3–27. London & New York: Routledge, 1998.

Grenville, Stephen. "Monetary Policy and the Formal Financial Sector". In *The Indonesian Economy During the Soeharto Era*, edited by Anne Booth and Peter McCawley, pp. 102–25. Kuala Lumpur: Oxford University Press, 1981.

Hill, Hal. *The Indonesian Economy in Crisis: Causes, Consequences and Lessons.* Singapore: Institute of Southeast Asian Studies, 1999.

Hunter, Alex. "Oil Exploration in Indonesia". *Bulletin of Indonesian Economic Studies* 1 (1965): 68–71.

International Monetary Fund (IMF). *The IMF and the Recent Capital Account Crisis — Indonesia, Korea, Brazil* (Washington, D.C.: Independent Evaluation Office, International Monetary Fund, 2003).

J.G. "Survey of Recent Developments". *Bulletin of Indonesian Economic Studies* no. 2 (1965): 1–15.

Johnson, Colin. "Survey of Recent Developments". In *Bulletin of Indonesian Economic Studies* 34 no. 2 (1998): 3–57.

Legge, John D. *Sukarno: A Political Biography*. Melbourne: Penguin Books, 1972.

McCawley, Peter. "The Growth of the Industrial Sector". In *The Indonesian Economy During the Soeharto Era*, edited by Anne Booth and Peter McCawley, pp. 62–101. Kuala Lumpur: Oxford University Press, 1981.

McLeod, Ross. "Indonesia". In *East Asia in Crisis: From Being A Miracle to Needing One?*, edited by Ross McLeod and Ross Garnaut, pp. 31–48. London & New York: Routledge, 1998.

Mackie, J.A.C. "The Indonesian Economy, 1950–63". In *The Economy of Indonesia — Selected Readings*, edited by Bruce Glassburner, pp. 16–69. Ithaca and London: Cornell University Press, 1971.

Manning, Chris. "Labour Market Adjustment to Indonesia's Economic Crisis: Context, Trends and Implications". In *Bulletin of Indonesian Economic Studies* 36 no. 1 (2000): 105–36.

Nidhiprabha, Bhanupong. "Economic Crises and the Debt-Deflation Episode in Thailand". In *Southeast Asia's Economic Crisis: Origins, Lessons, and the Way Forward*, edited by H.W. Arndt and Hal Hill, pp. 67–80. Singapore: Institute of Southeast Asian Studies, 1999.

Palmer, Ingrid. *The Indonesian Economy Since 1965: A Case Study of Political Economy*. London: Frank Cass, 1978.

Prawiro, Radius. *Indonesia's Struggle for Economic Development: Pragmatism in Action*. Kuala Lumpur: Oxford University Press, 1998.

Ramli, Rizal. "Life After the IMF". In *Van Zorge Report*, April 21 (2003): 10–18.

Ricklefs, M.C. *A History of Modern Indonesia Since c. 1300*. Second Edition, London: Macmillan, 1993.

S.A.; J.G. & L.C. "Survey of Recent Developments". *Bulletin of Indonesian Economic Studies* 1 (1965): 1–11.

Sadli, Mohamad. "The Indonesian Crisis". In *Southeast Asia's Economic Crisis — Origins, Lessons, and the Way Forward*, edited by H.W. Arndt & Hal Hill, pp. 16–27. Singapore: Institute of Southeast Asian Studies, 1999.

Thomas, K.D. and Panglaykim, J. *Indonesia — The Effect of Past Policies and President Soeharto's Plans for the Future*. P. Series no. 11, Committee for Economic Development of Australia (CEDA), November 1973.

Warr, Peter G. "Thailand". In *East Asia in Crisis: From Being A Miracle to Needing One?*, edited by Ross McLeod and Ross Garnaut, pp. 49–65. London & New York:. Routledge, 1998.

World Bank. *Indonesia: Sustaining Growth with Equity*. Report no. 16433-IND, Jakarta, 30 May 1997.

———. *Indonesia in Crisis: A Macroeconomic Update*. Jakarta, July 1998.

———. *Indonesia: Economic and Social Update*. Jakarta, November 2007.

———. *Indonesia: Economic and Social Update*. Jakarta, April 2008.

# 7

# THE IMPACT OF THE GLOBAL FINANCIAL CRISIS ON THE INDONESIAN ECONOMY AND THE PROSPECTS FOR THE RESUMPTION OF RAPID AND SUSTAINED GROWTH[1]

While in early 2008 the East Asian economies, including Indonesia, were tackling rising inflation caused by the surge in food and fuel prices, after the collapse of the Lehman Brothers in the U.S. on 15 September 2008 they were all confronted by an acceleration in the financial turbulence that had started in mid-2007. The collapse of Lehman Brothers sparked massive sell-offs on stock exchanges and foreign exchange markets (reflecting a flight to safety), including in Indonesia.

Fortunately, Indonesia, like the other middle-income East Asian countries, Malaysia, Thailand, and the Philippines withstood the financial turbulence well because they were better prepared for this shock after the Asian financial crisis of 1997/98. Over the past decade these countries, including Indonesia, strengthened their external balances, increased their foreign exchange reserves, reduced government debt to ensure fiscal sustainability, and improved banking supervision (World Bank, 2009a: 6).

In the fourth quarter of 2008 disruption in the global economy hit Indonesia through the trade channel as export-oriented industries contracted sharply, with adverse impacts on employment. The strong growth of non-oil and gas exports ended abruptly in the fourth (October–December) quarter of 2008, as did imports. The drop in exports, especially of non-oil and gas exports, was most evident in Indonesia's exports to China, which recorded the largest contraction, namely — 22.1 per cent. Exports to Japan, the U.S., the E.U., and the other ASEAN countries also declined (Patunru & Zetha, 2009: 3). Since Indonesia's exports are still dominated by primary commodities, the agricultural sector has also been adversely affected (Patunru & Zetha, 2009: 18).

However, in general Indonesia has thus far only suffered a relatively mild impact from the global financial crisis (GFC). Together with China and India, Indonesia was one of the only three Asian countries recording positive growth. Its economy grew at 4 per cent in the year to June 2009, displaying a more resilient response than some of its neighbours (Resosudarmo & Yusuf, 2009: 287). Although there was a mild decline in economic growth compared to the preceding seven years, this decline was lower than the global average (Hill, 2009: 5) and that of Indonesia's neighbours, including Malaysia, Singapore and Thailand which are much more export-oriented than Indonesia, since Indonesia's exports to GDP ratio is only 17 per cent (Resosudarmo & Yusuf, 2009: 289). Indonesia's economic performance during the GFC has also been much better than during the Asian financial crisis (Kuncoro, Widodo & McLeod, 2009: 151).

There are three reasons why Indonesia's vulnerability to the transmission of the GFC was less than that of its East Asian neighbours. First, its relatively low share of manufactures in its total exports; second, the relatively low share of inter-regional trade in total trade; and third, the relatively low degree of 'export-led' growth.

Compared to its Southeast Asian neighbours, the share of Indonesia's manufactured exports of its total exports was during the period 2005–06 rather low, only 12.5 per cent of its GDP, compared to Singapore's 156.8 per cent, Malaysia's 75.4 per cent, the Philippines' 34.7 per cent, and Thailand's 47.7 per cent. On the other hand, Indonesia's share of primary exports of its total merchandise exports was the highest, 43.7 per cent as compared to Malaysia's 17.8 per cent, the Philippines' 7.3 per cent and Thailand's 11.7 per cent (Goldstein & Xie, 2009: 26).

The reason why Indonesia's relatively low dependence on manufactured exports made it less vulnerable to the GFC was that manufactured exports have much higher income elasticities than primary exports. Hence, the demand for manufactured exports falls sharply during recessions in the major export markets (Goldstein & Xie, 2009: 27), as was the case with Indonesia's Southeast Asian neighbours.

A second reason why Indonesia was not as hard hit by the GFC as were the other Southeast Asian countries was the fact that it had not participated in a major way in the regional product fragmentation trade, the cross-border dispersion of parts and components production within vertically integrated production processes. This product fragmentation has been the outcome of the rapid expansion of the involvement of transnational corporations (TNCs) in the world economy. In East Asia it has been Japanese TNCs which have been largely involved in the regional fragmentation trade (Athukorala, 2007: 72, 88).

The low involvement of Indonesia in the regional product fragmentation trade is reflected by the fact that in 2003 the share of parts and components, including auto parts and electronic components, in Indonesia's manufactured exports was only 18.5 per cent, while that of Malaysia, the Philippines, Singapore and Thailand were respectively 55.7 per cent, 63.1 per cent, 49.2 per cent and 32.5 per cent (Athukorala, 2007: 82–83). The major reason for Indonesia's poor performance was its ambiguous attitude towards foreign direct investment (FDI) which made it a relatively unattractive place to invest for foreign investors.

However, when the GFC struck, Malaysia, the Philippines, Singapore and Thailand were much harder hit than Indonesia which was less export-oriented than these four former countries. In a sense, Indonesia's better performance during the GFC was to some extent more by default than by design.

A third reason why Indonesia was not as vulnerable to the transmission of the GFC was that Indonesia's economic growth was not as export-led as its Southeast Asian neighbours. First of all, Indonesia's *net* exports as a percentage of GDP in 2006 was only 9.6 per cent as compared to Malaysia's 13.1 per cent, Singapore's 20.4 per cent and Thailand's 15.4 per cent. For this reason the share of Indonesia's net exports' contribution to growth, that is its net exports to average GDP growth during 2000–2008, was only 7.7 as compared to the Philippines' 20, Singapore's 27.3 and Thailand's 10.4 (Goldstein and Xie (2009: 29). In other words, the contributions of domestic expenditures, including consumption (both private and government) and investment to growth were larger than Indonesia's Southeast Asian neighbours.

From the point of view of financial integration, a fourth reason why Indonesia was less vulnerable to the transmission of the GFC was that it benefited from not increasing its exposure (relative to its GDP) to banks in the U.S., E.U. and Japan in the decade preceding the GFC. Instead, it had relied more, although not too successfully, on relatively more stable FDI inflows, and from having avoided large credit exposures to sub-prime loans and securities originating in the U.S. (Goldstein and Xie, 2009: 38).

Fiscal stimulus measures, including tax cuts, skillful monetary policy, and direct cash transfers to the poor have also significantly contributed to softening the adverse impact of the crisis. The parliamentary elections in April 2009 and the presidential elections in July 2009 provided a further economic stimulus. Election-related spending by parliamentary candidates to the voters also contributed to household incomes, particularly of the poor. The stimulus measures helped maintain employment in the formal sector and the proportion of casual workers in the labour force (Resosudarmo & Yusuf, 2009: 287).

However, Indonesia's economic slowdown may last a little longer than people expect. The reason is the slowdown in the world, particularly the U.S., the E.U., and Japan, which used to be the main drivers of world economic growth. With the global economy in recession, global trade and and capital have naturally declined, hence causing emerging markets, including Indonesia, to scramble to attract any form of capital (Hill, 2009: 8). In contrast, in 1998 the world economy, including the U.S. economy, was growing strongly, enabling the crisis-affected countries, except Indonesia, to recover relatively quickly.

## PROSPECTS FOR A RESUMPTION OF RAPID AND SUSTAINABLE GROWTH

Despite the fact that Indonesia's economic performance during the GFC has been better than its Southeast Asian neighbours, this is no reason for complacency. It was argued above that this better performance has to some extent been more by default than by design, since Indonesia is less export-oriented than its Southeast Asian neighbours.

A worrisome feature of Indonesia's growth after the Asian economic crisis is that the non-tradable sectors have been growing more rapidly than the tradable sectors. Among the tradable sectors, the performance of the manufacturing sector has in particular been disappointing. Whereas during the Soeharto era, the manufacturing sector had been growing at double digit rates, after the Asian economic crisis the manufacturing sector has only been growing at low, single digit rates. For instance, in late June 2009 the year-on-year growth (at 2000 prices) of the manufacturing sector was only 1.5 per cent, with the non-oil and gas manufacturing subsector only growing at 1.8 per cent (Resosudarmo & Yusuf, 2008: 293).

Manufacturing growth, fueled by manufactured exports, has been particularly important after the end of the oil boom era in 1982, when the manufacturing sector since the late 1980s not only emerged as the largest source of export revenues, but also as the major engine of growth. When in the late 1980s low-skill, labour-intensive industries were established by foreign and domestic investors, the manufacturing sector also generated considerable manufacturing employment. Hence, a resumption of rapid growth of the manufacturing sector, including labour-intensive industries, is essential to fuelling rapid economic growth and generating employment and reducing poverty, as China's experience has shown.

With growth estimated to have grown by 4.5 per cent in 2009 (World Bank, 2009c: 10), Indonesia faces the possibility that it will only be able to achieve a respectable growth of 6 per cent plus, and at best 7 per cent, in the coming years, slightly less than which it recorded during the Soeharto era. Since the manufacturing sector, fuelled by manufactured exports, emerged as the major engine of growth after the end of the oil boom in the early 1980s, the sluggish growth of manufactured exports in recent years is worrisome. The reasons for this sluggish growth are the diminished prospects for labour-intensive manufactured exports, lack of progress in developing skill-intensive manufactured exports, and the great reliance on natural resource-intensive sectors (Coxhead & Li, 2008: 233). In fact, while the growth of manufactured exports, with a few exceptions, have been sluggish, its primary exports, including palm oil and coal, have been growing rapidly, at least until the onset of the GFC. As a result, primary exports has again emerged as an important source of export revenues, just as it was during the Dutch colonial period. However, relying mainly on commodity exports exposes the economy to the vicissitudes of the world economy and the adverse effects of the 'Dutch disease'.

A more serious aspect of relying too much on Indonesia's natural resource base for export revenues is that it deflects the attention of policy-makers from focusing their attention and efforts on building an internationally competitive manufacturing sector. As argued earlier, efforts to promote export-oriented industries were only made after the end of the oil boom era in 1982. It is not surprising that the resource-poor Northeast Asian countries, including Japan, South Korea and Taiwan, were able to develop a highly efficient, internationally competitive manufacturing sector because this was the only sector which could generate the needed foreign exchange revenues.

An even more serious aspect is that resource exploitation, which generates resource rents, has led to a proliferation of rent-seeking activities, not only during the Soeharto era, but also in the present. Although corruption takes place all over the world, it is not a surprise that the vast resource rents generated by resource exploitation, which were not adequately captured in resource rent taxes for the Indonesian state but diverted into the pockets of government officials and their business cronies, has contributed significantly to making Indonesia one of the most corrupt countries in the Asia-Pacific region.

In the late 1960s and early 1970s there were the considerable oil rents which were diverted from the Ministry of Finance to finance the operations, several of them of dubious economic value, of the state-owned oil company Pertamina. Since the mid-1970s unsound forestry policies have generated considerable forest rents, which was accomplished by undercharging the private loggers for the concessions and royalties in return for their financing of several development projects, some of which of dubious economic value, prioritised by President Soeharto (Ascher, 1998: 38).

Unfortunately, the continued over-exploitation of Indonesia's precious tropical hardwood forests has continued unabated up to the present because of weak governance. Because of this Indonesia is facing a major problem of suffering major losses from the adverse effects of climate change. Deforestation, peatland degradation, and forest fires have put Indonesia among the top three emitters of greenhouse gasses in the world after China and the U.S.. Emissions from deforestation and forest fires are five times those from non-forestry emissions (World Bank, 2007: 1).

While deforestation and forest fires already happened in the Soeharto era, particularly since the early 1990s, which adversely affected the health of the population on the islands of Sumatra and Kalimantan and neighbouring countries, particularly Malaysia and Singapore, they have arguably become worse in recent years as forests have been felled to make way for oil palm plantations which have expanded all over Indonesia.

However, Indonesia will experience significant losses because of climate change. Being an archipelago, Indonesia is very vulnerable to the adverse impacts of climate change. Prolonged droughts, increased frequency in extreme weather events, and heavy rainfall leading to big floods, are some of the glaring examples of climate change. This may lead to harmful effects on agriculture, fishery and forestry, resulting in serious threats to food security and livelihoods (World Bank, 2007: 1).

At the United Nations-sponsored Conference on Climate Change in Copenhagen in December 2009, Indonesia has committed itself to reduce its green house gas emissions by 26 per cent by 2020, and even by 41 per cent if it receives international aid. One important step to reduce its emissions from deforestation will be the moratorium on the expansion of oil palm plantations, and closely monitoring the operations of logging companies lest they fell trees in protected forests.

To strengthen its natural resource sector, Indonesia should endeavour to establish its own, but *efficient* resource-processing industries, if necessary with foreign investors. For instance, instead of exporting crude oil only, Indonesia should establish more and efficient oil refineries, so that it would not have to rely on imports of refined oil from Singapore.

While boosting the labour-intensive industries is crucial to Indonesia because it can still draw on a large labour surplus in the rural areas, developing skill-intensive industries in line with the growth of a skilled labour force is essential to sustain rapid industrial and economic growth. To this end, a top priority should be given to train a skilled labour force, including managers, engineers, technicians, and shop floor workers. The industrial and technological upgrading of the manufacturing sector also crucially depends on attracting new foreign direct investment (FDI). However, to achieve this, the government needs to make a much greater effort to improve the investment climate which, despite some efforts of the government, is still relatively unattractive compared to the other Southeast Asian countries.

With the global economy expected to grow sluggishly in the next few years, it would be imprudent for the manufacturing sector to rely mainly on manufactured exports. With rising per capita incomes, there would also be a significant domestic market for Indonesia's manufacturing industries. To ensure that their products are accessible to Indonesia's consumers, the manufacturing industries should endeavour to produce high quality products at the lowest cost possible which should be easily accessible to Indonesia's consumers all over Indonesia by better logistics, including more efficient container terminals and a more efficient inter-island shipping industry. Hence, in deciding on an appropriate industrial strategy, it is not merely a matter of choosing between export-oriented versus import-substituting industrialization, but ensuring *efficient* industrialisation, that is efficient export-oriented as well as efficient import-substituting industrialization. This implies that excessive import protection and export subsidies should be eschewed which will not only cost the country dear, but perpetuate inefficiencies in the manufacturing sector.

Tackling the dilapidated physical infrastructure is crucial to attracting more FDI, besides simplifying the still cumbersome administrative requirements, strengthening legal certainty and proper law enforcement, and making the rigid labour market more flexible. While during the Soeharto era considerable investment took place in the rehabilitation and expansion of physical infrastructure, including roads, bridges, harbours, electricity, communications, and irrigation networks, after the Asian financial crisis investment in infrastructure has lagged. In fact, Indonesia's investment-to-GDP ratio is currently lower than in its East Asian neighbours (OECD, 2008: 42). As a result, physical infrastructure has been crumbling at an alarming rate, and is one of the major impediments to attracting more domestic and foreign direct investment to Indonesia.

To the extent that the prospects for the product fragmentation trade are still good once the global economy recovers, it would be indeed be imperative for Indonesia to improve its investment climate for foreign investors. In fact, it were these foreign investors who established the supporting industries producing auto parts, electronic components and components for the electrical goods industries in Malaysia, the Philippines, Singapore and Thailand. In fact, one of the weak links in Indonesia's industrial structure that it has not been successful in the past decades to establish a broad and strong layer of supporting industries.

The steady appreciation of the rupiah *vis-a-vis* the U.S. dollar since April 2009 was mainly the result of Indonesia's strong trade balance due to a relatively good performance of the non-oil and gas exports (Resosudarmo & Yusuf, 2009: 299). However, a strong U.S. recovery and rebounding of the U.S. dollar against a basket of currrencies could exert renewed pressure on the *rupiah*/U.S. dollar exchange rate, which has been following the broader strengthening and weakening of the U.S. dollar very closely since the onset of the GFC (World Bank, 2009b: 8). Since the swings in the external value of the *rupiah* adversely affects the competitiveness of Indonesia's exports, including its manufactured exports, Bank Indonesia has been at pains to keep the real effective exchange rate at a competitive level by keeping inflation under control.

To realise its potential to rise further into the ranks of dynamic, middle-income economies, Indonesia can, just like India, benefit from a 'demographic dividend'. The reason is that with declining fertility rates and with the fraction of elderly persons yet to rise sharply, Indonesia has still a relatively young population. This implies that the working age population is still increasing relative to the rest of the population (World Bank, 2009c: 29).

In conclusion, one can state that Indonesia's challenge in the foreseeable future how to guard itself against future external shocks. The recurrence of internal shocks is unlikely, since sound macroeconomic policies have been firmly in place since the beginning of the Soeharto era up to the present. However, guarding against external shocks is much more difficult since Indonesia is now firmly embedded within the global economy with all its advantages, but also its risks of being affected by adverse external shocks, including the recent GFC. To guard against a recurrence of such an external shock, Indonesia by virtue of its membership in the G20 countries could help formulate the policies required to strengthen regulations to monitor and better regulate the financial institutions which were responsible for the GFC and the policies required to further liberalise international trade by reviving the stalled Doha Round and eschew beggar-thy-neighbour protectionist policies which would aggravate the global economic crisis.

## A FINAL, SPECULATIVE COMPARATIVE, LONG-TERM PERSPECTIVE

Despite its emergence as the third-largest democracy in the world after India and the U.S., its steady economic progress and inclusion in the G-20 biggest economies, Indonesia is still beset with doubts about its ability to achieve its national objective of becoming an economically strong, modern, and technology advanced country by 2030, if not 2025. This is, for instance, reflected in the grave concerns about the adverse effects of the ASEAN-China Free Trade Agreement which went into effect since 1 January 2010.

To achieve its national objective, Indonesia should put its own house in order: establish or strengthen its institutions, remove the sources of lucrative, rent-seeking activities and corrosive corruption, and address its structural weaknesses, such as its weakness in formulating and implementing sound policies, its poor investment climate, its dilapidated physical infrastructure, its uncompetitive manufacturing industries, and its failure in developing strong, highly skilled and highly motivated human resources.

If these goals are not achieved, Indonesia could well become 'a country with enormous potential which would always remain a country with enormous potential'. It could become a country like Argentina, which at the beginning of the 20th century was one of the two richest countries in the world besides Australia according to a book by Tim Duncan and John Fogarty: '*Australia and Argentina: on Parallel Paths*' While Australia, a resource-rich country, forged ahead, though not spectacularly, during the 20th century and by the early 21st century had remained one of the most prosperous countries in the world, Argentina, another resource-rich country, has up to the present remained 'an emerging economy' with a per capita income of about one-sixth of that of Australia when it persisted in continuing its protectionist, inefficient import-substituting industrialisation. It is up to us, the Indonesian government and the Indonesian people, whether by 2025 or 2030 we will be more like Australia rather than Argentina!

## Note

1.   Paper presented at the JBIC-LPEM Workshop on Strategies for Asia's Sustainable

Growth beyond the Global Crisis: Infrastructure, Environment and Finance, Jakarta, 15 February 2010.

## References

Ascher, William. "From Oil to Timber: The Political Economy of Off-Budget Development Financing in Indonesia". *INDONESIA* Vol. 65, April (1998): 37–62.

Athukorala, Prema-chandra. *Multinational Enterprises in Asian Development*. Edward Elgar: Cheltenham, UK, 2007.

Coxhead, Ian & Muqun Li. "Prospects for Skills-Based Export Growth in a Labour-Abundant, Resource-Rich Developing Country". *Bulletin of Indonesian Economic Studies* 44, No. 2, 2008: 199–228.

Dick, Howard, et al. *The Emergence of a National Economy: An economic history of Indonesia, 1800–2000*. Sydney: Allen & Unwin, 2002.

Goldstein, Morris and Daniel Xie. "The Impact of the Financial Crisis on Emerging Asia". Working Paper no. 09-11, Washington, D.C.: The Peterson Institute for International Economics, October 2009.

Hill, Hal. *The Indonesian Economy Since 1966*. Cambridge: Cambridge University Press, 1996.

———. "Indonesia's Three Crises: origins, impact and response". Paper presented at the seminar on The Indonesian Economy in International Perspective, Asian Development Bank, Manila, 3 May 2009.

International Monetary Fund (IMF). *The IMF and the Recent Capital Account Crisis: Indonesia, Korea, Brazil*. Independent Evaluation Office, Washington, D.C.: International Monetary Fund, 2003.

Kuncoro, Mudradjad; Tri Widodo and Ross H. McLeod. "Survey of Recent Developments". *Bulletin of Indonesian Economic Studies* 45, no. 2 (2009): 151–76.

McCawley, Peter. "Survey of Recent Developments". *Bulletin of Indonesian Economic Studies* 19, no. 1 (1983): 1–31.

Organization for Economic Co-operation and Development (OECD). *Indonesia — Economic Assessment*, OECD Economic Surveys, Volume 2008/17, Paris, July 2008.

Pangestu, Mari. *Economic Reform, Deregulation and Privatisation: The Indonesian Experience*. Jakarta: Centre for Strategic and International Studies, 1996.

Patunru, Arianto A. and Erna Zetha. "Crisis, Recovery, and Policy Response: The Case of Indonesia". Paper presented at the International Conference on the East Asian Economies: Crisis, Recovery, and Policy Response, Beijing, 22–23 October 2009.

Resosudarmo, Budy P. and Arief A. Yusuf. "Survey of Recent Developments". *Bulletin of Indonesian Economic Studies* 45, no. 3 (2009): 287–315.

Sadli, Mohammad. "The Indonesian Crisis". In *Southeast Asia's Economic Crisis:*

*Origins, Lessons and the Way Forward,* edited by H. Arndt and Hal Hill. Singapore: Institute of Southeast Asian Studies, 1999.

Thee, Kian Wie. The Indonesian Economic Crisis and the Long Road to Recovery, *Australian Economic History Review* 43, no. 3 (2003): 183–96.

———. "The Impact of the Two Oil Booms of the 1970s and the Post-Oil Boom Shock of the Eartly 1980s on the Indonesian Economy". In *Proceedings of the Third Afrasian International Symposium — Resources Under Stress: Sustainability of the Local Community in Asia and Africa,* edited by Yoshio Kawamura, et al. Kyoto: Afrasian Centre for Peace and Development Studies, Ryukoku University, 2008.

———. "Indonesia's Two Deep Economic Crises: the mid-1960s and late 1990s". *Journal of the Asia-Pacific Economy* 14, no. 1 (2009): 49–60.

World Bank. *Indonesia — Strategy for Growth and Structural Change.* Report no. 7758-IND, Washington, D.C., 3 May 1989.

———. *Indonesia: Sustaining High Growth with Equity.* Report no. 16433-IND, Washington, D.C., May 1997.

———. *Indonesia in Crisis: a Macroeconomic Update.* Washington, D.C., 6 July 1998.

———. *Making the New Indonesia Work for the Poor — Overview.* The World Bank Jakarta Office, Jakarta, November 2006.

———. *Executive Summary: Indonesia and Climate Change: Current Status and Policies.* Washington, D.C., July 2007.

———. *Battling the Forces of Global Recession — East Asia and Pacific Update.* Washington, D.C., April 2009a.

———. *Indonesia Economic Quarterly — Clearing Skies.* Washington, D.C. September 2009b.

———. *Indonesia Economic Quarterly — Back on Track?* Washington, D.C., December 2009c.

# 8

# INDONESIA AND THE BRICS[1]

The Indonesian economy managed to achieve solid growth after successfully weathering the Global Financial Crisis (GFC) in 2008. The economy grew at 4.5 per cent in 2009, and is likely to grow at 6.0 per cent in 2010 and 6.2 per cent in 2011. This kind of performance is making many Indonesians wonder whether Indonesia could soon join the BRIC group.

The term 'BRIC' was coined by in 2001, by Jim O'Neill of Goldman Sachs, to refer to Brazil, Russia, India and China, which were experiencing such rapid economic growth they were expected to overtake the U.S. by 2018. Since then, the term has come to symbolize the shift in global power away from the G-7 advanced economies (U.S., Japan, Germany, France, UK, Italy and Canada) toward the four BRIC economies.

IMF figures (below) show that over the period 2014–2030 the BRICs will grow so fast that their share of the world economy will increase from 19.4 per cent to 30.3 per cent, exceeding the economies of the U.S., the E.U. and Japan. In 2010, China overtook Japan as the second-largest economy in the world after the U.S., but with a projected 2030 GDP at 94 per cent of that of America, China's economy will not be far behind the U.S.

Indonesia still has a long way to go before it will be able to match the BRICs' economic size. In 2010 Indonesia's GDP only accounted for about one third of India's GDP, and will likely remain so in 2030.

Is the 'BRIC' grouping still relevant?

Since 2001, much has changed. For instance, Russia's low growth, pervasive corruption, and inability to diversify its economy away from its over-dependence on oil and gas exports, may mean that it can no longer be considered a BRIC economy.

And despite the fact that in 2007 the Indian economy was less than one half of that of Russia, by 2030 the Indian economy will be almost as large as Russia's because of its much higher growth rates. Thus, BRIC's relevance must be in doubt. If Indonesia maintains its rapid growth, the term 'BIIC' (Brazil, India, Indonesia, China) may be a more appropriate substitute.

Will Indonesia's rapid growth continue?

Collectively, the G-20 economies account for about 85 per cent of global Gross National Product (GNP). The G-20 group has grown in stature since the Washington summit in 2008 and the more recent G-20 summit in Seoul, Korea, in November 2010, and will therefore replace the G-8 countries (US, Japan, Germany, France, UK, Italy, Canada and Russia) as the main economic council of the 20 major economies in the world. As a member of the G-20, Indonesia is already reckoned as one of the 20 major economies in the world.

Indonesia weathered the Global Financial Crisis of 2008 well, with real GDP growth in 2009 the third-highest in the G-20 after China and India. The Indonesian economy is estimated to grow at around 6 per cent or slightly more in 2010 and 2011, due to its sound macroeconomic policies and economic resilience in the face of external shocks.

These two facts suggest that Indonesia will continue to grow relatively rapidly. Indonesia needs to address two development challenges if it aspires to this fast pace of faster.

First, Indonesia needs to invest much more in rebuilding its crumbling infrastructure, which is a serious impediment to faster growth. Increased investment in expanding and improving the quality of its health services and of its education at all levels, particularly in secondary and higher education will be a further aid to growth.

Indonesia must also improve its governance and institutions, particularly its bureaucracy and legal and judicial system. At present, Indonesia is one of the most corrupt countries in East Asia. Indonesia should needs to root out corruption, as a country with pervasive corruption cannot hope to become a dynamic and prosperous country.

Provided Indonesia tackles the issues of corruption and infrastructure, Indonesia will be the next 'BRIC' nation. And this will transform the group of BRIC into a more internationally influential 'BIIC.'

## Note

1    "Indonesia and the BRICs", by Thee Kian Wie, first published online at East Asia Forum <http://www.eastasiaforum.org/2010/12/12/indonesia-and-the-brics/>, Bureau of East Asian Economic Research, ANU College for Asia and the Pacific, School of Economics and Government, December 2010.

# PART IV
## INDUSTRIAL DEVELOPMENT

# 9

## INDONESIA'S INDUSTRIAL POLICIES AND DEVELOPMENT SINCE INDEPENDENCE[1]

### INTRODUCTION

Like in most other, newly independent countries, the leaders of newly-independent Indonesia considered industrialization as the best way to achieve a more balanced economy by lessening the country's dependence on agriculture and develop their country more rapidly. To this end, the then Minister of Trade and Industry, Professor Sumitro Djojohadikusumo, in 1951 introduced the Economic Urgency Plan (*Rencana Urgensi Perekonomian*) for a period of three years. Since this Plan focused on industrial development as the major engine of growth, the Plan was also referred to as the Industrial Urgency Plan.

Indonesia's post-independence industrialization did not start from scratch, but had already started in the late nineteenth century when Indonesia was still the Netherlands Indies. By 1900 a modern manufacturing sector had been set up, largely based in Java which was based upon the processing of primary commodities, both agricultural crops (particularly sugar) and raw materials (especially oil), associated with a large metals and machinery industry, supplemented by utilities and a modest range of light consumer goods and construction materials. During that period Java stood out within Southeast Asia as the area in which steam power was applied most intensively in the late nineteenth century (Dick, 1993: 123). However, because of the small domestic market and an open trade regime, which benefited the manufacturing industries in the Netherlands, particularly its textile industry, rather than the industries in the Netherlands Indies, the further development of a modern manufacturing sector in Indonesia was severely hampered (Dick, 1993: 138).

Another stimulus to industrial development took place in the 1920s. This incipient industrial development took mainly the form of engineering workshops for the large Dutch- and other Western-owned estates, mostly the sugar estates in Central and Eastern Java and the oil palm and rubber estates in Sumatra (Soehoed, 1967: 66). A third stimulus took place when the world economic depression of the early 1930s hit the Netherlands Indies very hard, particularly since the Netherlands Indies, just like The Netherlands, chose to stick with the gold standard, and only devalued the guilder in 1936. To cope with the crisis and stem cheap Japanese imports which flooded into the country, the Netherlands Indies government embarked on an import-substituting pattern of industrialization on densely-populated Java which provided strong protection against imports, particularly from Japan.

Because of its open-door policy to foreign direct investment, several foreign transnational companies (TNCs), such as Good Year (tyres), Unilever (soap, cooking oil and margarine), Eveready and National Carbon (flashlight and dry batteries), Bata (shoes) and large Dutch companies, such as Lindeteves (paint and varnish), Borsumij (bicycle assembling) as well as some small indigenous Indonesian companies, established plants in Java and to a lesser extent in Sumatra. A large consortium of about 50 Dutch companies also established a large textile plant, the Java Textile Company, in Tegal, Central Java, and a paper mill at Leces, East Java, in 1939 (Soehoed, 1967: 67).

After Indonesia's independence was achieved, the Indonesian government launched several development plans which included industrial development. Despite the launch of the Economic Urgency Plan, which focused on industrial development, for the period 1951–55, not much new industrial development took place during this period (Soehoed, 1967: 68). The main reason for this poor performance was that political turmoil and sharp political conflicts hampered the successive development plans from being realized. Hence, by the mid-1960s the industrial topography of Indonesia was like it was during the waning years of the Netherlands Indies in 1940. It was only after the advent of Soeharto's New Order regime in 1966 that industrial development really took off, as domestic and foreign investors, encouraged by a favourable investment climate, made large investments in the manufacturing sector.

In the following pages a more detailed account will be given of Indonesia's industrial development since the early years of independence up to the present.

## INDUSTRIAL DEVELOPMENT DURING THE EARLY
## INDEPENDENCE PERIOD, 1950–65

### a. Industrial policy during the early independence period

When Indonesia in 1950 was able to achieve effective sovereignty over its whole territory (with the notable exception of the disputed territory of West New Guinea (now consisting of the Papua and West Papua provinces) after a long armed struggle against the Dutch who wanted to reoccupy Indonesia, the Indonesian government was finally able to design a reconstruction and development plan for Indonesia. Like in many other, newly-independent nations, a high priority was put on industrialization to reduce the country's high dependence on agriculture and achieve a more balanced structure of the economy.

A few leaders, notably Sjafruddin Prawiranegara, the first Indonesian Governor of Bank Indonesia, the country's Central Bank, put a higher priority on developing agriculture first. Sjafruddin argued that manufacturing should be based on agriculture and on Indonesia's vast natural resources. This sequence was important since industralization would be not be easy if the agricultural sector was backward. Moreover, Indonesians would have first to be educated in technology and management before rushing into forced industrialization (Sjafruddin, 1987).

However, most of Indonesia's leaders shared Sumitro's view that Indonesia's economic development would require industrialization. To this end, Sumitro Djojohadikusomo, the Minister of Trade and Industry, in early 1950 introduced an Economic Urgency Plan (*Rencana Urgensi Perekonomian*) for three years, which was later extended to five years (1951–55). This plan focused on the rehabilitation of the productive apparatus, which had been destroyed during the Japanese occupation and the subsequent armed struggle against the Dutch army which wanted to reoccupy Indonesia, and the development of a modern manufacturing sector which was viewed as the engine of economic growth. For this reason the Economic Urgency Plan was sometimes referred to as Industrial Urgency Plan (*Rencana Urgensi Perindustrian*) (Siahaan, 1996: 190).

To design this Plan, a Committee for Industrialization (*Panitya Industrialisasi*) was appointed in March 1951 which submitted its report in August 1951. To design this Plan, the Committee members studied the papers and reports of Dutch officials and economists on the prewar industrialization of the Netherlands Indies and the Dutch plans for the postwar reconstruction, including the industrial development of the country, as well as Indonesia's earlier plans, as guidelines to design the plan.

The Plan's main objectives were:

1. To endeavour that Indonesia's economic activities would as far as possible be in the hands of the government, without neglecting the private sector;
2. To raise Indonesia's national income and achieve a more balanced economy;
3. The development and guidance of the manufacturing sector would be limited to small and medium-scale industries, while the development of large-scale industries would be done on a selective basis, with a view to stimulate the development of backward regions;
4. All industrial enterprises considered as 'key industries' would be government enterprises (Siahaan, 1996: 190–91).

The above stated objectives of the Plan reflected the prevailing views and ideology of Indonesia's policymakers which to a lesser or greater extent still persist up to the present. For instance, while the private sector is increasingly recognized as a dynamic and crucial player in Indonesia's economic development, many policymakers, politicians and influential segments of the population still harbour a suspicion of the private sector, a legacy from the Dutch colonial era. Instead, they emphasize the need for government ownership and control of the 'commanding heights of the economy', particularly the 'key industries', such as the basic industries, considered to be of strategic importance, including the defense-related industries.

In view of the wide gap between the modern, large-scale industries, which during the Dutch colonial era and postcolonial era dominated the Indonesian economy, including the manufacturing sector, and the more backward small and medium-scale industries (SMIs) on the other hand, there is a strong preference on the part of policymakers to favour the SMIs by providing them with preferential treatment, such as preferential access to subsidized credit. This view was underpinned by the fact that during the Dutch colonial era the modern, large-scale (assembling) industries were mostly owned and run by the Dutch and other Western transnational corporations (TNCs), such as Unilever, British-American Tobacco (BAT), Good Year, Heineken Beer, and Bata Shoes, and to a smaller extent by ethnic Chinese. On the other hand, the SMIs, particularly the SIs, were and still are largely owned and operated by indigenous Indonesian businessmen.

To achieve the above Plan objectives, industries had to be established which would lessen Indonesia's dependence on foreign products and thus save foreign exchange, for instance by establishing those industries which would process Indonesia's raw materials. To promote the cottage and small industries, they would be provided with cheap credit, while an Industrial Centre would provide them with extension services (Siahaan, 1996: 191).

During the Plan period a few industrial plants were built, including a few printing presses, a cement plant (which was built as a 'turn-key project' by an American company), a spinning plant which was completed in 1956, and four rubber remilling plants (Siahaan, 1996: 195–200). Despite the construction of these plants, in general the implementation of these plants was spotty. In appraising the progress of the large-scale industry programme, Sumitro, who had initiated the Plan, stressed bad organisation, incompetent management, cumbersome government administration and financial regulations, and lack of technical experts as the reasons for the lack of progress (Higgins, 1957: 75). The disappointing results of the Economic Urgency Plan, and growing concern about inflationary pressures caused by large development expenditures, led to the scrapping of the plan in 1956. To replace the Plan, a new development plan, Indonesia's First Five Year Development Plan for 1956–60, was prepared by the State Planning Bureau (Anspach, 1969: 163).

The Plan was a modest plan, and largely contained projections of what the various ministries were already doing. But even this plan was not fulfilled. In 1959 the National Planning Bureau issued a progress report on the Plan which attributed the lack of progress to the conflict with the Netherlands about the status of West Irian (which had subsequently led to the take-over and nationalization of all Dutch enterprises), the regional rebellions in West Sumatra and North Sulawesi, continuing budget deficits and the consequent rising inflation. By the end of 1958 only 42 of the planned 92 industrial projects had been completed, while 30 had not even been started (Higgins, 1968: 697).

As a result, the First Five Year Development Plan suffered the same fate as the Economic Urgency Plan. The Draft Plan submitted to the Parliament in 1956 was only approved in 1958 (Siahaan, 1996: 286). Although some of the planned projects were continued, the entire budgetary process fell into disarray, and the Five Year Plan had become largely irrelevant by 1958 (Mackie, 1971: 50).

When President Sukarno, vested with expanded executive power after the reintroduction of the 1945 Constitution, in 1959 introduced 'Guided Democracy and Guided Economy', he appointed a new National Planning

Council. This Council, which was a political rather than a technical body, was assigned to draw up a new plan, the Eight Year Overall Development Plan, appropriate to the new era of 'Indonesian-style socialism'. The Plan was manifestly unworkable, since it was based on unrealistic assumptions about government expenditures and inflation (Mackie, 1971: 52).

The Eight-Year Plan was a 'project plan' which contained projects proposed by the various ministries, including many of the unfulfilled projects of the old Five-Year Plan. The largest part of the proposed development budget was allocated to production, including 88 industrial projects (Higgins, 1968: 700).

However, by the early 1960s political developments, particularly the military West Irian campaign and the subsequent military campaign to 'crush' the newly-established Malaysian federation and the vast expenditures required to wage these campaigns, led to a new spurt of inflation in 1962–1963. These vast military expenditures and an austerity budget in 1963 had doomed the Plan to irrelevance, just like the preceding Five Year Plan (Mackie, 1971: 53).

## b. Industrial development during the early independence period

The above overview of Indonesia's industrial policies during the early independence period of the 1950s and early 1960s, as reflected in three successive plans, shows that the expected rapid industrial development of the country had not materialized. This disappointing performance was the outcome of several factors, including the lack of technical experts, incompetent management and organization, cumbersome government and financial regulations, and particularly the bitter political conflicts and regional rebellions which diverted policymakers from focusing their attention on economic issues.

Although the Netherlands Indies' government in the 1930s had launched a limited degree of import-substituting, protectionist pattern of industrialization to protect the Indonesian market against cheap Japanese imports (Dick, 2002: 160) which had flooded into the country, Indonesia after independence was still largely an agrarian economy. In fact, Indonesia's manufacturing sector was one of the weakest and least developed sectors sectors of the economy. It was estimated that in the 1950s the manufacturing sector only accounted for around 8–10 per cent of net national product, while the agricultural sector accounted for about 56 per cent (Paauw, 1963: 176–77). This estimate may have been an underestimate since much of handicraft production, which was largely produced by cottage industries, was either excluded or included in the contribution of small-scale agriculture (Paauw: 1963: 177).

Although in the early 1950s some new industries were established, more industries either stagnated, declined or just closed. This worrisome development was caused by several problems faced by several industries, including lack of safety, labour relations, lack of capital, lack of skilled personnel, lack of raw material, adequate water supply and electricity (Burger, 1975: 185). The shortage of raw materials and other imported inputs could not be solved because of the shortage of foreign exchange. The greatest difficulties were experienced by the small-scale industries because of their great shortage of capital and less efficient production methods (Burger, 1975: 185).

Promoting small-scale industry was considered more important than investments in large-scale industry which during the early 1950s was mostly foreign-owned, that is Dutch-owned or owned by ethnic Chinese who, while many of them were Indonesian citizens, were at the time still considered to be foreigners.

To improve the performance of small-scale industry, which by its nature was labour-intensive, the Indonesian government in the 1950s promoted a simple mechanization programme which had already been initiated by the Netherlands Indies' government in the 1930s. This mechanization program was implemented through a Loan and Mechanisation Programme which involved the lending of simple equipment to cottage and small industries on easy repayment terms (Mackie, 1971: 47; Dick, 2002: 177). In addition, industrial centres (Induk) were set up to provide credit, technical assistance, and marketing outlets to cottage industries, such as woodworking, ironworking, bronze, ceramics, textiles, leather, and umbrellas (Higgins, 1957: 68–69; Dick, 2002: 177). However, there were only a few of these centres, as reflected by the fact that in 1954 only eight of these centres were operating. These centres were also dispersed over various regions, and often so poorly managed that they were not effective in raising the welfare of the people (Dick, 2002: 177).

The planned development of large-scale industry progressed relatively better than that for small-scale industries. The few large-scale industries which were built were, like in most other developing countries embarking on industrialization, import-substituting industries. Some of these large-scale industries had already been planned during the waning days of the Netherlands Indies, when the Dutch colonial government had embarked on a 'crash program' of industrialization. These large-scale industries included rubber remilling, cotton spinning, cement, caustic soda and coconut flour. These industries were mainly established with government funds, for which the Indonesian government had allocated Rp. 160 million in 1952/53 alone. This amount was much larger than the much smaller amount of Rp. 30 million allocated for the establishment of small-scale industries and the Industrial Centres intended to assist these small-scale industries (Dick, 2002: 177).

Besides the various, above-mentioned technical problems faced by the various industries, the unstable political conditions in the 1950s and President Sukarno's increasing preoccupation since the late 1950s with 'completing the national revolution' rather than with economic development, made it extremely difficult, if not impossible, to realise the planned ambitious industrial projects. As a result, only few industrial projects planned during the 1950s and early 1960s were actually built. The few large-scale industrial projects which were established during this period included the first fertilizer plant (PT Pusri) in Palembang, South Sumatra, and the first large cement plant in Gresik, East Java (PT Semen Gresik). However, a steel plant to be built with Russian aid faced many problems and could not be built (Soehoed, 1988).

In almost all industries production declined during the early 1960s, except in a few cases, such as paper mills and salt factories where the decline was slowed down through the use of domestic raw materials and auxiliary materials. The data in Table 1 below clearly show the decline in production of several manufactured products by the mid-1960s. This was mainly the result of rising hyperinflation (which had reached almost 600 per cent in

**TABLE 1**
**Production of Selected Manufactured Products, 1961–1965**

| Products | Unit | 1961 | 1962 | 1963 | 1964 | 1965 |
|---|---|---|---|---|---|---|
| 1. Paper | Ton | 8,281 | 10,448 | 11,033 | 11,388 | 11,124 |
| 2. Cement | Ton | 445,768 | 510,689 | 429,499 | 438,647 | 389,478 |
| 3. Glass | Ton | 11,950 | 14,073 | 11,807 | 6,996 | 9.024 |
| 4. Oxygen | Cubic metres | 2,193,552 | 2,170,000 | 2,117,572 | 2,177,573 | 2,132,467 |
| 5. Carbon dioxide | Ton | 950 | 886 | 671 | 641 | 621 |
| 6. Tyres | Pieces | | | | | |
| a. Outer cover | | 97,138 | 189,762 | 47,839 | 84,798 | 76,594 |
| b. Inner tube | | 110,675 | 115,333 | 90,280 | 63,205 | 46,874 |
| 7a. Fine salt | Ton | 444,661 | 255,613 | 448,942 | 53,000 | 252,426 |
| b. Granulated salt | Ton | 67,850 | 53,585 | 69,801 | 44,688 | — |
| 8. Soda | Ton | 4,810 | 3,230 | 2,029 | 2,142 | 2,631 |
| 9. Fertiliser | Ton | — | — | — | — | 94,120 |

*Source*: Bank Indonesia: Report for the years 1960–65, Jakarta, 1 May 1968, table 75, p. 219, based on data provided by Bappenas, the National Planning Board, Jakarta.

1965), which greatly affected all fields of production, particularly industrial production (Bank Indonesia, 1968: 212).

Despite the generally poor performance of the manufacturing sector during the late Sukarno era (1960–65), Soehoed, Minister of Industry during the period 1978–1983, argued that during this early period a concept was already developed of first setting up large-scale, capital-intensive, state-owned basic industries, which could make use of available natural resources, after which the downstream, assembling industries could be established (Soehoed, 1988). Moreover, the few industrial plants set up during this period gave Indonesian engineers, managers and plant workers valuable industrial skills and experience in operating modern plants. Hence, the new government of General Soeharto, which had replaced Sukarno's government in 1966, did not start from scratch when it launched its own industrial drive in the late 1960s (Thee, 2003a: 18).

## INDUSTRIAL DEVELOPMENT DURING SOEHARTO'S NEW ORDER ERA, 1966–1998

### a. Industrial policies during the Soeharto era

Indonesia's rapid industrial growth and transformation during the Soeharto era can be roughly divided into three sub-phases, with each one corresponding to differing policy emphases and shaped in part by external economic developments (Hill, 1994: 78–80).

The *first sub-phase* was the period of rapid industrial growth from 1967 to 1973 which was mainly driven by trade and investment liberalization to normal economic conditions. Five factors were mainly responsible for the rapid growth in manufacturing after 1967 (Anwar, 1980: 210). First, there was a large excess capacity in 1967 and 1968, so that it was possible to increase production rapidly with existing capacity, Second, the enactment of a new Foreign Investment Law in 1967 and a Domestic Investment Law in 1968 led to rapid rise in foreign and domestic investment in manufacturing. These investments were further encouraged by various investment incentives, including tax holidays, and the introduction of an open capital account which would enable foreign investors to transfer their profits and dividends freely to their headquarters overseas. Third, the ready availability of foreign exchange because of the rapid rise of oil, other minerals and timber and new foreign aid flows made it possible again to purchase imported inputs. Fourth, domestic demand for manufactured products rose rapidly, not only with accelerating economic growth, but also to catch up with the scarcities of consumer and producer goods that had developed in the early 1960s because of very low imports and low domestic industrial production. Fifth, industrial growth accelerated from 1968 onwards from a situation where manufacturing only played a minor role in the Indonesian economy and where the self-sufficiency ratios of various manufactured products were small. This made it possible for industrial output for the domestic market to rise more rapidly than domestic demand in view of the large scope for import-substituting industrialization (Anwar, 1980: 210). During this period there was a shake-out of some traditional labour-intensive and cottage industries, but the broad-based industrial expansion which had taken place more than compensated for their decline (Hill, 1994: 80).

Initially, foreign investors showed most interest in the extractive sectors (forestry and mining), but subsequently they invested a substantial proportion in manufacturing projects, particularly textiles, a labour-intensive industry, and basic metals, a capital-intensive industry. Domestic investment showed a similar interest in manufacturing projects, particularly in the labour-intensive textile industry (McCawley, 1981: 67).

However, since 1975 growth in some industries slowed down. For instance, output growth in the textile industry fell from around 20 per cent per annum in the late 1960s and early 1970s to an average of 10 per cent per annum over the period 1975–1978. In some industries (automobile assembly and electronics) capacity had become such a problem that the government was considering plans to limit new entry (McCawley, 1981: 67).

There are a few reasons for this slowdown. The first was the virtual bankruptcy of Pertamina, Indonesia's state-owned oil company, which in early 1975 was unable to repay a short-term loan from a small bank in Texas, and subsequently turned out to be unable to repay other short-term loans from other foreign banks. As a result, the government had to bail out Pertamina, which was forced to stop its huge investment programme in some large-scale industries, including a steel industry. Another reason was that Indonesia's tradable industries, including many manufacturing industries, were suffering from the adverse effects of the 'Dutch disease' caused by the oil boom. A third reason was that in several industries (textiles, electronics, motor vehicles) the phase of 'easy' import substitution had come to an end. A fourth factor was the tight monetary policy pursued by Bank Indonesia to restrain inflationary pressures caused by the oil boom (McCawley, 1981: 67).

The *second sub-phase*, spanning roughly the period 1974–1981, was characterized by the impact of the two oil booms (1973/74 and 1978–1979) on industrial policy in Indonesia, which can be described as the phase of 'moving upstream' (Thee & Yoshihara, 1987: 327). During this period Indonesia pursued one of the most inward-looking patterns of industrialization among the developing countries (Naya, 1988: 87; Ariff and Hill, 1985: 17). Under this industrial strategy, nominal and effective rates of protection for consumer goods were among the highest among the Southeast Asian countries.

In the latter half of the 1970s the incentive regime for the manufacturing sector became even more restrictive and protectionist in nature. In many cases, the adoption of many policy instruments appeared to be an ad hoc response to requests from well-connected, private firms and manufacturers' associations. During this period the Indonesian government often protected domestic production from import competition if persuaded by the firms that domestic capacity was sufficient to meet local demand. Consequently, import bans were imposed on several products, including canvas fabrics, corrugated boxes, aluminium extrusion products, radios, television sets, completely assembled cars and weaving yarns. Not surprisingly, Indonesia's trade policy was biased towards import-substitution, and as a result, there was a strong incentive to invest in the protected industries (World Bank, 1981: 24).

One significant impact of the 'anti-export bias' of the protectionist trade regime in the 1970s was a *misallocation of resources toward production for the domestic market rather than exports and toward capital-intensive industries rather than labour-intensive ones* (my italics) (World Bank, 1981: 25). The data in Table 2 below clearly show that the highly protected import-competing industries use significantly less labour and more capital and skills than the least protected sectors. On the other hand, the labour requirements per unit of domestic value added in exportable industries is more than double that in import-competing industries. The capital-intensity of the import-competing industries is, on the average, also more than four times that of the exportable sectors. Hence, *the protectionist trade regime of the 1970s protected and encouraged import-competing industries, and thus slowed the growth of productive employment* (my italics) (World Bank, 1981: 30).

The capital-intensive bias of the protectionist trade regime of the 1970s was reinforced by government policies providing subsidized credit and various corporate tax incentives, such as investment allowances, various tax exemptions and holidays, and accelerated depreciation allowances (World Bank, 1981: 30).

When the phase of 'easy' or first phase of import substitution had come to an by the mid-1970s, the Indonesian government, instead of shifting to an export-promoting strategy of industrialization, launched an ambitious second phase of import-substitution, which involved moving upstream into basic, resource-processing industries and supporting industries, producing parts and components for the engineering goods, downstream assembling

### TABLE 2
### Labour and Capital Requirements in Indonesian Manufacturing by Tradable Category, 1975
### (millions of rupiah of domestic value added)

|                                       | Exportable industries | Importable industries |
|---------------------------------------|-----------------------|-----------------------|
| Labour requirements 1)                | 1,539                 | 715                   |
| Skill-days 2)                         | 175                   | 212                   |
| Capital requirements 3)               | 23.17                 | 47.03                 |
| Skill-days/per thousand man-days      | 113                   | 296                   |
| Capital-requirements per man-day      | 15.0                  | 65.8                  |

*Notes*:
1) Labour requirements are measured in man-days and reflect the labour used by all firms (including in cottage, small, medium and large establishments).
2) The measure of skill used is the product of the proportion of the daily average wage which exceeds the unskilled wage (Rp. 250/day) and the labour requirement per unit of domestic value added.
3) The proxy for capital requirements is kilowatt-hours.
*Source*: World Bank: *Indonesia — Selected Issues of Industrial Development and Trade Strategy — The Main Report*. Washington, D.C., 1981, table 3.3, p. 31.

industries, which amounted to pushing 'backward integration' (Thee and Yoshihara, 1987: 328).

The case for moving upstream was clearly outlined by a new forceful and articulate Minister of Industry, A.R. Soehoed, in 1978. In several papers written before and after his appointment as Minister of Industry, Mr Soehoed argued that

'the progress in import-substituting industrialization during the first two Five-Year Development Plans (1969-through 1979) had merely led to a *widening, rather than the deepening of the industrial structure* (my itallics). Industries expanded and grew more or less independently, and perhaps in some cases even in competition with each other, but at any rate not in general mutually reinforcing. Inter-industrial linkages, both backward and forward, generally are not very strong'. (Soehoed, 1981: 6–7)

Soehoed further argued that since:

'the phase of easy import substitution had been completed, the scope for further widening the structure of industry through import substitution along the past pattern is now more limited than in the last few years. In addition to the question of enlarging th size of the market for existing industries (including through exports), a stage has now been reached where the further development of industry will also necessitate the deepening of the industrial structure' (Soehoed, 1981: 6–7).

To realise his plan of deepening Indonesia's industrial structure, Soehoed promoted the development of upstream industries, specifically basic, resource-processing industries. Altogether, 52 basic industry projects were to be undertaken by state-owned enterprises (SOEs). Soehoed argued that SOEs had to take on these projects, because private enterprise was reluctant to enter the upstream sector because of the smaller margins and higher risks involved, as well as the huge capital requirements (Soehoed, 1988: 46). Another important reason for choosing SOEs to undertake and finance the resource-based, basic industries was that the Indonesian government in the late 1970s and early 1980s was awash in oil money because of the second oil boom. In addition to the government's oil money, several of these planned basic industries could also be financed by the considerable aid flows which Indonesia was receiving at the time. The downstream industries, on the other hand, could be left to the private sector (Soehoed, 1981: 6–7; Thee, 1989: 149).

Soehoed's industrial policy, which was referred to as the *'structuralist approach to industrialization'* because of its focus on natural resource-based, basic industries and need for inter-industrial linkages between upstream and downstream industries, reflects the influence of what Professor Deepak Lal in the context of India has called 'ecology' on the thinking of economic policy-makers (Lal, 1985: 29). Like in India, Indonesia's large population and varied natural resources induced Indonesia's industrial policymakers to push through the secondary and tertiary phases of import-substitution. Unlike India, the availability of large resource (oil) rent taxes made available by the oil booms in the 1970s and early 1980s made this 'structuralist approach to industrialisation' seem quite feasible (Thee, 1989: 150).

However, efficiency-minded economists argued that this 'structuralist approach to industrialization' neglected or glossed over considerations of economic efficiency by ignoring a comparison of production costs with border prices. Because of this, several economists, both Indonesian and foreign, expressed serious concern about the government's industrial deepening plan which was, as one foreign observer, noted:

> 'one masssive exercise in import substitution without any reference to efficiency or exportability considerations. Should this be the case, the potential damage to the economy would be far greater, as both the investment that would have to be protected and the number of downstream industries whose cost structures would be inflated by having to purchase higher-cost locally made inputs would be much greater than had been the case for

protected light manufacturing during the 'easy' phase of import substitution'
(Gray, 1982: 49).

In addition to promoting basic industries, Soehoed pushed the development
of the engineering goods industries, including the automotive industry, by
promoting the development of the supporting industries of the engineering
goods assembling industries. These supporting industries were to supply
locally-made parts and components to the assembling, engineering goods
industries. To stimulate the development of the supporting industries, the
Department of Industry launched several mandatory 'deletion programmes'
(local content programs), under which the engineering goods assembling
industries were required to use progressively more locally made parts and
components. These deletion programmes led to rapid but inefficient (and
ultimately unsustainable) industrial growth, since it was pushed under a
protectionist, import-substituting trade regime which did not provide both the
assembling as well as supporting industries the necessary scope for economies
of scale. In other words, since the domestic market was still relatively small,
the deletion programs were rarely, if at all, able to develop economically
viable supporting industries which were able to produce the high quality parts
and components required by export-oriented firms. As a result, in 1993 the
deletion programmes were discontinued (Thee, 2002: 223).

The *third sub-phase* in Indonesia's industrial development during the
Soeharto era started after the end of the oil boom era in 1982 and lasted
through 1996. While Indonesia was flush with oil money, the objections
of efficiency-minded economists to the high social costs of inward-looking
industrialization carried little weight. However, with the sharp decline in the
country's terms of trade in 1982 and the resultant sharp decline in the country's
balance of trade, the efficiency-minded economists, both inside and outside
the government, became more vocal in stressing the urgent need for a shift
from the highly protectionist import-substituting strategy of industrialization
towards an export-promoting strategy in order to encourage the growth of an
internationally competitive manufacturing sector (Thee, 1989: 151).

During the early post-oil boom years, roughly from 1983 through 1985,
the required shift from an import-substituting path of industrialization
to an export-oriented one was opposed by several vested interest groups
which waged an effective rearguard action against further reforms. For this
reason during this period the government's response was limited to prudent
macroeconomic management and a large devaluation in March 1983. In fact,
some of the thrusts of the oil boom period were still continued, including
huge state investments in oil and gas, which had been planned during the

oil boom era, were brought on stream, and the government even introduced more non-tariff barriers (Hill, 1994: 80), justifying these measures to keep the current account deficit from widening.

During this period some economic policymakers did not seem to realise that shifting to an export-oriented strategy required sacrificing the highly protected upstream industries, which penalised downstream, export-oriented assembly industries by forcing them to use more expensive, locally made inputs. Hence, the number of categories of products subject to quantitative import restrictions or outright bans actually increased. This was justified by the rising current account deficit, which could not yet be closed by non-oil exports, particularly manufactured exports (Thee, 2002: 211).

Only in 1986, when the price of oil fell even more steeply than in 1982, was the government finally forced to push through the policy reforms than had been urged by Indonesian and foreign economists. Indonesia's commodity terms of trade suddenly worsened by 34 per cent, resulting in a five per cent decline in national income (World Bank, 1987: 1–2) As a result, export promotion had become imperative.

The experience of the 'East Asian Tigers', particularly Korea and Taiwan, had shown that during the early stage of export-oriented industralisation a supportive trade regime was required which approximated free trade conditions for export-oriented firms. This implied that export-oriented firms should be able to purchase their inputs, whether imported or locally made, at world market prices (Little, 1979: 14, 34).

To this end the government introduced a series of deregulation measures to improve the investment climate for private, including foreign, investors, particularly for those planning to invest in export-oriented projects. The government also launched a series of trade reforms to reduce the *'anti-export bias'* of its trade regime. A major step was the introduction of a duty exemption and drawback scheme in May 1986. Firms exporting at least 85 per cent (subsequently lowered to 65 per cent) of its output were exempted from all import duties on restrictive regulations on importing their inputs (Muir, 1986: 22) Further measures to improve the trade regime were introduced in October 1986, January and December 1987, November 1988 and at the end of May 1990.

In addition to a supportive trade regime to reduce, if not eliminate, its 'anti-export bias', a successful export promotion policy also requires a supportive exchange rate policy. Managing the exchange rate correctly is crucial to maintaining the competitiveness and profitability of exports as well as induce entrepreneurs to invest in export-oriented industries (World Bank, 1986: 107). By keeping inflationary pressures under control, and by pursuing an active managed float policy through a steady depreciation of the *rupiah* against the falling US dollar since the 31 per cent devaluation in September 1986, Bank Indonesia was quite successful in depreciating the real effective exchange rate (World Bank, 1989: 4–5). In turn, the steady depreciation of the *rupiah*'s real effective exchange rate led to an upsurge of non-oil exports, particularly manufactured exports, which started after 1987 (Thee, 1990: 74). This manufactured export surge was so remarkable, since it was the first time in Indonesia's modern economic history that Indonesia began to experience a broadly-based export expansion (Hill, 1987: 29).

As a result of the manufactured exports surge, Indonesia's manufacturing sector since the late 1980s emerged as the major engine of growth and the major source of export earnings, at least until Indonesia was hit in 1997/98 by the Asian financial and economic crisis. To a large extent the rapid growth of the manufacturing sector since the late 1980s was due to the rapid growth of manufactured exports, particularly labour-intensive exports (textiles, garments and footwear) and resource-intensive exports (particularly plywood and other processed wood products).

To a significant degree this surge of manufactured exports was due to a surge of direct investments by domestic and foreign investors in export-oriented projects which occurred since the late 1980s. This development was quite in contrast to the preceding period of the 1970s and early 1980s when the bulk of domestic and foreign investment took place in domestic market-oriented activities. This domestic market orientation was not surprising in view of the 'anti-export bias' of the protectionist trade regime.

The data in Table 3 show the rising trend in export-oriented, approved domestic and foreign direct investment since the mid-1980s.

Both 'pull' and 'push' factors were at work which accounted for the rising trend towards export-oriented investments by domestic and foreign direct investment, particularly by the Asian newly-industrializing economies (NIEs), specifically South Korea and Taiwan. On the part of Indonesia, the '*pull*' factors were the easing of restrictions on foreign investment and the series of trade reforms to reduce the 'anti-export bias' of the trade regime. Most of the export-oriented projects by the foreign investors, particularly from South Korea and Taiwan, took place in labour-intensive industries (garments and footwear). On the part of the source countries, specifically South Korea and Taiwan, the '*push*' factors were the substantial appreciation of their currencies and rapidly rising real wages in these countries, which rendered the labour-intensive industries less competitive in export markets (Thee, 1991: 58–62).

**TABLE 3**
**Number and Percentage of Newly-approved Investment Projects in Indonesia, 1986–1989**

| | 1986 Total approved projects | 1986 Approved export-oriented projects | 1987 Total approved projects | 1987 Export-oriented projects | 1988 Total approved projects | 1988 Export oriented projects | 1989 Total approved projects | 1989 Export-oriented projects |
|---|---|---|---|---|---|---|---|---|
| | A | B | A | B | A | B | A | B |
| Domestic investment projects | 316 | 166 | 565 | 370 | 845 | 594 | 863 | 623 |
| B as % of A | | 53% | | 65% | | 70% | | 72% |
| Foreign investment projects | 50 | 19 | 70 | 37 | 145 | 105 | 294 | 231 |
| B as % of A | 38% | 53% | 72% | 79% | | | | |

*Source:* Thee Kian Wie: The Surge of Asian NIC Investment into Indonesia, in *Bulletin of Indonesian Economic Studies* 27, no. 3, table 2, p. 64. (derived from data of the Capital Investment Coordinating Board (BKPM), Jakarta.

However, the surge of manufactured exports proved to be short-lived, since these exports began to grow at a more sluggish rate since 1993. While manufactured exports during the period 1989–1993 grew at an average annual rate of 20–30 per cent, they grew only at an average annual rate of 11.3 per cent during the period 1994–96 (Biro Pusat Statistik, 1997).

In view of these developments, Indonesia's policymakers became concerned that the country was losing its comparative advantage in labour- and resource-intensive manufactured exports in view of the disappointing performance of its largest manufactured exports, namely textiles, garments and footwear., and its largest resource-intensive manufactured exports, namely wood and wood products. Some policy-makers therefore argued that that to sustain the growth of manufactured exports, Indonesia could no longer rely on its traditional sources of comparative advantage, namely its large supplies of relatively cheap but mostly low skill labour and natural resources (Thee, 2000: 37–38).

In response to this challenge, the Department of Industry, which had become more outward-looking in its policy orientation after the end of the oil boom era in the early 1980s, launched a 'broad-based' strategy of export-oriented industrialisation which they termed a '*broad spectrum*' strategy to promote the various export-oriented industries. On the other hand, the powerful Minister of State for Research and Technology, Dr B.J. Habibie, strongly promoted the development of 10 selected state-owned '*strategic industries*', notably the hi-tech state-owned aircraft industry, *PT Industri Pesawat Terbang Nusantara, IPTN*, and the shipbuilding industry, *PT PAL*, both of which were targeted to achieve international competitiveness within a reasonable (but not explicitly targeted) period of time (Thee & Pangestu, 1998: 262).

These 'strategic industries' were nurtured by strong protection, assured government procurement, and substantial amounts of explicit and implicit government subsidies. Unfortunately, by pursuing this 'dual track' industrialization strategy, the government did not take account of the possible trade-offs between the promotion of the costly 'strategic industries' pursued by Dr Habibie and the 'broad spectrum' export-oriented industrialization strategy pursued by the Department of Industry (Thee & Pangestu, 1978: 262). Until the onset of the Asian economic crisis, these two contending views about Indonesia's industrial policy were never satisfactorily reconciled to the detriment of Indonesia's industrial performance.

## b. Industrial development during the Soeharto era

During the 32 years of the Soeharto era the Indonesian economy experienced rapid and generally sustained growth of around 7 per cent a year. As a result of this rapid growth, Indonesia was graduated from the ranks of one of the poorest developing countries in the mid-1960s to one of the eight 'high performing Asian economies' (HPAEs) in the early 1990s, along with Japan, the four 'Asian Tigers' (Korea, Taiwan, Hong Kong and Singapore), and Indonesia's two Southeast Asian neighbours, Malaysia and Thailand (World Bank, 1993: 1, 37). With the Indonesian economy growing at an average annual rate of around 7 per cent during the New Order era, Indonesia's real gross national product roughly doubled every 10 years over this period.

Rapid economic growth during this period was driven by the expansion of the three main sectors of the economy, namely agriculture, manufacturing and services. Since the manufacturing sector throughout this period was growing at double digits, much faster than the two other sectors which were only growing at single digits, the Indonesian economy also underwent a rapid transformation, as reflected by the relative decline of agriculture in the economy and a rapid rise in the relative importance of manufacturing (Table 4). By 1991 manufacturing's contribution to GDP had exceeded the contribution of the agricultural sector (Aswicahyono, 1997: 25).

TABLE 4
**Economic Growth and Transformation in Indonesia, 1965–1997**

| | Average annual growth rate | | | Percentage of GDP | | |
|---|---|---|---|---|---|---|
| | 1965–80 | 1980–90 | 1990–97 | 1965 | 1980 | 1997 |
| GDP | 7.0 | 6.1 | 7.7 | | | |
| Agriculture | 4.3 | 3.4 | 2.8 | 51 | 24 | 16 |
| **Manufacturing** | **12.0** | **12.6** | **10.8** | **8** | **13** | **26** |
| Services | 7.3 | 7.0 | 7.2 | 36 | 34 | 41 |

*Source*: World Bank: Successive issues of *World Development Indicators*.

Although during the 1950s until the mid-1960s industrial development in Indonesia had, as we have seen, been sluggish, rapid industrial development during the New Order era had made Indonesia's manufacturing sector the largest in terms of manufacturing value added among the ASEAN-4 countries (Table 5).

The data in Table 5 show that while Indonesia by 1996 had the largest manufacturing sector among the ASEAN-4 countries because of its double digit growth throughout the New Order era, its economic transformation was less rapid than that of Malaysia and Thailand. However, the economic

**TABLE 5**
**Indonesia's Industrial Development in ASEAN Perspective, 1965–1997**

| | Manufacturing value added (millions of US$) | | Average annual growth rate (%) | | | Manufacturing value added as a percentage of GDP (%) | | Manufactured exports as a percentage of total exports (%) | |
|---|---|---|---|---|---|---|---|---|---|
| | 1970 | 1996 | 1965–80 | 1980–90 | 1990–96 | | | | |
| Indonesia | 994 | 58,244 | 12.0 | 12.6 | 11.1 | 8 | 26 | 4 | 42 |
| Malaysia | 500 | 34,030 | — | 8.9 | 13.2 | 9 | 34 | 6 | 76 |
| Philippines | 1,652 | 18,908 | 11.2 | 0.2 | 2.6 | 20 | 22 | 6 | 45 |
| Thailand | 1,130 | 51,525 | — | 9.5 | 10.7 | 14 | 29 | 3 | 71 |

*Source:* World Bank: Successive issues of *World Development Indicators.*

transformation of the Philippines was much inferior to Indonesia, as reflected by the fact that the contribution of its manufacturing sector to GDP had hardly increased over a time span of three decades. The data in Table 5 also show that by 1997 Indonesia had become a significant exporter of manufactured products, while in 1965 the bulk of its exports were largely primary commodities. For this reason the World Bank in its famous but controversial report on the 'East Asian Miracle' also classified Indonesia as one of the three East Asian 'newly industrializing economies' (NIEs) along with Malaysia and Thailand (World Bank, 1993: 1).

While, as indicated above, manufactured exports grew at an average annual rate of 27 per cent with the whole manufacturing sector growing at an average annual rate of 22 per cent, manufactured exports in 1992 and 1993 slowed down to 15 and 12 per cent respectively (Kuncoro, 2000: 2). During the period 1994–1997 manufactured export growth slowed down further to an average annual rate of 12 per cent, with the whole manufacturing sector declining to an average annual rate of 12 per cent (UNIDO: 2000: 1).

The slowdown of the early 1990s was particularly evident in the case of the wood-based products (particularly plywood) and textile and garment exports which were Indonesia's most important manufactured exports. The concern that Indonesia's low skill labour-intensive manufactured exports were becoming less competitive in the face of strong price competition from the other low wage Asian countries was warranted by the fact that Indonesia's textile and garment exports in 1994 had declined most sharply in the non-quota markets (James, 1995: 22–25).

Textile industry circles attributed this export competitiveness to the mandatory steep rises in minimum wages which over the period 1991–1996 rose by a staggering 350 per cent. This steep was until 1993 matched by a corresponding rise in labour poductivity (Tanudjaja, 1999: 7). However, between 1993 and 1994 the minimum wage rose by about 10 per cent faster than labour productivity (World Bank, 1996: 75). As a result, per unit labour costs began to rise, which adversely affected employment growth as well as the competitiveness of labour-intensive, export-oriented industries, including the textile, garment and footwear industries, most of which were located in the Greater Jakarta and surrounding regions in West Java (Thee, 2000a: 422).

Despite these adverse factors, the labour-intensive textile and garment exports were still able to grow because they benefited from the Multi Fibre Agreement (MFA) which conferred unused export quotas on the country, enabling them to 'compete' internationally with the industrially more advanced East Asian NIES (Korea, Taiwan, and Hong Kong). However, when quotas became binding for Indonesia's fabric and garment exports, the trend towards higher values appeared to accelerate in the late 1980s as a result of the quality upgrading of these exports (Hill, 1997a: 106–07). This quality upgrading included improvement in productivity and efficiency, as the producers acquired more knowledge of technology and trends in international markets, often from overseas buyers or from Japan and the Asian NIEs (Hill, 1997a: 107), particularly from the business partners of Japanese or NIE (Korean and Taiwanese) — Indonesian joint ventures. In addition, labour-intensive manufactured exports were also still able to grow because they were broadening in composition as many new manufactured exports had emerged since the late 1980s, including footwear, electronics, furniture, toys and sporting goods (Hill, 1995: 12–13).

In spite of these moderately positive developments, there was real concern among the major industrial policymakers about the slowing down of Indonesia's manufactured exports. This period witnessed a vigorous intellectual debate about the required policy reforms, and also a reorientation in thinking among senior government officials, particularly at the Department of Industry (Hill, 1995: 16).

To get manufactured exports growing rapidly and in a sustained way, several economists, including foreign advisers, recommended that Indonesia would have to transform its export base by moving gradually towards the exports of more sophisticated manufactured products (HIID, 1995: 6). In other words, Indonesia would have to gradually reduce its reliance on its traditional sources of competitiveness, namely cheap labour and natural resources, and develop a more sustainable source of competitiveness through a wider diffusion of technological capabilities and organizational competence (Ernst, Ganiatsos, and Mytelka, 1998: 1).

The need to broaden and transform Indonesia's manufactured export base was also underlined in a report prepared by the late Professor Sanjaya Lall of Oxford University and Kishore Rao prepared at the request of the Asian Development Bank (ADB) in 1995 and subsequently submitted to Bappenas, Indonesia's National Planning Board. In their report Lall and Rao recommended that in the face of emerging international environment of accelerating technological change and globalization of production, and the entry of many low-cost competitors, the sustainability of Indonesia's manufactured export growth would require a broadening and deepening of its competitive advantages. This in turn would require upgrading existing export products, increasing their local content, and promoting the emergence of new, more highly value added export products and activities (Lall and Rao, 1995: 3).

The need to increase local content by developing efficient and economically viable supporting industries was obvious in the face of few backward linkages and the resulting high import dependence of Indonesia's assembling industries. For example, in 1997 the value of imported raw materials, intermediate inputs, parts and components ranged from 45 per cent in the chemical industry, 56 per cent in the transport equipment industry, and 70 per cent in the electrical goods industry. This high import dependence was even evident in the labour-intensive, export-oriented industries, where the value of imported raw materials, intermediate inputs, parts and components ranged from 40–43 per cent in the textile, garment and leather industries to 56 per cent in the footwear industry (UNIDO, 2000: 3).

In hindsight it is debatable whether the generally sensible policy recommendations contained in the HIID and ADB reports would have been carried out by the government. Even if there had been serious plans to take the necessary steps to implement the recommendations, the onset of the Asian economic crisis in 1997/98 made the recommendations largely irrelevant for the time being, as the government tried to cope with the severe socio-economic impact of the crisis.

## THE PERFORMANCE OF THE MANUFACTURING SECTOR AFTER THE ASIAN ECONOMIC CRISIS

The severe financial and economic crisis which hit Indonesia in 1997/98 had a severely adverse impact on the Indonesian economy, including the manufacturing sector. Although the crisis hit Indonesia in mid-1997, its most devastating impact was only felt in 1998 when the economy contracted by an unprecedented –13.1 per cent, while the manufacturing sector contracted by –11.4 per cent. While manufacturing slightly recovered in 1999 when it grew by a sluggish 3.9 per cent and to six per cent in 2000, it kept only growing at low single digits from 2001 through 2003. When the economy grew faster in 2004, manufacturing also grew slightly faster at 6.4 per cent. However, in 2005 and 2006 manufacturing's growth rate fell again to 4.6 per cent (Table 6).

From December 2006 through March 2008 quarterly growth rates of the manufacturing sector continued to be less than five per cent. The disappointingly slow growth of manufacturing can to a large extent be attributed to the business-unfriendly labour regulations which were introduced after the fall of Soeharto in 1998. These labour regulations, such as governing the large severance payments which have to be paid even to workers voluntarily

## TABLE 6
## Growth of the Indonesian Economy and
## Its Manufacturing Sector, 1997–2007
### (in percentages)

|  | 1997 | 1998 | 1999 | 2000 | 2001 | 2002 | 2003 | 2004 | 2005 | 2006 |
|---|---|---|---|---|---|---|---|---|---|---|
| GDP | 4.7 | –13.1 | 0.8 | 4.9 | 3.8 | 4.3 | 4.8 | 5.0 | 5.7 | 5.5 |
| Manufacturing | 5.3 | –11.4 | 3.9 | 6.0 | 3.3 | 5.3 | 5.3 | 6.4 | 4.6 | 4.6 |
| Oil and gas industry | –2.0 | 3.7 | 6.8 | –1.7 | –6.2 | 2.5 | 0.8 | –1.9 | –5.9 | –1.2 |
| Non-oil and gas industries | 6.1 | –11.4 | 3.5 | 7.0 | 4.9 | 5.7 | 6.0 | 7.5 | 5.9 | 5.3 |

*Note*: After 2000 the real growth rates were computed on the basis of 2000 constant prices.
*Source*: National Income of Indonesia, successive issues, Badan Pusat Statistik (Central Agency of Statistics), Jakarta.

resigning from their jobs and to workers who were fired because of crimes (such as stealing) have naturally adversely affected labour-intensive industries (McLeod, 2008: 186).

In short, growth of the manufacturing sector during the post-crisis decade has consistently recorded only a one digit growth, quite unlike the three decades of the Soeharto era when the manufacturing sector was growing at double digit rates, both during the import-substitution phase as well as the export promotion phase.

The data in Table 6 show that Indonesia's manufacturing sector consists of the oil refining and gas liquefaction industries and the non-oil and gas industries. During the oil boom era of the 1970s and early 1980s the oil and gas industries were the largest sub-sector of the manufacturing sector. However, after the oil boom had ended, the non-oil and gas industries emerged as the most important sub-sector as it was generally growing at much higher rates than the oil and gas sub-sector, even during the post-crisis years.(Table 6). In 2002 the oil and gas sub-sector only accounted for 11 per cent of the non-oil and gas sub-sector (Thee, 2006: 345).

The impact of the Asian financial crisis on the real sectors, especially the the manufacturing sector, was largely transmitted through two channels in the socio-economic system. The impact transmitted through the first channel was caused by substantial capital outflows, steep depreciation of the *rupiah*, and the contractionary effects of tight fiscal and monetary policies on the economy and its various constituent sectors, including the manufacturing sector. The sharp contraction of the manufacturing sector in 1998 (as well as other labour-intensive sectors such as construction), many of them geographically located in or near urban areas, led to many lay-offs (Daimon and Thorbecke, 1999: 2). The impact transmitted through the second channel was caused by the substantial shifts in relative prices, as the prices of tradable goods, including manufactured products, rose steeply vis-a-vis the non-tradable goods and services as a result of the steadily depreciating *rupiah* in early 1998. As a result, inflation rose steeply in early 1998 (Daimon and Thorbecke, 1999: 2). Lay-offs of hundreds of thousands of workers formerly employed in the manufacturing sector and other real sectors and the high rate of inflation led to a sharp decline in the purchasing power of Indonesian consumers which, in turn, contributed to sharply reduced demand for tradable goods, including manufactured products (Thee, 2000b: 428).

Although Indonesia possesses a strong potential comparative advantage in *resource-based industries* because of its diverse resource base, their post-crisis performance continues to be sluggish, except for the food-processing and crude palm oil (CPO) industries. The food-processing industries have thrived because of the inelastic demand for food products and the rupiah depreciation after the crisis (Aswicahyono, Narjoko and Hill, 2008: 6). CPO exports have been booming, particularly because of the large demand from China, India and other countries. However, the wood-processing industries, particularly plywood, have been experiencing great difficulties because of the large shortage of raw materials, mainly because of the rampant smuggling of logs, mostly to China. The worst-affected wood-processing industry has been the plywood industry, which over the past quarter of a century has benefited from capturing the rents from the artificially depressed domestic timber prices (caused by the total ban on log exports introduced since the early 1980s), but which has not used the opportunity to develop an efficient processing industry (Aswicahyono and Hill, 2004: 288–89). The pulp and paper industries have also grown slowly in spite of the high international prices. Like the wood-processing industries, the problems faced by the pulp and paper industries lie on the supply side, as access to raw material supplies have become a serious constraint. (Aswicahyono; Narjoko and Hill, 2008: 5).

The growth of the '*traditional*', *low skill, labour-intensive, largely export-oriented industries,* notably the textile, garment and footwear industries, the exports of which surged since the late 1980s through the early 1990s, has been largely sluggish after the crisis. These industries appear unable to compete effectively with China and other low-cost producers in the region, such as Vietnam. Even though per unit labour costs in the garment industry remain competitive, Indonesia has been losing its 'competitiveness' in the garment industry and other labour-intensive industries (Table 7). Foreign direct investment (FDI) in the low skill, labour-intensive industries, which

## TABLE 7
### Revealed Comparative Advantage (RCA) Measures for
### Labour-Intensive Product Categories (2000–04 average)

| Product category | SITC Code | Revealed Comparative Advantage (RCA) | | | | | |
|---|---|---|---|---|---|---|---|
| | | Indonesia | China | Malaysia | Philippines | Thailand | Vietnam |
| Travel goods, handbags, etc. | 83 | 0.87 | 5.12 | 0.06 | 2.48 | 2.00 | 4.33 |
| Garments and accessories | 84 | 2.28 | 4.12 | 0.68 | 2.15 | 1.61 | 3.88 |
| Footwear | 85 | 3.02 | 4.59 | 0.13 | 0.24 | 1.51 | 13.42 |

*Notes*: RCA values greater than one indicate comparative advantage
SITC = Standard International Trade Classification
*Source*: Ian Coxhead and Muqun Li. "Prospects for Skill-Based Export Growth in a Labour-Abundant in a Resource-Rich Developing Economy". *Bulletin of Indonesian Economic Studies* 44, no. 2, 2008, table 1, p. 213.

surged in the late 1980s, has largely been absent after the crisis (Aswicahyono and Hill, 2004: 290).

The data in Table 7 show that Indonesia still has a revealed comparative advantage in garments and accessories and footwear, but not in travel goods and handbags. Since Malaysia at present is a labour-scarce economy where real wages have increased rapidly, it is not surprising that this country does not have a comparative advantage anymore in the production of labour-intensive products. The data in Table 7 also indicate that Indonesia faces strong competition in the overseas markets for these products from low wage, efficient producers, such as China and Vietnam. Countries, such as Indonesia, that to a large extent depend on exports of low skill, labour-intensive products, have during the past few years been directly and negatively affected by strong competition from China, by far the largest exporter in the above three labour-intensive products (Coxhead and Li, 2008: 212–13).

Despite widely-held views on the part of some government officials, businessmen and academic economists that Indonesia's garment industry is a 'sunset industry' with little prospect of future dynamic development, there is a strong case for strengthening and upgrading the garment industry to increase its international competitiveness in the post-MFA era. With more moderate rises in minimum wages accompanied by rising labour productivity which will restrain rises in per unit labour costs, Indonesia still has quite a strong comparative advantage in its low skill, labour-intensive industries, including the garment and footwear industries. In view of the growing unemployment problem (with around 10 per cent of the labour force of 105 million being openly unemployed), it makes good economic sense to strengthen and upgrade labour-intensive industries, including the garment industry (Thee, 2008).

Facing strong international competition in its export and domestic markets, Indonesia's garment industry should gradually move away from the lower end of the market garments where international competition is fierce, and shift to up-market, high quality garments, including designer clothes and beach wear popular with tourists, as the Bali case has shown. To make this possible, the garment industry should send its qualified staff to study design in, for instance, Hong Kong's well-known design institute (Thee, 2008).

Since skill levels of workers in the garment industry are quite low, the garment industry could establish joint training centres to improve their skills, particularly in the operation and maintenance of high-tech equipment. This is training is very important since garment producers are being asked to use cutting-edge computer technology to provide designs and patterns to the rich country buyers (USAID & Senada, 2006: 88).

Since one of the fastest growing trade areas for garments now take place within preferential trading arrangements, the Indonesian government can also assist the garment industry by playing an active role in trade negotiations with Indonesia's most important trading partners to obtain tariff preferences through production sharing arrangements or through preferential trade agreements (Aswicahyono, et al. 2005: 55).

Lastly, the government can help the manufacturing sector, including the low skill labour-intensive industries, such as the garment industry, by taking effective steps to improve the country's poor investment climate which is generally rated as the worst in East Asia. By improving the investment climate by substantially simplifying the cumbersome and time-consuming licensing procedures, providing legal certainty, issuing more business-friendly labour regulations which are in accordance with the legitimate labour demands for adequate wages and good working conditions, and clamping down on corruption by the government bureaucracy, particularly the customs service, the government could do a great deal to help manufacturing firms, including the low skill labour-intensive firms, such as the garment firms, to reduce the high transaction costs which contribute to making these industries less competitive (Thee, 2008).

## CONCLUSION

This paper has presented a broad overview of Indonesia's industrial policies and industrial development since the early years of independence in the 1950s up to the present. However, Indonesia's industrial development after independence did not start from scratch, since the Netherlands Indies government had already initiated a modest industrialization programme in the 1920s and a slightly more ambitious import substitution programme in the 1930s to ward off strong import competition from Japan.

Although the new Indonesian government in the early 1950s launched an ambitious industrialization plan (Economic Urgency Plan), for the period 1951–1955, not much new industrial development took place during this period. The main reason for this poor performance was that political turmoil and sharp political conflicts hampered the successive development plans from being realized. Hence, by the mid-1960s the industrial topography of Indonesia was like it was during the waning years of the Netherlands Indies in 1940.

It was only with the advent of Soeharto's New Order regime that the development of a modern manufacturing sector took off. During the oil boom years of the 1970s, the government pursued an import-substitution program which started in the late 1960s through he mid-1970s. When the phase of 'easy' import substitution was completed around the mid-1970s, the government, instead of shifting to an export promotion strategy, opted to launch a second stage import substitution policy, involving the establishment of large-scale, upstream, state-owned basic industries, such as a steel and aluminium ingot industry.

This ambitious state-led industrialization programme had to be abandoned when the price of crude oil dropped in 1982. With the sharp decline in the country's terms of trade in 1982 and the resultant sharp decline in the country's balance of trade, the efficiency-minded economists, both inside and outside the government, became more vocal in stressing the urgent need for a shift from the highly protectionist import-substituting strategy of industrialisation towards an export-promoting strategy in order to encourage the growth of an internationally competitive manufacturing sector.

To this end the government introduced a series of deregulation measures to improve the investment climate for private, including foreign, investors, particularly for those planning to invest in export-oriented projects. The government also launched a series of trade reforms to reduce the '*anti-export bias*' of its trade regime. A major step was the introduction of a duty exemption and drawback scheme in May 1986. Firms exporting at least 85 per cent (subsequently lowered to 65 per cent) of its output were exempted from all import duties on restrictive regulations on importing their inputs.

In addition to a supportive trade regime to reduce, if not eliminate, its '*anti-export bias*', a successful export promotion policy also requires a supportive exchange rate policy. Managing the exchange rate correctly is crucial to maintaining the competitiveness and profitability of exports as well as induce entrepreneurs to invest in export-oriented industries. By keeping inflationary pressures under control, and by pursuing an active managed float policy through a steady depreciation of the *rupiah* against the falling US dollar since the 31 per cent devaluation in September 1986, Bank Indonesia was quite successful in depreciating the real effective exchange rate. In turn, the steady depreciation of the *rupiah*'s real effective exchange rate led to an upsurge of non-oil exports, particularly manufactured exports, which started after 1987, and ended when the Asian economic crisis hit Indonesia.

The severe financial and economic crisis which hit Indonesia in 1997/98 had a severe adverse impact on the Indonesian economy, including the manufacturing sector. Although the crisis hit Indonesia in mid-1997, its most devastating impact was only felt in 1998 when the economy contracted by an unprecedented –13.1 per cent, while the manufacturing sector contracted by –11.4 per cent.

From December 2006 through March 2008 quarterly growth rates of the manufacturing sector continued to be less than five per cent. The disappointingly slow growth of manufacturing can to a large extent be attributed to the business-unfriendly labour regulations, particularly the Labour Law of 2003, which were introduced after the fall of Soeharto in 1998.

The growth of the 'traditional', low skill, labour-intensive, largely export-oriented industries, notably the textile, garment and footwear industries, the exports of which surged since the late 1980s through the early 1990s, has been largely sluggish after the crisis. These industries appear unable to compete effectively with China and other low-cost producers in the region, such as Vietnam. Even though per unit labour costs in the garment industry remain competitive, Indonesia has been losing its 'competitiveness' in the garment industry and other labour-intensive industries. Foreign direct investment (FDI) in the low skill, labour-intensive industries, which surged in the late 1980s, has been sluggish after the crisis.

To boost the growth of the manufacturing sector in the face of strong competition from other, low wage producers in the region, the Indonesian government has to make a more determined effort to improve the investment climate of the country, for both domestic and foreign investors alike. New foreign direct investment is particularly important, since it not only brings in capital, but also new technology and modern management methods and access to export markets. Indonesia can not continue to rely on its cheap labour and natural resources, but needs to make a more serious and determined effort to develop and upgrade the technological capabilities of its manufacturing firms in order to meet the strong competition of its competitors.

## Note

1.  "Indonesia's Industrial Policies and Development since Independence", by Thee Kian Wie, paper presented at the Workshop on Labour-Intensive Industrialization in Southeast Asia. Kyoto: Center for Southeast Asian Studies, Kyoto University, 22 February 2008.

## References

Anspach, Ralph. "Indonesia". In *Underdevelopment and economic nationalism in Southeast Asia*, edited by Frank Golay, Ralph Anspach, M. Ruth Pfanner and Eliezer B. Ayal, 111–202. Ithaca and London: Cornell University Press, 1969.

Anwar, M. Arsyad. "Trade Strategies and Industrial Development in Indonesia". In *ASEAN in a changing Pacific and world economy*, edited by Ross Garnaut, 207–30. Canberra: Australian National University, 1980.

Ariff, Mohamed and Hal Hill. *Export-Oriented Industrialization: The ASEAN Experience*. Allen & Unwin, Crows Nest, NSW, Australia, 1985.

Aswicahyono, Haryo. "Transformation and Structural Change in Indonesia's Manufacturing Sector". In *Waves of Change in Indonesia's Manufacturing Industry*, edited by Mari Pangestu and Yuri Sato, 1–28. Tokyo: Institute of Developing Economies, 1997.

Aswicahyono, Haryo and Hal Hill. "Survey of Recent Developments". *Bulletin of Indonesian Economic Studies* 40, no. 3 (December 2004): 277–05.

Aswicahyono, Haryo, Raymond Atje and Thee Kian Wie. *Indonesia's Industrial Competitiveness: A Study of the Garments, Auto Parts And Electronic Components Industries*. Report to the Development Economics Research Group, The World Bank, Jakarta, March 2005.

Aswicahyono, Haryo, Dionisius Narjoko and Hal Hill. *Industrialisation after a Deep Economic Crisis: Indonesia*. First draft, May 2008.

Bank Indonesia. *Report for the years 1960–1965*. Jakarta, 1 May 1968.

Booth, Anne and Peter McCawley, eds. *The Indonesian Economy During the Soeharto Era*. Oxford University Press, Kuala Lumpur, 1981.

Burger, D.H. *Sociologisch-Economische Geschiedenis van Indonesia, Deel II: Indonesia in de 20e Eeuw* (Sociological-Economic History of Indonesia — *Vol. II: The twentieth century*). KITLV, Leiden; Royal Tropical Institute, Amsterdam & School of Agriculture, Division of Agrarian History, Wageningen, 1975.

Coxhead, Ian and Muqun Li. "Prospects for Skill-Based Export Growth in a Labour-Abundant in a Resource-Rich Developing Economy". *Bulletin of Indonesian Economic Studies* 44, no. 2 (December 2008): 209–38.

Dick, Howard. "Nineteenth century industrialization: A missed opportunity". In *New Challenges in the Modern Economic History of Indonesia*, edited by J. Th. Lindblad, 123–48. Leiden: PRIS, 1993.

Dick, H.W. "Formation of the Nation-state, 1930s–1966". In *The Emergence of a National Economy in Indonesia, 1800–2000*, edited by H.W. Dick, V.J.H. Houben, J.Th. Lindblad and Thee Kian Wie, 153–93. Sydney: Allen and Unwin, 2002.

Dick, Howard. Vincent Houben, J. Thomas Lindblad and Thee Kian Wie. *The Emergence of a National Economy: An economic history of Indonesia, 1800–2000*. Allen and Unwin, Crows Nest, NSW, Australia, 2002.

Ernst, Dieter, Tom Ganiatsos and Lynn Mytelka. *Technological Capabilities and Export Success in Asia*. London and New York: Routledge, 1998.

Garnaut, Ross. *ASEAN in a Changing World Economy*. Canberra: Australian National University Press, 1980.

Glassburner, Bruce. *The Economy of Indonesia: Selected Readings*. Ithaca and London: Cornell University Press, 1971.

Golay, Frank H., Ralph Anspach, M. Ruth Pfanner & Eliezer B. Ayal. *Underdevelopment and Economic Nationalism in Southeast Asia*. Ithaca and London: Cornell University Press, 1969.

Gray, C.S. "Survey of Recent Developments". *Bulletin of Indonesian Economic Studies* 18, no. 3 (November 1982): 1–51.

Higgins, Benjamin. *Indonesia's Economic Stabilization and Development*. New York: Institute of Pacific Relations, 1957.

————. *Economic Development: Problems, Principles, and Policies* (Revised Edition) New York: W.W. Norton & Co., 1968.

HIID (Harvard Institute for International Development). *Prospects for Manufactured Exports during Repelita VI*. Draft report submitted by the HIID to the Department of Industry, Republic of Indonesia, Jakarta, 1995.

Hill, Hal. "Survey of Recent Developments". *Bulletin of Indonesian Economic Studies* 23, no. 3 (December 1987): 1–33.

————. "The Economy". In *Indonesia's New Order: The Dynamics of Socio-Economic Transformation*, edited by Hal Hill, 54–122. St. Leonards: Allen & Unwin, 1994a.

————. *Indonesia's New Order: The Dynamics of Socio-Economic Transformation*. St. Leonards: Allen & Unwin, 1994b.

————. *Indonesia's Industrial Policy and Performance: 'Orthodoxy' Vindicated*. Economics Division Working Papers no. 95/1, Research School of Pacific and Asian Studies. Canberra: The Australian National University, 1995.

————. "The Garment and Textile Industries". In *Indonesia's Industrial Transformation*, edited by Hal Hill, 83–121. Singapore: Institute of Southeast Asian Studies, 1997a.

———. *Indonesia's Industrial Transformation*. Singapore: Institute of Southeast Asian Studies, 1997b.

James, William E. "Survey of Recent Developments". *Bulletin of Indonesian Economic Studies* 31, no. 3 (December 1995): 3–38.

Kuncoro, Ari. "Regional Specialization, Industrial Competition and Finance: The Case of the Indonesian Manufacturing Sector". Paper presented at the Second IRSA International Conference on Indonesia's Regional Development: Challenges in the New Millenium, Jakarta, 28 February 2000.

Lal, Deepak. "Ideology and Industrialisation in India and East Asia". Paper prepared for the Workshop on Industrialization in East and Southeast Asia, Canberra, September 1985.

Lall, Sanjaya & Kishore Rao. *Indonesia: Sustaining Manufactured Export Growth, Vol. 1, Main Report*. Report submitted to the Asian Development Bank, Manila, 1995.

Lindblad, J. Thomas. *New Challenges in the Modern Economic History of Indonesia*. Leiden: Programme of Indonesian Studies, 1993.

Little, I.M.D. *The Experience and Cause of Rapid Labour-Intensive Development in Korea, Taiwan, Hong Kong and Singapore and the Possibilities of Emulation*. Bangkok: International Labour Organisation, 1979.

Mackie, J.A.C. "The Indonesian Economy, 1950–1960". In *The Economy of Indonesia: Selected Readings*, edited by B. Glassburner, 16–69. Ithaca NY: Cornell University Press 1967.

McCawley, Peter. "The Growth of the Industrial Sector". In *The Indonesian Economy during the Soeharto Era*, edited by A. Booth and P. McCawley, 62–101. Kuala Lumpur: Oxford University Press, 1981.

McLeod, Ross. "Survey of Recent Developments". *Bulletin of Indonesian Economic Studies* 44, no. 2 (August 2008): 277–305.

McVey, Ruth. *Indonesia*. New Haven: HRAF Press, 1963.

Muir, Ross. "Survey of Recent Developments". *Bulletin of Indonesian Economic Studies* 22, no. 2 (August 1986): 1–27.

Naya, Seiji. "The Role of Trade Policies in the Industrialization of Rapidly Growing Asian Developing Countries". In *Achieving Industrialization in East Asia*, edited by Helen Hughes, 64–94. Canberra: Australian National University, 1988.

Paauw, Douglas S. "From Colonial to Guided Economy". In *Indonesia*, edited by Ruth McVey, 155–247. New Haven: Human Relations Area Files, 1963.

Pangestu, Marie E. and Yuri Sato eds., *Waves of Change in Indonesia's Manufacturing Industry*. Tokyo: Institute of Developing Economies, 1997.

Sastromihardjo, Sanjoto and Norio Mihira eds. *Indonesia's Non-Oil Exports: Performance and Prospects*. Tokyo: Institute of Developing Economies, 1990.

Siahaan, Bisuk. *Industrialisasi di Indonesia: Sejak Hutang Kehormatan sampai Bantiing Stir* (Industrialisation in Indonesia: Since the Debt of Honour to the Turn-Around), Pustaka Data, Jakarta, 1996.

Sjafruddin Prawiranegara. "Recollections of My Career". *Bulletin of Indonesian Economic Studies* 23, no. 3 (December 1987): 100–08.

Soehoed, A.R. "Manufacturing in Indonesia". *Bulletin of Indonesian Economic Studies*, no. 8, October (1967): 65–84.

———. "Japan and the Development of the Indonesian Manufacturing Sector". *Indonesian Quarterly*, No. 10, 1981.

———. "Reflections on Industrialization and Industrial Policy in Indonesia". *Bulletin of Indonesian Economic Studies* 24, no. 3 (December 1988): 43–57.

Takeshi, Daimon and Erik Thorbecke. "Mitigating the Social Impact of the Indonesian Crisis: Lessons from the IDT Experience". Unpublished paper, 1999.

Tanudjaja, Sunjoto. "Efforts in Revitalizing the Real Sector". Paper presented at the Conference on the Economic Issues Facing the New Government. Jakarta, 18–19 August 1999.

Thee Kian Wie. "Industrialization in India and Indonesia". *ITINERARIO — Special Issue — India and Indonesia: General Perspectives*, no. 1 (1989): 133–54.

———. "Indonesia's Manufactured Exports: Performance and Prospects". In *Indonesia's Non-Oil Exports: Performance and Prospects*, edited by Sanjoto Sastromihardjo and Norio Mihira, 69–99, 1990.

———. "The Surge of Asian NIC Investment into Indonesia". *Bulletin of Indonesian Economic Studies* 27, no. 3 (December 1991): 55–88.

———. "Raising Indonesia's Industrial Competitiveness". *Economics and Finance in Indonesia* 48, no. 1 (2000a): 35–61.

———. "The Impact of the Economic Crisis on Indonesia's Manufacturing Sector". *The Developing Economies* 38, no. 4 (December 2000b): 420–53.

———. "The Soeharto Era and After: Stability, Development and Crisis, 1966–2000". In *The Emergence of a National Economy in Indonesia, 1800–2000*, edited by H.W. Dick, V.J.H. Houben, J.Th. Lindblad and Thee Kian Wie, 194–243. Sydney: Allen & Unwin, 2002.

———. "Introduction". In *Recollections: The Indonesian Economy 1950s–1990s*, Thee, editor, 2003a, pp. 3–43.

———. "Introduction". *Recollections: The Indonesian Economy 1950s–1990s*, edited by Thee Kian Wie. Singapore: Institute of Southeast Asian Studies. Singapore, 2003b.

———. "Policies Affecting Indonesia's Industrial Technology Development". *ASEAN Economic Bulletin* 23, no. 3 (December 2006): 341–59.

———. "Indonesia's Garment Industry Before and After the Expiry of the MFA". *Journal of Contemporary Asia — Special Issue on the Garment Industry in East Asia*. London: Taylor & Francis, 2008.

Thee Kian Wie and Kunio Yoshihara. "Foreign and Domestic Capital in Indonesian Industrialisation". *Southeast Asian Studies* 24, no. 4 (March 1987): 327–49.

Thee Kian Wie and Mari Pangestu. "Technological capabilities and Indonesia's manufactured exports". *Technological capabilities and export success in Asia*, edited by Dieter Ernst, Tom Ganiatsos, and Lynn Mytelka, 211–65. London; New York: Routledge, 1998.

UNIDO. *Strategy for Building Manufacturing Capability and Competitiveness of Indonesian Firms: Summary of Preliminary Findings and Implications.* United Nations Industrial Organization, Jakarta Office, 25 May 2000.

USAID and SENADA. *Indonesia's Competitive Environment: Current Conditions.* Jakarta, March 2006.

World Bank. *Indonesia — Selected Issues of Industrial Development and Trade Strategy — The Main Report.* East Asia and Pacific Regional Office, Washington, D.C., 15 July 1981.

———. *Indonesia: Adjusting to Lower Oil Revenues.* Washington, D.C., 21 May 1986.

———. *Indonesia: Strategy for Economic Recovery.* Washington, D.C., 1987.

———. *The East Asian Miracle: Economic Growth and Public Policy.* New York: Oxford University Press, 1993.

———. *Indonesia: Dimensions of Growth.* Washington, D.C., 7 May 1996.

# 10

# POLICIES AFFECTING INDONESIA'S INDUSTRIAL TECHNOLOGY DEVELOPMENT[1]

## INTRODUCTION

The competitive environment for Indonesia's manufacturing industries has changed a great deal in years following the Asian economic crisis. The major factors in the global environment which have adversely affected Indonesia's competitiveness in its manufactured exports include increasing economic openness, shorter product cycles and continuous technological improvements (World Bank, 2003: 4). For countries, like Indonesia, which are highly dependent on foreign trade and therefore deeply integrated in the global economy, it is vital to monitor regularly the productivity and international competitiveness of their industries, which are of great importance to their economies.

Other major factors which have adversely affected or may adversely affect the competitiveness of Indonesia's manufacturing industries are China's rise as a formidable competitor in the world markets for manufactured exports and as an attractive host country for foreign direct investment (FDI); the emergence of global contract manufacturers in Singapore, Malaysia and Thailand; the expiry of the Multifibre Agreement (MFA) in early 2005; trade liberalization within the ASEAN countries; and the WTO mandated reduction in tariff barriers (World Bank, 2003: 3).

This paper discusses Indonesia's low industrial competitiveness and the steps which could be taken to remedy this problem. A brief overview will first be given of Indonesia's industrial development before and after the Asian economic crisis. This will be important to understand why Indonesia's industrial competitiveness is relatively low compared to its competitors in the region.

## INDONESIA'S INDUSTRIAL DEVELOPMENT BEFORE AND AFTER THE ASIAN ECONOMIC CRISIS: AN OVERVIEW

### a. Industrial development during the Soeharto Era

During the 32 years of "New Order" rule (1966–98) the Indonesian economy experienced rapid and sustained growth, which enabled Indonesia to graduate from the ranks of one of the poorest countries in the mid-1960s to one of the eight "high-performing Asian economies" (HPAEs) in the early 1990s, along with Japan, the four "Asian Tigers", and Indonesia's two Southeast Asian neighbours, Malaysia and Thailand (World Bank 1993: 1, 37).

Rapid economic growth averaging 7.0 per cent during the period 1965–97 was driven by the expansion of the three main sectors of the economy, namely agriculture, manufacturing, and services. As the manufacturing sector throughout this period was growing at double digits, much faster than the two other sectors which were growing at single digits, the Indonesian economy underwent a rapid transformation, as reflected by the rapid rise in the relative importance of the manufacturing sector (Table 1). By 1991 manufacturing's contribution to GDP exceeded the contribution of the agricultural sector (Aswicahyono 1997: 25).

During the late 1960s and early 1970s Indonesia's rapid industrial growth was fuelled by the liberalization of economic policies, and the return to normal economic conditions after the political turmoil and economic chaos

### TABLE 1
### Economic Growth and Transformation in Indonesia, 1965–97

|  | Average annual growth rate (%) | | | % of GDP | |
|---|---|---|---|---|---|
|  | 1965–80 | 1980–90 | 1990–97 | 1965 | 1997 |
| GDP | 7.0 | 6.1 | 7.7 |  |  |
| Agriculture | 4.3 | 3.4 | 2.8 | 51 | 16 |
| Manufacturing | 12.0 | 12.6 | 10.8 | 8 | 26 |
| Services | 7.3 | 7.0 | 7.2 | 36 | 41 |

*Source*: For the period 1965–80: World Bank: *World Development Report 1992*, Oxford University Press, 1992, table 2, p. 220; table 3, p. 222. For the periods 1980–90 and 1990–96: *World Development Indicators 1999*, Development Data Center, table 4.1, p. 189; table 4.2, p. 193.

of the early 1960s. During the oil boom period (1974–81) rapid industrial growth was facilitated by protectionist import-substituting policies. During this oil boom era the liberal economic policies were largely replaced by more interventionist policies, when the Indonesian government, flush with windfall revenues from the oil booms, initiated an ambitious, second phase import-substitution policy after the 'easy' phase of import-substitution had been completed by the mid-1970s (McCawley 1979: 13). This second phase of import-substituting industrialization involved the establishment of various upstream, state-owned, capital-intensive, basic industries.

Even though many Indonesian and foreign economists were concerned about this costly and inefficient pattern of upstream import-substituting industrialization, which largely ignored comparison of production costs with border prices (Gray 1982: 41), the large oil boom revenues enabled the Indonesian government to ignore their criticisms. However, by 1983 the end of the oil boom forced the Indonesian government to shift to export-promoting policies by introducing a series of deregulation measures to improve the investment climate for private, including foreign, investors to encourage them to invest in export-oriented projects. These deregulation measures also included a series of trade reforms to reduce the '*anti-export bias*' of the protectionist trade regime, including the introduction of a '*duty exemption and drawback scheme*' in May 1986. This scheme provided export-oriented firms with the opportunity to purchase inputs, whether actually imported or locally made, at international prices. This scheme turned out to be a crucial factor in facilitating the rapid growth of manufactured exports.

The trade reforms and the reintroduction of liberal foreign investment policies, combined with a supportive exchange rate policy aimed at keeping the real effective exchange rate at a competitive level, and underpinned by sound macroeconomic policies, proved to be successful. Since 1987 the manufacturing sector generated a surge in manufactured exports, particularly low skill labour-intensive exports. For this reason the World Bank study on '*The East Asian Miracle*' classified Indonesia as one of the three East Asian '*newly-industrializing economies*' (*NIEs*) along with Malaysia and Thailand (World Bank 1993).

As a result of the surge in manufactured exports, Indonesia's manufacturing sector, specifically the non-oil and gas manufacturing sub-sector, by the late 1980s emerged as the country's major engine of economic growth (World Bank 1994: 1) and major source of export revenues. During the period 1985–88 the manufacturing sector grew at an average annual rate of 13 per cent, while manufactured exports grew at an average annual rate of 27 per cent. During the period 1989–92 the manufacturing sector surged at a much faster rate of 22 per cent, while manufactured exports continued to grow at an average of 27 per cent (Dhanani 2000: 28). Since 1993, however, up to the crisis year of 1997 the growth of the manufacturing sector slowed down to an average 12 per cent, while manufactured exports grew only at a sluggish 7 per cent (Dhanani 2000: 28).

The slowdown in the growth of manufactured exports was in a sense understandable, since these exports started from a narrow base in the mid-1980s. Nevertheless, this slowdown aroused concern among Indonesia's economic policymakers that Indonesia was losing its export competitiveness and that this might adversely affect the prospects of sustained rapid economic growth. One indication of the loss of export competitiveness was the loss of market share of Indonesia's textile and garment exports in 1993–94 in the non-quota markets where Indonesia's exports faced head on the competition from other exporting countries (James, 1995: 23–25).

To study the sustainability of manufactured export growth, the Indonesian government commissioned some studies to look into this problem. In a study on the '*Prospects for Manufactured Exports During Repelita VI*' conducted by the Harvard Institute of International Development (HIID) in 1995 for the Department of Industry and Trade, the HIID report found that Indonesia was behind its international competitors in laying the foundation for developing skill- and capital-intensive exports (HIID 1995: 7). Like these countries, for Indonesia the only basis for modernizing the export base was to achieve continued gains in the productivity of workers, capital, and the firms themselves (HIID 1995: 1). Hence, the challenge facing Indonesia's manufacturing sector was to achieve a sustained increase in total factor productivity (TFP).

TFP growth rates in Indonesian manufacturing are greatly affected by the policy environment as indicated by the findings of studies by Hill, Aswicahyono, & Bird; and Timmer (Table 2).

The study by Hill, Aswicahyono, and Bird (1997) study found that TFP growth rates in Indonesian manufacturing varied according to three distinct policy periods, namely the period of import-substituting industrialization during the oil boom (1976–81), the immediate post-oil boom period when existing policies were reassessed (1982–85), and the period marked by a more decisive shift to export-promotion policies (1986–91). Average annual TFP growth was low during the first period, then rose during the second period, and then rose faster during the third period (Hill, Aswicahyono and Bird 1997: 78). Evidently, the more favourable policy environment since the mid-1980s had a positive impact on TFP growth.

A more recent study by Marcel Timmer on aggregate TFP growth in Indonesian manufacturing came up with largely similar findings. Subdividing

**TABLE 2**
**Average Annual TFP Growth in Indonesian Manufacturing, 1975–95**

| Period | Average annual TFP growth (%) (1) | Period | Average annual TFP growth (%) (2) |
|--------|-----------------------------------|--------|-----------------------------------|
| 1976–81 | 0.7 | 1975–81 | 1.0 |
| 1982–85 | 1.1 | 1982–85 | 0.1 |
| 1986–91 | 2.1 | 1986–90 | 7.9 |
|  |  | 1991–95 | 2.1 |
|  |  | 1975–95 | 2.8 |

*Source*: For (1), Hill, Aswicahyono, and Bird (1997), table 3.8; and for (2) Timmer (1999), table 4, p. 87.

the period studied into five-year intervals, Timmer found, like Hill, Aswicahyono, and Bird, that average annual TFP growth rate was low during the import-substituting phase of the late 1970s-early 1980s. However, after the policy reforms since the mid-1980s TFP growth accelerated steeply in the late 1980s (Timmer, 1999: 84–87). During the first half of the 1990s, TFP growth declined again, although it was still higher than during the import-substitution phase of the late 1970s-early 1980s.

The differences between the estimates of Hill, Aswicahyono, and Bird and of Timmer on TFP growth, including on the period 1986–91, are largely due to the way the factor inputs, notably the capital stock, were measured and the extent and scope of quality improvements were accounted for. This in turn was dependent on the availability and choice of data, with the greatest problem lying in the measurement of physical and human capital (Timmer, 1999: 76).

Despite the soundness of the recommendations in the HIID report, the government had on the eve of the Asian economic crisis not yet completed the necessary deregulation of international trade, including further tariff reductions and relaxation of non-tariff barriers (NTBs), which would have reduced the production costs of manufacturing firms and raised their international competitiveness (World Bank 1997: 112). In addition, extensive regulations and restrictions on domestic competition also added to the costs of doing business in Indonesia, thereby further reducing the efficiency of private firms (World Bank 1997: 118).

One major reason why the Indonesian government had by 1997 not yet taken the necessary steps, obvious to economists, to further deregulate international trade and lift the policy-generated barriers to domestic competition, was the influence of well-connected, vested interests. These interests had benefited from the rents created by the barriers to import and domestic competition.

Another reason why the government did not take the necessary steps to raise the country's industrial competitiveness, as suggested by the HIID and other studies, was the political influence of Dr B.J. Habibie, the powerful Minister of State for Research and Technology. Unlike most economists, Habibie, an aeronautic engineer by training, argued that Indonesia should no longer depend on labour-intensive industries, which in his view were 'sunset industries', the international competitiveness of which were declining (Thee 1998: 33). To compensate for the decline of these 'sunset industries', Habibie advocated the development of 'strategic industries', including the state-owned, 'hi-tech' aircraft industry, which in his view would yield more foreign exchange earnings than the 'sunset industries'. To develop these 'strategic industries', these industries needed to be temporarily protected and subsidized (Thee 1998: 133).

Habibie's views were criticized by economists, who argued that these costly 'strategic industries', particularly the aircraft assembling industry, were imposing high social opportunity costs on the country. However, because of Habibie's strong influence on President Soeharto, his views prevailed. Hence, during the 1990s up to the crisis of 1997/98 the Indonesian government pursued a dual track industrial policy by pursuing a 'broad spectrum policy of outward-looking industrialization, as advocated by a more export-oriented Department of Industry and Trade, and the promotion of Habibie's strategic industries' (Thee & Pangestu 1998: 262).

## b. Industrial Development after the Asian Economic Crisis

After the Asian economic crisis, growth of Indonesia's manufacturing sector slowed down sharply. While manufacturing in 1996 had grown at almost 12 per cent, it slowed to 5.3 per cent in 1997 and in 1998 contracted by −11.4 per cent. (Table 3)

Although manufacturing growth recovered to a sluggish 3.9 per cent in 1999 and to 6.0 per cent in 2000, it slowed down from 2001 through 2003. In 2004 it rose to 6.4 per cent in line with more rapid economic growth. However, in 2005 growth of GDP and manufacturing declined again due to the sharp increase in fuel prices and interest rates.

To some extent, the sluggish growth of manufacturing after 2000 was due to the lower output of the oil and gas industries, specifically the petroleum refineries. It should be borne in mind that the relative importance of the oil and gas industries after the end of the oil boom era in 1982 has steadily

## TABLE 3
### Growth of Indonesia's GDP and Manufacturing Sector, 1997–2005

|  | 1997 | 1998 | 1999 | 2000 | 2001 | 2002 | 2003 | 2004a | 2005b |
|---|---|---|---|---|---|---|---|---|---|
| GDP | 4.7 | –13.1 | 0.8 | 4.9 | 3.8 | 4.3 | 4.8 | 5.1 | 5.6 |
| Manufacturing | 5.3 | –11.4 | 3.9 | 6.0 | 3.3 | 5.3 | 5.3 | 6.4 | 4.6 |
| Oil and gas industry | –2.0 | 3.7 | 6.8 | –1.7 | –6.2 | 2.5 | 0.8 | –1.9 | –5.3 |
| Non-oil and -gas industries | 6.1 | –13.1 | 3.5 | 7.0 | 4.9 | 5.7 | 6.0 | 7.5 | 5.9 |

*Notes*: Data from 1997–99 at constant 1999 prices; Data from 2000 onwards at constant 2001 prices.
a. Preliminary figures
b. Very preliminary figures
*Source*: Badan Pusat Statistik (BPS), Jakarta.

declined. In 2002, the oil and gas manufacturing sub-sector accounted for only 11 per cent of the non-oil and -gas manufacturing sub-sector.

Looking at the performance of the non-oil and -gas industries, which generated the bulk of the surge of non-oil exports since the late 1980s through 1996, we see that the growth of the non-oil and gas manufacturing sub-sector also declined steadily from a high of 7.0 per cent in 2000 to 4.0 per cent or less from 2001 through 2003. However, in 2004 the non-oil and gas manufacturing sub-sector grew at 7.5 per cent, which was the highest rate after the crisis. However, in 2005 growth of the non-oil and gas manufacturing sector declined again because of the adverse impact of higher fuel prices and interest rates. This is a matter of concern, since rapid growth of the manufacturing sector, driven by rapid growth of manufactured exports, have fuelled economic growth and created new jobs.

At present the prospects for rapid growth of the manufacturing sector, particularly manufactured exports, are still cloudy because of various adverse domestic factors rather than external factors. Four adverse factors in particular account for the post-crisis sluggish growth of manufactured exports. These are the decline in cost competitiveness, decline in investment, increased international competition and poor trade facilitation (World Bank, 2004: ii–iii).

### ad i. Loss in cost competitiveness

The stronger rupiah and higher domestic cost inflation, including higher labour costs, have eroded Indonesia's competitiveness in the world markets.

According to an IMF estimate, the unit labour costs in US dollars, a key indicator of competitiveness, are now 35 per cent higher than before the crisis. This adverse development has eroded the competitiveness of Indonesia's labour-intensive exports. This rise in unit labour costs is caused by the steady rise in minimum wages which have exceeded the rise in labour productivity.

### ad ii. Decline in investment

Indonesia's investment climate has deteriorated considerably after the demise of the 'New Order', and now ranks as one of the worst in the East Asian region. This poor investment climate has deterred new investments, particularly foreign direct investment (FDI), which are important for product upgrading and generating new manufactured exports and new jobs.

### ad iii. Increased international competition

In recent years China and Vietnam have emerged as strong competitors to Indonesia, since they export the same low skill labour-intensive products. While Indonesia's key exports, such as fabrics and footwear, experienced a decline, both China and Vietnam recorded a rapid growth in these manufactured exports. In Japan, which was not a signatory to the Multi-Fibre Agreement (MFA), Indonesia lost 40 per cent of its market share in textiles to lower cost competitors (World Bank, 2004: ii), even before the expiry of the MFA in early 2005 (World Bank, 2004: ii).

### ad iv. Poor trade facilitation

Port and other infrastructure bottlenecks, such as congested highways to the ports and occasional blackouts of electricity, substantially raise the domestic costs of manufactured exports. After the Asian economic crisis Indonesia's physical infrastructure has greatly deteriorated because of the decline in public investment. Although responsibility for maintaining physical infrastructure has partly been handed over to the regional governments since the introduction of regional autonomy in early 2001, implementation has been patchy because of ill-defined coordination arrangements and divisions of authority between the central and regional governments (Bird & Hill, 2006: 369).

Because of the low efficiency of Indonesia's ports, including the Jakarta International Container Terminal (JICT), the main container terminal of Tanjung Priok, Indonesia's largest port, virtually all of Indonesia's container traffic is transshipped through Singapore and Malaysia. According to World

Bank estimates, Indonesia could increase its exports by 18 per cent if port logistics and procedures were just half as efficient as in the average APEC country (World Bank, 2004: iii).

To increase Indonesia's exports, the government should therefore focus its efforts on tackling the above adverse factors, including efforts to lower the costs of exporters; improve the investment climate for private, including foreign, investors, by improving governance, particularly in the judiciary, tax and custom offices; assisting exporters in penetrating new export markets; and tackling the port and other infrastructure bottlenecks.

## SOME ASSESSMENTS OF INDONESIA'S TECHNOLOGICAL COMPETENCE

Although Indonesia's rapid industrial transformation during the past three decades has been accompanied by technological upgrading, as reflected by rising TFP levels (Table 2) since the mid-1980s, the development of Indonesia's industrial technological capabilities (ITCs) has lagged behind that of the Asian Tigers, particularly Korea and Taiwan, and even behind the two other East Asian NIEs, Malaysia and Thailand. Improved technological capabilities are crucial to sustain Indonesia's manufactured export growth.

Indonesia's low industrial technological capabilities (ITCs) is, amongst others, reflected by the low percentage of its high technology manufactured exports, as compared to those of the other East Asian countries (Table 4).

Although definitions of what constitute high technology exports are not perfect, since they also include assembled products with low local value added, such as consumer electronics, they can serve as a rough indicator of a country's technological competence. Hence, the data in Table 5 which show the much lower percentage of Indonesia's high technology manufactured exports as compared to those of the other East Asian countries indicate how far Indonesia still has to go in developing technology- and skill-intensive products.

Indonesia's relatively low ITCs have also been confirmed by qualitative, firm-level surveys conducted by international consulting firms (e.g. SRI International, 1992) and academic economists. In a comparative study sponsored by UNCTAD's Technology Program on the link between manufactured exports and technological capabilities in Korea, Taiwan, Indonesia, Thailand, and Vietnam (Ernst, et al., 1998), this comparative study indicated that Indonesia's ITCs, even in export-oriented manufacturing firms, were still limited to the basic production or operational capabilities required for the smooth functioning of the plants and, to a lesser extent, to

## TABLE 4
## Indonesia's High Technology Exports in Regional Perspective, 2003

| Country | High technology manufactured exports (US$ billion) | High technology exports as a percentage of total manufactured exports (%) |
|---|---|---|
| Indonesia | 4,580 | 14 |
| Malaysia | 47,042 | 58 |
| Singapore | 71,421 | 59 |
| Thailand | 18,203 | 30 |
| China | 107,543 | 27 |
| South Korea | 57,161 | 32 |

*Note*: High technology exports are products with a high R & D intensity, as in aerospace, computers, pharmaceuticals, and scientific instruments.
*Source*: World Bank: *World Development Indicators, 2005*, table 5.12, pp. 314–18.

## TABLE 5
## Indonesia's Record in Education in Regional Perspective

| Country | Public expenditure on education | Gross enrollment ratio, 2004 (% of relevant age group) | | |
| | | Primary | Secondary | Tertiary |
| | % of total government expenditure, 2004 | | | |
|---|---|---|---|---|
| Indonesia | 9.0 | 116 | 62 | 16 |
| Malaysia | 20.3 | 93 | 70 | 29 |
| Philippines | 17.8 | 113 | 84 | 29 |
| Thailand | 27.5 | 99 | 77 | 41 |
| South Korea | 15.5 | 105 | 91 | 89 |

*Source*: World Bank: World Development Indicators, 2006, table 2.10, pp. 85–86; table 2.11, pp. 89–90.

adaptive or minor change capabilities, specifically in regard to introducing minor changes in process technologies to adapt to local conditions. None of Indonesia's firms, however, had as yet developed the more demanding innovative (major change) capabilities that enable firms to make major changes in process or product technologies. Development of these latter capabilities, the study concluded, was essential to the ability of Indonesian firms to achieve and maintain international competitiveness (Thee and Pangestu, 1998).

In a critical assessment of Indonesia's technology policies, Sanjaya Lall pointed out the relatively low level of Indonesia's ITCs. Lall observed that Indonesia's industrial structure had several weaknesses in terms of technology. These weaknesses, if not overcome, would hamper Indonesia's long-term industrial growth and upgrading (Lall, 1998: 136). Among the technological weaknesses cited were the shallow and backward technological base, particularly compared to that of the East Asian Tigers; weak and narrow domestic capabilities for absorbing and improving upon complex imported technologies; an underdeveloped capital goods sector; and the relatively small amount of technological effort, which was concentrated and distorted (because of the focus on the highly subsidized and protected "hi-tech" industries promoted by Dr Habibie (Lall, 1998: 136).

In the following pages the policies to enhance Indonesia's industrial competitiveness through improved technological capabilities will be discussed.

## RAISING INDONESIA'S INDUSTRIAL COMPETITIVENESS THROUGH INDUSTRIAL TECHNOLOGICAL DEVELOPMENT

International experience, particularly of the East Asian NIEs, has indicated that raising Indonesia's export competitiveness requires the effective development of technological and associated managerial capabilities. Developing these technological capabilities does not mean innovation in the sense of 'reinventing the wheel' to create technologies that are available elsewhere, often at lower cost. It does mean learning to use existing technologies efficiently, a daunting task (Lall & Weiss, 2003: 4).

Developing these technological capabilities is particularly important for raising Indonesia's export competitiveness, since thus far its manufactured exports has mainly consisted of resource- and low skill labour-intensive products, which generally involve less effort, risk, and externalities. Although Indonesia for the foreseeable future still retains a comparative advantage in labour-intensive manufactured exports because of its large labour surplus, there is general agreement that technology development is crucial to raise the efficiency and international competitiveness of Indonesia's manufacturing industries and sustain the growth of these industries. However, inadequate attention has been paid to mechanisms to promote broad, effective diffusion of best practice technologies which could help Indonesia's manufacturing sector to improve its international competitiveness (World Bank, 1996: i).

International experience has shown that an industrial technology development strategy requires that certain basic and enabling conditions have to be met (World Bank, 1996: 2–5; Lall, 1992: 165–86; Hill, 2001: 6–9).

The *basic conditions* for industrial technology development in Indonesia are:

1. The pursuit of sound macroeconomic policies, as low inflation encourages firms to make long-term investments in technology development;
2. The pursuit of pro-competition economic policies, since a competitive environment is conducive to drive firms to invest more in technology upgrading to raise their competitiveness;
3. The upgrading of the quality of human resources, which is imperative for technology development (World Bank, 1996: ii).

In addition to these basic conditions, a number of *enabling conditions* should be met through policies that:

1. Improve Indonesia's access to foreign technologies, including through foreign direct investment (FDI), as a tool for technology development;
2. Improve the availability of adequate finance for technology development;
3. Improve the effectiveness and performance of the technology support services (World Bank, 1996: i).

Sound macroeconomic policies and pro-competition policies shape the *incentive system* facing manufacturing firms to encourage them to invest in technology development. On the other hand the upgrading of human resources as well as the access to foreign technologies, finance and technology support services determine the *supply-side capabilities* of these firms.

The policies to meet the basic and enabling conditions are discussed below.

*a. The basic conditions*
*1. Pursuing sound macroeconomic policies*
From the outset the 'New Order' government under General, later President Soeharto (1966–98), put a high priority on pursuing sound macroeconomic policies. After the reckless deficit-financing policies of President Sukarno which led to hyperinflation in the mid-1960s, the 'New Order' government realized that maintaining macroeconomic stability was crucial to encourage firms to undertake the long-term capital investments necessary for rapid and sustained economic growth. Hence, during the Soeharto era Indonesia's

record on controlling inflation has been fairly good, although Indonesia's inflation during the mid-1980s through the mid-1990s was always slightly higher than that of its East Asian neighbours, except for the Philippines (Hill, 1996: 7).

Macroeconomic stability in 1997/98 was severely disrupted because of the Asian economic crisis. As a result of the steep depreciation of the rupiah, inflation rose steeply to 80 per cent in early 1998. However, in the course of 1998 the hyperinflation was gradually brought under control because of tight monetary policies (Hill, 1999: 29).

Whatever the political differences between the post-Soeharto governments (Habibie, Abdurrachman Wahid, Megawati Sukarnoputri, and currently Susilo Bambang Yudhoyono), all these governments realized the great importance of sound macroeconomic policies to maintain macroeconomic stability. Under the able stewardship of Dr Boediono, Minister of Finance in the Megawati administration (2001–04), macroeconomic stability was strengthened, as reflected by a stable inflation rate of 6 per cent in 2004 (World Bank, 2005: ii). However, in late 2005 inflation rose steeply to over 17 per cent because of the large fuel price increases. To control these inflationary pressures, Bank Indonesia raised interest rates which, together with a 6 per cent appreciation of the rupiah, led to a much lower cumulative inflation of 2.4 per cent over the period January–May 2006 (World Bank, 2006b: 3–4).

## 2. Pursuing pro-competition economic policies

The experience of the East Asian NIEs has shown that a competitive environment for firms has been an important prerequisite for technology upgrading. In these countries competition has been an important stimulus to drive firms to invest in their technological development (World Bank, 1996: 3).

The overall competitive environment is determined by the foreign trade regime and domestic competition. After the end of the oil boom era 1982 the 'New Order' government introduced a series of trade reforms to reduce the 'anti-export bias' of the protectionist trade regime. These trade reforms included a gradual but steady reduction in tariff protection and non-tariff barriers (NTBs), specifically quantitative import restrictions, and a duty exemption and drawback scheme for export-oriented firms, which proved to be effective in encouraging firms to export. However, by the time the 'New Order' government had introduced its last trade reforms in early 1997, remaining import protection still accounted for a lower, though still significant 'anti-export bias' of the trade regime (Thee, 1998: 118–19).

While the trade reforms from the mid-1980s through 1996 led to greater import competition, domestic competition and trade were still subject to extensive regulations and restrictions introduced by the central and provincial governments, and occasionally by officially sanctioned trade and industry associations (Thee, 2002: 332). These restrictions took many forms, including entry controls, price controls, provisions for public sector dominance, the sanctioning of cartels, and ad hoc interventions favouring specific firms or sectors (Iqbal, 1995: 14).

Only after the Asian economic crisis was the Indonesian government forced, as part of its first agreement with the IMF in early November 1997, to lift the policy-generated barriers to domestic competition and trade. In its second agreement with the IMF in January 1998, a wider range of structural reforms were included, which provided for a further deregulation of the foreign trade and foreign investment regimes as well as the domestic competition regime (Thee, 2002: 332).

Aside from the deregulation policies to promote competition in the local and national markets, in early 1999 the new Indonesian government under President Habibie enacted a competition law, the Law Banning Monopolistic Practices and Unfair Competition. This competition law was intended to protect and maintain free and open market competition by preventing anti-competitive business practices by firms. With this competition law, Indonesia had in place, at least on paper, a comprehensive competition policy, encompassing both the various deregulation measures and a competition law (Thee, 2002: 333).

Since the appointment of a Business Competition Supervisory Commission in late 1996, many cases, particularly bid rigging or closed tenders, have already been investigated by this Commission.

While some of its decisions have been criticized, it has been quite active in pursuing and investigating cases where anti-competitive business conduct was suspected.

Unfortunately, the deregulation policies of the recent past have been offset by the proliferation of new regulations by local governments since regional autonomy was introduced in early 2001. Many of these regulations restrict or tax trade within or between districts (kabupaten) and provinces. Obviously, these taxes and restrictions interfere in domestic trade and undermine domestic competition and internal market efficiency (World Bank, 2005: 41). Hence, in terms of domestic competition, the new local restrictions on domestic trade and competition have undermined the pro-competition policies of recent years.

*3. Expanding education and upgrading the quality of human resources*
A well-trained labour force, an effective training system, good quality science and engineering faculties of universities, and good management training programs are key elements for sustaining Indonesia's industrial technology development (World Bank, 1996: ii). Despite the progress in expanding education during the Soeharto era, Indonesia's record in education, as reflected by its public expenditures on education and gross enrollment ratios at all levels of education, is generally still inferior compared to that of its Southeast Asian neighbours and South Korea (Table 5). Aside from this, the quality of Indonesia's education at all levels is generally inferior to that of its East Asian neighbours.

The data in Table 5 show that Indonesia is far behind its Southeast Asian neighbours and South Korea in terms of its public expenditures on education and participation in education, particularly at the secondary and tertiary levels.

Aside from the fact that Indonesia's public expenditure on human resource development is even lower than the average low income country, let alone the average middle income country, the current education and training system in general does not meet the needs of industry. The reason is that the general secondary education system relies on rote learning, and does not develop adequate mastery of basic literacy, basic numeracy, and thinking and creative skills. Hence, high school graduates are not adequately equipped with the knowledge and skills required for a more complex and diversified manufacturing sector, and also cannot take advantage from on-the-job training (Dhanani, 2000: 11).

Moreover, the senior secondary technical vocational schools, two thirds of which are privately-funded and -operated, are poorly staffed and equipped, and thus do not equip the graduates with adequate practical knowledge. Post-secondary vocational technical education, on the other hand, is mainly provided by the government (Dhanani, 2000: 11), which currently lacks the resources to expand education and improve the quality of education, particularly technical education.

Indonesia's record in health too lags behind that of its East Asian neighbours, as reflected by some indicators on health expenditure and the health status of its population (Table 6).

The data in Table 6 show that public expenditure on health as a percentage of total health expenditure is the lowest in Indonesia as compared to that of its East Asian neighbours. Not surprisingly, the incidence of tuberculosis in Indonesia, for instance, is, together with the Philippines, one of the highest

## TABLE 6
### Health Status of Indonesia's Population in Regional Perspective, 2003–04

|  | Public health expenditure (% of total), 2004 | Prevalence of undernourishment (% of population), 2001–03 | Incidence of tuberculosis per 100,000 people, 2004 | Life expectancy at birth, 2004 |
|---|---|---|---|---|
| Indonesia | 35.9 | 6 | 245 | 67 |
| Malaysia | 58.2 | 3 | 103 | 73 |
| Philippines | 43.7 | 19 | 293 | 71 |
| Thailand | 61.6 | 21 | 142 | 71 |
| South Korea | 49.4 | Less than 3 | 90 | 77 |

*Source*: World Bank: World Development Indicators, 2006, table 2.14, pp. 101–02; table 2.17, pp. 113–14; table 2.18, pp. 117–18; table 2.19, pp. 121–22.

in East Asia. Life expectance at birth in Indonesia is also the lowest in East Asia. Interestingly, however, the prevalence of undernourishment in Indonesia is lower than in the Philippines and Thailand.

Aside from the above basic conditions required to promote industrial technology development, enabling conditions should be in place to facilitate technological development.

### b. The enabling conditions
### 1. Facilitating manufacturing firms' access to foreign technologies
Like other developing countries, Indonesia is a net importer of advanced technologies developed in the advanced industrial countries. These advanced technologies are crucial to enhance a country's technological capabilities to produce more efficiently and competitively. The experience of Japan and the East Asian NIEs, particularly Korea and Taiwan, has shown that the acquisition of foreign technologies, the assimilation and adaptation of these technologies to local conditions, and the subsequent improvement of these imported technologies have been crucial to raising these countries' technological capabilities. (Chen 1983: 63).

In view of the economic importance of these imported technologies, it is important to identify the major channels through which these technologies have been transferred to Indonesia, particularly to its manufacturing sector. Studies on international technology transfer in Indonesia's manufacturing sector indicate that foreign direct investment (FDI), technical licensing agreements, capital goods imports and the related transfer of skills by technical experts of foreign supplier firms, and the technical and marketing assistance by foreign buyers who acted as consultants to export-oriented firms, have been the major channels for international technology transfer to Indonesia (Thee, 2005: 218–19).

### i. Foreign direct investment (FDI)

While Indonesia since the early 1990s through 1996 experienced sizable net FDI inflows, after the Asian economic crisis it experienced net FDI outflows which persisted through 2003. This development was in sharp contrast to developments in Malaysia, Thailand and South Korea which, although also hard hit by the Asian economic crisis, did not experience net FDI outflows, but in fact experienced rising net FDI inflows (Table 7).

Even the positive net FDI inflow which Indonesia experienced in 2004 was much smaller than the large net FDI inflows during the late 1980s through 1996. This positive figure was also caused by the fact that Bank Indonesia has recently included privatisation of state-owned enterprises (SOEs), specifically the sale of these SOEs to foreign investors, and bank restructuring, specifically the sale of distressed banks to foreign investors, as part of FDI inflows.

### TABLE 7
### Net FDI flows into Indonesia, Malaysia, Thailand and
### South Korea, 1990–2004
### (millions of US$)

|      | Indonesia | Malaysia | Thailand | South Korea |
|------|-----------|----------|----------|-------------|
| 1990 | 1,093     | 2,332    | 2,444    | 789         |
| 1991 | 1,482     | 3,998    | 2,014    | 1,180       |
| 1992 | 1,777     | 5.183    | 2,113    | 728         |
| 1993 | 2,004     | 5,006    | 1,804    | 588         |
| 1994 | 2,109     | 4,341    | 1,366    | 809         |
| 1995 | 4,345     | 4,178    | 2,068    | 1,776       |
| 1996 | 6,194     | 5,078    | 2,336    | 2,325       |
| 1997 | 4,667     | 5,137    | 3,895    | 2,844       |
| 1998 | −356      | 2,163    | 7,315    | 5,412       |
| 1999 | −2,745    | 3,895    | 6,103    | 9,333       |
| 2000 | −4,550    | 3,788    | 3,336    | 9,283       |
| 2001 | −2,798    | 554      | 3,892    | 3,528       |
| 2002 | 145       | 3,203    | 953      | 2,392       |
| 2003 | −597      | 2,473    | 1,949    | 3,526       |
| 2004 | 423       | 4,624    | 1,412    | 8,189       |

*Source*: Data on the net FDI flows obtained from the balance of payments data from Bank Indonesia, Bank Negara Malaysia, Bank of Thailand and Bank of Korea, as quoted in: *ICSEAD: East Asian Economic Perspectives*, Vol. 17, no. 1, February 2006, table 7.2 (Indonesia), table 8.2 (Malaysia), table 11.2 (Thailand), and table 5.2 (South Korea).

The lack of interest of foreign investors to undertake new greenfield investments after the Asian economic crisis can be attributed to Indonesia's poor investment climate, which currently ranks among the worst in the East Asian region. Various factors account for this poor investment climate, including the lack of legal certainty and adequate law enforcement; labour problems, mainly caused by a business-unfriendly labour law enacted in 2003; confusion about overlapping authorities between the central and regional governments caused by the regional autonomy introduced in early 2001; widespread corruption which raise the costs of doing business in Indonesia; and crumbling physical infrastructure due to the lack of proper maintenance after the Asian economic crisis. The net effect of these problems is uncertainty, higher costs and many demands for bribes (World Bank, 2003: 29).

The fact that a small amount of FDI only flowed into Indonesia since 2004, while Korea and Thailand, the two other East Asian countries worst affected by the Asian economic crisis, already experienced rising net FDI inflows in 1998, meant that these two latter countries experienced not only a strengthening of their currencies, but also an acceleration of much needed corporate restructuring, and important infusions of new technologies and modern management methods (World Bank, 2000: 6). Indonesia, on the other hand, was unable to obtain these benefits, as FDI instead flowed out of the country.

*ii. Technical licensing agreements*

In Indonesia a major 'unpackaged' (non-equity) mode of technology transfer from advanced country firms to Indonesian firms has been technical licensing agreements (TLAs). Although no quantitative data are available on the number of these TLAs, circumstantial evidence indicates that these TLAs often involve the transfer of older and mature technologies that do not offer the recipient country a long-term competitive advantage in the global market (Marks 1999: 6). However, for a late-industrializing economy like Indonesia, acquiring and mastering these older technologies first is a good way to develop the important basic industrial technological capabilities (ITCs), namely the production, investment and adaptive capabilities.

*iii. Imports of capital goods and the transfer of skills by technical experts of foreign supplier firms*

Imports of capital goods provide another way of acquiring the means of production without the transactional costs involved in FDI or TLAs (Dahlman, Ross-Larson & Westphal 1987: 768). Capital goods imports are actually embodied technology flows entering a country. They introduce into the production processes new machinery, other capital equipment and components that incorporate technologies which do not always incorporate high or frontier technologies, but are nevertheless new to the recipient firm (Soesastro 1998: 304).

These imported capital goods can be a cheap way of developing local TCs if they can be used as models for reverse engineering to produce the machines locally (Dahlman, Ross-Larson & Westphal 1987: 768). However, Indonesian firms have in general not engaged in 'reverse engineering' on a large scale to develop their ITCs, as Korean firms have done. However, the import of capital goods, particularly modern machinery, is often accompanied by technical advice provided by technical experts of the foreign supplier firm to the employees of the local firm on how to properly maintain or repair the machinery. In this way the import of capital goods contribute to the development of local technological capabilities.

*iv. Technical assistance by foreign buyers*

Since the mid 1970s an important informal channel of international technology transfer for Indonesian firms, including small and medium-scale enterprises (SMEs), has been provided by their participation in world trade, specifically through exporting their products. This informal channel was utilised effectively by local firms, particularly electronics firms, in the four East Asian NIEs, including Korea, Taiwan, Hong Kong and Singapore which, based on low wage rates, were able to build up basic operational (production) capabilities through simple assembly of mature products for exports, often developed through technical assistance provided by foreign buyers (Hobday, 1994: 335; World Bank 1996: 4). These local NIE firms successfully coupled export and technological development, allowing export market needs (the needs and design and product specifications of their overseas buyers) to focus their investment in technological upgrading and to provide a channel for them to acquire foreign technologies from their overseas buyers. This process of coupling exports with technology development has been referred to as '*export-led technology development*' (Hobday, 1994: 335).

Although not as technologically advanced as the East Asian NIEs's 'export-led technology development', the remarkable export performance which the garment industry and other export industries in Bali and Jepara, Central Java, have experienced since the mid-1970s is somewhat similar to the experience of these East Asian firms. The remarkable growth of Bali's export industries, starting with the garment industry in the mid-1970s, and subsequently the silver jewelry, wood carving, quilting, leather products, bamboo furniture, ceramics, and stone carving industries, was based on vital information flows which these Balinese firms, received through strategic business alliances with foreign firms and businessmen (Cole 1998: 257).

Through the vital information transfer and technical and managerial assistance (for instance on designs and plant lay-out, advice on the purchase of the most appropriate machines, and strict quality control) provided by the foreign buyers who often also acted as technical consultants to the largely small Balinese firms, these firms were able to achieve high levels of efficiency and accuracy. This assistance was provided on a for-profit basis, as it was specifically tied to tangible product output results (Cole 1998: 275; Thee & Hamid 1997). The ongoing interaction of these two parties started a virtuous cycle of technological improvements and learning that was self-replicating and largely self-financing, and which led to rapid and sustained export growth (Cole 1998: 275).

*2. The availability of finance for technology development*
Another important element of industrial technology development is the availability and access to finance. The availability and access to term finance for investments in technology upgrading would be facilitated if the capacity of the banking system to appraise such investments could be strengthened. In Indonesia the government during the late Soeharto era also attempted to improve the tax treatment of venture capital funds (World Bank, 1996: iv).

Unfortunately, even before the Asian economic crisis, finance for investments in technology development was scarce. Indonesia never had a financing firm for technology development as Korea had, namely the Korea Technology Development Corporation (KCTC) (World Bank, 1996: 29). A state-owned venture capital firm, the PT Bahana Pembinaan Usaha Indonesia (Bahana PUI), was mainly entrusted to guide and develop small-and medium enterprises (SMEs) (FIAS: 1996: 54).

After surviving banks had recovered from the Asian economic crisis, the bulk of their loans has been provided for private consumption, which indeed has been the main driver of economic growth during the past few years. At present banks and non-financial institutions have provided large amounts of loans for housing loans and credit card lending. Bank consumer credit has grown rapidly since 2000, and in 2004 grew at an average year-on-year rate of over 30 per cent (Soesastro & Atje, 2005: 35). Under these conditions little is left to finance technology development, even if banks are willing to overcome their risk aversion. It is therefore not surprising that the bulk of R&D activities in the manufacturing sector is financed by the private firms themselves (Table 8).

**TABLE 8**
**Spending on R & D in Indonesian Manufacturing by**
**Source of Funds, 1994 and 1999**
**(billions of rupiah)**

| Source of funds | 1994 | 1999 |
|---|---|---|
| Government | 38.79 | 0.68 |
| Other firms | 27.56 | 1.04 |
| Own firm | 159.61 | 228.92 |
| Overseas | 17.59 | 7.57 |
| Other | 1.29 | 9.52 |

*Source*: LIPI and Office of the Minister of State for Research and Technology, 2004, based on surveys by the Central Agency for Statistics, held in 1994 and 1999.

The above date show that even before the Asian economic crisis, the bulk of R&D funding was financed by the manufacturing firms themselves. After the crisis R&D funding by the firms themselves became even more important, both in absolute and in relative terms.

*3. Improve the performance of technology support services*
To assist firms to improve their technological capabilities, effective technology support services are needed. These technology support services include metrology, standards, testing and quality support services (MSTQ services). These services include the dissemination of information on international standards and assistance to firms to get ISO 9000 certification. It also includes industrial extension services to assist firms to improve productivity, quality, product designs and delivery times. Other important technology support services include technology information services to provide firms with information on best practices, that is globally competitive technologies (World Bank, 1996: v).

During the Soeharto era the performance of the available technology support services, particularly the MSTQ services, was rated as inadequate by many firms. To some extent this was caused by the fact that many firms did not realise that their products needed to conform to strict standards (e.g. technical and sanitary standards) and performance requirements (e.g. ISO 9000), both national and international, particularly if they wanted to enter export markets (Thee, 1998: 127).

The available technology support services, particularly the important MSTQ services, are public institutes. If these services were rated as inadequate before the Asian economic crisis, the range and quality of these public institutes have likely declined further after the crisis, as public funds to upgrade these services have been reduced. It has been suggested that these technology support services should be privatised, but it appears unlikely that at present the private sector is interested in taking charge of these services.

The performance of the public sector research institutes, consisting of the R&D institutes of the Department of Industry and the research institutes under the coordination of the Minister of Research and Technology, particularly the Indonesian Institute of Sciences (LIPI) and the Agency for Technology Assessment and Application (BPPT), in developing Indonesia's ITCS is in general also not satisfactory. The 12 national R&D laboratories and several regional laboratories of the Department of Industry are primarily engaged in training and product testing and certification rather than in R&D, and have little or no linkages with industry. The staff is generally neither well- trained nor highly motivated because of low salaries, while the laboratories operate with outdated equipment (Lall, 1998: 153–54).

The laboratories of LIPI and BPPT are in general better funded and staffed than those of the Department of Industry. However, their contribution to technology development is also limited, since their R&D activities are supply- rather than demand-driven, and often lack behind world technological frontiers. For this reason they have not been able to establish linkages with private industry. The internal management and procedures of these institutes also tend be bureaucratic (Lall, 1998: 154).

The performance of these public research institutes has hardly changed after the Asian economic crisis. In fact, because of the shortage of funds of the government, it has been difficult to improve the performance of these institutes. Because of the relatively low salaries, many researchers tend to moonlight instead of working full-time on research.

## CONCLUSION

The above overview of the required basic and enabling conditions to encourage Indonesian firms to invest in their technological development to raise their competitiveness indicates that in general these conditions have not been adequately met. While sound macro economic policies have in general been pursued with great success, pro-competition policies were only introduced to a limited degree through the liberalization of the trade and the foreign investment regimes. However, during the late Soeharto era various restrictions on domestic competition and trade were introduced which adversely affected the business environment for bonafide entrepreneurs.

Although in March 1999 an anti-monopoly and fair competition law was introduced, these pro-competition policies have recently been undermined by new restrictions on domestic competition and trade introduced by various regional governments after the introduction of regional autonomy in early 2001. Because of these restrictions, the business environment has deteriorated again.

Human resource development in Indonesia has generally lagged behind its East Asian neighbours before the Asian economic crisis, and have lagged even farther after the Asian economic crisis. Technical education at the secondary and tertiary level has been inadequate in imparting to the students the necessary technical skills to support technological development. The health status of the Indonesian population is in general not as good as that of the populations in the other East Asian countries.

Indonesian firms have access to foreign technologies mainly through foreign direct investment (FDI), technical licensing agreements, capital goods imports, and exporting. However, in the past Indonesia has not been able to take sufficient advantage from the presence of foreign firms to promote industrial and technological upgrading. At present the lack of interest of foreign investors to invest in Indonesia because of the country's poor investment climate has prevented Indonesia from benefiting from the infusions of new technologies and advanced management methods. Although technical licensing agreements have been a good means to get access to foreign technologies, these purchased technologies are generally older, mature technologies. The import of capital goods has also been a good channel to get new embodied technology, the use of which can be enhanced by technical assistance provided by technicians of the foreign suppliers of these capital goods. Gaining access to new product designs, technologies and export markets through the advice and assistance of foreign buyers/consultants of Indonesian products has also been helpful to several exporting firms, including SMEs, in upgrading their technical performance. The downside of this development is the continuing reliance on foreign buyers/consultants for the introduction of new product designs, technologies, and access to foreign markets.

Although finance for industrial technological development is important to firms willing to invest in this development, the performance of the financial sector in providing loans to firms willing to invest in technology development was disappointing even before the Asian economic crisis. After the crisis the prospects for getting more finance from the financial sector have become worse, as risk-averse banks prefer to provide loans for consumption purposes or use their deposits to purchase Bank of Indonesia certificates which earn a high interest.

To assist firms to improve their technological capabilities, effective technology support services are needed. The available technology support services, including the important metrology, standardization, testing and quality assurance (MSTQ) services, are public institutes. These services were generally rated as inadequate before the Asian economic crisis. After the crisis the range and quality of these public institutes have likely declined further, since public funds to upgrade these services were reduced. For this reason it has been suggested to privatise these technology support services. However, it appears unlikely that at present the private sector is interested in running these services themselves.

The performance of the public research institutes, including the laboratories of the Department of Industry and the research institutes of the Indonesian Institute of Sciences (LIPI) and the Agency for the Assessment and Application of Technology (BPPT), in technology development has also not been satisfactory. The laboratories of the Department of Industry are poorly staffed and poorly funded and mostly equipped with obsolete equipment. The laboratories of LIPI and BPPT are better staffed and funded, but their research is mostly supply- rather than demand-driven. For this reason these research institutes have in general not been able to establish linkages with private industry.

The above overview of the state of basic and enabling conditions for industrial technology development in Indonesia indicates that in general these important conditions have not been fully met during the Soeharto era, and even less so after the Asian economic crisis. Besides a more serious and determined effort to improve the investment climate, the Indonesian government has to focus its industrial and technology policies on meeting the above conditions for industrial technological development, if it is serious in raising Indonesia's industrial competitiveness. However, these efforts have to be accompanied by a serious effort to tackle the various, mainly domestic, problems which are a burden to private industry, namely the loss in cost competitiveness, the poor investment climate, increased international competition, and the poor trade facilitation caused by port and other infrastructure bottlenecks.

## Note

1. "Policies Affecting Indonesia's Industrial Technology Development", by Thee Kian Wie, first published in *ASEAN Economic Bulletin* 23, no. 3 (December 2006): 341–59. The author would like to acknowledge the valuable comments

and suggestions of the two anonymous referees of this paper. However, I alone am responsible for shortcomings and errors in this paper.

## References

Aswicahyono, Haryo. "Transformation and Structural Change in Indonesia's Manufacturing Sector". In *Waves of Change in Indonesia's Manufacturing Industry*, edited by Mari Pangestu and Yuri Sato, pp. 1–28. Tokyo: Institute of Developing Economies, 1997.

Bird, Kelly and Hal Hill. "Indonesia's Industrial Policies: Before and After the Crisis". In *The East Asian High-Tech Drive*, pp. 335–75. Cheltenham, U.K.: Edward Elgar, 2006.

Chen, Edward K. Y. *Multinational Corporations, Technology and Employment*. London: Macmillan Press, 1983.

Chu, Yun-Peng and Hal Hill, eds. *The East Asian High-Tech Drive*. Cheltenham, U.K.: Edward Elgar, 2006.

Cole, William. "Bali's Garment Export Industry". In *Indonesia's Technological Challenge*, edited by Hal Hill and Thee Kian Wie, pp. 255–78. Canberra and Singapore: Research School of Pacific and Asian Studies, Australian National University, and Institute of Southeast Asian Studies, 1998.

Dahlman, Carl, Bruce Ross-Larson, and Larry Westphal. "Managing Technological Development: Lessons from the Newly-Industrialising Countries". *World Development*, no. 15 (1987), pp. 759–75.

Dhanani, Shafiq. *Indonesia: Strategy for Manufacturing Competitiveness, Vol. II, Main Report*. Jakarta: United Nations Industrial Development Organization, November 2000.

Ernst, Dieter, Tom Ganiatsos, and Lynn Mytelka, eds. *Technological Capabilities and Export Success in Asia*. London and New York: Routledge, 1998.

FIAS. Indonesia: *A Pilot Project to Promote Backward Linkages: A Private–Public Partnership*. Washington, D.C.: Foreign Investment Advisory Service, June 1996.

Gray, Clive S. "Survey of Recent Developments". *Bulletin of Indonesian Economic Studies* XVIII, no. 3 (November 1982): 1–51.

HIID (Harvard Institute of International Development). "Prospects for Manufactured Exports During Repelita VI". Report to the Department of Industry and Trade, Republic of Indonesia, Jakarta, 1995.

Hill, Hal. *The Indonesian Economy Since 1966: Southeast Asia's Emerging Giant*. Cambridge and Melbourne: Cambridge University Press, 1996.

———. *Indonesia's Industrial Transformation*. Singapore: Institute of Southeast Asian Studies, 1997.

———. *The Indonesian Economy in Crisis: Causes, Consequences and Lessons*. Singapore: Institute of Southeast Asian Studies, 1999.

———. "Technology and Innovation in Developing East Asia: An Interpretive

Survey". Working Papers in Trade and Development, no. 2001/11, Division of Economics, Research School of Pacific and Asian Studies and Asia Pacific School of Economics and Management, The Australian National University, November 2001.

Hill, Hal, Haryo Aswicahyono, and Kelly Bird. "What Happened to Industrial Structure during the Deregulation Era". In *Indonesia's Industrial Transformation*, edited by Hal Hill, pp. 55–80. Singapore: Institute of Southeast Asian Studies, 1997.

Hill, Hal and Thee Kian Wie, eds. *Indonesia's Technological Challenge*. Canberra: Research School of Pacific and Asian Studies, Australian National University, and Singapore: Institute of Southeast Asian Studies, 1998.

Hobday, Mike. "Export-Led Technology Development in the Four Dragons: The Case of Electronics". *Development and Change* 25, no. 2 (1994).

ICSEAD (International Centre for the Study of East Asian Development). *East Asian Economic Perspectives: Recent Trends and Prospects for Major Asian Economies.* Kitakyushu 17, no. 1 (February 2006) Special Issue.

Iqbal, Farrukh. *Deregulation and Development in Indonesia*. Paper presented at the Conference on Building on Success: Maximising the Gains from Deregulation, Jakarta, 20–28 April 1995.

James, William E. "Survey of Recent Developments". *Bulletin of Indonesian Economic Studies* 31, no. 1 (1995): 3–38.

Lall, Sanjaya. "Technological Capabilities and Industrialisation". *World Development* 20, no. 2 (1992): 165–86.

————. "Technology Policies in Indonesia". In *Indonesia's Technological Challenge*, edited by Hal Hill and Thee Kian Wie, pp. 136–68. Canberra: Research School of Pacific and Asian Studies, Australian National University, and Singapore: Institute of Southeast Asian Studies, 1998.

Lall, Sanjaya and John Weiss. *Industrial Competitiveness: The Challenge for Pakistan.* Asian Development Bank Institute, December 2003.

LIPI and The Office of the Minister of State for Research and Technology. *Buku Saku Indikator IPTEK Indonesia* [Pocket book of Indicators on Science and Technology in Indonesia]. Jakarta, December 2004.

McCawley, Peter. *Industrialization in Indonesia: Developments and Prospects.* Occasional Paper no. 13. Canberra: Development Studies Centre, The Australian National University, 1979.

Marks, Stephen. *Foreign Direct Investment in Indonesia and its Management through Government Policy*. Partnership for Economic Growth, Department of Industry and Trade, Jakarta, March 1999.

Pangestu, Mari and Yuri Sato, eds. *Waves of Change in Indonesia's Manufacturing Industry*. Tokyo: Institute of Developing Economies, 1997.

Soesastro, Hadi. "Emerging Patterns of Technology Flows in the Asia-Pacific Region: The Relevance to Indonesia". In *Indonesia's Technological Challenge*, edited by Hal Hill and Thee Kian Wie, pp. 303–25. Canberra: Research School of Pacific and Asian Studies, Australian National University, and Singapore: Institute of Southeast Asian Studies, 1998.

Soesastro, Hadi and Raymond Atje. "Survey of Recent Developments". *Bulletin of Indonesian Economic Studies* 41, no. 1 (2005): 5–34.

Thee Kian Wie. "Determinants of Indonesia's Industrial Technology Development". In *Indonesia's Technological Challenge*, edited by Hal Hill and Thee Kian Wie, pp. 117–35. Canberra: Research School of Pacific and Asian Studies, Australian National University, and Singapore: Institute of Southeast Asian Studies, 1998.

———. "Competition Policy in Indonesia and the New Anti-Monopoly and Fair Competition Law". *Bulletin of Indonesian Economic Studies* 38, no. 3 (December 2002): 331–42.

———. "The Major Channels of International Technology Transfer to Indonesia: An Assessment". *Journal of the Asia-Pacific Economy* 10, no. 2 (2005): 214–36.

Thee Kian Wie and Ahmad Hamid. "Perkembangan Industri Garmen di Bali sesudah tahun 1990" [The development of the garment industry in Bali after 1990]. Paper presented at the Conference of the Association of Indonesian Economists (Ikatan Sarjana Ekonomi Indonesia), Malang, 19 December 1997.

Thee Kian Wie and Mari Pangestu. "Technological Capabilities and Indonesia's Manufactured Exports". In *Technological Capabilities and Export Success in Asia*, edited by Dieter Ernst, Tom Ganiatsos, and Lynn Mytelka, pp. 211–65. London and New York: Routledge, 1998.

Timmer, Marcel. "Indonesia's Ascent on the Technology Ladder: Capital Stock and Total Factor Productivity in Indonesian Manufacturing, 1975–95". *Bulletin of Indonesian Economic Studies* 35, no. 1 (April 1999): 75–89.

World Bank. *The East Asian Miracle: Economic Growth and Public Policy.* New York: Oxford University Press, 1993.

———. *Indonesia: Industrial Policy: Shifting into High Gear.* Washington, D.C.: World Bank, 1994.

———. "Indonesia: Industrial Technology Development for a Competitive Edge". Report no. 15451-IND. Washington, D.C., 29 May 1996.

———. "Indonesia: Sustaining High Growth With Equity". Report no. 16433, Washington, D.C., 30 May 1997.

———. "Indonesia: Accelerating Recovery in Uncertain Times". Report no. 20991-IND, Jakarta, 13 October 2000.

———. "Comparative Study of Industrial Competitiveness in East Asia: A Research Proposal". Development Economics Research Group (DERG), 9 January 2003.

———. "Making Indonesia Competitive: Promoting Exports, Managing Trade". Report no. 30535. Washington, D.C., 2004.

———. "Indonesia: New Directions". CGI Brief, Report no. 31335-IND. Jakarta, January. 2005a.

————. *World Development Indicators, 2005*. Washington, D.C.: Development Data Center, 2005*b*.

————. *World Development Indicators 2006*. Washington, D.C.: Development Data Center, 2006*a*.

————. "Investing for Growth and Recovery". Report no. 35423-IND, Washington, D.C., 14 June. 2006*b*.

# 11

# THE MAJOR CHANNELS OF INTERNATIONAL TECHNOLOGY TRANSFER TO INDONESIA: AN ASSESSMENT[1]

Like other developing countries, Indonesia is a net importer of advanced technologies developed in the industrial countries. These technologies are crucial to generate and sustain the rapid economic growth necessary to raise the standards of living of the Indonesian people. In view of the economic important function of imported technologies, it is important to identify the major sources and channels through which these technologies are transferred to Indonesia and to assess the extent to which the transfer has indeed contributed to the development of local technological capabilities. At its present relatively low level of industrial and technological development, Indonesia should focus its technology strategy on importing those technologies most relevant to its development needs, at the most favourable terms, and to assimilate, adapt and improve these imported technologies, very much like Japan and later the East Asian NIEs — particularly Korea and Taiwan — successfully did in earlier decades. Several studies on technology transfer in Indonesia's manufacturing sector have indicated that foreign direct investment, technical licensing agreements without equity involvement by the foreign licensor, capital goods imports, and participation in world trade through exports have been the major channels of international technology transfer to Indonesia.

## INTRODUCTION

Like other developing countries, Indonesia is a net importer of advanced technologies developed in industrial countries. These technologies are crucial to drive and sustain the rapid economic growth necessary to raise the standard of living of the Indonesian people. For this reason it is important that such technologies are transferred to developing countries, such as Indonesia (Chen, 1983, p. 63). In view of the economic importance of imported technologies, we need to identify the major channels through which they are transferred to Indonesia, particularly to the manufacturing sector. An important issue is whether these imported technologies have been fully assimilated and mastered by the recipients, i.e. Indonesian firms. It is therefore important to assess whether and to what extent the various channels of international technology transfer have contributed to Indonesia's industrial technology development (ITD), i.e. the development of local (indigenous) technological capabilities (TCs) required in manufacturing. The successful development of local TCs will determine whether the imported technologies can be successfully applied in Indonesia.

## BASIC CONCEPTS

It is useful to start out with a definition of technology, technology transfer, technological capability and technological effort. If technology is defined as the knowledge and machinery needed to run an enterprise, it would include both software (blueprints and operating manuals) and hardware (machinery and other capital equipment). Technology transfer can then be defined as the transfer of skills and technical know-how as well as the transfer of machinery and other capital equipment (embodied technology) (Chee, 1981, p. 2). As such a transfer usually involves the transfer of modern technologies from advanced to developing countries, this concept implies the international or cross-border transfer of technology. While international technology transfer is crucial to developing countries for gaining access to modern technologies, the great challenge facing developing countries, including Indonesia, is how its nationals can eventually master the transferred or imported technologies. 'Mastering' means acquiring and developing the capabilities of using the new technologies effectively and efficiently.

Technological capabilities (TCs) in manufacturing can be defined as the skills — technical, managerial and institutional — that enable manufacturing enterprises to utilize capital equipment and technical information efficiently (Lall, 1996, p. 28). As virtually all advanced technologies are imported from industrial countries, technological capability can also be defined as the ability to make effective use of imported technologies (Bell et al., 1984, pp. 107–08). At a more advanced stage of industrial and technological development, technological capability should enable a firm to create new technology and to develop new products and processes in response to a changing economic environment (Kim, 1997, p. 4). To acquire this technological capability, a technological effort is required. This effort usually takes the form of purposeful investments by a firm in training its employees (managers, engineers, technicians and plant workers), searching for new technical and other relevant knowledge, and developing the organizational knowledge to create, communicate, and diffuse knowledge internally within the firm itself. At a more advanced level of industrial development, absorption and mastery of new technologies also requires investment in R&D (research and development) (Lall, 1993, p. 100). The acquired TCs are firm-specific, i.e. they constitute institutional knowledge that has been accumulated and developed over time by the combined skills of the firm's employees (Lall, 1996, p. 28). Development of TCs is crucial to promote and sustain the growth of an internationally competitive manufacturing sector.

We now turn to the various modes of international technology transfer. As in other developing countries, there are numerous channels open to Indonesia. We differentiate between formal or market-mediated channels and informal or non-market-mediated channels (Kim, 1999, pp. 125–27; World Bank, 1996, p. 4). The former involves formal arms-length transactions between buyer and seller mediated by the market including:

(a) Foreign direct investment;
(b) Technology (technical) licensing agreements;
(c) Imports of capital goods;
(d) Foreign education and training;
(e) Turnkey plants;
(f) Technical consultancies.

Through informal channels, foreign technology is transferred to local buyers without mediation by the market. Technology transfer then takes place without formal agreements and payments (Kim, 1999, p. 126). Such channels include:

(a) Technical assistance by foreign buyers;
(b) Technical assistance by foreign vendors;
(c) Copying or 'reverse engineering';
(d) Information from trade journals;
(e) Technical information services provided by public agencies.

As in most other developing countries, the bulk of international technology transfer to Indonesia takes place in the private sector, i.e. from private firms in industrial countries to private Indonesian firms, although some transfer has also occurred between foreign firms and Indonesian state-owned enterprises (SOEs). In addition, international technology transfer has taken place in the public sector through the technical assistance programmes of individual donor countries or multilateral aid agencies, including the World Bank, the United Nations Industrial Development Organization (UNIDO) and the United Nations Development Programmme (UNDP) (Thee, 1994, p. 41). However, in Indonesia, technology transfer through the public sector has been far less important than through the private sector.

For purposes of assessment it is crucial to distinguish between the various types and levels of technological capability. The following classification of elements of technological capabilities is derived from the work of Sripaipan (1990), Kim (1997, pp. 4–6) and Ernst et al. (1998, pp. 17–18):

(1) Production or operational capability, i.e. the knowledge and skills required for the efficient operation and control of the production process and the machinery in the plants, including maintenance and repairs. It includes both production management (overseeing the operation of the plant), production engineering (providing the required information to optimize the operation of the plant) and repair and maintenance of capital equipment.

(2) Investment or acquisitive capability, i.e. the knowledge and skills required to search, assess, negotiate and procure relevant technologies and install and start up the newly set-up production facilities. This acquisitive or investment capability includes manpower training to impart the various necessary skills as well as the ability to conduct proper analysis of the feasibility of investing in a certain project and the ability to implement the project.

(3) Adaptive or minor change capability refers to the knowledge and skills required to digest the transferred technologies and to carry out minor modifications or improvements in the existing process or product technologies in response to changing circumstances and/or to raise productivity.

(4) Innovative or major change capability, i.e. the capability required to carry out significant in-house research and development (R&D), to make radical or major process or product modifications, and develop new products or processes. Innovative capability includes the capability to invent, innovate and improve existing technology beyond original design parameters.

These four elements of technological capability will be used as criteria to assess the extent to which international technology transfer to Indonesian nationals through the various channels has succeeded in developing local TCs. This classification is also helpful in suggesting a sequential ordering of priorities for industrial and technological strategies of late industrializing countries. It implies that a developing country at a relatively early stage of export-oriented industrialization, such as Indonesia is in now, may have to spend much of its initial technological effort on developing the more basic production, investment, and adaptive capabilities (Ernst et al., 1998, p. 17). In more advanced newly-industrializing countries, for instance Korea and Taiwan, technological efforts have to focus more on developing the more demanding innovative capabilities in order to remain internationally competitive. Hence, the TCs that a firm needs to master depend on the stage of development reached by the economy in which it operates (Ernst et al., 1998, pp. 17–18).

## INDONESIA'S CHALLENGE AS AN IMPORTER OF TECHNOLOGY

As a technology-importing country, Indonesia faces the challenge of maximizing the international transfer of the most relevant technologies on the best available terms. The technologies that are actually transferred do not only involve the purchase of capital equipment or acquisition of blueprints but, more importantly, also the development of the capacity to use, adopt, replicate, modify or further expand the knowledge and skills developed elsewhere (Soesastro, 1998, p. 304). With many firms in Indonesia highly dependent on imports of 'ready-made' technology, sustained industrial growth will greatly depend on the country's ability to move from a passive dependence on technology transfer to a more active role in mastering and building upon imported technologies (Lall, 1998, p. 137). At its present level of industrial and technological development, technology development in Indonesia should first focus on developing the required technological capabilities (TCs), specifically the capabilities to make effective use of transferred technologies (Bell et al., 1984, pp. 107–08). Development of these TCs does not only come from experience (although experience is important), but to an even higher extent more from the technological efforts of firms.

Development of TCs is crucial as Indonesia, facing sharp competition in international markets from other, rapidly industrializing countries, notably China, can no longer continue to rely only on its traditional sources of comparative advantage, including its large supplies of relatively cheap, but mostly low-skilled labour and its natural resources. In fact, in view of the large overlap of China's and Indonesia's labour intensive exports in the

United States market (the largest market for both China's and Indonesia's manufactured exports), Indonesia is highly vulnerable to China's strong export competitiveness in manufactured exports, particularly in labour-intensive manufactured exports. Indonesia will therefore have to develop a more sustainable source of comparative advantage in order to raise the international competitiveness of its manufacturing industries. To achieve this, Indonesia's manufacturing firms, including small- and medium-scale enterprises (SMEs), will, just as in South Korea and Taiwan a few decades earlier, have to make a serious effort on developing technological and related organizational capabilities in order to develop more technology- and skill-intensive, higher value added industries.

The need of Indonesia's manufacturing industries to develop TCs is crucial since the technological base is shallow and backward compared with that of the East Asian newly-industrialized economies (NIEs), particularly Korea and Taiwan. Compared with these NIEs, Indonesia's capacity to absorb and improve upon complex imported technologies is narrow and weak; its capital goods sector, a crucial element of industrial deepening, is relatively underdeveloped, and its relatively modest technological effort (even before the Asian economic crisis) was distorted and excessively concentrated, mostly on state-owned strategic industries, in particular the costly aircraft assembling enterprise, PT Dirgantara Indonesia (Lall, 1998, p. 136).

Various studies on international technology transfer in Indonesia's manufacturing sector indicate that foreign direct investment, technical licensing agreements, imports of capital goods, and technical and marketing assistance from foreign buyers of manufactured exports, have been the four major channels for international technology transfer in Indonesia. Each will be reviewed in detail. However, whereas several firms have obtained technical and managerial advice from foreign consultancies, no comprehensive data are available on the number or costs and benefits of such transactions.

## Foreign direct investment

Since the late 1980s, Indonesia experienced a surge in foreign direct investment (FDI), particularly in export-oriented FDI, which lasted up to the onset of the Asian economic crisis. The surge of FDI actually consisted of two surges. The first one occurred during the years 1987–1990 and was largely due to a favourable confluence of 'pull'- and 'push'-factors, resulting in a large inflow of export-oriented FDI from East Asian NIEs, particularly Korea and Taiwan. A significant part of these NIE investments took place in low-skill, labour-intensive industries, including textiles, garments, footwear and consumer electronics. The second surge of FDI started in early 1994 and was partly driven by the worldwide boom in FDI (World Bank, 1996, p. 12).

As a result of the surge in export-oriented FDI, Indonesia since the late 1980s experienced a rapid expansion of manufactured exports. This expansion was a remarkable achievement considering that in 1981 manufactured exports had accounted for only 7 per cent of Indonesia's total merchandise exports. By 1996 manufactured exports accounted for 53 per cent of total exports. However, the expansion of manufactured exports was mainly limited to the low-skill labour-intensive manufactured exports, including textiles, garments, footwear and consumer electronics. Ramstetter (1999) has shown that export-oriented FDI did contribute a great deal to the expansion of Indonesia's manufactured exports during the first half of the 1990s. He found that foreign-controlled plants tended to have higher trade propensities than domestically owned plants. Ramstetter's study indicates that firms with a high foreign equity share had by far the highest export propensities, followed by plants with a moderate foreign ownership and plants with low foreign ownership (Ramstetter, 1999, p. 57).

Since the onset of the Asian economic crisis, Indonesia has even experienced net FDI outflows that have persisted until the present (Table 1). The continuing net FDI outflow can be largely attributed to Indonesia's poor investment climate. Various factors account for the poor investment climate, including the lack of legal certainty, lack of security, labour militancy and business-unfriendly labour regulations, confusion caused by the process of devolving autonomy to the regional level, as well as concerns about the re-emergence of macroeconomic instability, policy uncertainty and widespread corruption. The net effect is uncertainty, higher costs and many demands for bribes (MacIntyre & Resosudarmo, 2003, p. 146; World Bank, 2003, p. 29). The continuing net FDI outflows from Indonesia are a source of great concern, as the two other worst-afflicted Asian countries, Korea and Thailand, are already experiencing net FDI inflows (World Bank, 2000, p. 5). The fact that practically no new FDI has entered Indonesia since the Asian crisis also implies that no new infusions of modern technologies into Indonesia through FDI are taking place.

## Technical licensing agreements

In Indonesia, a major 'unpackaged' (non-equity) mode of technology transfer from advanced country firms to Indonesian firms has been technical licensing agreements (TLAs). Several foreign firms concluding TLAs with Indonesian firms might have preferred to export their products to Indonesia or to invest

**TABLE 1**
**Net In- and Outflows of FDI in Indonesia,**
**1986–2002 ($ millions)**

| Year | Net FDI |
|------|---------|
| 1986 | 258 |
| 1987 | 385 |
| 1988 | 576 |
| 1989 | 682 |
| 1990 | 1093 |
| 1991 | 1482 |
| 1992 | 1777 |
| 1993 | 2004 |
| 1994 | 2109 |
| 1995 | 4346 |
| 1996 | 6194 |
| 1997 | 4667 |
| 1998 | –356 |
| 1999 | –2745 |
| 2000 | –4551 |
| 2001 | –5887 |
| 2002 | –7066 |
| 2003(Q1) | –2651 |

*Source*: Bank Indonesia, Indonesian Financial Statistics (successive issues).

directly in Indonesia but abandoned such plans because of difficulties in exporting due to high import barriers or unexpected difficulties in undertaking investment (Thee, 1990, pp. 205, 209). Some foreign firms were reluctant to enter into licensing agreements with Indonesian firms out of concern that the terms of agreement would not be faithfully observed by the licensees in light of the country's weak protection of intellectual property rights. For this reason, foreign firms have preferred to choose large and bona fide domestic firms with a good reputation rather than small firms largely unknown to them.

The TLAs often involve the transfer of older technologies that do not offer the recipient country a long-term competitive advantage in the global market (Marks, 1999, p. 6). However, for a late-industrializing economy such as Indonesia, acquiring and mastering older technologies first is a good way to develop important basic TCs, i.e. production, investment and adaptive capabilities. However, sometimes restrictions are attached to the TLAs, including clauses obliging the licensee to purchase materials, components or equipment from the licensor (often at prices considered excessive), limitation of sales to the domestic market and grant-back provisions (provisions giving the licensor all rights to improvements) (Frank, 1980, p. 79). The available evidence from a number of Indonesian firms shows that TLAs indeed often contain restrictive conditions such as bans on exports (Thee, 1990).

## IMPORTS OF CAPITAL GOODS

Imports of capital goods provide another way of acquiring the means of production without the transactional costs involved in FDI or TLAs (Dahlman et al., 1987, p. 768).

Capital goods imports are actually embodied technology flows entering a country. They introduce into the production processes new machinery, other capital equipment and components that incorporate technologies that do not necessarily incorporate high or frontier technologies, but are nevertheless new to the recipient firm (Soesastro, 1998, p. 304). Imported capital goods can prove a cheap way to develop local TCs if they can be used as models for reverse engineering to produce the machines locally (Dahlman et al., 1987, p. 768). Imitative reverse engineering of existing foreign products became the backbone of Korea's industrialization up to the mid-1980s (Kim, 1997, p. 38). Korea's dynamic small firms continue to focus mainly on developing operational capabilities by producing imitative goods through reverse engineering (Kim, 1997, p. 206). However, Indonesian firms have in general not engaged in 'reverse engineering' on a large scale.

Capital goods imports also contain a significant disembodied element as foreign suppliers of capital goods, in particular machinery, often send technical experts to Indonesian firms to train the workers of these firms how to operate, maintain and repair the imported machinery. This kind of technology and skill transfer by technical experts from foreign firms to Indonesian employees has been quite significant with most foreign machinery suppliers to Indonesian firms. Training is crucial as mere imports of capital goods do not automatically lead to an enhancement of local TCs.

If imports of capital goods are accompanied by effective training of local workers, such imports may indeed lead to the development of operational capabilities and, over time, also to the development of adaptive capabilities, specifically to carry out minor process adaptations. Historically, there has been a close association between capital investment in Indonesia and imports of capital goods due to the fact that Indonesia's capital goods industry is still relatively small and backward, not only compared with the other large Asian countries, such as China and India, but even compared with neighbouring Malaysia. Backwardness and lack of dynamism in Indonesia's capital goods industry are attributed to the industry being coddled for too long as an 'infant industry' enjoying high rates of effective protection and non-tariff protection, at any rate until the mid-1990s (World Bank, 1994, pp. 26–27). As a result, the bulk of capital goods required in production processes still needs to be imported (Table 2).

Table 2 shows an impressive increase in capital goods imports during the investment boom, including the FDI surge in the first half of the 1990s. The data on capital goods imports are aggregate figures and do not reveal to which industries the various capital goods are channelled. Not surprisingly, the sharp decline in manufacturing investment after the onset of the Asian economic crisis is also reflected in a steep decline in capital goods imports. The Asian economic crisis has clearly led to a greatly reduced inflow of new technologies embodied in capital goods. Moreover, since the use of newer capital goods has generally been accompanied by a higher labour productivity, the reduced inflow of capital goods may have adversely affected the growth in labour productivity and efficiency in Indonesian manufacturing.

### TABLE 2
### Imports of Capital Goods into Indonesia, 1986–2001 ($ billions)

| Year | Imports of capital goods (Jan.–March) |
|------|---------------------------------------|
| 1986 | 1.9 |
| 1987 | 2.4 |
| 1988 | 2.6 |
| 1989 | 3.8 |
| 1990 | 6.1 |
| 1991 | 7.7 |
| 1992 | 7.4 |
| 1993 | 7.1 |
| 1994 | 7.4 |
| 1995 | 8.7 |
| 1996 | 9.6 |
| 1997 | 9.3 |
| 1998 | 5.8 |
| 1999 | 3.1 |
| 2000 | 4.7 |
| 2001 | 4.8 |
| 2002 | 4.4 |
| 2003 (Jan.–July) | 3.8 |

*Source:* Badan Pusat Statistik [Central Bureau of Statistics], Economic Indicators (successive issues).

## TECHNICAL AND MANAGERIAL ASSISTANCE FROM FOREIGN BUYERS

Since the mid-1970s, an important informal channel of international technology transfer for Indonesian firms, including small and medium-scale enterprises (SMEs), has been their participation in world trade. This informal channel was utilized effectively by local export firms, particularly electronics firms, in the four East Asian NIEs, including Korea, Taiwan, Hong Kong and Singapore which, based on low wage rates, were able to build up basic operational capabilities through simple assembly of mature products for exports, often developed through technical assistance provided by foreign buyers (Hobday, 1994, p. 335; World Bank, 1996, p. 4). These local NIE firms successfully coupled exports and technological development, allowing export market needs (the needs and design and product specifications of their overseas buyers) to focus their investment in technological upgrading and to provide a channel for them to acquire foreign technologies from their overseas buyers. Such a process of coupling exports with technology development is labelled 'export-led technology development' (Hobday, 1994, p. 335). Although not as technologically advanced, the impressive export performance of the garment industry and other export industries in Bali since the mid-1970s is somewhat akin to the experience of the firms in these NIEs. The remarkable growth of Bali's export industries, starting with garments in the mid-1970s, and subsequently the silver jewellery, wood carving, quilting, leather products, bamboo furniture, ceramics, and stone carving industries, was based on vital information flows that these Balinese firms received through strategic business alliances with foreign firms and businessmen (Cole, 1998, p. 257). The remarkable thing about this success is that the industries in question mostly consisted of rural based small and micro-enterprises, largely owned and run by pribumi (indigenous) Indonesian entrepreneurs. Another remarkable feature is that these export industries were able within a relatively short time to produce highly competitive products for the international market and that these products were largely made from domestic material inputs. Moreover, unlike many large domestic firms, which were able to benefit from government protection or implicit or explicit subsidies, Bali's export industries did not receive any specific government support. In fact, the rapid growth of these export industries was neither anticipated nor planned by the government (Cole, 1997, p. 2).

The major factor that triggered the success in the Bali export industry was the presence of foreign buyers or entrepreneurs from Australia and later from the United States, Western Europe and Japan, many of whom initially arrived as tourists, and who were able to establish direct contacts with local entrepreneurs. Through the vital information transfer and technical and managerial assistance, including strict quality control, provided by the foreign buyers or entrepreneurs, the Bali firms were able to achieve high levels of efficiency and accuracy. This assistance was provided on a for-profit basis, as it was specifically tied to tangible product output results (Cole, 1998, p. 275; Thee & Hamid, 1997). The ongoing interaction of these two parties started a virtuous cycle of technological improvement and learning that was self-replicating and largely self-financing resulting in a rapid and sustained export growth (Cole, 1998, p. 275). This export performance could be sustained even after the onset of the Asian economic crisis since these foreign buyers or entrepreneurs, unlike foreign investors, still kept visiting Bali after the crisis, as this island was largely spared the unrest and breakdown in safety, law and order that afflicted some other regions in Indonesia, at least until the devastating bomb attack in Bali on 12 October 2002. Not surprisingly, this bomb attack has led to a much reduced inflow of foreign tourists, including foreign buyers and entrepreneurs.

Another case of successful export-led technology development, similar to Bali's experience, is the export-oriented furniture industry in the Jepara district (kabupaten), Central Java. This industry actually consists of industry clusters including about 100 large and medium-scale firms and about 2000 small firms and mobile skilled craftsmen, which have been responsible for the rapid growth of this export industry. This clustering has made possible an efficient division of labour between the larger firms and the small firms, in which the larger firms concentrated their operations on specific and essential stages in the production process while recruiting small firms as subcontractors to specialize on other, simpler stages, which they could do more efficiently than the larger firms. During the period 1989–1998, Jepara furniture exports rose from $3.8 million to $97 million in 1996 and to $147 million in 1998 (Sandee et al., 2000, pp. 1, 5). A crucial event which led this industry to focus on export markets was the participation of a number of Jepara furniture producers in a trade fair in Bali in 1989, which led to contacts with prospective foreign buyers who started visiting Jepara to have a look at the operations of these furniture producers. Just as in the case of the Bali garment industry, the foreign buyers or entrepreneurs played an important role as intermediaries between Western customers and local producers. The foreign buyers played a major role in introducing new, higher value-added designs, teaching quality control methods, standardizing output required for the rapid expansion of order-driven production tailored to the quickly changing preferences of foreign buyers, and opening up new export markets for modern Jepara furniture. As a result, the quality of Jepara furniture has been steadily upgraded (Sandee et al., 2000, pp. 5–7). The economic crisis of 1997/98 forced the Jepara furniture industry to orientate their operations even more towards export markets, which then became easier because of the steep depreciation of the rupiah. Unlike many other industries, this industry is also not heavily dependent on expensive imported raw materials and capital goods. However, just as in the case of the Bali export industries, this export trade was not really driven by the Indonesian firms themselves, but by the foreign buyers or entrepreneurs (Sandee et al., 2000, pp. 8–10).

Participation in world trade has clearly allowed Indonesian firms to gain access to foreign technologies, enabling them to improve their competitiveness by upgrading their TCs, in particular their operational capabilities and, to some extent, also adaptive capabilities. However, as the export-oriented activities in Bali and Jepara were almost exclusively initiated by foreign buyers or consultants, the Bali and Jepara firms were in general not able to develop the acquisitive capabilities, let alone innovative capabilities. Moreover, the experiences of Bali and Jepara and that of other export-oriented manufacturing firms, for instance garment firms in Bandung, indicate a continuing reliance on foreign buyers. It therefore reflects a 'passive' stance both in regard to gaining access to world markets and to foreign designs and technologies. To reduce this vulnerability, Indonesian firms need to make a serious effort themselves to establish close links with overseas buyers to quickly identify changes in consumer preferences.

Studies on the impact of FDI on technology transfer have largely adopted one of two approaches, i.e. an econometric approach, which has in recent years been increasingly used by quantitative economists, and a more traditional, micro-approach that is largely qualitative and based on in-depth interviews at the firm-level (Hill & Athukorala, 1998, p. 42). The former approach uses a large secondary data set in which foreign and domestic firms are separately identified. These studies focus on productivity (either total factor or labour productivity) trends among the two groups of firms and across industries to find out whether the presence of foreign firms has affected the productivity levels and growth rates of the domestic firms. The main concern is with the issue of whether or not technologies have been transferred, rather than with the mechanism of transmission itself. These studies are unable to estimate the relative importance of FDI among other factors accounting for the productivity growth of domestic firms. However, they do provide presumptive evidence of causation (Hill & Athukorala, 1998, p. 42).

The second, more qualitative approach usually involves case studies of firms in which the assessment of the impact of FDI on technology transfer in the recipient firms is based on case studies of individual firms, the information of which are obtained from questionnaire surveys and in-depth interviews with managers. One advantage of this approach is that it offers a greater understanding of the mechanism of technology transfer or diffusion. The disadvantage of such an approach is that its findings may be considered merely indicative rather than explanatory. Moreover, as these case studies are based on interviews with the managers of firms that have, in general, not been randomly selected, the findings of these studies cannot be generalized. Results using both of these approaches are presented in the following two sections.

## FINDINGS FROM ECONOMETRIC STUDIES

An econometric study conducted by Fredrik Sjöholm on technology transfer and spillovers from foreign-controlled establishments to domestic establishments in a number of Indonesia's manufacturing industries found that foreign-controlled establishments had higher total factor productivities (TFPs) than establishments of domestic firms. This empirical evidence indicates that TNCs had transferred more advanced technologies to their Indonesian affiliates. The study also found that the structure of ownership, whether fully-owned subsidiary, joint venture with foreign majority ownership or joint venture with foreign minority ownership, had no effect on TFP levels (Sjoholm, 1999, p. 611). This is not surprising since in most cases foreign partners were able to maintain management control, even if majority equity ownership had been transferred to the Indonesian partner. If the amount of loan capital provided by the foreign partner to the joint venture was larger than the total amount of equity capital, it was relatively easy for the foreign partner to retain management control. By retaining management control, the foreign partner was generally able to maintain high productivity levels (Thee, 2001b, p. 10).

Technologies used by the foreign-controlled establishments also appeared to have benefited domestic establishments through favourable technological spillovers since domestic establishments in industries with relatively high levels of FDI were found to have comparably high levels of factor productivity. Insofar as the strong presence of foreign-controlled establishments in a number of manufacturing industries is associated with higher factor productivities of the domestic establishments in these industries, Sjoholm's findings indicate that the gradual liberalization of Indonesia's foreign investment regime was beneficial for the country's manufacturing sector in terms of technological spillovers (Sjöholm, 1999, p. 611). Therefore, the favourable technological spillovers indicate that technology transfer from these foreign-controlled establishments and its subsequent diffusion did take place in these industries, amongst others, through the turnover of labour from foreign-controlled to domestic establishments and the support of local supplier firms (Sjöholm, 1999, p. 589).

A more recent econometric study by Sadayuki Takii on productivity spillovers from foreign-controlled establishments in manufacturing in Indonesia came up with slightly different conclusions. Takii found that positive spillovers were smaller in industry-year combinations in which the foreign equity share was relatively high. This result could be caused by the fact that plants where the foreign partner held majority equity ownership were able to control the diffusion of firm-specific assets better than other foreign-controlled plants and that, as a result, the magnitude of spillovers from these plants was smaller (Takii, 2001, p. 19). Takii's study also found that spillovers tended to be relatively large in industries where the technological gap between foreign-controlled and locally-owned firms was relatively small in the initial year. This suggests that technological levels in locally-owned firms were not high enough in some industries to facilitate large spillovers from foreign-controlled firms. These results indicate that encouraging more FDI by transnational corporations (TNCs) does not necessarily lead to more favourable spillovers, especially in technologically backward industries (Takii, 2001, p. 20).

## FINDINGS FROM SELECTED CASE STUDIES

The following presentation is limited to the findings of two recent studies conducted by the present author in cooperation with other researchers. It surveys three branches of manufacturing, i.e. textiles, garments and electronics, as well as a study specifically focusing on transfers of Japanese technology. The sectoral approach was applied in a study for UNCTAD's Technology Program conducted by Thee & Pangestu whereas the country-specific approach was chosen in a study undertaken by Lindblad & Thee.

### The textile industry

The study by Thee & Pangestu of two Japanese-Indonesian textile joint ventures (JVs) found that the investment (acquisitive) capabilities of Indonesian employees of the JVs were lower than those employed in private domestic firms without foreign equity involvement. In the former firms, active involvement of Indonesian employees in the procurement of relevant technologies was minimal. However, the Indonesian employees were actively involved in the installation and start-up of the production facilities, including discussions on the layout of the plant, purchase of machinery and other capital equipment, construction of the plant and the start-up of the production process. Through this involvement they were able to acquire some degree of investment capability.

In the course of the longstanding operations of these two textile JVs, dating back to the early 1970s, the Japanese managers and technical experts were able to transfer the basic production (operational) capabilities to their local employees, specifically in the spinning and weaving operations. These local production capabilities were acquired through an active involvement in various processes, including production planning, material and component sourcing, production management and engineering, quality control and the maintenance and repair of capital equipment. However, the fact that even after 20 years of operations both JVs still employed 10 or more Japanese expatriates suggests that the transfer of technology in these JVs has been less than complete. While a number of the senior Indonesian staff had been promoted to senior managerial positions in both JVs, they still had to be supported and advised by Japanese advisers (Thee & Pangestu, 1998, pp. 236–38).

The same study, by Thee & Pangestu, of two large, domestic, export-oriented textile firms showed that through a package agreement, including technical licensing, with a Japanese textile firm as well as a Japanese general trading company, the firms in question had been able to gain access to new textile technology, new capital equipment and experienced technical experts from the Japanese partner. Although these two firms enjoyed access to new technology provided by the Japanese textile firm, it was not the newest technology. The senior manager of these firms attributed this to the fact that the Japanese technical experts attached to these firms were mostly retired people over 50 years old who may not have followed the latest development in textile technology, but who were nevertheless still able to provide adequate expertise to these firms. Under the package agreement, the Japanese textile firm had carried out the original feasibility study, designed the plant layout, supplied the textile machinery, constructed the plant and also set up the production lines. In addition, the Japanese textile firm had also provided suppliers' credit to the Indonesian firm to purchase modern textile machinery. During the early years of operation, the Japanese textile firm supplied the Indonesian firm with eight Japanese senior managers and technical experts to assist the Indonesian managers and technical experts. As a result, after some time, the Indonesian managers and technical experts were able to operate the plants by themselves, even though the firm still relied on Japanese experts for quality control, since the bulk of its exports was handled by the Japanese general trading company. This meant that these two domestic textile companies greatly relied on the Japanese general trading company for overseas marketing (Thee & Pangestu, 1998, pp. 237–38).

The experience of these two large domestic textile firms indicates that while, through their technical licensing agreement with a Japanese textile firm, new textile technologies were continuously transferred, their technological effort was mostly focused on mastering basic production capabilities, enabling them to operate the plants efficiently. Having as its production director an experienced Indonesian textile engineer who had studied textile engineering in Japan and who had worked in a Japanese textile firm for 8 years, enabled one of these firms to acquire greater TCs, including adaptive (minor change) capabilities. This was reflected by the fact that before this firm installed new capital equipment, its production director was actively involved in discussing with the overseas equipment suppliers the exact design and technical specifications of the capital equipment to make it suitable for local conditions (Thee & Pangestu, 1998, p. 237). However, by relying on the Japanese textile firm to carry out the feasibility study, design the plant lay-out, supply the textile machines, construct the plant and set up the production lines, these two domestic textile firms failed to develop basic investment capabilities. By relying on their Japanese partners in marketing their output overseas, these firms also did not have the incentive to increase their marketing abilities. As they found it profitable to rely on their association with the Japanese firms, the two firms did not have the incentive to make a determined effort to lessen their technological dependence on their Japanese partners.

## The garment industry

Thee & Pangestu's study also included one export-oriented Korean-Indonesian joint venture (JV) in the garment industry. This JV made overcoats and jackets under OEM (Original Equipment Manufacturing) arrangements with its overseas buyers in Western Europe. The Korean partner held a 95 per cent majority share, while all the senior managers were Koreans. The only two Indonesian managers were in charge of accounting and personnel respectively, i.e. none of them was involved in actual production. As production management and engineering, repair and maintenance of the capital equipment and quality control were all carried out and led by the Korean managers, no significant transfer of the basic production capabilities appeared to have taken place. Since the procurement of the relevant technologies and the installation and the start-up of the plant had also been carried out by the

Korean managers, no local investment capabilities were acquired. However, this absence of significant technology transfer may have been due to the fact that, at the time of the interview, this JV had only been in operation for three and a half years (Thee & Pangestu, 1998, p. 241).

## The electronics industry

Thee & Pangestu's study on the TCs of consumer electronics firms indicated that foreign-controlled JVs were prevalent among large electronics firms. Indonesian employees in an older, well-established Japanese–Indonesian JV (dating back to the early 1970s) were found to have been more involved in the search and procurement of relevant technologies and the instalment and start-up of production facilities than those employed in newer, majority-owned JVs, mostly Japanese–Indonesian and Korean– Indonesian JVs established in the late 1980s and early 1990s. While the Indonesian employees in the former firm were able to acquire some investment capabilities, those in the latter did not. However, even in the former case, the staff of the Indonesian partner had only been involved in product selection, site selection, and processing of the required licences, without much involvement in the more essential investment activities, such as product specification, process technology, design and plant lay-out. Since the newer JVs had experienced difficulties in recruiting experienced local engineers and managers, many top positions were still being occupied by expatriates. The middle-level and lower positions, however, were filled by recent graduates from local universities who, upon recruitment, were trained in-house, at the head office of the principals in their home country or in the subsidiaries in Singapore and Malaysia. As a result, at the time of the interviews, the local employees in these new JVs had not yet fully mastered the basic production capabilities (Thee & Pangestu, 1998, pp. 250–51).

Thee & Pangestu's study also included case studies of four JVs making electronics components, including a majority-owned Japanese–Indonesian JV, two Singaporean– Indonesian JVs and a Korean–Indonesian JV. In the case of the Japanese–Indonesian JV, the Indonesian engineers and workers were trained at the Japanese partner's plant in Japan, which enabled them to acquire the basic production capabilities from the Japanese staff. However, maintenance and repair of the capital equipment and quality control were still done under the supervision of Japanese staff. Since this JV still relies on Japanese expertise, the Indonesian employees have, aside from some basic production capabilities, not developed the investment and adaptive capabilities. Three other JVs making integrated circuits (ICs) were JVs with Indonesian majority ownership, including two Indonesian–Singaporean JVs and one Korean–Indonesian JV. Unlike the Japanese majority-owned JV, the Indonesian staff of the Korean–Indonesian JV and one Singaporean–Indonesian JV had to search and procure the relevant technologies as well as install and start up the production facilities themselves. In doing so, they were able to develop basic investment and production capabilities. The other Singaporean–Indonesian JV was previously owned by National Semiconductor. As the workers of the former American owner had stayed on, this JV was able to acquire the basic production capabilities which, over time, they built up further, including the capability to source important inputs (machinery and other capital equipment), to learn to use the new equipment, and to keep up with the rapid changes in IC technology (Thee & Pangestu, 1998, pp. 250–51).

Thee & Pangestu's study also described the experience of a domestic, private electronics firm producing industrial electronics products (sound systems and computer monitors) under licence from a Taiwanese electronics firm. Under the technical licensing agreement, this firm not only obtained the technology and product designs from its licensor but was also able to send its engineers and plant workers to Taiwan for special training at the headquarters of the Taiwanese firm. This latter firm dispatched two of its technical experts to work in the licensee's plant in charge of quality control. For marketing its products overseas, the licensee relied on its licensor, although it had also begun to make its own marketing efforts by opening up a marketing office in Singapore. Before its establishment, this firm had searched, assessed, negotiated and procured the relevant technologies, which had led to the licensing agreement with the Japanese firm. Over time, this domestic electronics firm was able to develop its investment and production capabilities (Thee & Pangestu, 1998, pp. 250–51).

## Transfer of Japanese technology

A recent study by Lindblad & Thee on technology transfer in a number of Japanese–Indonesia joint ventures (JVs) came up with similar findings to the UNCTAD study. This study found that among the six manufacturing firms that were interviewed, four JVs had been able to transfer full production (operational) capabilities to their Indonesian employees, while the remaining two firms had only been able to transfer partial production capabilities to their Indonesian employees (Lindblad & Thee, 2002, p. 29). The study also found that of the six JVs, only three had been able to transfer adaptive (minor change) capabilities to their Indonesian employees, particularly in regard to process technologies. However, among the six JVs, only two had been able to transfer investment (acquisitive) capabilities to their Indonesian employees. As was to be expected, in none of the six JVS had innovative capabilities been transferred. It would be too much to expect that foreign-controlled enterprises would be willing fully to transfer innovative capabilities to their local staff, since these innovative capabilities are crucial to the international competitiveness of the foreign principals. Moreover, the establishment of R&D facilities in Indonesia would require a sufficiently large scale of operations and a minimum reservoir of scientific skills. Yet, even if these conditions could be met in Indonesia (and they are not), local R&D in the foreign-controlled JV would remain a mere dependency of the fully-fledged R&D department at the headquarters of the foreign principal (Lindblad & Thee, 2002, pp. 29–30).

## Assessment of Technology Transfers

The findings of the case studies mentioned above on technology transfer through FDI and technical licensing agreements and the discussion on the two other main channels of technology transfer in Indonesia are summarized in Table 3.

The data in Table 3 indicate that, in general, the international technology transfer through FDI projects has resulted in the development of basic production capabilities, occasionally also adaptive capabilities, primarily by introducing minor process adaptations to local conditions, particularly in older, well-managed FDI projects where experienced Indonesian local employees have worked for a long time. On the other hand, minor product adaptations have usually not been allowed by foreign licensors, especially if

**TABLE 3**
**Major Chanels of International Technology Transfer to Indonesia**

|  | Technological capabilities Channel | | | |
|---|---|---|---|---|
|  | Production | Investment | Adaptive | Innovative |
| FDI | S | OS | OS | NS |
| TLA | S | S | S | NS |
| Capital goods imports | S | NS | OS | NS |
| Technical assistance from foreign buyers | S | NS | OS | NS |

*Note*: FDI = foreign direct investment, TLA = technical licensing agreements, S = successful, OS = occasionally successful, NS = not successful.

the foreign licensors were large, well-known TNCs that had a large stake in upholding the reputation of the brand names of their products. In many FDI projects, however, local employees are not always or only partly involved in the procurement of the relevant technologies and the installation and start-up of the production facilities. Therefore, local employees did not have the opportunity to develop the basic acquisitive abilities. In view of the relatively small scale of Indonesia's domestic market, it does not make economic sense to undertake R&D activities in these FDI projects, particularly as such activities are very costly and also need a large number of highly qualified and experienced scientists and engineers who are in short supply in Indonesia. For this reason, FDI projects in Indonesia in general do not have fully fledged R&D units, but at most small laboratories for product testing and quality control. As a result, local conditions do not yet provide foreign-controlled firms with the proper incentive to develop local innovative capabilities.

Without doubt, FDI is often the only way to obtain the latest technologies from abroad, and hence the only way to ensure a rapid transfer of technology. FDI can therefore play a vital role in the industrial and technological upgrading of Indonesia. However, even if TNCs find it feasible and profitable to conduct R&D in a developing country, R&D may provide relatively few external benefits. The reason is that R&D at TNCS is likely to be tightly interwoven into the global R&D networks of the TNCs concerned, and also narrowly specialized in certain segments of the innovative process. Moreover, R&D by TNCs is unlikely to raise significantly the TCs of local firms (Lall, 1991, p. 6). Relying on FDI from developed countries to lead the economy into an advanced industry, as Singapore has done, also makes the development of local TCs highly dependent on foreign investors, and thus runs the risk of being subject to forces outside the country's control (Lall, 1991, pp. 5–6). A large country like Indonesia therefore needs to devote much of its technological effort to developing its own indigenous TCs in order to take full advantage of the presence of FDI. To achieve a more effective transfer of technology from FDI, Indonesia will have to take a more pro-active approach in attracting the kind of FDI it needs for more effective technology transfer. Indonesia also needs to make a far greater effort to build up a pool of broadly skilled workers in order to raise the country's absorptive capacity for more advanced technologies.

Technology transfer through technical licensing agreements between foreign firms (licensors) and domestic firms (licensees) has generally provided a better opportunity for domestic firms to acquire the basic production and, to a lesser extent, the basic investment and adaptive capabilities. The reason is that domestic firms have to make a much greater technological effort to actively develop the required basic TCs, including investment and adaptive capabilities, than in the case of FDI projects. Local employees have to be actively involved from the outset of the investment project in the search for, assessment and procurement of, relevant foreign technologies and in the installation and start-up of the production process. Through their active involvement in all these activities, these local employees are able to develop basic investment capabilities.

In the case of domestic firms producing under licence from foreign licensors, the local employees also have to make a greater effort to develop the basic adaptive capabilities themselves, particularly with regard to minor process adaptations to local conditions, which in the case of FDI projects are often carried out by the expatriates. However, for the same reasons as mentioned above, domestic firms producing under licence have not established fully-fledged R&D units but only small laboratories for product testing and quality control. Hence, these domestic firms have not been able to develop local innovative capabilities.

Capital goods imports cannot by themselves raise a domestic firm's TCs unless such imports are accompanied by technical advice and instructions provided by technical experts from the suppliers about how to operate, maintain and repair the imported machinery and other capital equipment. Technical instructions and manuals are a crucial element accompanying embodied foreign technology inflows that should enhance the production capabilities of local employees. However, while these capital goods imports provide a good opportunity to raise the local production capabilities, the outcome will ultimately depend on the skills and motivation of the local employees working with these capital goods. Firms planning to utilize the technical experts of their foreign suppliers more intensively to raise their TCs can, through them, also develop their adaptive capabilities.

Exporting through OEM arrangements has also offered domestic firms a good opportunity to develop their basic TCs as reflected by the favourable experiences in Bali and Jepara. The important information flows and technical advice provided by foreign buyers, who often acted as consultants to the firms in Bali and Jepara, contributed to the development of the basic production and, to a lesser extent, the adaptive capabilities of these firms, most of which included small and micro-enterprises. However, as the export-oriented activities were almost exclusively initiated and organized by foreign buyers/consultants, these firms have in general not been able to develop investment nor marketing capabilities. Through these foreign buyers acting as technical consultants, however, they can occasionally develop their adaptive capabilities.

## CONCLUSION

This account of international technology transfer to Indonesia argues that Indonesia, like other developing countries, is a net technology importer. It therefore needs to have free and unhampered access to foreign technologies from advanced and newly industrialized economies (NIEs) in order to enable it to improve the productivity, efficiency and competitiveness of its economy, notably its manufacturing industries. As Indonesia could choose from the large stock of available foreign technologies to decide which it should import on the best available terms, it would be technically and economically not feasible, except in a few cases, to attempt to invent technologies at its present relatively low level of scientific and technological development. Instead, Indonesia should focus its technology strategy on importing those technologies most relevant to its development needs at the most favourable terms, assimilate, master and adapt and wherever possible improve on these imported technologies, very much like Japan and later Korea and Taiwan have done so spectacularly in earlier decades.

Unlike the East Asian NIEs, however, Indonesia has thus far not yet been able to take full advantage of the various channels of international technology transfer open to it to develop and raise its TCs, notably through FDI and exporting through OEM arrangements. In the case of FDI, Indonesia has not been able to take full advantage of FDI because of the frequent changes in policies towards foreign investment, which reflects that Indonesia's policy-makers did not have a clear idea of what they specifically expected of FDI. Even with technology transfer, there was a lack of understanding of how this process could be encouraged beyond exhortations and regulations designed to prod foreign-controlled firms to accelerate the 'Indonesianization' of their senior expatriate staff by replacing them with local staff and by providing training to local employees at all levels. A major factor which has often hampered the efficient international transfer of technology through FDI and other channels has been the country's lack of absorptive capacity, specifically the shortage of adequately trained and skilled local employees able to fully comprehend and master the technologies transferred to them. This shortage is often caused by the poor quality of education in Indonesia at all levels.

Although FDI is a crucial source of international technology transfer, only relying on FDI for a country's development runs the risk of making a country's technological development too dependent on foreign investors, and thus runs the risk of being subject to forces outside the country's control. To prevent such an excessive dependence, the Indonesian government needs to encourage domestic firms to spend much of their technological effort on developing local TCs, to avoid excessive dependence on FDI as a vehicle for technological development. This would require a proper incentive system, consisting of sound macroeconomic policies and pro-competition policies (specifically an export-promoting trade regime and sound domestic competition policies), and a much greater investment in human resources in order that these firms have access to better trained and skilled workers which, in turn, would enhance the firms' 'supply-side capabilities'. Other important factors to enhance a firm's supply-side capabilities are easy access to finance and adequate technology support services. Access to finance, notably venture capital funds, is important as technology development requires long-term and risky investments in new technologies. Technology support services provided by a country's science and technology (S&T) institutes and institutes providing metrology, standardization, testing and quality (MSTQ) services are also very important to diffuse technological information and to assist firms, including SMEs, in making effective use of imported technologies, keeping up with technology trends, and assisting these firms to use this information effectively to improve their competitiveness (World Bank, 1996, p. 5). Unfortunately, both with regard to adequate access to sources of finance and adequate provision of technology support services, the performance of the relevant agencies and institutes in Indonesia are still far from satisfactory (Thee, 1998).

Capital goods imports and the related transfer of skills by the technical experts of the supplier firms as well as technical assistance by foreign buyers through exporting has enabled many domestic firms to get access to valuable foreign technologies, including design capabilities. However, the export orientation of several domestic firms, particularly the SMEs, has largely been the result of active approaches by foreign buyers with access to, and knowledge of, export markets rather than through the efforts of domestic firms themselves to identify promising potential export markets, gather the necessary market information about prospective customers in the export markets, identify their specific tastes and preferences, establish the necessary distribution channels in their export markets and establish an adequate after sales service. In order to reduce the great dependence on foreign buyers, domestic, export-oriented firms also need to develop the important marketing capabilities. By developing the marketing capabilities themselves, domestic firms would be able to gain continuing access to foreign technologies without being dependent on foreign buyers. In this respect, Indonesia could learn a great deal from the important role which Japan's sogoshosha (general trading companies) have played in gathering the important information about foreign markets for Japan's export-oriented firms, including SMEs, and in providing the valuable marketing channels to export markets.

## Note

1. "The Major Channels of International Technology Transfer to Indonesia: An Assessment", by Thee Kian Wie first published in *Journal of the Asia-Pacific Economy* 10, no. 2 (May 2005). This article is a substantially revised, updated and abbreviated version of Thee (2001a). The author is grateful to the International Centre for the Study of East Asian Development (ICSEAD), Kitakyushu, for permission to publish parts of it.

## References

Bell, M., Ross-Larson, B. & Westphal, L. E. "Assessing the performance of infant industries". *Journal of Development Economics* 16, no. 1–2 (1984): 101–28.

Chee Peng Lim. "EEC investment in ASEAN and the transfer of technology: a Malaysian case study". Paper presented at the First Conference on ASEAN-EEC Economic Relations, Singapore, 6–8 August 1981.

Chen, E. K. Y. *Multinational Corporations, Technology and Employment.* London: Macmillan, 1983.

Cole, W. "Bali's garment industry: an Indonesian case of successful strategic alliances". Unpublished paper, Jakarta, 1997.

———. "Bali's garment export industry". In *Indonesia's Technological Challenge*, pp. 255–78, edited by H. Hill & Thee KianWie. Singapore: Institute of Southeast Asian Studies, 1998.

Dahlman, C. J., Ross-Larson, B. & Westphal, L. E. "Managing technological development lessons from the newly industrializing countries". *World Development* 15 (1987): 759–75.

Ernst, D., Mytelka, L. & Ganiatsos, T. "Technological capabilities in the context of export-led growth: a conceptual framework". In *Technological Capabilities and Export Success in Asia*, pp. 5–45, edited by D. Ernst, T. Ganiatsos & L. Mytelka. London: Routledge, 1998.

Frank, I. *Foreign Enterprise in Developing Countries.* Baltimore and London: John Hopkins University Press, 1980.

Hill, H. & Athukorala, P. "Foreign investment in East Asia: a survey". *Asian-Pacific Economic Literature* 12, no. 2 (1998): 23–50.

Hobday, M. "Export-led technology development in the four dragons: the case of electronics". *Development and Change* 25, Issue 2 (1995): 361–93.

Kim, L. *Imitation to Innovation: The Dynamics of Korea's Technological Learning.* Boston: Harvard Business School Press, 1997.

———. "Pros and cons of international technology transfer: a developing country's view". In *Learning and Innovation in Economic Development*, pp. 125–141, edited by L. Kim. Cheltenham: Elgar, 1999.

Lall, S. "Emerging sources of FDI in Asia and the Pacific". Paper presented at the

Roundtable on Foreign Direct Investment in Asia and the Pacific, Honolulu, 26–28 March 1991.

————. "Promoting technology development: the role of technology transfer and indigenous effort". *Third World Quarterly* 14 (1993): 95–108.

————. "Understanding technology development". In *Learning from the Asian Tigers: Studies in Technology and Industrial Policy*, pp. 27–58, edited by S. Lall. London: Macmillan, 1996.

————. "Technology policies in Indonesia". In *Indonesia's Technological Challenge*, pp. 136–68, edited by H. Hill and Thee Kian Wie. Singapore: Institute of Southeast Asian Studies, 1998.

Lindblad, J. Th. & Thee Kian Wie. "Indonesian economic development and Japanese technology". ICSEAD Working Paper Series 2002-09. Kitakyushu: International Centre for the Study of East Asian Development [with a supplement by B. Purwanto & Dj. Suryo], 2002.

MacIntyre, A. & Resosudarmo, B. P. "Survey of recent developments". *Bulletin of Indonesian Economic Studies* 39, no. 2) (2003): 133–56.

Marks, S. *Foreign Direct Investment in Indonesia and its Management through Governmental Policy*. Jakarta: Department for Industry and Trade, 1999.

Ramstetter, E. D. "Trade propensities and foreign ownership shares in Indonesian manufacturing". *Bulletin of Indonesian Economic Studies* 35, no. 2 (1999): 43–66.

Sandee, H., Andadari, R. K. & Sri Sulandjari. "Small firm development during Indonesia's economic boom and crisis: the Jepara furniture industry". Unpublished paper, Amsterdam and Salatiga, 2000.

Sjoholm, F. "Joint ventures, technology transfer and spillovers: evidence from Indonesian establishment data". In *Economic Planning Agency, Papers and Proceedings of the International Symposium on Foreign Direct Investment in Asia*, pp. 587–616. Tokyo: Government of Japan, 1999.

Soesastro, H. "Emerging patterns of technology flows in the Asia-Pacific region: the relevance to Indonesia". In *Indonesia's Technological Challenge*, pp. 303–25, edited by H. Hill & Thee Kian Wie. Singapore: Institute of Southeast Asian Studies, 1999.

Sripaipan, Ch. "Constraints to technology development in a rapidly growing economy: the case of Thailand". *TDRI Quarterly Review* 5, no. 3) (1990): 6–11.

Takii Sadayuki. "Productivity spillovers and characteristics of foreign multinational plants in Indonesian manufacturing, 1990–1995". ICSEAD Working Paper Series 2001-14 Kitakyushu: International Centre for the Study of East Asian Development, 2001.

————. "Indonesia: Technology transfer in the manufacturing industry". In *Technological Challenge in the Asia-Pacific Economy*, pp. 201–232, edited by H. Soesastro & M. Pangestu. Sydney: Allen & Unwin, 1990.

————. "Technology transfer from Japan to Indonesia". In *The Transfer of Science and Technology between Europe and Asia, 1780–1880*, pp. 30–59, edited by Yamada Keiji. Kyoto: International Research Center for Japanese Studies, 1994.

————. "Determinants of Indonesia's industrial technology development". In *Indonesia's Technological Challenge*, pp. 117–134, edited by H. Hill & Thee Kian Wie. Singapore: Institute of Southeast Asian Studies, 1998.

Thee Kian Wie. "Channels of international technology transfer to Indonesia: a brief survey". ICSEAD Working Paper Series 2001-31. Kitakyushu: International Centre for the Study of East Asian Development, 2001a.

Thee Kian Wie. The role of foreign direct investment in Indonesia's industrial technology development, *International Journal of Technology Management* 10, (2001b): 1–16.

Thee Kian Wie & Hamid, A. "Perkembangan industri garmen di Bali sesudah tahun 1990 [The development of the garment industry in Bali after 1990]". Paper presented at the Conference of the Ikatan Sarjana Ekonomi Indonesia [Association of Indonesian Economists], Malang, 19 December 1997.

Thee Kian Wie & Pangestu, M. "Technological capabilities and Indonesia's manufactured exports". In *Technological Capabilities and Export Success in Asia*, pp. 211–65, edited by D. Ernst, T. Ganiatsos & L. Mytelka. London: Routledge, 1998.

World Bank. *Indonesia: Industrial Policy Shifting into High Gear.* Washington, DC: World Bank, 1994.

————. *Indonesia: Industrial Technology Development for a Competitive Edge.* Washington, DC: World Bank [Report no. 15451-IND], 1996.

————. *Indonesia: Accelerating Recovery in Uncertain Times.* Washington, DC: World Bank: East Asia Poverty Reduction and Economic Management Unit, [Report no. 20991-IND], 2000.

————. *Indonesia: Beyond Macroeconomic Stability.* Washington, DC: World Bank, [Report no. 27374-IND], 2003.

# 12

---

# THE INDONESIAN WOOD PRODUCTS INDUSTRY[1]

This chapter analyses the development of Indonesia's wood products industry, particularly the plywood industry, which from a small base emerged in the 1980s as one of Indonesia's major manufacturing industries. This account is of interest since it provides a good example of 'export-substitution', that is the enforced development of the wood products industry by limiting the exports of logs through prohibitive export taxes and subsequently by a partial and later by a total ban on log exports. However, because of the difficulties which the wood products industry, particularly the plywood industry, has experienced over the past decade, the question arises whether 'export substitution' provides the proper incentives to develop an efficient manufacturing industry.

## INTRODUCTION

The following account outlines the development of Indonesia's wood products industry, particularly the plywood industry, which from a small base emerged in the 1980s as one of Indonesia's major manufacturing industries. This account is of interest since it provides a good example of successful *'export-substitution'*, that is the enforced development of the wood products industry by limiting the exports of logs through prohibitive export taxes and subsequently by a partial and later by a total ban on log exports.

As a result of this 'export substitution', by the early 1990s Indonesia had become the largest manufacturer of hardwood plywood in the world. The exports of wood-based products were even more impressive, as plywood exports increased from US$1 billion in 1985 to US$4 billion in 1992, while pulp and paper exports during the same period rose from US$28 million to US$400 million. As a result, during this period the wood products industry became the second most important contributor to the rapid growth of the manufacturing sector after the textile and textile products industry (World Bank, 1994: 24).

However, by the early 2000s the wood products industry experienced great difficulties because of the problem of accessing adequate raw material supplies, allegedly due to the rampant smuggling of logs, mainly to China. The industry most adversely affected by this smuggling is the plywood industry (Aswicahyono & Hill, 2004: 288–89). As of today this problem still besets the plywood industry. However, aside from this problem, this industry over the past few years has been experiencing strong competition from China's plywood industry. This may indicate that Indonesia's plywood industry has not been able to enhance its international competitiveness when it was still the dominant producer in the world market.

Because of the difficulties which the wood products industry, particularly the plywood industry, has experienced over the past decade the question arises whether 'export substitution' is the right way or provides the proper incentives to develop an efficient manufacturing industry. The reason for this doubt is that the ban on log exports has led to the artificial lowering of the domestic prices of the timber. This has enabled the wood products industry to capture the considerable rents from it, reducing the incentive to develop an efficient, internationally competitive wood-processing industry. This paper tries to address this question in the following pages.

## THE DEVELOPMENT OF THE FORESTRY SECTOR IN INDONESIA SINCE THE EARLY 1970s

When Soeharto's New Order government assumed power in the late 1960s, it badly needed new sources of government revenues to finance the rehabilitation of the dilapidated infrastructure and productive apparatus which had been neglected during the final years of the Sukarno government. To this end, the lush forests in Sumatra, Kalimantan and the other islands in the Indonesian archipelago with their tropical hardwood (*Dipterocarp*) trees looked like a valuable natural resource which could be easily exploited and sold in the export markets. For this reason the New Order government in 1967 issued the Basic Law on Forestry.

This Law was prepared in a hurry, since it did not reflect an awareness that tropical hardwood, although a renewable natural resource, is not a resource which can be quickly renewed. The contents of the Law also did not reflect an awareness of the adverse effects of the indiscriminate felling of trees on the environment. Only in the 1980s did an increasing public concern arise in Indonesia about the adverse effects of rapid deforestation, but this concern did not result in effective action on the part of the government to halt or slow down this rapid deforestation.

By the late 1980s it already became increasingly evident that forest depletion was proceeding rapidly, as Indonesia was losing forest at a rate of one million hectares annually, a worrisome development since Indonesia has an estimated 98 million hectares of tropical rain forests, which is more than one half of Indonesia's total land area and second in area only to Brazil. Since the more accessible, higher-yielding forest areas were targeted for logging before the less accessible ones, the loss of one million hectares of the total forested area a year is of much greater economic significance for future supplies of timber than it might appear at first glance (Ascher, 1993: 1).

Right from the outset the development of the wood products industry there were some worrisome issues related to the efficiency and allocation of forestry resources and marketing arrangements that had serious implications on the efficiency and future prospects of the industry. These serious issues were related to rent dissipation, price distortions, and disincentives for reforestation (World Bank, 1994: 24).

It should be borne in mind that the level of natural resource rent extraction is one of the most important forestry sector policies. With regard to rent dissipation in the exploitation of Indonesia's forest policies, the most serious weakness of the royalty and taxation system was the low proportion of the natural resource rent captured by the combined fees, royalties and taxes accruing to the government. The low level of rent captured by the government encouraged over-harvesting and put considerable resources in the hands of well-connected individuals and companies without any incentive to re-invest them in the Indonesian economy (Ascher, 1993: 5).

The government's concession policy provided for a concession period for natural forests under the Selective Logging System of 20 years, with the possibility of renewal. The problem with this concession policy was that the length of the concession period was not chosen to correspond to the regeneration cycle of the most commonly harvested tree species. Moreover, the 20-year period, combined with the widespread perception that renewals were by no means automatic, did not contribute to ensuring sustainable forestry practices by the timber companies (Ascher, 1993: 4).

The development of Indonesia's timber industry can be divided into three phases. During the first phase, covering the period 1967–1979, the industry was focused on the export of logs. The production of logs did not require much capital investment, while exporting logs was very profitable because the efficient wood-processing industries in Japan, the largest export market for Indonesia's log exports, were willing to pay high prices for imported logs (Hardjono, 1994: 211).

The position of Indonesia as an important exporter of logs was due to the fact that Southeast Asia, particularly Indonesia, Malaysia and the Philippines, had vast tropical hardwood forests, the timber of which were in large demand in Japan, South Korea, Taiwan and Singapore. During the 1950s the Philippines was the most important exporter of tropical hardwood, but when its forests were exhausted, Malaysia emerged as a significant exporter after the mid-1950s. Indonesia only emerged as an important exporter of logs after the advent of the New Order government since the late 1960s (Takeuchi, 1974: 4).

There were two other regions in the world with tropical hardwood forests, namely West Africa and Latin America. However, the importance of West Africa as an important exporter of logs had declined by the early 1970s because of the vast deforestation it had experienced during the past years. Latin America has an even larger area with tropical hardwood forests, but compared to the forests in Southeast Asia, its forests compared unfavourably because of two factors. First, the forests in Latin America on the average produced a smaller volume of logs because its forests had more heterogeneous species than the more homogeneous and uniform species in Southeast Asia's forests. Moreover, the access to Latin America's vast forests was more difficult than to Southeast Asia's forests. For this reason the per unit costs of production of Latin America's tropical hardwood were much higher than those of Southeast Asia. The easier access to Southeast Asia tropical hardwood forests, including those of Indonesia, and the more uniform quality of Southeast Asia's timber exports accounted for the higher prices which Southeast Asia's timber exports were able to fetch in the export markets. These higher prices also meant that that Southeast Asia's timber exports yielded a high economic rent (Takeuchi, 1974: 6–7).

During the first phase of Indonesia's timber development, specifically the period 1967–1973, log exports doubled every year, making Indonesia the largest exporter of logs in the world in 1973. During this period an investment boom took place when timber companies from Japan, South Korea, the Philippines, Malaysia and the United States made largest investments in Indonesia's forestry sector. To access the vast forests in Sumatra and Kalimantan, the foreign timber companies undertook large investments in physical infrastructure, particularly roads which linked their timber concessions with the ports. However, during this period these foreign timber companies did not undertake investments in wood-processing activities, such as sawmills, because of the large overseas demand for logs (Ascher, 1998: 51).

During the period 1966–1970 log exports emerged as one of Indonesia's major export commodities, surpassing all traditional export commodities, except for natural rubber and petroleum (Table 1).

### TABLE 1
### Indonesia's Major Primary Exports, 1966–1970
### (millions of US$)

| Year | Logs | Rubber | Copra | Tin | Tobacco | Palm oil | Petroleum |
|------|------|--------|-------|-----|---------|----------|-----------|
| 1966 | 3.6  | 233    | 15    | 31  | 19      | 33       | 203       |
| 1967 | 6.3  | 167    | 14    | 49  | 24      | 24       | 340       |
| 1968 | 11.5 | 177    | 35    | 27  | 15      | 20       | 298       |
| 1969 | 25.3 | 198    | 18    | 25  | 14      | 15       | 373       |
| 1970 | 86.1 | 213    | 24    | 49  | 3.5     | 22       | 450       |

*Source*: Chris Manning: The Timber Boom, *Bulletin of Indonesian Economic Studies* 7, no. 3 (November 1971): 30 (based on data from Statistics Indonesia's monthly Economic Indicators, successive issues.

During the first phase of Indonesia's timber industry development the surge in log exports was characterised by three features: first, the production of logs was only concentrated in a few regions, particularly in East Kalimantan; secondly, almost all wood exports were log exports; thirdly, most of the log exports were absorbed by Japan. Moreover, almost all of the production of logs was undertaken by private firms, including foreign firms (Manning, 1971: 31, 33).

## THE EMERGENCE OF THE WOOD PRODUCTS INDUSTRY

The overriding factor affecting the development of the wood products industry were, as we will see below, the policies affecting this industry, specifically the prohibitive export taxes on log exports and sawn timber. These taxes ranged from $1,000/m3 to $4,800/m3, and effectively banned the exports of logs and sawn wood. As a result, they significantly reduced the returns to log producers and saw millers by forcing them to sell these products in the domestic market at lower prices (HIID, 1995: 4).

During the second phase of Indonesia's timber industry development, spanning roughly from 1980 through the early 1990s, log exports were steadily replaced by processed wood exports. This happened because the Indonesian government, dissatisfied with the actual receipts of log exports which were considered lower than the potential export receipts, in 1978 raised the export tax on log exports from 10 per cent to 20 per cent. This measure was taken to encourage the establishment of domestic wood-processing mills in order to raise the domestic value added of timber exports as well as the revenues from export taxes and foreign exchange earnings. It was hoped that the establishment of wood-processing mills would also increase employment and raise their marginal productivity because of the higher capital-labour ratio in the wood-processing mills (Lindsay, 1989: 111–12).

There was certainly an economic rationale for developing a wood products industry, since wood is the single most important cost component (over 50 per cent) for a wood products industry, followed by labour. Labour costs were relatively low in the early 1980s and were likely to remain low in the medium term. For this reason Indonesia had a strong comparative advantage in wood products since its forestry base was (and likely still is) among the richest in the world (although rapidly dwindling because of continued deforestation to produce logs, much of which is smuggled overseas, and to make way for the establishment of vast oil palm estates). Moreover, in the 1980s Indonesia was situated in the fastest growing region in the world which generated a strong and growing demand for wood products (World Bank, 1994: 24), as mentioned above.

On the other hand, it should also be pointed out that the ban on log exports forced the loggers to sell their logs to the down-stream wood-processing industries even when domestic prices were low. In addition, the government also provided tax incentives to the wood-processing industries. This policy led to inefficient processing that was vulnerable both to international competition and to the reduction in inputs from domestic logging (Ascher, 1993: 5).

Because of the sharp increase in the export tax, log exports declined sharply after 1978). On the other hand, the exports of processed wood, specifically plywood and sawn wood, rose from 70,000 cubic metres respectively 756,000 cubic metres in 1978 to 245,000 cubic metres, respectively 1,203,000 cubic metres in 1980, an increase of 250 per cent respectively 60 per cent in only two years (Lindsay, 1989: 112).

Because the Indonesian government was still not satisfied with the increase in processed wood exports, it issued two regulations in 1980 which were implemented in 1981. The first regulation stipulated that log exports had to be gradually reduced from 6.2 million cubic metres in 1981 to virtually zero in 1985. The second regulation stipulated that the export tax on log exports would be steadily raised, while export quotas would only be given to forest concession holders which already had or were already in the process of building wood-processing facilities. Forest concession holders which did not have wood-processing facilities or did not yet have plans to establish wood-processing facilities were prohibited from exporting logs. In February 1982 this regulation was followed up by a total ban on log exports (Hunter, 1984: 98).

In 1980 the Indonesian government also started reducing the role of foreign forest concession holders, which in 1984 was followed up by a total ban on foreign timber companies to hold forest concessions. Henceforth, foreign timber companies would only be allowed to participate in forest exploitation if they established a joint venture with an Indonesian timber company. With this new regulation foreign timber companies, which had initially been invited to participate in forest exploitation, were henceforth prohibited from felling trees (Ascher, 1982: 52).

As result of the ban on log exports, domestic and foreign timber companies established wood-processing facilities, particularly plywood mills, which subsequently led to a surge in plywood exports. In fact, since the mid-1980s through 1990 plywood exports emerged as the most important non-oil export commodity. However, in 1991 textile and textile products, particularly garments, emerged as the most important non-oil exports (Hardjono, 1994: 211).

The clear shift from log exports to plywood exports over time is evident from the data in Table 2 which show the amount of log exports and plywood exports over the period 1971–2008 (Jan–June).

The data in Table 2 clearly show that because of the partial ban on log exports in 1980 and the total ban in 1982, log exports declined sharply until it reached zero in 1990. On the other hand, as a result of large investments in the establishment of many plywood mills by both domestic and foreign timber companies, plywood exports steadily rose from a modest amount in 1981 until it reached a peak in 1993 when plywood exports amounted to more than $4.2 billion. Hence, within a relatively short time span, Indonesia was transformed from being the largest log-exporting country in the world in 1980 into the largest plywood-exporting country in the world in the course of the 1980s (Hardjono, 1994: 211). However, the data in Table 2 also show a worrying downward trend in Indonesia's plywood exports since it shows that since 2001 Indonesia's plywood exports has been steadily declining.

In view of the increasing importance of the plywood industry in the course of the 1980s, the development of this industry will be discussed in greater detail below.

## TABLE 2
## Log and and Plywood Exports from Indonesia, 1971–2007
### (millions of US$)

| Year | Log exports | Plywood exports |
|---|---|---|
| 1971 | 161.4 | — |
| 1972 | 228.7 | — |
| 1973 | 573.6 | — |
| 1974 | 724.9 | — |
| 1975 | 954.2 | — |
| 1976 | 780.5 | — |
| 1977 | 954.2 | — |
| 1978 | 995.0 | — |
| 1979 | 1,796.7 | — |
| 1980 | 1,852.5 | — |
| 1981 | 873.9 | 161.4 |
| 1982 | 331.8 | 269.9 |
| 1983 | 290.7 | 509.4 |
| 1984 | 172.4 | 667.9 |
| 1985 | 8.9 | 824.7 |
| 1986 | 2.1 | 1,002.4 |
| 1987 | 1.7 | 1,759.3 |
| 1988 | 0.5 | 2,073.7 |
| 1989 | 0.3 | 2,350.9 |
| 1990 | — | 2,725,5 |
| 1991 | — | 2,871.0 |
| 1992 | — | 3,230.2 |
| 1993 | — | 4,257.0 |
| 1994 | — | 3.716.4 |
| 1995 | — | 3,462.0 |
| 1996 | — | 3,595.4 |
| 1997 | — | 3,410.6 |
| 1998 | — | 2.077.9 |
| 1999 | — | 2,256.3 |
| 2000 | — | 1,988.8 |
| 2001 | — | 1,838.0 |
| 2002 | — | 1,748.4 |
| 2003 | — | 1,662.9 |
| 2004 | — | 1,576.7 |
| 2005 | — | 1,374.7 |
| 2006 | — | 1,506.6 |
| 2007 | — | 1,524.7 |
| 2008 (Jan–June) | — | 774.3 |

Source: Statistics Indonesia: Economic Indicators, successive issues.

## RAPID GROWTH OF THE PLYWOOD INDUSTRY

The plywood industry is the most important part of Indonesia's wood products industry. Aside from the plywood industry, the wood products industry also includes saw mills, block board plants, particle board plants, woodworking plants, furniture plants, chip mills, and cement-bonded plants. However, because of the much larger importance of the plywood industry, this paper will focus mainly on the development of this industry.

The larger importance of the plywood industry is, for instance, reflected by the fact that, according to a Department of Industry study, in 1987 of the approximately 337,000 people employed in the wood products industry, some 135,000 workers or 40 per cent of the total were employed in the plywood industry. Unlike the generally small-scale establishments of sawmills, woodworking plants and furniture plants, the average plywood mill is a large-scale plant, on the average employing 1,300 workers in the late 1980s. Of the 101 plywood mills in operation in 1987, the bulk were located in Kalimantan (56 mills), particularly in East Kalimantan, and in Sumatra (27 mills) (Wood Industry Development Partnership, 1987).

The plywood industry started to develop in 1973 with the establishment of two mills with an installed capacity of 28,000 cubic metres. During the following years the plywood industry expanded steadily, though not remarkably, until it began to grow rapidly as a result of the stimulus it received when the Indonesian government in 1980 introduced a partial ban on the exports of logs, which was subsequently followed by a total ban on the export of logs in 1982.

This ban on log exports was introduced in order to develop the wood products industry, particularly the plywood industry, in view of the large demand for plywood in the export markets. As a result, by 1986 the plywood industry accounted for almost 11 per cent of Indonesia's total manufacturing value added and for 10 per cent of total manufacturing employment (Apkindo, 1986: 51). The data in Table 3 show the remarkable development of the plywood industry during its early years.

The above data show that while the plywood industry gradually expanded in terms of capacity, production and domestic sales (although much less in terms of exports), it surged after the ban on log exports in 1980, both in terms of installed capacity, production and particularly in terms of exports.

While sales to the domestic market increased steadily through 1985, sales to the export markets increased even more rapidly. Sales to the export market began to exceed sales to the domestic market in 1982, and rose even further until they accounted for 80 per cent of total output in 1986. On the

## TABLE 3
## Development of the Indonesian Plywood Industry, 1973–1986
### (in thousands of m3)

| Year | Number of mills | Capacity | Production | Domestic sales | Exports | Imports |
|------|-----------------|----------|------------|----------------|---------|---------|
| 1973 | 2 | 28 | 9 | 7.5 | 15 | 14 |
| 1974 | 5 | 103 | 24 | 24 | 24 | 10 |
| 1975 | 8 | 305 | 107 | 105 | 2 | 7 |
| 1976 | 14 | 405 | 214 | 204 | 10 | 5 |
| 1977 | 17 | 535 | 279 | 261 | 17 | 4 |
| 1978 | 19 | 799 | 424 | 341 | 83 | 3 |
| 1979 | 21 | 1,809 | 624 | 498 | 126 | 0.8 |
| 1980 | 29 | 1.949 | 1,011 | 728 | 283 | — |
| 1981 | 40 | 2,601 | 1,552 | 778 | 774 | — |
| 1982 | 61 | 3,292 | 2,140 | 890 | 1,250 | — |
| 1983 | 79 | 4,477 | 2,943 | 943 | 2,000 | — |
| 1984 | 95 | 5,327 | 3,820 | 810 | 3,010 | — |
| 1985 | 101 | 6,228 | 4,983 | 1,200 | 3,783 | — |
| 1986 | 111 | 6,500 | 5,000 | 1,000 | 4,000 | — |

Source: APKINDO: Directory of the Indonesian Plywood Industry, 2nd Edition, 1986, table 2, p. 51.

other hand, plywood imports, never large in the first place, steadily declined during the 1970s and in 1980 ended. However, this surge in plywood exports was not a successful case of export promotion efforts, but a case of 'export substitution' in which log exports were replaced by the exports of wood products, particularly plywood, as a result of the partial and subsequently total ban on log exports

When in 1982 the Indonesian government introduced a total ban on log exports, a major realignment of the world plywood industry took place. Many plywood mills in Japan, South Korea and Taiwan were forced to close down or relocate their plywood operations to Indonesia. In fact, the surge in plywood exports can be attributed to the large investments in the establishment of wood-processing plants, particularly plywood mills, which initially were quite competitive compared to its competitors in other countries. As a result, Indonesia became the major plywood producer and exporter in the world. While in 1980 Indonesia's share of plywood exports in the world market was only 4 per cent, in 1983 this share had already risen to 24 per cent (UNIDO, 1987: 47). By the late 1980s Indonesia supplied about 80 per cent of the world demand for plywood, since many of the higher cost producers in Asia (Japan, South Korea and Taiwan) ceased production (World Bank, 1988: 40).

In the following years Indonesia's plywood industry continued to grow rapidly because of the growing demand in the world market, particularly from Japan, which kept world prices at a high level. To ensure that plywood exports remain high, a World Bank report (in hindsight prophetically) pointed out that a higher production of plywood and other wood panel products could only be sustained if the management of Indonesia's forests would have to be improved, and that output growth of timber would have to be reduced over the longer term. The reason for this recommendation was obvious, since the actual exploitation of Indonesia's forests was higher than the reported levels, so that excessive logging and damage to existing timber stocks was widespread (World Bank, 1988: 40, 94). Hence, the World Bank report recommended that the government would have to take a number of measures to ensure that the area designated as permanent production forest would have to be maintained in order to sustain current levels of timber production, or at most permitting only slight increases. However, by 1994 timber supply to the plywood industry had already reached the limits of sustainability. In addition to serious raw material constraints, plywood exports also began to face market access constraints of environmental nature (World Bank, 1994: 14).

Great concern about the environmental impact of severe deforestation was not only expressed in foreign countries. In Indonesia itself since the early 1990s a rising concern arose about the long-term risks associated with these large investments in the timber industry if timber supplies would continue to dwindle because of the continuing deforestation (Ascher, 1993: 1). This concern about the long-term prospects of Indonesia's turned out to be justified, since from 1994 through 2005 plywood exports steadily declined because of the dwindling supplies of logs. As a result of this dismal export performance, of the 1,800 exporters of plywood and other wood products registered with the Agency for the Revitalisation of the Forest Industry (*Badan Revitalisasi Industri Kehutanan, BRIK*), by mid- 2007 only about 800 exporters were still actively engaged in the export of wood products (Kompas daily, 5 August 2007: 17).

In the importing countries, particularly in the advanced countries, there was rising concern about the link between timber exports from the developing countries exporting wood products made from tropical hardwood and the worsening deforestation in these countries, particularly their impact on the environment and global warming. For this reason since the 1980s popular pressure in the advanced, importing countries arose for a ban on importing wood products made from tropical hardwood if the production of these wood products was not done according to methods which guaranteed the sustainability of these tropical forests. Although these movements were initially not successful and considered controversial, in the end this popular pressure led to the introduction of a regulation which required that wood export products made from tropical hardwood would have to be accompanied by an eco-label, that is a mandatory *tropical timber certification* (*TC*) certificate to gain market access to the importing countries. This mandatory eco-label was considered to be a more effective means to promote a more sustainable felling of tropical hardwood trees, that is which would better guarantee sustainable forest resources (Crossley, et al., 1997: 228).

Various parties, including the governments of several advanced and developing countries, multilateral agencies and NGOs, were also attracted to the TC scheme since they saw in the scheme a way to meet the objectives of the consumer in the advanced countries through a market-based, consumer-driven instrument. It was also hoped that through the eco-labelling requirement, trade disputes between the advanced and developing countries could be minimised (Crossley, 1997: 228).

In spite of the eco-labelling requirement, according to the Indonesian Eco-Label Institute (*Lembaga Ekolabel Indonesia, LEI*) thus far only 11 timber companies have obtained the TC certificate. The area of the operations of these 11 companies cover only 1.04 hectares which amounts to only 1.5 per cent of Indonesia's total forest area (LEI, March 2007). The above data show that even with the mandatory TC certificate, the efforts to halt deforestation has not been successful. The worsening export performance of the plywood industry and other wood-processing plants can also be attributed to the total ban on log exports. This ban amounted to an implicit subsidy to the plywood industry and other wood-processing facilities, because this measure enabled the plywood and other wood-processing plants firms to purchase logs at prices lower than the international prices. A clear indication of the magnitude of the subsidy was the substantial difference between the prices of logs in Indonesia and in world markets (HIID, 1995: 4–5). As a result, logs were smuggled overseas, while domestic supplies of logs also declined because of the worsening deforestation (Ascher, 1998: 50).

## THE THIRD PHASE IN THE DEVELOPMENT OF INDONESIA'S TIMBER INDUSTRY

The third phase in the development of Indonesia timber industry development occurred in the early 1990s with the emergence of a pulp and paper industry which from the outset grew rapidly. As mentioned earlier, after the end of the oil boom era in 1982 the Indonesian government shifted from an import substitution industrialization policy to an export-promoting one. As part of this shift, the Department of Industry and Trade promoted the development of a large-scale pulp and paper industry which, it was hoped, could replace the oil sector as an important source of export earnings and employment generation (van Dijk, 2005: 72). This expectation was met when pulp and paper exports rose from only $28 million in 1985 to $400 million in 1992 (World Bank, 1994: 23).

Another important consideration to promote the development of a pulp and paper industry was the importance attached to encouraging resource-based industrialization. Because Indonesia had tropical hardwood forests, the development of a pulp and paper industry was considered feasible in order to establish an integrated, upstream to downstream wood products industry. A large-scale pulp and paper industry was also expected to play an important role in solving the serious problem of deforestation. The pulp and paper industry could still make use of small, unfelled trees as raw materials for the industry (van Dijk, 2005: 72).

From its early beginnings in the early 1980s the pulp and paper industry grew rapidly because of rising domestic demand and, to a lesser extent, growing exports from a small base. Although Indonesia has a potential comparative advantage in pulp wood supply, which is the most important input to the pulp and paper industry, the growth of the paper industry has been more policy-driven, since about one half of the fibre consumption was imported. Since the required investment for a modern paper mill is very large, the tariff structure, which protects paper products (with a high effective rate of protection of 50 per cent) while allowing free imports of pulp, assured investors that they could produce for the domestic paper market with high prices and low cost subsidized inputs. For this reason the market became highly concentrated (World Bank,1994: 25).

The pulp and paper industry is competitive in most segments of the market and had the potential to become a major exporter of pulp and paper. However, the industry also faced structural problems, including a number of companies with small, inefficient, not viable units. Since this industry exhibits large economies of scale, the pricing and tariff policies kept these inefficient companies alive, while the few large companies had the opportunity to charge high prices in the domestic market (World Bank, 1994: 25).

Since the early beginnings of the pulp and paper industry, exports of paper and paper products have steadily increased over the years, making it one of Indonesia's major manufactured exports. It has not, however, replaced the oil and gas sector as the major source of export earnings, as the Department of Industry had hoped. The data in Table 4 show that in general there has been a steady increase in the exports of paper and paper products over the period

## TABLE 4
### Exports of Indonesia's Paper and Paper Products, 1994–2008 (January–June) (millions of US$)

| | |
|---|---|
| 1994 | 671.2 |
| 1995 | 1,011.4 |
| 1996 | 955.3 |
| 1997 | 938.5 |
| 1998 | 1,425.8 |
| 1999 | 1,965.6 |
| 2000 | 2,291.2 |
| 2001 | 2,034.3 |
| 2002 | 2,097.4 |
| 2003 | 2,007.3 |
| 2004 | 2,228.9 |
| 2005 | 2,324.8 |
| 2006 | 2,859.3 |
| 2007 | 3,374.8 |
| 2008 (Jan–June) | 1,935.1 |

*Source*: Statistics Indonesia: Economic Indicators, successive issues.

1994 through 2007, even though in some years there was a decline in exports which however, was succeeded by increased exports in the following years.

The establishment of the pulp and paper industry, however, was again characterized by the same problems of rent dissipation, price distortions and disincentives for reforestation which have afflicted the other wood products industries, including the plywood industry. The forcible removal of the local population by the authoritarian New Order authorities to make way for the forest concessions given to the few large pulp and paper companies has also generated huge social costs to the affected local communities, as the account below shows, which up to the present continue to protest the activities of these large pulp and paper companies.

The pulp and paper industry received various facilities from the government, in particular in gaining access to the tropical hardwood forests. This blatant, preferential treatment was evident from the experience of the two largest pulp and paper companies in Indonesia, namely PT Indah Kiat Pulp and Paper (IKPP) and PT Inti Indorayon Utama. In 1984 the Sinar Mas conglomerate established the Indah Kiat Pulp and Paper (IKPP) company, which built a pulp plant in Perawang, Riau Province, Sumatra. The Indonesian government supported this company by giving the company exclusive rights to a forest concession (Sonnenfeld, 1998: 115).

This company produced pulp and paper from tropical hardwood which it obtained from its forest concession, and subsequently planted other, fast-growing trees. Although IKPP paid royalties to the government for the timber it got from its forest concessions, the relatively low royalty for the use of this timber actually amounted to a subsidy from the government for the initial operations of this government. Worse, the rural population living in the area of this concession but did not own a document of ownership were forced to leave their dwellings (Sonnenfeld, 1998: 115).

In 1987 the Raja Garuda Mas (RGM) conglomerate, particularly its timber company PT Inti Indorayon Utama, built a pulp plant after winning a tender for a government project to use pinus trees (planted in the 1960s with Japanese aid) in the hills surrounding Lake Toba in the province of North Sumatra. Although the Indorayon company was obliged to use the pinus trees, the company built roads to gain access to these trees. However, during the rainy season these roads became very muddy, which caused erosion and land slides. At one time a whole village was covered with mud because of the bad road construction by Indorayon. The local population staged a protest when the company tried to establish a new pinus estate on land which was used by the local population to grow food and cash crops or for their cattle to graze. Not surprisingly, Indorayon from the outset was involved in various conflicts with the local population because of environmental problems or problems which threatened the livelihood and the economic activities of the local population. This experience clearly showed that the Indonesian government had given permission for the establishment of a pulp and paper company without first consulting the local population. As a result, the local population had to suffer the adverse effects of the operations of the pulp and paper plant (Sonnenfeld, 1998: 116) which has persisted up to the present.

However, in newly democratic Indonesia, these collusive relationships between corrupt central and local power holders and the companies concerned are now slowly being unraveled. At present the owner and top management of Indorayon are being investigated by the Tax Office for huge amounts of tax avoidance, but have apparently fled the country.

## CONCLUSION

After initial successes in export performance, Indonesia's wood products industries, particularly the important plywood industry, are now suffering from serious shortages in raw material supplies, particularly logs, which they blame on the rampant smuggling of logs, mainly to China. The industry most adversely affected is the plywood industry, which over the past two decades since a log export ban was imposed, had been a vehicle for capturing the rents from the artificially depressed domestic timber prices, rather than using the opportunity to develop an efficient processing industry (Aswicahyono and Hill, 2004: 288–89).

Although addressing the rampant rent dissipation, price distortions and disincentives for reforestation associated with the faulty forestry policies and poor governance of the forestry sector which has led to severe deforestation, is politically very difficult, they are essential to raising the efficiency and competitiveness of the wood products industries, particularly the plywood and pulp and paper industries. This applies particularly to the plywood industry which could still enhance its international competitiveness through better product design and quality and more vigorous marketing in the international markets.

The sustainability of the more competitive pulp and paper industry could also be ensured if the Indonesian government stops providing the industry with preferential treatment and forces the industry to adhere to the country's strict environmental obligations. Equally important, the industry should seriously address the grievances of the local population lest its position does not become politically untenable in newly-democratic Indonesia.

## Note

1.  "The Indonesian Wood Products Industry", by Thee Kian Wie, first published in *Journal of the Asia-Pacific Economy* 14, no. 2 (2009): 138–49.

## References

APKINDO (Indonesian Wood Panel Association). *Directory of the Plywood Industry in Indonesia.* 2nd Edition, Jakarta: Asosiasi Panel Kayu Indonesia, 1986.

Ascher, William. *Political Economy and Problematic Forestry Policies in Indonesia: Obstacles to Incorporating Sound Economics and Science.* Center for Tropical Conservation. Duke University: Durham, NC, 1993.

―――. "From Oil to Timber: The Political Economy of Off-Budget Development Financing in Indonesia". *Indonesia*, Issue no. 65 (April 1998): 37–61.

Aswicahyono, Haryo and Hal Hill. Survey of Recent Developments. *Bulletin of Indonesian Economic Studies* 40, no. 3 (December 2004): 277–305).

Booth, Anne. "Survey of Recent Developments". *Bulletin of Indonesian Economic Studies* 24, no. 1 (April 1988): 1–35.

Crossley, Rachel, Carlos Primo Braga and Panayotis Varangis. "Is there a Commercial Case for Tropical Timber Certification". In *Eco-Labelling and International*

*Trade*, edited by Zarrilli, Simonetta, Veena Jha and René Vossenaar. London: Macmillan Press, 1997.

Hardjono, Joan. "Resource Utilization and the Environment". In *Indonesia's New Order: The Dynamics of Socio-economic Transformation*, edited by Hal Hill. NSW: Allen & Unwin Pty Ltd, 1994.

HIID. *Prospects for Manufactured Exports During Repelita VI*. Report submitted to the Department of Industry, Republic of Indonesia, Harvard Institute for International Development, Jakarta, 1995.

Hill, Hal. *Indonesia's New Order: The Dynamics of Socio-Economic Transformation*. St. Leonards, NSW: Allen and Unwin, 1994.

Hunter, Lachlan. Tropical Forest Plantations and Natural Stang Management: A National Lesson from East Kalimantan? *Bulletin of Indonesian Economic Studies* 20, no. 1 (April 1984): 98–116.

*Kompas* daily, 7 August 2007.

Lembaga Ekolabel Indonesia (LEI). *LEI luncurkan Sistem Sertifikasi Hutan Bertahap* (LEI launches the Forest Certification Scheme in Stages). News/Info, Lembaga Ekolabel Indonesia, 28 March 2007.

Lindsay, Holly. The Indonesian Log Export Ban, An Estimation of Foregone Export Earnings. *Bulletin of Indonesian Economic Studies* 25, no. 2 (August 1989): 111–13.

Manning, Chris. The Timber Boom: With Special Reference to East Kalimantan. *Bulletin of Indonesian Economic Studies* 7, no. 3 (November 1971): 30–60.

Sonnenfeld, David A. Logging versus Recycling: Problems in the Industrial Ecology of Pulp Manufacturing in Southeast Asia, *Greener Management International (GNI)* Summer (1998): 108–22.

Statistics Indonesia. *Economic Indicators*. Successive issues.

Takeuchi, Kenji. *Tropical Hardwood Trade in the Asia-Pacific Region*. World Bank Staff Occasional Papers no. 17, Baltimore & London: John Hopkins University Press, 1974.

Thee, Kian Wie. "Pengaruh Ekolabel Terhadap Perdagangan Internasional Indonesia (The Impact of Ecolabelling on Indonesia's International Trade in Wood Products)". Unpublished paper Pusat Penelitian Ekonomi, Lembaga Ilmu Pengetahuan Indonesia (P2E-LIPI), Jakarta, 6 September 2007.

UNIDO. *Indonesia: Changing Industrial Priorities*. Industrial Development Review Series, United Nations Industrial Development Organization, Vienna, October 1987.

Van Dijk, Michiel. *Industry Evoloution and Catch Up: Th Case of the Indonesian Pulp and Paper Industry*. Ph.D. thesis, Technische Universiteit Eindhoven, 23 February 2005.

Wood Industry Development Partnership. *Wood-Processing Industry Sector Study Indonesia — Main Report* (draft). Atlanta, Hamburg and Inproma, Jakarta, May 1987.

World Bank. *Indonesia: Adjustment, Growth, and Sustainable Development*. Report no. 7222-IND, May 1988.

———. *Indonesia: Industrial Policy-Shifting Into High Gear*. Washington, D.C., 1994.

Zarrili, Simonetta; Veena Jha and Rene Vossenaar (editors). *Eco Labelling and International Trade*. UN-UNCTAD, Macmillan Press, 1997.

# 13

# THE DEVELOPMENT OF LABOUR-INTENSIVE GARMENT MANUFACTURING IN INDONESIA[1]

Indonesia's garment industry is a relatively young industry which only emerged as a factory activity around the mid-1970s. This was in response to an expanding domestic market and growing export opportunities. Before the 1970s garment production was largely conducted in small tailor shops all over the country. Since the mid-1980s up to the Asian economic crisis of 1997–98 the garment industry emerged as one of the most important export-oriented industries, generating increasing foreign exchange revenues and job opportunities for low skill, mostly women workers, because of its labour-intensive production process. After the Asian economic crisis garment exports declined because of declining competitiveness in the face of strong competition from other developing countries, particularly China and Vietnam. Unfortunately, due to its relatively low international competitiveness, Indonesia's garment industry was not able to take full advantage of the expiry of the Multi-Fibre Arrangement in early 2005 to increase its exports.

Since the mid-1980s, Indonesia's garment industry emerged as one of the most important export-oriented industries, generating a rising stream of foreign exchange earnings and many job opportunities, mostly for low skilled, predominently women workers because of its labour-intensive production process. Except for a temporary decline in garment exports in the first two years after the Asian economic crisis, post-crisis garment exports until the expiry of the Multi-Fibre Arrangement (MFA, also known as the Agreement on Textile and Clothing) have generally been higher than before the crisis, despite the concern that the competitiveness of Indonesia's garment industry had declined in the face of strong competition from other developing countries, particularly China, Vietnam, India and Bangladesh. However, while garment exports after the expiry of the MFA have slightly increased, there is as yet no strong evidence yet that the garment industry will be able to take full advantage of the expiry of the MFA to substantially raise its garment exports.

This paper will first give a detailed overview of the development of the garment industry since the 1970s up to the expiry of the MFA. The paper will then discuss the development of this industry after the expiry of the MFA in early 2005, the problems it is facing at present, and the prospects for a revitalisation of this industry.


## PRE-MFA DEVELOPMENTS

### The period of rapid growth

Indonesia's garment industry is a relatively young industry, as it only began to grow rapidly during the early years of the Soeharto era in the early 1970s. The garment industry emerged as a factory activity only since the mid-1970s, responding to growing export opportunities and the expanding domestic market. Up to the early 1970s, garment production was largely conducted in the many small tailor shops found all over the country (Hill, 1992: 8).

While Indonesia's weaving industry until the late 1980s was the largest industry among the three sub-sectors of the textile industry (i.e. the up-stream, highly capital-intensive, large-scale synthetic fibre industry; the mid-stream capital-intensive, large scale spinning industry and the labour-intensive weaving and fabric producing industry; and the down-stream, highly labour-intensive garment industry) in terms of output and employment, since 1989 the garment industry emerged as the largest industry in terms of employment (Pangestu, 1997: 30).

Growth of the garment industry was quite rapid from the late 1970s in response to rapidly rising demand in the domestic market and improving growth opportunities in the export market (Pangestu, 1997: 31). The export orientation of garment firms was also encouraged by Indonesia's comparatively low labour costs and because of its unutilised quota for the large quota-constrained export markets in the US and the European Community (Wymenga, 1991b: 212).

By 1975 there were 72 industrial establishments in the garments sector, in which 2,804 workers were employed. In the same year about 4,800 persons, mostly women, were also employed in small-scale garment production.

However, in 1986, there were already 565 large- and medium-scale garment plants in operation which altogether employed an estimated 63,576 workers, most of them women. There were also 6,963 registered small-scale garment establishments which employed about 46,940 workers. In addition to these small, medium, and large establishments, there were numerous cottage or home establishments engaged in garment production (Wymenga, 1991b: 212).

Production capacity in the garment industry increased rapidly in the 1980s due to the rapid increase in the number of garment plants (Pangestu, 1997: 33) and the corresponding rapid increase in the number of sewing machines during the period 1980–90. There was also a rapid increase in the number of workers from 14,350 to 105,007, a seven-fold increase. Fabric consumption by the garment industry also rose by 78 per cent between 1985 and 1990 (World Bank, 1994: 21). As a result, garment output increased from 50,400 tons in 1978 to 171,250 tons in 1989. When the garment industry became export-oriented in the late 1980s, the value of garment exports during the same period rose rapidly from US$42.9 million to US$1,248 million (Sastromihardjo, 1991). By 1989, garment exports, together with plywood, ranked as Indonesia's two most important manufactured exports, with plywood accounting for 21.3 per cent and garments accounting for 10.6 per cent of total manufactured exports.

To get a better idea of Indonesia's garment industry in the early 1990s, Table 1 presents the main features of the garment industry in the early 1990s.

### TABLE 1
### Characteristics of the Garment Industry, Indonesia, Early 1990s

| Indicators | Features |
|---|---|
| History | Very new (as plants) in the early 1990s |
| Factor proportions | Very labour-intensive |
| Scale economies | Unimportant (except in export-oriented plants) |
| Ownership | Mainly private domestic, but also a number of foreign-owned, export-oriented plants established in the late 1980s, mainly from Korea |
| Vertical integration | Rare |
| Size distribution | Many small and medium-scale domestic firms, but a number of large-scale, foreign-owned and a few domestic firms |
| Market orientation | Mainly export-oriented, except for a few large, domestic market-oriented domestic firms |
| Location | Mainly in the Greater Jakarta region, Bandung, and Bali |

*Source*: Adapted from Hill (1992:2).

Table 2 gives an idea of the relative importance of the garment industry in Indonesia's manufacturing sector over the period 1990-2002. Although in terms of gross manufacturing value added, the garment industry is not very significant, it is an important employment generator contributing 10 per cent of manufacturing employment in 2002 (see Table 2).

**TABLE 2**
**Garment Manufacturing Value Added and Employment, 1990–2002**

| Industry | Gross value added (billions of rupiah) | | | Employment (thousands of workers) | | |
|---|---|---|---|---|---|---|
| | *1990* | *1996* | *2002* | *1990* | *1996* | *2002* |
| Garments | 820.8 | 2,721.4 | 9,300 | 240.1 | 363.6 | 446.3 |
| | (3.6%) | (3.2%) | (3.4%) | (9.0%) | (8.6%) | (10.2%) |
| Total manufacturing | 2,843.9 | 85,241.4 | 269,000 | 2,662.8 | 4,214.9 | 4,385.9 |
| | (100%) | (100%) | (100%) | (100%) | (100%) | (100%) |

*Source*: Statistics Indonesia (*Economic Indicators*, various issues).

Unlike the spinning and weaving industries where foreign equity accounted for 26 and 16 per cent of total equity respectively, the garment industry is dominated by domestic private firms. However, since the late 1980s, foreign firms have also entered garment manufacturing in large numbers, particularly companies from Korea, Taiwan and Hong Kong, responding to "push" factors, particularly higher wage and land costs at home, as well as their appreciating currencies. "Pull" factors were also at work, specifically a series of deregulation measures introduced by the Indonesian government, from the mid-1980s, meant to improve the investment climate for private investors as well as the series of trade reforms which proved to be successful in attracting new export-oriented foreign direct investment (FDI) from the East Asian newly industrialized economies (Thee, 1991a: 64). Before the mid-1980s, the bulk of FDI took place in domestic-market-oriented projects as a result of the protectionist import substitution policies.

Most of these labour-intensive operations in Indonesia set up by the Asian newly-industrialised economy (NIE) firms consist of garment and footwear plants. For instance, according to data provided by the Jakarta office of the Korean Trade Association, 50 of the 100 Korean plants operating in Indonesia in 1990 consisted of 35 garment plants and 15 footwear plants. The data in

Table 3 show the percentage of ownership of garment firms by local private, government and foreign ownership during the period 1990–93.

Table 3 shows that during the first half of the 1990s local private firms dominated the garment industry, although their relative dominance slightly decreased when many East Asian NIE-invested firms entered the industry to use Indonesia as a lower cost export platform. However, the number of government garment firms was miniscule.

### TABLE 3
### The Relative Share of Local Private, Government and Foreign Firms in Indonesia's Garment Industry, 1990–93 (%)

|       |           | Local private | | Government | | Foreign | |
|-------|-----------|------|------|------|------|------|------|
| ISIC  | Commodity | 1990 | 1993 | 1990 | 1993 | 1990 | 1993 |
| 32210 | Garments  | 91.9 | 84.6 | 0.4  | 0.5  | 7.7  | 14.9 |

*Source*: Pangestu (1997: 35).

The increasing export orientation of the domestic private firms since the mid-1980s was mainly caused by the increasing attractiveness of the export market and the sluggish growth of the domestic market following the end of the oil boom era in 1982. Exporting became a profitable undertaking with the shift from import-substituting to export promotion policies in the mid-1980s after the oil boom had ended. In support of the export promotion policies, since the mid-1980s, the Indonesian government introduced a series of trade reforms to reduce the "anti-export bias" of its highly protectionist trade regime and also pursued a realistic exchange rate policy to maintain the effective real exchange rate at a competitive level (Thee, 1991a: 7).

The most important trade reform came with the May 1986 deregulation package which introduced a duty exemption and drawback scheme which enabled export-oriented manufacturing firms (defined as firms exporting at least 85 per cent of their output; subsequently lowered to 65 per cent of their output) to purchase their inputs, whether imported or locally made, at international prices. Export-oriented garment firms, particularly the new garment firms, were able to benefit from this scheme because they imported most of their raw materials (Wymenga, 1988: 6). The opportunity of importing raw materials without adhering anymore to restrictive import licenses as provided by the duty exemption and drawback scheme was therefore very helpful for the export-oriented garment firms. Particularly the new garment firms were now able to import their raw materials directly (Wymenga, 1991b: 213).

In addition to the trade reforms and the sensible exchange rate policy, other factors contributed to making garment exports attractive. First, the availability of under-utilised import quotas as provided under the MFA in the major export markets for garments, namely the US and, to a lesser extent, the European Community (EC), was a strong incentive to produce garments for the export market even before the mid-1980s. The availability of these unutilised import quotas and the strong comparative advantage of Indonesia's garment industry, which was largely based on its low labour costs, attracted garment firms from the East Asian NIEs, notably Hong Kong, South Korea and Taiwan, to set up new garment plants in Indonesia. These garment plants thus served as 'export platforms' to supply the quota countries, including the US, Canada, and the EC countries, as well as the non-quota countries, including Japan, Australia, New Zealand, Singapore and the countries in the Middle East (Thee et al, 1989: 22).

However, by the end of the 1980s the quota ceilings set under the MFA for a variety of garment categories had been reached, and therefore became an important constraint on further export growth, particularly for the cheaper garments at the lower end of the market. Since about 90 per cent of Indonesia's garment exports at the time were directed at the MFA-constrained markets, particularly the US and the EC (Hill, 1992), redirection of Indonesia's garment exports to non-MFA constrained markets was imperative. The great dependence of garment exports on one single export market, the US, is indicated by the fact that, in 1989, 49 per cent of these exports were directed at the US, while the second-largest market, West Germany, absorbed only 8.5 per cent, with the Netherlands occupying third place, absorbing 6.3 per cent of the garment exports (Statistics Indonesia, 1989). As a result of the successive deregulation measures and trade reforms, garment exports rose steadily over the period 1986–96, although after 1993 growth became more uneven (Table 4).

Indonesia's leading garment exports included shirts of synthetic fibre for men and boys, blouses for women and girls made of synthetic fibre, and trousers and breeches of cotton for men and boys. Fabrics and other raw materials were imported for high quality garments. For standard garments raw materials were usually sourced in Indonesia (Wymenga, 1991a: 213).

Despite the fact that since the mid-1980s quite a lot of new export-oriented garment plants were established, notably in the Bandung area in West Java province and in the Cakung Export Processing Zone in the vicinity of Jakarta's Tanjung Priok harbour, many garment firms in the late 1980s still catered

**TABLE 4**
**Garment exports, Indonesia, 1986–96**

| Year | Value (US$ million) |
|------|---------------------|
| 1986 | 519 |
| 1987 | 598 |
| 1988 | 796 |
| 1989 | 1,169 |
| 1990 | 1,670 |
| 1991 | 2,290 |
| 1992 | 3,189 |
| 1993 | 3,395 |
| 1994 | 3,226 |
| 1995 | 3,388 |
| 1996 | 3,576 |

*Note*: Rounded figures.
*Source*: Statistics Indonesia (Economic Indicators, various issues).

mainly to the domestic market (Thee et al. 1989: 21). For instance, in 1986, only about 36 per cent of the value of gross output of the garment industry was exported. Garment firms oriented towards the domestic market consisted mainly of small firms catering mainly to local or individual requirements. For this reason these small firms were playing an important role in tailoring, sub-contracting to large garment firms, and in producing textile handicrafts (Wymenga, 1988: 3).

That the garment industry even after the trade reforms of the late 1980s was still largely domestic market-oriented was due to the fact that both the textile and garment industries continued to enjoy tariff protection and various import restrictions, such as import surcharges, import licensing procedures and selective tariff exemptions. Although *nominal* tariffs had been falling since the mid-1980s, the *effective* rates of protection on import-competing goods remained higher than on export-competing goods, thus imparting a persistent bias in favour of firms selling in the domestic market rather than in export markets (see Table 5).

While export-oriented garment firms could purchase their tradable inputs at international prices (whether imported or locally-made), they still had to purchase their non-tradable intermediate inputs at "above free trade prices," with the result that their export sales received negative effective protection. However, garment firms selling in the domestic market continued to enjoy a high level of effective protection on their value added. Hence, because of

**TABLE 5**
**Effective Rates of Protection in Textiles and**
**Garments, Indonesia, 1989**

| Industry | Total sales | Domestic sales | Exports |
|----------|-------------|----------------|---------|
| Textiles | 84.9 | 109.4 | −2.0 |
| Garments | 16.5 | 101.4 | −1.3 |

Source: Wymenga (1991a: 140).

this dual structure of protection, there was a sharp dichotomy between the firms that were internationally competitive and export and those firms which were not competitive and therefore served the domestic market (World Bank, 1994: 22).

Other types of regulations also penalised export-oriented textile and garment firms. These included the imposition of a compulsory levy on garment exports to countries applying quota restrictions, granting a single designated firm the sole right to import cotton and synthetic fibres required by the spinning industry (rescinded after industry complaints), and the operation of a non-transparent system for the allocation of export quotas (Thee and Pangestu, 1998: 218).

A survey by the World Bank revealed that several export-oriented garment firms mentioned that the MFA was a major obstacle to their future growth. While some firms appeared to experience no problem in obtaining quota, other firms complained of the lack of transparency and premiums having to be paid. On paper the general allocation of quota, 80 per cent was based on past export performance and 20 per cent went to new exporters and small firms. The annual increase in quota was given to these new exporters and small firms (World Bank, 1994: 22).

Given the remaining "anti-export bias" of the trade regime in the late 1980s and other restrictive measures, the question that arises is why garment exports were nevertheless able to increase so rapidly since the mid-1980s. The most important factor appeared to be the above-mentioned duty exemption and drawback scheme which enabled export-oriented firms to procure their intermediate inputs at international prices with few bureaucratic hurdles. In this way these firms were able to operate as though they were in an export-processing zone (Hill, 1992: 31–33). Another important factor in the surge of manufactured exports, including garment exports, since 1987 was Bank Indonesia's ability to maintain the real effective exchange rate at a competitive level (Thee and Pangestu, 1998: 219).

Two other factors accounting for the rapid expansion of Indonesia's garment exports were the strong linkages with foreign buyers which were established since the mid-1980s and the improved reputation among these foreign buyers about the garment industry's ability to provide quality products and keep to tight delivery schedules (HIID, 1995: E.5). The linkages with foreign buyers were established when buying agents from Hong Kong, acting on behalf of foreign buyers (mostly department stores in the developed countries in the US, the EC and Japan) in the mid-1980s were looking for low-cost garment suppliers in Southeast Asia, including Indonesia (Thee, Hamid and Wiranta, 1989). During their visits to Indonesia, they approached several local garment firms to start exporting garments according to the specific designs of the foreign buyers. This kind of producing for the export market was one of the first cases of "original equipment manufacturing" in Indonesia, since these domestic garment firms had to make the garments according to the strict specifications of the overseas buyers in regard to design, fabrics, buttons, quality and delivery schedules.

The crucial role of foreign buyers is particularly evident with the interesting case of the garment industry in Bali which since the mid-1970s through the early 1990s experienced rapid export growth. The remarkable growth of Bali's export-oriented was based on crucial information flows which these Balinese firms received through strategic business alliances with foreign firms and businessmen (Cole, 1998: 257).

The remarkable thing about the export success of Bali's garment industry is that they mostly consist of rural-based small and micro enterprises largely owned and run by *pribumi* (indigenous) Indonesian entrepreneurs. Another remarkable feature of the Bali export garment industry was that this industry was able, within a relatively short time, to produce highly competitive products for the international market, and that these products were largely made from domestic material inputs. Moreover, unlike many large domestic firms which were able to benefit from government protection or implicit or explicit subsidies, Bali's garment industry did not receive any government subsidy. In fact, the rapid growth of this industry had neither been anticipated nor planned by the government (Cole, 1997: 2).

The major factor which triggered this success was the presence of foreign buyers/entrepreneurs from Australia and later from the U.S., Europe and Japan, many of whom initially came as tourists, who were able to establish direct contacts with local entrepreneurs. Through the vital information transfer and technical and managerial assistance (for instance in plant lay-out, advice on the purchase of the most appropriate machines, and quality control techniques), provided by the foreign buyers/entrepreneurs to the small and micro Balinese firms, these firms were able to achieve high levels of efficiency and accuracy. This assistance was provided on a for-profit basis, as it was specifically tied to tangible product output results (Cole, 1998: 275; Thee and Hamid, 1997).

The ongoing interaction of these two parties started a cycle of technological improvements and learning that was self-replicating and largely self-financing, which led to rapid and sustained export growth (Cole, 1998: 275). This export performance could be sustained even after the onset of the Asian economic crisis, since these foreign buyers/entrepreneurs, unlike foreign investors, still kept visiting Bali after the crisis as this island was largely spared the unrest and breakdown in safety, law and order which afflicted some other regions in Indonesia, at least until the devastating terrorist bomb attacks in Bali in 2002 and again in 2005. Not surprisingly, these attacks led to a much reduced inflow of foreign tourists and foreign buyers.

As regards the relative export orientation of the garment firms in Indonesia, three categories of garment firms can be distinguished, namely local private firms, government (state-owned) firms and foreign-invested firms. Since foreign garment firms which had established their plants in Indonesia to serve primarily the export markets, it is not surprising that they were more export-oriented (in the sense of having a higher export-output ratio) than the local private firms (Table 6).

Table 6 shows that foreign firms are more export-oriented than the local private firms. The surprising thing, however, is that the very few government garment firms were the most export-oriented compared to the local private and foreign firms. Many of the best equipped garment plants with modern cutting equipment were joint ventures, mostly with South Korean and Taiwanese garment firms. About 90 per cent of the local, private, export-oriented garment firms worked on a cut, make and trim basis for overseas buyers with little local design input. While the local garment firms' lack of a design department kept part of the overhead costs down, and therefore the

**TABLE 6**
**Export-output Ratio with the Local Private, Government and Foreign Garment Firms, Indonesia, 1990–93 (%)**

|  | Commodity | Local private | | Government-owned | | Foreign-owned | |
|---|---|---|---|---|---|---|---|
| ISIC |  | 1990 | 1993 | 1990 | 1993 | 1990 | 1993 |
| 32210 | Garments | 38.5 | 37.8 | 46.2 | 73.4 | 57.4 | 65.3 |

Source: Pangestu (1997: 35).

selling price, this fact also limited the scope of the firm offering alternative ideas and working on a more equal basis with the foreign buyers. However, some firms, particularly the joint ventures, started to invest in computer aided design equipment. For several garment firms one constraint in expanding garment output and maintaining product quality was the difficulty they faced in recruiting skilled and experienced middle management and technicians. As a result of the excess demand for skilled technicians, their pay was in many instances higher than that of their counterparts in Thailand or Singapore (World Bank, 1994: 22).

## The period of sluggish growth

Since 1994 through 1996 the garment industry grew at a more sluggish rate, as reflected by the slowdown in garment exports which stopped growing at a steady rate. Garment exports slowed down since 1993, declined in 1994, slightly recovered in 1995, but then declined again in 1996 (Table 4). These disappointing results were primarily a result of falling prices, quota limitations and sharp international competition (HIID, 1995, E.1). Interviews conducted by an HIID team in 1995 with several garment exporters revealed that faced serious difficulties because of the intensified international competition, causing many garment firms to close or relocate to lower cost sites in other countries, such as Vietnam. Press reports from that period reported that as many as 76 garment firms had closed in 1994. Hong Kong-owned garment firms also reported that their garment factories in China were making profits, while their Indonesian plants were struggling to survive (HIID, 1995: E.5).

Actually, a slowdown in the growth of garment exports was not surprising. The surge of garment exports which started in the late 1980s was possible because of the unfulfilled quotas in the US and the EC. However, these quotas were mostly utilised by the mid-1990s (Pangestu, 1997: 49). The export opportunities that opened up as a result of the relocation of garment plants from South Korea and Taiwan had by the early 1990s also been exploited (HIID, 1995: E.5).

However, quota limitations alone could not account for the sluggish growth of garment exports, because after an agreement between the Indonesian and American governments, quota allocations for Indonesia were increased by more than 35 per cent (Thee and Pangestu, 1998). As a result, for some garment categories there were some unfulfilled quotas. Actually, the biggest decline in garment exports took place in the non-quota markets caused by strong competition from other low-wage countries, including China, India and Bangladesh. The relative competitiveness of Indonesian garment exports was further eroded because of the government's mandatory minimum wage policy which led to an increase of 40 per cent in minimum wages during the period 1994–96. In 1996 alone wage costs rose by over 30 per cent. However, this increase was not matched by a corresponding rise in labour productivity (Pangestu, 1997: 49). As a result per unit labour costs rose relative to those of Indonesia's competitors.

Another source of difficulty for the export-oriented garment firms was that much garment production depended on imported fabric. Hence, delays in the delivery of imported fabric seriously hampered the tight turn-around times required for the production of the mid- and high-end garments. Unfortunately, local sourcing of fabrics was hampered because of the lack of good textile finishing capacity, general lack of export quality fabrics, lack of high quality cotton fabrics for export garment production, the unwillingness of textile manufacturers to service the needs of garment exporters for small, frequent orders, difficulties with the tax office in reclaiming the value added tax on domestic purchases of fabrics, and the protection enjoyed by fabric producers which allowed them to get higher prices from domestic market-oriented firms than from export-oriented firms, thus limiting their incentive to serve the export-oriented garment firms (HIID, 1995: E.12).

Yet another factor accounting for the reduced competitiveness of the garment industry was the lack of new investments in the industry. Instead of investing the large profits they had earned during the boom years, several large garment firms expanded horizontally outside their core business and ventured into sectors outside their core business and moved into sectors unrelated to the garment industry (Aswicahyono et al., 2005: 53).

One important indication of the garment industry's reduced competitiveness was revealed by a study in late 1995 which found that Indonesia's garment exports had declined most sharply in the non-quota markets, with a small decline in volume accompanying a larger decline in unit value (James, 1995: 22–25). In contrast, declining volumes in quota markets exceeded unit value declines. Garment exports since 1994 experienced a decline in market share, indicating that Indonesia was facing increasingly tough competition from Vietnam, the Philippines, China, India, Pakistan, Sri Lanka and Bangladesh.

Assessing the weakness of the Indonesian garment industry, a report submitted by Sanjaya Lall and Kishore Rao to Indonesia's National Development Planning Board (Bappenas) in 1995, concluded that the industry had to raise its productivity, design and local content of the industry in order to raise its export competitiveness. In addition, the domestic market-oriented firms had to be encouraged to also produce for the export markets, which required that their base of domestic skills and technology had to be raised (Lall and Rao, 1995: 139).

To upgrade the garment industry, Lall and Rao recommended that steps had to be taken in the fields of investment and financing and the improvement of market analysis. In regard to investment and financing, the declining rate of equipment imports by the industry had to be developed so that more value-added activities could be undertaken within Indonesia.

Improving market analysis was also strongly recommended because the Indonesian firms had to keep close track on trends in different garment categories and markets in the industry. While the large firms had few problems in doing market analysis, the smaller firms were generally unable to undertake the investment required, and thus remained completely dependent on the foreign buyers. For these firms, a detailed market share analysis and comparisons with major competitors would be crucial to devising coherent and timely responses to changing competitive needs (Lall and Rao, 1995: 139).

A World Bank (1994: 23) study concluded that to achieve sustained growth, the garment industry would also have to shift its market position from simple to higher quality products, with more own design content to achieve higher value added. Since the industry had already gone through the basic skills learning curve, it would henceforth need to strengthen its market position by improving its skills in production process management, product quality improvement, and logistics, and also add an element of own design input.

## After the Asian crisis

The severe Asian economic crisis that hit Indonesia in 1997 and 1998 had a devastating impact on the Indonesian economy. The crisis struck in mid-1997, but its greatest impact was only felt in 1998 when the economy contracted by an unprecedented 13.1 per cent. The manufacturing sector, which after the end of the oil boom era in 1982 had emerged as the major engine of growth and the major source of export revenues by the late 1980s, contracted by 11.1 per cent, while the textile, leather and footwear industry (ISIC 32) contracted by 14.9 per cent.

The economy slightly recovered in 1999 with a positive but miniscule growth rate of 0.8 per cent, while the manufacturing sector grew at 3.9 per cent and the textiles, leather products and footwear industry grew at 8.5 per cent. In the following years, growth rates picked up, with the economy growing at an average annual rate of 4.6 per cent over the period 2000–04, compared to the average annual growth rate of 7 per cent during the 30 years of the Soeharto era.

During the same period of 2000–04 the manufacturing sector grew at an average annual rate of 5.2 per cent, while the textile, leather products and footwear industry grew at an average annual rate of 4.9 per cent (Statistics Indonesia, *National Income of Indonesia*, 2000-04), while during the Soeharto era the manufacturing sector was on the average growing at double digit rates. Hence, the performance of the manufacturing sector, including the textiles, leather products and footwear industry, after the Asian economic crisis up to the present continues to be modest compared to the rapid growth rates achieved during the Soeharto era.

The vibrant textile, garments, and footwear industries, which spearheaded Indonesia's labour-intensive, export-oriented industrialization drive since the late 1980s up to the Asian economic crisis, are now facing great difficulties. During the short period immediately after the crisis, export oriented firms, including the garment industry benefited from the sharp but short-lived real exchange rate depreciation. However, since 2000 export growth has been rather sluggish, since these firms, including the export-oriented garment firms, seem unable to compete with China and other low-cost producers, such as Vietnam. The problem is that while international competition in the garment industry has intensified, Indonesia's garment industry has become less competitive (Aswicahyono and Hill, 2004: 289–90).

The size and dynamism of the Chinese economy, its cost advantages and its large pool of labour resources have changed the rules of international competition (James, Ray and Minor, 2003: 93). For Indonesia, in particular with its dependence on low skill labour-intensive exports, China's increasingly dominant position as a supplier of textiles and garments is a matter of great concern. This has been evident with the very large and growing overlap between China's labour-intensive exports and the labour-intensive exports of Southeast Asian countries, particularly Indonesia and Thailand, to the US market (see Table 7). For both China and the Southeast Asian countries, particularly Indonesia, the US market is the largest market for their manufactured exports, particularly labour-intensive manufactured exports, including Indonesia's garment exports. The fact that the Southeast Asian countries' labour-intensive manufactured exports are competing in the same categories with China's highly competitive labour-intensive manufactured exports in the demanding American market is therefore a source of great concern to these former countries (see Table 7).

## TABLE 7
### Overlap of Labour-intensive Manufactured Exports from Southeast Asian Countries with China's Labour-intensive Exports to the United States, 1990–2000 (%)

| Country | 1990 | 1995 | 2000 |
|---|---|---|---|
| Indonesia | 85.3 | 85.5 | 82.8 |
| Malaysia | 37.1 | 38.9 | 48.7 |
| Philippines | 46.3 | 47.8 | 46.1 |
| Thailand | 42.2 | 56.3 | 65.4 |

*Source*: World Bank (2003: 4).

Table 7 shows that in view of the large overlap (over 80 per cent) between China's and Indonesia's labour-intensive manufactured exports, including garments, in the US market, Indonesia among the Southeast Asian countries is the most exposed to the strong competition from China. In the face of open competition from China, Indonesia's garment industry is likely to lose market share in its export markets if it is not able to improve competitiveness.

Strong competition in the export markets for garments will not only come from China, but from other Asian developing countries as well. For instance, India has been pursuing a revitalisation program for its garment industry by establishing 15 model parks based on China's special economic zones. The parks will be equipped with infrastructure and worker training centres in order to attract investment from large-scale garment producers under the "dereservation" policy. This means that garment production will no longer be reserved for small-scale enterprises. Under this "dereservation" policy, the garment industry will be open to investment in large- and medium-scale production facilities (James; Ray and Minor, 2003: 100; 103).

Moreover, Vietnam secured access to the US market under a bilateral trade agreement in 1999 and has also been able to attract major investments in its integrated textile and garment production facilities from Formosa Plastics, Taiwan's largest textile producer. Other Asian countries, including Pakistan, Sri Lanka, Bangladesh and Cambodia, have also had negotiations with the US and the EU for increased preferential access to their markets (James; Ray and Minor, 2003: 100).

The Constant Market Shares Analysis of the garment industry conducted by Aswicahyono and colleagues in 2005, indicated that Indonesia's garment industry was indeed losing its competitiveness long before the Asian economic crisis. However, the garment industry's unit labour costs (wage costs adjusted for labour productivity) appeared to remain competitive. However, the garment industry was not able to translate Indonesia's labour cost advantage into growing penetration into the export markets (Aswicahyono and Hill, 2004: 290; Aswicahyono, Atje and Thee, 2005).

## Post-MFA Developments

With the phase-out of the MFA at the end of 2004, trade in garments as of January 2005 was conducted under the rules of the World Trade Organization. This meant that Indonesia's garment industry since that date was facing strong competition in all its export markets, including in its former protected quota markets where it is now facing strong competition from its competitors. A worrying development has been that Indonesia's garment industry has in recent years lost not less than 40 per cent market share in Japan, the world's largest non-quota (non-MFA) import market before the expiry of the MFA (Aswicahyono and Hill, 2004: 292). In addition, with the trade liberalisation in the ASEAN markets in the framework of the ASEAN Free Trade Agreement, Indonesia's garment industry within the ASEAN market at present is also facing strong competition from lower wage countries, such as Vietnam and Cambodia.

Another problem facing Indonesia's garment industry is that in the global trading system, preferential trade agreements (PTAs) that liberalise trade among members, but discriminate against non-members, have been proliferating in recent years. Countries constituting the major export markets have been negotiating new PTAs that divert trade away from low-cost, non-member countries, such as Indonesia (James, Ray and Minor, 2003: 93). Thus far, however, Indonesia, unlike some of its ASEAN neighbours, such as Thailand, has not been very active in concluding PTAs with its major trading partners.

Indonesia's ability to respond to these demand-side pressures is constrained by rising domestic transaction costs. Under the regional autonomy legislation introduced in January 2001, both textile and garment firms have been and are increasingly burdened with new taxes (often referred to as "nuisance taxes" by businessmen) imposed by the regional governments, charges and other levies, as local governments look for ways to increase their own-source revenues (James, Ray and Minor, 2003: 93–94). Although the central government has recently issued a decree that the regional governments are now only allowed to impose a limited number of taxes, the effectiveness of this decree has yet to be tested in the field.

Moreover, under the new freedoms introduced after the fall of Soeharto, many new labour unions have been created which have created many labour problems since are now much more vocal and aggressive in demanding higher minimum wages, higher severance payments and better working conditions. The government has also introduced regulations on costly dismissal procedures and on social security which has increased the costs of employing labour in Indonesia (Aswicahyono and Hill, 2004: 291).

The new political freedoms which has led to the creation of many new labour unions as well as the enactment of a new labour-friendly Labour Law in 2003 has led to many industrial disputes and lost working days. A recent effort by the government to revise the controversial Labour Law of 2003 has led to mass labour demonstration, including during the 1 May Labour Day celebrations in 2005 when many workers left their jobs, causing billions of rupiah losses to the plants, including garment plants, which could not operate.

Despite the problems faced by the garment industry, garment exports after the expiry of the MFA have, at least thus far, steadily increased compared to the years just before this expiry. However, some industry representatives remain doubtful whether this steady growth can be sustained in the next few years (see Table 8).

The data in Table 9 presents more data on various aspects of the development of Indonesia's garment industry in the few years immediately after the expiry of the MFA in late 2004. Table 9 indicates that while the

**TABLE 8**
**Garment Exports, Indonesia, 1997–2008**

| Year | Garment exports (US$ million) |
|------|-------------------------------|
| 1997 | 2,876 |
| 1998 | 2,588 |
| 1999 | 3,818 |
| 2000 | 4,703 |
| 2001 | 4,477 |
| 2002 | 3,887 |
| 2003 | 4,038 |
| 2004 | 4,352 |
| Post-MFA | |
| 2005 | 4,967 |
| 2006 | 5,608 |
| 2007 | 5,713 |
| 2008 (Jan–Oct) | 5,062 |

*Note*: Rounded figures
*Source*: Statistics Indonesia (*Economic Indicators*, various issues).

**TABLE 9**
**Capacity of the Garment Industry, Indonesia, 2001–05**

| Item | Unit | 2001 | 2002 | 2003 | 2004 | 2005 |
|------|------|------|------|------|------|------|
| No. of companies | | 860 | 849 | 855 | 861 | 860 |
| Capital investment | Billions of rupiah | 2,808 | 2,913 | 2,958 | 2,978 | 2,975 |
| No. of machines | | 279,546 | 285,136 | 290,838 | 292,878 | 292,538 |
| Employment | Persons | 376,584 | 350,901 | 352,457 | 353,590 | 353,179 |
| Production capacity | Thousands of tons | 584 | 591 | 590 | 666 | 685 |
| Production | Thousands of tons | 565 | 462 | 461 | 517 | 383 |
| Exports | Thousands of tons | 380 | 328 | 332 | 324 | 345 |

*Note*: Rounded figures
*Source*: Statistics Indonesia (*Large and Medium Manufacturing Statistics, Vol. I*, various issues); and data provided by the Indonesian Textile Association.

number of companies, the amount of capital investment, and the number of sewing machines before and after the expiry of the MFA were about the same, the number of workers in 2005 was slightly lower compared to that of 2004 and more than 20,000 lower than in 2001. However, the data on production capacity and the volume of output in 2005 as compared to the years before the MFA expiry indicate that while in 2001 the garment plants were operating at almost full capacity, in the following years before the expiry, these plants were operating at steadily lower levels of capacity. After the MFA expiry in early 2005, the capacity utilisation level of the garment industry as a whole declined to only 57 per cent. The data also show that in that year the bulk of the output of garments was exported. Hence, the recent increased garment exports can be largely attributed to price rather than to volume increases, as indicated by the data in Table 9.

The fact that the bulk of garment output had to be exported should be attributed to widespread smuggling of garments since the locally-made garments cannot compete with the cheaper garments smuggled or imported illegally. Over the years conditions have worsened because of the flood of smuggled garments in the domestic market. Since a value added tax is levied on the sale of locally made garments, these garments cannot compete with the cheaper, illegally imported garments (Gita, 2007a: 2).

To combat widespread smuggling of garments and other manufactured products (including consumer electronics), the government has submitted a draft law on customs which imposes a 20-year prison sentence and hefty fines on smugglers, including corrupt custom officials who allow the illegal imports of garments, for instance by tolerating the under-invoicing of imported garments (Gita, 2007b: 2). However, whether this law will be effective will ultimately depend on the effective enforcement of this law by honest rather than corrupt custom officials. Unfortunately, the customs service has been one of the most corrupt government agencies in Indonesia. However, more recently the minister of finance, who oversees the customs service, has recently taken drastic steps to clean up the customs service by firing the most corrupt officials and imposing a strict code of conduct for the remaining officials.

Aside from the problem of smuggling, Indonesia's garment industry does suffer from a lack of international competitiveness. However, since the expiry of the MFA, Indonesia has not been fully able to take advantage of the opportunities open to it to better penetrate the rich export markets of the US and the EU because of the imposition of safeguard measures against the imports of garments from China after the MFA expiry.

## CONCLUSIONS

Despite widely-held views on the part of several government officials, businessmen and academic economists that the garment industry is a "sunset industry" with little prospect of future dynamic development in Indonesia, there is a strong case for strengthening and upgrading the industry to increase its international competitiveness in the post-MFA expiry era. With more moderate rises in minimum wages accompanied by rising labour productivity which will restrain rises in per unit labour costs, Indonesia still has a strong comparative advantage in labour-intensive industries, including the garment industry. In view of the growing unemployment problem (with 9 per cent of the labour force of 110 million being openly unemployed), it makes good economic sense to strengthen and upgrade labour-intensive industries, including the garment industry.

Facing strong international competition in its export and domestic markets, Indonesia's garment industry should gradually move away from the lower end of the market garments where international competition is fierce, and shift to up-market, high quality garments, including designer clothes and beach wear popular with tourists, as the Bali case has shown. To make this possible, the garment industry should send its qualified staff to study design in, for instance, Hong Kong's well-known design institute.

Although the garment industry is generally regarded as a low skill labour intensive industry, the garment industry in the advanced countries, such as Japan and the US, has during the past two decades experienced important technological developments. In Japan the Ministry of Economy, Trade, and Industry in the early 1980s introduced a Flexible Manufacturing System for fully automated garment production in which the labour input has been reduced to one-tenth of its former level, while the lead time has been shortened through the computerised control in design, cutting, patterning and sewing which has led to a considerable reduction in costs (Yamazawa, 1982: 7).

In the US the most important technological development has been the application of microelectronics to garment production (process) technology. The application of these microelectronics-based innovations, however, has been mainly limited to the large firms (Hoffman, 1985: 376).

Although the equipment which embodies these technological developments are very expensive, the government may be able to assist garment firms, in first instance the larger, better endowed firms but also smaller firms grouped in cooperatives to purchase this equipment, for instance by providing subsidised loans.

Since skill levels of workers in the garment industry are quite low, the garment industry could establish joint training centres to improve their skills, particularly in the operation and maintenance of high-tech equipment. This training is very important since garment producers are being asked to use cutting-edge technology computer technology to provide designs and patterns to the rich country buyers (USAID and Senada, 2006: 88).

Since one of the fastest growing trade areas for garments now take place within preferential trading arrangements, the Indonesian government can also assist the garment industry by playing an active role in trade negotiations with Indonesia's most important trading partners to obtain tariff preferences through production sharing arrangements or through preferential trade agreements (Aswicahyono et al., 2005: 55).

Lastly, the government can help the manufacturing sector, including the garment industry, by taking effective steps to improve the country's poor investment climate which is generally rated as the worst in East Asia. By improving the investment climate by substantially simplifying the cumbersome and time-consuming licensing procedures, providing legal certainty, issuing more business-friendly labour regulations which are in accordance with the legitimate labour demands for adequate wages and good working conditions, and clamping down on corruption by the government bureaucracy, particularly the customs service, the government could do a great deal to help manufacturing firms, including the garment firms, to reduce the high transaction costs which contribute to making the garment industry less competitive.

## Note

1.  "The Development of Labour-intensive Garment Manufacturing in Indonesia", by Thee Kian Wie, first published in *Journal of Contemporary Asia* 39, no. 4 (2009): 562–78.

## References

Aswicahyono H. and H. Hill. "Survey of Recent Developments," *Bulletin of Indonesian Economic Studies* 40, no. 3 (2004): 277–305.

Aswicahyono, H., R. Atje and K.W. Thee. *Indonesia's Industrial Competitiveness: A Study of the Garments, Auto Parts and Electronic Components Industries*. Jakarta: Report to the Development Economics Research Group, World Bank, March 2005.

Cole, W. (1997) *Bali's Garment Industry: An Indonesian Case of Successful Strategic Alliances*. Jakarta, unpublished paper.

Cole, W. (1998) "Bali's garment export industry", H. Hill and K.W. Thee (eds.), *Indonesia's Technological Challenge*. Canberra: Research School of Pacific and Asian Studies, The Australian National University and Singapore: Institute of Southeast Asian Studies, pp. 255–78.

Gita, R. "2006 TNC Report and Forecast for 2007". *TITAS*. Jakarta, 5 February 2007a.

———. "Parliament: Punishment for Smugglers". *TITAS*. Jakarta, 6 February 2007b.

IIIID. "Prospects for Manufactured Exports During Repelita VI". Report submitted to the Department of Industry and Trade, Republic of Indonesia. Jakarta: Harvard Institute of International Development, 1995.

Hill, H. "Indonesia's Textile and Garment Industries: Developments in an Asian Perspective". Singapore: ASEAN Economic Research Unit, Institute of Southeast Asian Studies, 1992.

Hoffman, K. "Clothing, Chips and Competitive Advantage: The Impact of Microelectronics on Trade and Production in the Garment Industry". *World Development* 13, no. 3 (1985): 371–92.

James, W.E. "Survey of Recent Developments". *Bulletin of Indonesian Economic Studies* 31, no. 3 (1995): 3–38.

James, W., D. Ray and P. Minor. "Indonesia's Textiles and Apparel: The Challenges Ahead". *Bulletin of Indonesian Economic Studies* 39, no. 1 (2003): 93–103.

Lall, S. and K. Rao. *Indonesia: Sustaining Manufactured Export Growth*. Jakarta: Report Submitted to the National Development Planning Board (BAPPENAS), August 1995.

Pangestu, M. "The Indonesian Textile and Garment Industry: Structural Change and Competitive Challenges". In *Waves of Change in Indonesia's Manufacturing Industry*, edited by M. Pangestu and Y. Sato. Tokyo: Institute of Developing Economies, 1997.

Sastromihardo, S. "The Indonesian Textile Industry". In *Indonesia's Non-Oil Exports: Performance and Prospects*, edited by N. Mihira and S. Sastromihardjo. Tokyo: Institute of Developing Economies, 1991.

Statistics Indonesia. *Indonesia's Foreign Trade Statistics: Exports 1989*, Vol. II. Jakarta: BPS, April 1990.

————. (various years). *Economic Indicators*. Jakarta: BPS.

————. (various issues). *Large and Medium Manufacturing Statistics,* Vol. I. Jakarta: BPS.

————. (various issues), *National Income of Indonesia*, Jakarta, BPS.

Thee, K.W. "The Surge of Asian NIC Investment into Indonesia". *Bulletin of Indonesian Economic Studies* 27, no. 3 (1991a): 55–88.

————. *Technological Development and Its Implications for Indonesia's Garment Industry*. Paper presented at the Trade and Development Seminar, organised by the Economics Division, Research School of Pacific Studies, The Australian National University, Canberra, 9 July 1991b.

Thee, K.W., Ahmad Hamid and Sukarna Wiranta. *Employment Consequences of the Plywood and the Textile Products Export Surge*. Jakarta: Report prepared for the International Labour Organisation, Jakarta Office, 1989.

Thee K.W. and Ahmad Hamid. *Perkembangan Industri Garmen di Bali sesudah tahun 1990* [The development of the garment industry in Bali after 1990]. Paper presented at the Conference of the Association of Indonesian Economists (Ikatan Sarjana Ekonomi Indonesia), Malang, 19 December 1997.

Thee, K.W. and Pangestu M. "Technological capabilities and Indonesia's manufactured exports". In *Technological Capabilities and Export Success in Asia*, pp. 211–65, edited by Ernst, T. Ganiatsos. and L. Mytelka. London: Routledge, 1998.

USAID and SENADA. *Indonesia's Competitive Environment: Current Conditions*, Jakarta, March 2006.

World Bank. *Indonesia: Industrial Policy-Shifting into High Gear*. Washington, DC: World Bank, 1994.

————. *Comparative Study of Industrial Competitiveness in East Asia: A Research Proposal*. Washington, DC: Development Economics Research Group, January 2003.

Wymenga, P. *The Textile Industry in Indonesia*. Jakarta: Industry Planning Project. Centre for Data Processing and Analysis, Department of Industry, 1988.

————. "The Structure of Protection in Indonesia in 1989". *Bulletin of Indonesian Economic Studies*, 27, no. 1 (1991a): 127–49.

————. "The Textile and Garment Industry". In *Prospects of Industrial Development in Indonesia,* edited by P. Wymenga. Centre for Data Processing and Analysis. Jakarta: Department of Industry and Netherlands Economic Institute, pp. 211–21, July 1991b.

Yamazawa, I. *Renewal of the Textile Industry in Developed Countries and World Textile Trade.* RUEE Working Paper no. 82-6, July 1982.

# 14

## INDONESIA'S AUTO PARTS INDUSTRY[1]

This chapter on Indonesia's auto parts industry, a medium-tech industry, assesses the past and present performance of this industry, including its export performance, and its prospects in the coming years. The reasons for its successful performance, or the lack of it, is investigated using qualitative interviews of 20 selected firms in the auto parts industry. The interviews were designed to elicit from the surveyed firms the nature and degree of competitive pressures, whether and how they were responding to these pressures, and how their own actions were affected by industry-wide and macroeconomic factors. The interviews were also expected to yield a forward-looking perspective on how these auto parts firms saw their advantage shifting relative to their perceived competitors, and how they intended to remain competitive in the future.

This study found that because of its largely domestic market orientation which caters largely to the domestic car assemblers and the important local aftermarket, it appears unlikely that the Indonesian auto parts industry will develop into a strong, export oriented, internationally competitive industry. However, those auto parts producers that are joint ventures with foreign auto parts producers, specifically Japanese producers, have better prospects of becoming internationally competitive, export oriented firms. These auto parts producers, particularly if they are among the most efficient parts producers in the region, can utilize the marketing channels of their foreign principals to export to other countries and may even become the major auto parts producers in the ASEAN region.

## INTRODUCTION

This study on the auto parts industry aims at making an assessment of its performance, including its export performance, and its prospects in the coming years. The reasons for its successful performance, or the lack of it, would be investigated using qualitative interviews of 20 selected firms in the auto parts industry. The interviews would be designed to elicit from the surveyed firms the nature and degree of competitive pressures, whether and how they were responding to these pressures, and how their own actions were affected by industry-wide or macroeconomic factors. The interviews were also expected to yield a forward-looking perspective on how these auto parts firms saw their advantage shifting relative to their perceived competitors, and how they intended to remain competitive in the future (World Bank, 2003: 1–2).

## INDONESIA'S AUTO PARTS INDUSTRY: A HISTORICAL OVERVIEW

Indonesia's automotive industry dates back to the early 1930s, when General Motors established a car assembly plant on the outskirts of colonial Batavia (present-day Jakarta). However, the auto parts industry only started in earnest after the introduction of a mandatory deletion (local content) programme for the automobile assembling industry in 1974. But even before this deletion programme, some auto parts firms were already established during the early 1970s, mostly by Japanese-Indonesian joint ventures (Tarmidi, 1998: 44), with most of these firms catering to the after (replacement) market. By 1975, more than thirty auto parts firms were already in operation, producing a variety of parts and components, mostly universal components, including automobile paint, tires, radiators, car batteries, leaf springs, wheel rims, window panes, and chassis. During the second half of the 1970s, the production of car batteries experienced the most rapid development, rising from 220,000 units in 1975 to 800,000 units in 1978 (Chalmers, 1988: 187).

In 1976, Indonesia's Department of Industry introduced a mandatory deletion programme for the car assembly industry, particularly commercial vehicles (buses and trucks), with a view to developing supporting (local supplier) industries to make needed auto parts. The government gave preference to the development of a commercial vehicle industry because these vehicles were required to expand transportation options for low-income passengers, using buses and minivans, and for goods, transported in bulk in trucks. Commercial vehicles, being more robust than passenger cars, were also more suitable for the relatively poor conditions of most roads in Indonesia. Promoting passenger cars was deemed less suitable for a low-income country like Indonesia, where the number of high- and upper-middle-income people able to purchase expensive passenger cars was small.

The promotion of commercial vehicles was supported by the imposition of lower import duties on the components required for the assembly of commercial vehicles and lower value-added taxes on assembled commercial vehicles (Aswicahyono, et al., 2000a: 215). However, one result of this distortionary policy was that commercial vehicles, particularly the smaller-sized ones, were converted into passenger cars, referred to as Multi-Purpose Vehicles (MPVs), which could be sold more cheaply than passenger cars. As a result, demand for commercial vehicles that had been converted into passenger cars increased sharply when rapid economic growth during the Suharto era led to a burgeoning middle class. The Asian economic crisis led to a steep drop in the sales of motor vehicles in 1998, including both commercial vehicles and passenger cars, but after the economy gradually recovered after 1999, production of cars (including passenger cars and commercial vehicles) again started rising rapidly. (Table 1)

The steep decline in car production in 2006 was caused by the adverse impact of the steep rise in fuel prices. However, after the economy had adjusted to the higher fuel prices, car production rose again in 2007 as interest rates has also come down, and rose steeply in 2008. However, as a result of the adverse impact of the Global Financial Crisis (GFC) in 2008 on the Indonesian economy, production of cars declined again in 2009. As the Indonesian economy started recovering rapidly by late 2009, production of cars is estimated to rise again rapidly in 2010 as will be the auto parts industry. In fact, by June 2010 production of auto parts has risen by 70 per cent compared to the previous year (GIAMM, July 2010).

Despite the progress of Indonesia's auto parts industry over the past two decades, in comparative perspective production of auto parts in Indonesia has lagged behind that of its Southeast Asian neighbours, except Malaysia (Table 2).

The data in Table 2 show that the ASEAN-5 countries still account for a very small share of the world auto parts production, only around 2.7 per cent of the world total. Indonesia's share of 0.37 per cent is still miniscule, while Thailand is the largest producer of auto parts in the ASEAN-5 region, producing around 2.5 times the value of Indonesia's auto parts output.

## PROGRAMMES AND POLICIES TO DEVELOP THE AUTO PARTS INDUSTRY

The major programmes and policies introduced since the early 1970s to develop Indonesia's auto parts industry are outlined in Table 3 below.

**TABLE 1**

**Production of Cars (Passenger Cars and Commercial Vehicles, 2000–09)**

| 2000 | 2001 | 2002 | 2003 | 2004 | 2005 | 2006 | 2007 | 2008 | 2009 |
|---|---|---|---|---|---|---|---|---|---|
| 299,000 (est) | 299,629 | 317,942 | 354,334 | 483,295 | 500,710 | 296,608 | 411,638 | 600,628 | 464,816 |

*Source:* GAIKINDO (Association of Indonesia's Automotive Industries), July 2010.

TABLE 2
World Auto Parts Production, 2006
(US dollars)

| Country | Amount (US$) | Percentage |
|---------|-------------|------------|
| Indonesia | 908, 518,800 | 0.37 |
| Malaysia | 425,247,062 | 0.17 |
| Philippines | 1,394,311,669 | 0.57 |
| Singapore | 1,502,264,511 | 0.61 |
| Thailand | 2,506,163,687 | 1,03 |
| Rest of the World | 237,718,314,037 | 97.24 |

*Source*: Johnson, 2007, p. 2.

TABLE 3
Major Programmes and Policies to Develop the
Auto Parts Industry, 1974 – present

| Programme | Policy |
|-----------|--------|
| Compulsory Deletion Programme (1974–1993) | 1. Step by step localization, specifying the parts to be made locally<br>2. Applicable only to commercial vehicles (trucks, buses, minivans) |
| Incentive Programme (1993–1999) | Gradual increase of local content by offering lower import duties on imported parts if a specified level of local content is achieved |
| National Car Programme (1996–1999) | Promotion of 'National Car', a small Korean-designed passenger car exempted from import duties on imported parts if a 60 per cent local content was achieved within 3 years |
| Harmonized System (1999–Present) | 1. Abolition of local content programmes due to WTO-mandated TRIM (trade-related investment measures)<br>2. Liberalization of policy on automotive industry |

*Source*: Adapted from Gunadi (2007), p. 4.

## a. The deletion programme

Under the mandatory deletion programme, a compulsory, step-by-step deletion schedule was drawn up on an item-by-item basis, under which the car assembly firms were required to gradually delete a number of specified parts and components from the imported CKD (completely knocked down) kit and instead procure progressively more and more locally made parts and components in the assembly of commercial vehicles. However, the deletion programme was not applied to passenger cars.

In the following years more decrees were issued specifying in further detail the parts and components that had to be made locally. For the time being, the Department of Industry chose to disregard the fact that several of the components intended to be made locally were products that had to be assembled from imported parts and subcomponents. Hence, the deletion programmes did not lead to a substantial saving of foreign exchange.

The main purpose of the mandatory deletion programme (or local content programme) in the late 1970s was to foster the growth of an Indonesian auto parts industry. The introduction of this programme was based on the expectation that it would foster the development of Japanese-style, stable, durable, and intense subcontracting relationships between the large car assembling firms and the local auto parts supplier firms, most of which were expected to be small- or medium-scale enterprises (SMEs). It was hoped that through these subcontracting relationships, the car assembly firms, being joint ventures between automobile companies from advanced countries and local firms, would transfer modern technologies to their subcontractors (Aswicahyono, Basri, and Hill, 2000a: 233).

However, these subcontracting relationships did not develop into stable, durable relationships, since the local supplier firms, faced with a segmented and relatively small domestic market for automobiles, were forced to supply several car assemblers if they wanted to achieve scale economies. However, the proliferation of many brands and car models assembled by a relatively large number of assembling firms for Indonesia's relatively small domestic market has prevented car assemblers from reaping the benefits of scale economies. As a result, auto parts firms, having to produce auto parts in relatively small quantities, have also been unable to achieve scale economies.

In 1981, Mr A. R. Soehoed, the then Minister of Industry, attempted to rationalize the automotive industry by requiring the car assemblers to reduce the number of car brands and models they assembled. However, this policy could not be effectively implemented in the face of strong opposition by vested interests in the industry. On their part, car assemblers in general tended to avoid durable relationships with large numbers of small-and medium-scale subcontractors making low-quality replacement parts because of these firms' high mortality rates and the difficulties of appropriating returns from investment in enhancing these firms' skills (Aswicahyono, Basri, and Hill, 2000a: 233). The only durable relationships that developed between car assemblers and auto parts producers were the joint ventures between foreign auto parts producers and local firms. These subcontracting relationships were particularly strong between car assemblers, which were joint ventures between Japanese automotive firms and local firms, and auto parts firms, which were also joint ventures between the Japanese parts supplier to the Japanese car assembling firm and a local firm. Most, if not all, of these joint venture auto parts firms were first-tier subcontractors to the car assembling firm. However, compared to the large number of locally owned auto parts firms, the number of joint venture auto parts firms is relatively small.

Initially, the deletion programme was resisted by the car assembling firms, all of which were either joint ventures between foreign, mostly Japanese, automotive transnational corporations (TNCs) and their local partners or which were assembling the cars under license of their foreign principal. Their reluctance to implement the deletion programme was because there were virtually no local firms able to produce sufficient amounts of the components specified by the deletion programme (Chalmers, 1988: 188) according to the strict specifications of the car-assembling firms. However, after the Minister of Industry issued Decree No. 307 in 1976, requiring the car assembling firms to gradually delete a number of specified components from the imported CKD kit and replace them with locally made parts and components, specifically for commercial vehicles, these firms did not have any choice but to procure those locally made parts and components as specified in the deletion programme.

Unlike the pyramid-shaped, three-tiered structure of subcontractors in Japan, in which the first tier of a relatively small number of main component makers is supplied by a larger number of second-tier producers of subcomponents, which in turn are supplied by an even large number of third-tier parts producers, the structure of subcontractors in Indonesia is quite different (Table 4).

The above table shows that the largest number of auto parts firms consists of second tier subcontractors (225 firms), with a much smaller number of

### TABLE 4
### Structure and Number of Auto Parts Firms in Indonesia, 2007

| Level (tier) | Number of auto parts firms |
| --- | --- |
| First tier | 11 firms |
| Second tier | 225 firms |
| Third tier | Exact number of third tier firms unknown, but estimated to be quite few |

*Source*: Gunadi, 2007, p. 4.

first-tier, large subcontractors (11 firms), and an unknown, but relatively small number of third-tier subcontractors (Gunadi, 2007: 7). Hence, Indonesia's auto parts industry still lacks the broad base of third-tier subcontractors which should largely consists of small- and medium-scale enterprises (SMEs) like in Japan.

The first tier auto parts makers, almost all of them joint ventures with foreign (mostly Japanese) auto parts makers, produce axles, brakes, clutches, transmissions, steering wheels, and shock absorbers, while the second tier auto parts makers produce pressed parts, glass sheets, radiators, mufflers, electric parts, rubber and plastic parts. When highly qualified suitable local auto parts makers were not available, the car assembling industry, consisting of 14 joint venture firms with foreign automotive companies, established in-house manufacturing facilities, including eight stamping plants, eight engine manufacturing plants, two transmission manufacturing plants, axle and propeller shaft plants, five steering system plants, two plastic injection plants, four die casting plants, and two ferro casting plants, requiring a total capital investment of around US$4 to 5 billion (Gunadi, 2007: 7).

However, by the early 1990s it had become increasingly clear that the deletion programme had not been very successful in developing viable supporting industries for the car assembling industry, particularly at the second and third tier levels. Several factors account for this lack of success, including the generally low technological capabilities of the local supplier firms; the lack of economies of scale due to the relatively small and fragmented domestic market; the reluctance of the foreign principals to procure locally made parts; and the large amount of investment often needed to set up local supplier firms (Tarmidi, 1998: 54; Aswicahyono, Anas, and Rizal, 2000b: 4).

## b. The incentive programme

Because of the lack of success of the deletion programmes, and faced with the pressure of global trade liberalization to abandon non-tariff trade protection (Tarmidi, 2003: 135), as reflected by the mandatory deletion programme, the Indonesian government in 1993 terminated the deletion programme. Instead, it introduced an incentive programme to encourage, rather than require, the car assembly firms to continue raising the local content of the assembled cars, specifically the commercial vehicles. This programme allowed assemblers to import components and parts not yet made locally at progressively lower import duties , the higher the local content of their cars. This incentive programme turned out to be relatively successful in encouraging the car assembling firms to raise the local content of their assembled cars.

However, by 1996 this incentive programme was overshadowed by the highly controversial and blatantly preferential 'national car' programme which conferred unfair tax exemptions to the Timor company owned by President Suharto's youngest son.

## c. The 'national car' programme

Under the controversial 'national car' programme, a 'national car' joint venture company, owned by President Suharto's youngest son and KIA Motors from South Korea, was allowed to import auto parts duty free provided that within an unlikely short period of three years it was able to achieve a 60 per cent local content. However, this 'national car' programme had to be terminated in 1999 when the WTO ruled that this programme violated WTO rules.

## d. The harmonized system

After the termination of the 'national car' programme in 1999, a so-called 'harmonized system' was introduced which, under WTO rules, specifically the 'trade-related investment measures' (TRIMS), removed the local content programmes. The protectionist policies governing the automotive industry were abolished and replaced by market liberalization. Under this trade liberalization, completely-built-up (CBU) cars, including passenger cars, could now be imported, albeit at very high import duties.

## e. Assessment of the deletion and incentive programmes

Over time, both the deletion programme and the subsequent incentive programme did succeed in raising the local content ratios, which to a large extent was made possible by the entry of new local supplier firms, many of them owned by local entrepreneurs, as well as the entry of foreign auto parts firms. Since the late 1980s, the product range and quantity of locally made parts and components also expanded rapidly, while the quality of these locally made parts also improved rapidly.

Like the car assembling firms, most auto parts producers are largely oriented toward the domestic market, although in recent years it has been quite successful in exporting several kinds of auto parts. To a large extent, this has been the consequence of the highly protectionist policies for the car assembly industry. As all the assembly firms are joint ventures with foreign automotive TNCs, the technical licensing agreements signed by these joint ventures and their foreign principals contained provisions banning or restricting the exports of these assembled cars, except to a few small countries, such as Brunei Darussalam. As a result, most of the auto parts producers mainly supply the auto parts to the domestic market, including both the local assembly firms and the important replacement or after market. This aftermarket is supplied mainly by repair shop retailers, and is able to thrive as an alternative for customers who do not want or are unable to purchase the expensive, high value, high quality branded parts which are supplied by the first tier auto parts makers (SENADA, 2007: 5), almost all of which are joint ventures with foreign, mostly Japanese, auto parts makers.

A survey on the major problems faced by the auto parts industry identified three problems: first, the firms' inadequate technological capabilities; second, the shortage of skilled workers; and third, the high dependence on imported inputs (Tarmidi, 1998: 74–75), specifically the sub-parts assembled by the auto parts firms into locally-made auto parts. The inadequate technological and design capabilities of many auto parts firms is thus a major factor why these firms in general lack international competitiveness. For this reason, exports of the locally made parts and components remained minimal until the mid-1990s.

## THE IMPACT OF THE ASIAN ECONOMIC CRISIS

The Asian economic crisis badly affected the auto parts industry, since the production of passenger cars and commercial vehicles declined steeply from 387,000 in 1997 to only 58,000 in 1998 (Farrell and Findlay, 2001: 64). As the auto parts producers are largely oriented to the domestic market, the steep decline in car production led to a steep decline auto parts production. However, as the Indonesian economy gradually recovered in 1999, the production of passenger cars and commercial vehicles steadily increased again (see Table 1) in response to rising demand for motor vehicles. Consequently, the production of auto parts also rose steadily.

As a result of the Asian economic crisis, the exports of auto parts and components also rose from only US$48.1 million in 1995 to US$109.3 million in 1999 (Aswicahyono, Anas, and Rizal, 2000b). A field survey conducted by Feridhanusetiawan, Aswicahyono, and Anas found that this good export performance was due to the sharp depreciation of the rupiah. Their survey also showed that the auto parts producers that had developed industrial or trade networks with foreign partners had gained the most. When they were struck by the crisis, they were able to switch their sales from the domestic to the export market. However, only relatively few of these auto parts producers had in this way access to the export market (Feridhanusetiawan, Aswicahyono, and Anas, 2000: 40; 49–50) since most of the auto parts makers, particularly the second and third tier auto parts makers which were not joint ventures with foreign auto parts makers did not have this access to the industrial and trade networks with foreign partners.

In spite of the general view that the deletion and incentive programmes have not been effective in raising the technological capabilities of the local supplier firms, some recent studies have indicated that these two programmes did lead to improved technological capabilities in a number of small- and medium-scale local auto parts firms. According to Hayashi's survey of locally owned small- and medium-scale metalworking and machinery enterprises supplying parts to car and motorcycle assembling firms, improvements in technological capabilities were made possible through technical support provided by the big automotive assembler firms to their local auto parts firms. The most valuable technical support provided by the assembler firms was the quality control (QC) audit, through which the quality of management and production management was periodically assessed by experts dispatched by the assembler firms. These experts give the auto parts firms valuable advice on how to improve the quality of their products and meet the strict delivery schedules (JIT, just-in-time system) for their products (Hayashi, 2005: 136).

Despite these improvements in the technological capabilities of many auto parts supplier firms, many of these firms still lack international competitiveness. In the early 1990s, only a small percentage of the relative large number of the auto parts firms were capable of efficiently manufacturing original equipment market (OEM) products. According to a World Bank study on Indonesia's manufacturing sector at the time, Indonesia would need significant engineering development before it would be capable of supplying efficient, competitive inputs to the local auto parts (World Bank, 1994: 28). However, this engineering development has thus far not yet made a lot of headway.

The general lack of international competitiveness in the Indonesian auto parts industry has largely been the result of the government's protectionist policies regarding the car assembly industry. As a result of these protectionist policies, the car assembly firms have oriented their production towards the domestic market. This orientation has been further strengthened because the car assembly firms are all joint ventures with foreign principals. generally prohibited the export of assembled cars. In other words, domestic market demand has historically been the driver for both the car assembling and auto parts industries. This pattern has persisted until the present, since the auto parts industry has been sustained by the strong growth in the domestic market for cars (see Table 1), as well as a subsequent growth of the replacement parts market (aftermarket) (Senada, 2007: 7).

## INDUSTRIAL ORGANIZATION

Since the auto parts industry, compared with the car assembly industry, is in general more labor-intensive and less dominated by a small number of very large firms, industrial concentration in the auto parts industry is much lower than in the car assembly industry. (Table 5) Because of the entry of new auto parts firms, including joint ventures, during the 1990s up to the Asian financial crisis, the industrial concentration ratio of the auto parts industry steadily declined, in contrast to the concentration ratios in the car assembly industry, which have, to the present, remained very high. After the crisis, the industrial concentration ratio in the auto parts industry rose again to 72 per cent, as some of the largest firms took over some of the distressed firms. However, since the auto parts industry is still a relatively young industry, the concentration ratios may decline again with further growth. Since barriers to entry and exit are relatively low in the auto parts industry, rapid growth in the car assembly industry in response to rising domestic demand for motor cars will also stimulate further growth of the auto parts industry through

### TABLE 5
### Industrial Concentration Ratios in the
### Automotive Industry, 1975–2001
### (%)

| Year | Car Assembling Industry | Auto Parts Industry |
|------|-------------------------|---------------------|
| 1975 | 85 | 57 |
| 1980 | 81 | 61 |
| 1985 | 81 | 45 |
| 1990 | 83 | 61 |
| 1996 | 92 | 58 |
| 1998 | 93 | 44 |
| 2001 | 93 | 72 |

*Note*: The data refer to the sum of added values of the four largest firms (CR4) in, respectively, the car assembly and auto parts industries, as a percentage of the total value added of these industries.

*Source*: 1. For the period 1975 to 1996, see Haryo Aswicahyono, M. Chatib Basri and Hal Hill, "How Not to Industrialise? Indonesia's Automotive Industry", in *Bulletin of Indonesian Economic Studies* 36, no. 1 (April 2000): Table 11, p. 237 (derived from BPS's *Statistik Industri*, selected issues).

2. For 2001, see Badan Pusat Statistik: *Survey Industri*, 2002, Jakarta.

the entry of new firms, both local and foreign. With the entry of new firms, concentration ratios are likely to decline again in the next few years.

As many car assembly establishments, assembling various brands and models of cars, are owned by one of the three largest automobile enterprises in Indonesia, the above concentration ratios actually understate the real seller concentration in this industry. Unlike the car assembly industry, however, the auto parts industry is not so dominated by these large automobile enterprises, even though several auto parts firms are either owned by the car assembly firms as part of their vertical integration strategy or are joint ventures with the Japanese first-tier subcontractors belonging to the same keiretsu group of joint venture assembly firm principals. Hence, ownership in the auto parts industry is more diversified, as several auto parts firms are owned by enterprises without any relationship with the large automobile enterprises. As the many auto parts firms make a wide range of quite different products, seller concentration ratios in this industry would be even lower if the various firms were grouped according to the particular products they make. However, the increase in seller concentration ratio after the Asian financial crisis indicates that several distressed, unaffiliated firms may have been acquired by larger firms.

As the auto parts industry consists of three tiers or layers — namely, the first-tier supplier firms making the main components, the second-tier firms making sub-components for the first-tier firms, and the third-tier firms making parts and sub-subcomponents for the second-tier firms, the seller concentration ratios in these three tiers of supplier firms would be different. Unfortunately, no data are available on the industrial concentration ratios in the three tiers of the auto parts industry.

## EXPORTS AND IMPORTS

Despite the largely domestic market orientation of most auto parts firms, a number of these firms, particularly the first tier auto parts makers producing under OEM (original equipment manufacturing) arrangements (Johnson 2007: 3), have nevertheless been able to export part of their output. These exports were largely been carried out by the first tier auto parts firms which are joint ventures with foreign firms (Tarmidi, 2003: 141). Through the overseas marketing channels of the foreign principals, these joint venture auto parts firms were able to export part of their output.

Locally made auto parts are highly dependent on imported parts. In fact, producing locally made auto parts in general merely amounts to assembling imported inputs, that is sub-parts which the auto parts makers assemble into whole parts. Not surprisingly, auto parts imports far exceed the exports of locally made auto parts, as shown in Table 6.

In interpreting the data in Table 6, a caveat is in order, as the SITC 784 category includes both auto and motorcycle parts. Unfortunately, BPS, the Central Agency for Statistics, does not have a separate SITC category for auto parts.

The data in Table 6 clearly show the high dependence of Indonesia's auto parts exports on imported inputs. As auto parts exports steadily increased after the Asian economic crisis, so did auto parts imports, keeping the auto parts trade balance unfavourable for Indonesia.

### TABLE 6
### Exports and Imports of Auto Parts, 1998–2006
### (millions of US$)

| Year | Exports | Imports |
|------|---------|---------|
| 1998 | 141 | 460 |
| 1999 | 209 | 352 |
| 2000 | 302 | 1,240 |
| 2001 | 475 | 1,838 |
| 2002 | 561 | 1,639 |
| 2003 | 665 | 1,878 |
| 2004 | 964 | 2,395 |
| 2005 | 1,355 | 3,033 |
| 2006 | 1,668 | 2,442 |

*Source*: SENADA report, 2007, p. 11.

At present Indonesia auto parts makers, particularly the second- and third tier producers, face increasing competition from Chinese, Taiwanese, Thai and Vietnamese low-priced imported parts at the bottom end of the aftermarket. Indonesia's second- and third tier auto parts makers, unable to compete in price with these cheap imported parts, have responded to this challenge by moving into a nascent mid-market, mid-value domestic aftermarket segment which has started to grow quite rapidly (SENADA, 2007: 5).

As indicated above, it is mainly the first-tier auto parts makers, mainly joint ventures with foreign (primarily Japanese) auto parts makers which exports their products through OEM (original equipment manufacturing) arrangements. Under these OEM arrangements the buyers specify the designs of the products they buy, the materials to be used, the exact delivery times, and other specifications which need to be strict adhered to by the sellers, in this case the auto parts makers.

The advantages of OEM arrangements to access the export market are that the costs and risks of exporting are reduced; and that the auto parts makers can get access to foreign investment and other financial resources, new technologies and customers in export markets, and innovative managerial practices. However, these OEM arrangements also carry disadvantages for the auto parts makers since a large part of the profits accrue to the foreign buyer. There is also a minimal transfer of standards and skilled personnel into the local auto parts makers (Johnson, 2007: 4).

## FACTORS INFLUENCING THE DYNAMICS OF THE AUTO PARTS INDUSTRY

### a. Government policy

Among the various factors influencing the development of Indonesia's auto parts industry, government policy has, as pointed earlier, played a decisive role through its strongly protectionist and interventionist policies. Since the role of government policy has already been discussed in detail above, this role will not be discussed again.

### b. Production Networks

The structure of an efficient automotive industry should, as in Japan, be like a pyramid, with quite a few assembling firms at the top that procure their auto parts from a relatively small number of first-tier component supplier firms just below. In turn, these supplier firms procure their inputs from several supporting industries, consisting of a larger number of second-tier supplier firms that, in turn, procure their inputs from an even larger number of third-tier supplier firms. In Indonesia, however, the industry structure resembles an inverted pyramid, with a relatively large number of assembler firms and a shaky base due to the absence of a strong tier of supporting industries (World Bank, 1994: 28). Unlike Japan's automobile industry, Indonesia's layer of third-tier subcontractors is quite narrow due to the great shortage of qualified small and medium supplier firms able to meet the strict QCD (quality, cost and delivery schedules) requirements imposed by the higher tier subcontractors. Even the layer of qualified second-tier subcontractors is relatively narrow compared to Japan's.

When it issued the deletion programme in the late 1970s, Indonesia's Department of Industry hoped the programme would foster development of industries to support a car assembly industry that, just like Japan's, would consist mostly of small and medium enterprises (SMEs). As all the car assembling firms were joint ventures with automotive corporations from the advanced countries, it was hoped that the deletion programme would lead to the transfer of advanced technologies to Indonesia's small and medium enterprise supplier firms. In this way, the deletion programme could foster the development of efficient and viable supporting industries that, it was hoped, would consist mostly of SMEs.

The establishment of viable supporting industries, however, was hampered by market fragmentation caused by the relatively large number of commercial vehicle assemblers, which, because they assembled several models, were prevented from standardizing within the context of a small domestic market. This situation resulted in small orders for local parts and component firms, preventing them from growing into viable supplier firms, especially those who might have benefited from economies of scale (Thee, 1993: 17).

It was this situation that led the Japanese partners (principals) in the joint ventures to pursue in-house manufacture of the important auto parts they needed by establishing their own supplier firms. A look at the capital structure of these Japanese-Indonesian joint venture supplier firms, as listed in the Directory of Japanese companies in Indonesia, published annually by the JETRO Jakarta Center, show that most of these joint venture auto parts firms are majority-owned by the Japanese companies, with Japanese serving as top management and Indonesians serving as vice president directors. However, interviews with several of these joint venture auto parts firms, conducted as part of the survey of 20 auto parts firms, were always held with Indonesian managers, who were very knowledgeable about the operations of their firms. This fact indicates that over the years substantial technology and managerial transfer had taken place from the Japanese staff to the local Indonesian staff.

As the auto parts industries in all the ASEAN4 countries (Indonesia, Malaysia, the Philippines, and Thailand) are small and fragmented, the Japanese automotive companies and their first-tier subcontractors have been trying to foster regional specialization, including in Indonesia, using the complementation schemes adopted by the ASEAN countries. For instance, Nippon Denso has chosen Indonesia as the center of production of compressors and spark plugs (Farrell and Findlay, 2001: 44–45). However, because of Indonesia's current poor investment climate, rated far worse than those of Malaysia, Thailand, and China (World Bank, 2003: 28–29), it is not certain that the planned investments in these component operations will actually take place.

Like the auto parts firms in the other ASEAN countries, Indonesia's auto parts firms, particularly those firms affiliated with Japanese car assembly or component firms, need to access the global supply chains by forming linkages with module suppliers to original equipment manufacturers (OEMs) by making use of the existing keiretsu systems. However, because some of the Japanese parent firms are now partly owned by non-Japanese auto firms, the traditional keiretsu system may be eroding (Farrell and Findlay, 2001: 45). The advantages of having links with foreign firms, including Japanese car assembling or auto parts firms, is indicated by the findings of a study by Feridhanusetyawan, et al., that the auto parts firms with established trade networks with foreign firms, including Japanese firms, were able to survive during the Asian economic crisis by switching their sales from the depressed domestic market to the export market (Feridhanusetyawan, et al., 2000: 49).

It will be much more difficult, if not impossible, for Indonesia's independent (unaffiliated) auto parts firms to become regional, let alone global, suppliers of auto parts, since they need to incorporate more complex technologies or less standard production processes, which they can only acquire if these technologies are transferred to these firms (Farrell and Findlay, 2001: 48). Whether this will actually happen depends on the evolving regional or global strategies of the big automotive firms and the absorptive capacity of the Indonesian auto parts firms.

## c. Foreign Direct Investment

Indonesia's car assembling industry is dominated by foreign, particularly Japanese, automotive firms. None of the car assembling firms is operating independently of foreign principals (Aswicahjyono, Basri, and Hill, 2000a: 217). Because of this, just looking at the foreign share of ownership in this industry understates the importance of foreign principals.

Besides the Japanese automotive firms, German automotive firms, namely Daimler and BMW have also set up assembly plants for passenger cars on a small scale since the early years of the Suharto era. Among these German firms, only Daimler assembles commercial vehicles, particularly large buses, besides assembling luxury passenger cars for the domestic market. Since the 1980s Korean automotive firms, namely Hyundai and KIA Motors, have also invested in Indonesia's car-assembling industry. These Korean firms have mainly focused on assembling passenger cars and large SUVs (sport utility vehicles). General Motors also re-entered the Indonesian market by assembling Chevrolet cars which are made in Korea since General Motors acquired the bankrupt Daewoo car company. Since October 2006 a Chinese automobile firm has also started investing in Indonesia on a small scale, assembling the small Cherry car for the domestic market.

Despite these new entrants, the Japanese car makers retain a dominant share of the domestic market for cars, including passenger cars and commercial vehicles, accounting for almost 96 per cent of the domestic car market (Table 7).

Due to the deletion programme and the subsequent incentive programme, several foreign auto parts firms, notably Japanese firms, established affiliates or subsidiaries in Indonesia, often as joint ventures with domestic firms. The termination of the deletion programme in 1993, and the prospect of a growing domestic market for cars as a result of rapid economic growth since the late 1980s, encouraged many domestic and foreign auto parts firms to enter the auto parts industry (Ito, 2000: 7). The large majority of these foreign auto parts makers were Japanese firms, as Table 8 shows.

According to the Directory of Japanese Companies and Representative Offices in Indonesia, published annually by the JETRO (Japan External Trade Organization) Jakarta Center, 73 Japanese auto parts firms were operating in Indonesia in 2003. With 236 auto parts firms officially registered as GIAMM members, Japanese-controlled auto parts firms thus account for a sizable 31 per cent of the registered auto parts firms.

The data in Table 8 show the number of Japanese auto parts firms that entered Indonesia from the early 1970s through 2002.

### TABLE 7
### Percentage of Automobile Market Shares by
### Country of Principal, 2006

| Country of Principal | Percentage |
|---|---|
| Japan | 95.6 |
| Germany | 0.6 |
| South Korea | 2.2 |
| USA | 1.4 |
| China | 0.1 |

*Note*: Rounded figures.
*Source*: Gunadi Sindhuwinata, 2007, p. 7.

## TABLE 8
### The Number of Japanese Auto Parts Firms According to the Period of Entry into the Indonesian Auto Parts Industry, 1970s–2002

| Period | Number of Japanese firms entering the Indonesian auto parts industry |
|--------|:--:|
| 1970s | 14 |
| 1980s | 7 |
| 1990–1996 | 34 |
| 1997–2002 | 18 |
| Total | 73 |

*Source*: JETRO, Jakarta Center: Directory of Japanese Companies and Representative Offices in Indonesia, 2003, Jakarta, April 2003.

The data in Table 8 show that the introduction of the mandatory deletion programme in the 1970s led to the first entry of Japanese firms into the Indonesian auto parts industry. During the 1980s, not many Japanese auto parts firms entered Indonesia, but during the 1990s up to the Asian economic crisis, a large number did so. This surge of Japanese direct investment into the Indonesian auto parts industry was largely due to the positive effects of rapid economic growth on the demand for cars, including commercial vehicles converted into passenger cars. With rising demand for cars, the demand for locally made auto parts rose as well. The data in Table 8 also show that even after the Asian economic crisis, a smaller number of Japanese auto parts firms continued to invest in Indonesia in anticipation of continued rising demand for cars and the derived demand for auto parts once economic recovery was achieved.

According to Mr. Hadi Surjadipradja, Executive Director of GIAMM, the auto parts industry association, the auto parts industry can roughly be divided into two categories: first, the better managed, more efficient and productive firms possessing more advanced technological (including design) capabilities and operating better equipped modern plants; and, second, the less efficient and productive firms with lower technological (including design) capabilities and operating less modern and less well-equipped plants. In general, the first category consists largely of joint venture firms between foreign and local auto parts firms, while the second category consists almost exclusively of domestic firms (Surjadipradja, 2004).

The gap between the larger, technologically more advanced and efficient, mostly foreign-controlled auto parts firms, on the one hand, and the smaller, technologically less advanced and efficient, mostly domestic firms, on the other hand, is also reflected by the high percentage of turnover accounted for by, respectively, the top ten and top twenty auto parts producers, as shown in Table 9.

The data in Table 9 clearly show that the 10 largest auto parts firms alone accounted for 53 per cent of the total sales of auto parts, while the top 20 firms accounted for 70 per cent of total sales. Taking into account that the auto parts industry consists of around 236 first- and second-tier auto parts firms, the data in Table 9 suggest that the sales of the remaining 200-plus smaller auto parts firms account for only 30 per cent of total sales.

The important question regarding the impact of the foreign-controlled auto parts firms in Indonesia is whether they have exerted a positive impact on the development of the auto parts industry. A study by Professors Okamoto and Sjoholm found that these foreign firms have not become an engine of growth for the Indonesian auto parts industry for two reasons. First, the number of these foreign firms is, as indicated in Table 9, smaller compared to the number in Thailand, where 111 Japanese-controlled auto parts firms have been established (Okamoto and Sjoholm, 2000: 69).

Second, although the foreign-controlled auto parts firms were more productive than were the domestic firms, it appears that the foreign firms have not generated substantial spillovers on the domestic firms, as reflected by the latter firms' persistent poor productivity (Okamoto and Sjoholm, 2000: 69). One possible explanation may be that many foreign auto parts firms were only established since the mid-1990s as a result of the attraction of a rapidly growing economy, the introduction of the incentive programme in 1993, and a further liberalization of the foreign investment regime in 1994 (Ito, 2002: 11). For this reason, more time was needed before they were able to operate efficiently and before the domestic auto parts firms were able to benefit from their superior production technology and managerial competence (Okamoto and Sjoholm, 2000: 71).

### TABLE 9
### Turnover of the Top Ten and Top Twenty Auto Parts Firms, 2002

|                                        | Amount (billions of rupiah) | Percentage ( %) |
| -------------------------------------- | --------------------------- | --------------- |
| 1: Turnover of top 10 auto parts firms | 6, 741                      | 53.1            |
| 2: Turnover of top 20 auto parts firms | 8,883                       | 70.0            |
| Total sales of GIAMM members           | 12,688                      | 100.0           |

*Source*: GIAMM.

# CONCLUSIONS

Because of its largely domestic market orientation and associated lack of scale economies, dependence on principals for access to new technologies, weakness in product design capability, relatively low quality of workers, the competitive threat from auto parts firms from other ASEAN countries in view of AFTA, and, last but not least, the unfavorable investment and business environment created by burdensome and restrictive regulations and an inefficient and corrupt government bureaucracy, one would be inclined to conclude that the long-term prospects for Indonesia's auto parts industry do not appear to be favorable.

Against these negative factors, however, stands one factor that might promote rapid growth of the auto parts industry, namely steadily rising domestic sales of passenger cars and commercial vehicles after the Indonesian economy recovered from the Asian economic crisis and the associated rise in the demand for locally-made auto parts, and a modest but steady rise in auto parts exports.

With the resumption of more rapid economic growth after the adverse effect of the Global Financial Crisis has largely been overcome, the medium-term prospects for the car assembly and auto parts industries look quite good. The fact that quite a large number of Japanese auto parts firms have established operations after the Asian economic crisis lends support to a more optimistic assessment of the prospects for Indonesia's auto parts industry. Without a careful analysis of the market potential of auto parts in Indonesia, it is unlikely that these Japanese auto parts firms would have established operations in Indonesia. Some of these Japanese auto parts makers have also made plans to make their Indonesian operations as the base to supply the whole ASEAN market under the AFTA (ASEAN Free Trade Area) arrangements.[2]

Nevertheless, the high dependence of most auto parts firms on car assemblers with a domestic market orientation has constrained the development of Indonesia's auto parts industry into an internationally competitive industry, due to the relatively low efficiency and low technological (including design) capabilities of local, specifically domestic, auto parts firms. From the early 1970s until the present, the Indonesian car assembly industry has hitched its fortunes to a high dependence on its foreign principals, particularly the automotive TNCs from Japan and, to a much lesser extent, from Europe (Germany), and, more recently, from Korea. Because of this high dependence on its foreign principals, it should have been evident from the outset that the Indonesian car assembly industry could not develop into an independent, internationally competitive industry able to stand on its own in the world market against its former foreign principals. The reasons for this were the restrictive conditions set by the industry's foreign principals in their technical licensing agreements with their local automotive joint venture partners, mostly established during the Suharto era. The most important of these was the total or limited ban on exporting joint venture products to other countries, meant to prevent these exports from competing head on with the same cars produced under license from these same principals in other countries.

In view of the largely domestic market orientation of the auto parts industry, which caters largely to the domestic car assemblers and, to the important local aftermarket, it appears unlikely that the Indonesian auto parts industry will develop into a strong, export oriented, internationally competitive industry. However, those auto parts producers that are joint ventures with foreign auto parts producers, specifically Japanese producers, have become more competitive, export oriented firms. These auto parts producers, particularly if they are among the most efficient parts producers in the region, can utilize the marketing channels of their foreign principals to export to other countries and may even become the major parts producer in the ASEAN region. This could, among other arrangements, occur under the regional division of labour arranged by Toyota Motors, which has designated Thailand as the hub of its regional operations. Under Toyota's regional division of labor scheme, those Indonesian auto parts producers considered to be the most efficient in the ASEAN region will be allowed to export their products to the whole ASEAN market and perhaps even to non-ASEAN markets as well.

In a recent interview with the Executive Director of GIAMM, the major challenges facing the auto parts industry were identified, namely:

1. Maintaining competitiveness by improving productivity and efficiency and the quality of the products;
2. Improving product development (design) capability; and
3. Penetrating the export market by improving competence in the distribution network and in labor relations (Surjadipradja, 2004).

A recent survey by a Phillipino consultant on the current conditions of Indonesia's second- and third-tier auto parts makers found that these firms have in general a weak engineering capacity (Castro, 2007), as reflected by:

1. Weak product design development
2. Weak production engineering
3. Weak quality control.

These local auto parts makers apply only minimal process standards, unless they are demanded by the OEM (original equipment manufacturing) buyers. The reasons for this lack of process standards by the local auto parts makers are:

1. Since most of these firms produce for the local aftermarket, there is minimal end-market demand from customers to adopt and implement process standards;
2. Lack of a culture of quality, since these firms do not see the value-added benefits in improving their process systems;
3. These auto parts makers have difficulty accessing and understanding complex processes and product standards requirements of the OEM buyers versus what is acceptable in the domestic market;
4. Lack of standardization throughout the industry.
   (Castro, 2007: 2).

To promote a market-driven standardization and upgrading, it is therefore crucial for the second and third tier auto parts firms to acquire a seal of certification to promote process standardization and upgrading. (Castro, 2007: 3–4). Through these certified standards, the auto parts firms could increase their competitiveness and obtain broader domestic access. Through the seal of quality certification, these auto parts makers would not only be able to systematize a healthier and safer environment for their workers, but also develop a stronger design engineering capability for product development, and their production engineering and quality controls.

## Notes

1. "Indonesia's Auto Parts Industry", by Thee Kian Wie is an abbreviated and updated version of part 3 of the Final Report on *Indonesia's Industrial Competitiveness: A Study on the Garments, Auto Parts and Electronic Components Industries*, written by Haryo Aswicahyono, Raymond Atje and Thee Kian Wie for the Development Economics Research Group, The World Bank, March 2005.
2. Personal communication to the author by a Japanese-controlled auto parts maker, June 2003.

## References

Aswicahyono, Haryo, M. Chatib Basri & Hal Hill. "How not to Industrialise? Indonesia's Automotive Industry". *Bulletin of Indonesian Economic Studies* 36, no. 1 (2000a): 209–41.

Aswicahyono, Haryo, Titik Anas and Jose Rizal. "The Indonesian Automotive Industry". Paper presented at the PECC Conference, August 2000.

Aswicahyono, Haryo and Titik Anas. "Understanding the Pattern of Trade in the ASEAN Automotive Industry in the First Half of the 1990s". Unpublished Report, Jakarta, 2000.

Castro, Doreen M. "Process Standardization and Certification: Taking the next Step Towards Domestic and Export Market Penetration". Presentation at the Round Table Discussion on Best Practices in Indonesian Automotive Component Export Promotion And Process Standards Upgrading. Jakarta, 18 September 2007.

Chalmers, Ian. "Economic Nationalism, the Third World State, and the Political Economy of the Indonesian Automotive Industry, 1950–1984". Ph.D. thesis, The Faculties, The Australian National University, Canberra, 1988.

Farrell, Roger and Christopher Findlay. "Japan and the ASEAN4 Automotive Industry: Developments and Inter-Relationships in the Regional Automotive Industry". ICSEAD Working Paper Series, 24 August 2001.

Feridhanusetiawan, Tubagus, Haryo Aswicahyono and Titik Anas. *The Economic Crisis an the Manufacturing Industry: The Role of Industrial Networks*. Jakarta: Centre for Strategic and International Studies (CSIS), 2000.

Gunadi Sindhuwinata. "Indomobil Automotive Component Domestic and Export Market Penetration". Presentation at the Round Table Discussion On Best Practices in Indonesian Automotive Component Export Promotion and Process Standards Upgrading. Jakarta, 18 September 2007.

Hayashi, Mitsuhiro. *SMEs, Subcontracting and Economic Development in Indonesia: With Reference to Japan's Experience*. Tokyo: Japan International Cooperation Publishing Co. Ltd., 2005.

JETRO. *Directory of Japanese Companies and Representative Offices in Indonesia, 2009*. Jakarta: JETRO Jakarta Center, April 2009.

Johnson, Dan R. "Alternative Model for Indonesian Automotive Export Promotion". Presentation at the Round Table Discussion on Best Practices in Indonesian Automotive Component Export Promotion and Process Standards Upgrading. Jakarta, 18 September 2007.

Okamoto, Yumiko and Fredrik Sjoholm. "Productivity in Indonesia's Automotive Industry". *ASEAN Economic Bulletin* 17, no. 1 (2000): 60–73.

Perhimpunan Alumni Jerman. *Daya Saing Industri Indonesia* (Indonesia's Industrial Competitiveness). Jakarta, 1998.

Radhi, Fahmy. "Technology Transfer and Industrial Development: A Case Study of the Indonesian Automotive Industry". Unpublished Ph.D. thesis, The University of Newcastle, NSW, Australia, 2002.

SENADA. *Automotive Component Value Chain Overview, Market Justification and Strategies for Domestic Component Market Upgrading, (June 2007–2008)*, USAID and SENADA — Indonesia Competitiveness Programme. Jakarta, 2007.

Suryadipradja, Hadi. "Overview of the Indonesian Automotive Component Industry". Presentation at the Indonesian Investment Seminar, 23–25 March 2004.

Tarmidi, Lepi. "Industri Komponen Otomotif (The Automotive Components Industry)". *Perhimpunan Alumni Jerman* (1998): 36–98.

———. *Indonesian Industrial Policy in the Automobile Sector with Focus on Technology Transfer.* Mimeo, Jakarta, 2003.

World Bank. *Indonesia: Industrial Policy-Shifting Into High Gear.* Washington, D.C., 1994.

———. *Comparative Study of Industrial Competitiveness in East Asia — A Research Proposal.* Development Economics Research Group, 9 January 2003.

# INDEX